G. M. TREVELYAN

Also by David Cannadine

G. M. Trevelyan, circa 1930. Leonard Woolf described him as 'a large, craggy, looming figure, with a curious clumsiness of body and intellectual ferocity which could be intimidating to anyone who did not know him well, or had any kind of intellectual wobble'.

G. M. TREVELYAN

A LIFE IN HISTORY

David Cannadine

HarperCollins*Publishers*

HarperCollins*Publishers*
77–85 Fulham Palace Road
Hammersmith, London W6 8JB

Published by HarperCollins*Publishers* 1992

1 3 5 7 9 8 6 4 2

Copyright © David Cannadine 1992

David Cannadine asserts the moral right to
be identified as the author of this work

A catalogue record for this book is
available from the British Library

ISBN 0 00 215872 8

Photoset in Linotron Janson by
Rowland Phototypesetting Ltd
Bury St Edmunds, Suffolk

Printed and bound in Great Britain by
HarperCollinsManufacturing Glasgow

Trevelyan . . . is now at the nadir of his reputation . . . His revival will come when he is seen more strongly in the context of his age, and then, I suspect, he will loom over the twentieth century as Macaulay looms over the early nineteenth.

J. H. PLUMB, 'The True Voice of Clio',
Times Literary Supplement, 2 May 1980

FOR LINDA – AT LAST!

Contents

List of Illustrations

Garden Corner, West Road. Trevelyan's Cambridge house from 1928 until his death in 1962: a suburban dwelling of forbidding drab brick and of best-forgotten unloveliness.

Preface

I have written a very short *Autobiography* ... It is not
memoirs of my life and all the interesting people I have met,
for I do not think I should be very good at describing them.
It is really confined to an account of those circumstances
and experiences which led me to be an historian, and to
write each particular book. It is just what I am ready to have
known about me. The rest of my life is not the business of
the public.

> G. M. Trevelyan to Sir Charles Trevelyan,
> 19 January 1948.

One of the penalties of great fame is that, after a time, the
public had [sic] a right to pry into your intimacies.

> G. M. Trevelyan to Arthur Bryant, 16 August 1932.

A man's reputation with the world at large is usually at its
lowest exactly a hundred years after his birth, especially in
the realm of letters.

> G. M. TREVELYAN, 'George Meredith, 1828–1928',
> *The Nation and Athenaeum*, 11 February 1928, p. 713.

THE HOUSE ONCE KNOWN as Garden Corner, West Road,
Cambridge, England, is a suburban dwelling of forbidding
drab brick and of best-forgotten unloveliness. The uninspired
façade is disfigured by too many windows, and by too many drainpipes,
and the roof is an unhappy jumble of ill-assorted gables and chimneys.
Inside, the rooms are badly proportioned, there is an excess of lin-
oleum, and it is easy to imagine the place filled with ugly and uncom-
fortable furniture. Thus described, this might be any one of a thousand
homes which the English middle classes built and bought between the
late nineteenth century and the Second World War. But in this particular case, it is distinguished by the commemorative plaque which is so

discreetly placed above the front door that few passers-by actually notice it, and even fewer pause to read it. The inscription recorded there is as follows:

GEORGE MACAULAY TREVELYAN
LIVED HERE
DURING THE PERIOD 1928–1962

The historian thus modestly celebrated is scarcely a familiar name in most late twentieth-century households. Indeed, Trevelyan's reputation and readership were both in decline for almost a decade before his death, and that trend has only intensified in the thirty years since 1962. Today, his many volumes rest undisturbed on the shelves of our great libraries, or gather dust in secondhand bookshops, and he himself belongs to that marginal band of superannuated stars he once described as 'the great unread'.[1] Most history students at British universities obtain their degrees without opening a book that Trevelyan wrote. When I presented an early version of my second chapter to the Cambridge University seminar in modern British history, the majority of graduate students admitted to having never read him (though this did not prevent them making extremely helpful comments and much-appreciated suggestions). And most full-time historians are too busy with their own research, trying to keep up with the mass of new publications in their own specialized fields, and with their burdensome teaching and administrative obligations, to spend their limited leisure hours perusing the works of an author often regarded in their profession with indifference or contempt.

Yet during the first half of the twentieth century Trevelyan was the most famous, the most honoured, the most influential and the most widely read historian of his generation. He was a scion of the greatest historical dynasty that this country has ever produced. He wrote books which were readily acclaimed for the soundness of their scholarship, for the brilliance of their style, for the wisdom of their insights, and for the matchless quality of their poetic imagination. He knew and corresponded with many of the greatest figures of his time, not just historians and intellectuals, but also politicians and men of affairs on both sides of the Atlantic. He was devoted to the countryside, was an ardent conservationist, and played a significant part in the affairs of the National Trust. He cared deeply about contemporary events, in Britain and in Europe, and his books and letters reveal his lifelong

struggle to make sense of them in the light of history. For fifty years,
Trevelyan acted as a public moralist, public teacher and public benefactor, wielding unchallenged cultural authority among the governing and
the educated classes of his day.[2] To his contemporaries, he was Clio's
truest and most trusted voice.

Inevitably, Trevelyan's life and work have attracted a certain amount
of attention, from relatives, admirers, scholars and critics. At the time
of his death, appreciative obituary notices were produced by Lord
Adrian, Sir George Clark and J. R. M. Butler.[3] Since then, there
have been memoirs by his daughter, Mrs Mary Moorman, and by
his kinsman Humphrey Trevelyan.[4] And there have also been more
reflective recollections by some of his friends and protégés: Lord
Briggs, Professor Owen Chadwick, Dr G. Kitson Clark, Professor Sir
John Plumb, Dr Brian Wormald, Professor John Clive and Dr A. L.
Rowse.[5] There is a perceptive study of Trevelyan by Joseph M.
Hernon, but it is of too small a compass to do adequate justice to the
subject.[6] There are essays by Walter L. Arnstein, John W. Osborne
and Henry R. Winkler, but these add little to Trevelyan's own account
of his life and work.[7] There was an early attack, disclaimed at the time,
and disowned a decade later, by Herbert Butterfield, which has more
recently been disinterred by Maurice Cowling, and which cannot pass
uncommented upon.[8] And there have been intemperate caricatures
and hostile misrepresentations by Sir Geoffrey Elton, Professor J. P.
Kenyon, Dr J. C. D. Clark and Professor Arthur Marwick, which will
be dealt with, as appropriate, towards the end of this book.[9]

All these writers, even the most admiring and uncritical, or the most
unsympathetic and vituperative, have something to offer the scholar
in search of the authentic historical Trevelyan. But as its subtitle
implies, this book is the first full-scale attempt to understand him, and
to present him, neither as an icon to be revered nor as an Aunt Sally
to be scorned, but as a substantive and significant historical personality
who deserves to be recognized and understood for what he was: one
of the towering figures in the political, cultural and intellectual life of
twentieth-century Britain. For Trevelyan's was a life in history in both
the senses in which that phrase may be understood: the past was his
inheritance, his passion, his calling, his duty, his art; but he was as
much the child of his own day as any other scholar, or any other
person. Like most historians, Trevelyan's life and work cannot be
properly understood without reference to the time in which he lived.
But like very few historians, the time in which he lived cannot be

properly understood without reference to Trevelyan's life and work. Therein lies the true measure of his importance and the justification for this book.

Although Trevelyan loved writing biographies, this is not a work conceived in a biographical mode. In his will, he gave instructions that 'no life or memoir of me is to be written.'[10] But since this injunction has already been disregarded by members of his own family, it is not out of deference to it that I have eschewed a conventionally biographical approach. The details of Trevelyan's life are already well known, and the pages which follow contain no significant or sensational revelations. Instead, they provide the first sustained analysis of his work, his attitudes, his influence, and his achievements, based on a thorough examination of the appropriate and available sources. I have adopted a thematic, rather than a chronological approach, partly in the hope of doing full justice to the richness and range of Trevelyan's work and interests, and partly so as to locate him more satisfactorily in the context of his time. By setting Trevelyan against the broader background of twentieth-century events, I have sought to throw light not only on the man, the historian and the phenomenon, but also on his world, his era, and his generation. For he touched life at so many points that he may be regarded as a prism through which we may view – and better understand – his age.

Trevelyan destroyed all his own papers, but there exists an abundance of material about him. Much may be learned from his vast output: not just his books, but also his lectures, essays, articles, and reviews. A great deal of his correspondence has survived, not only in the Trevelyan family papers in Cambridge and Newcastle, but also scattered in archives throughout Britain and the United States. Trevelyan once claimed that he 'never wrote a private letter worth printing', and insisted that his 'scrawls' were 'never to be published'.[11] But his father was surely nearer to the mark in describing Trevelyan's letters as 'excellent literature', and I make no apology for having quoted extensively from this source.[12] And I have also learned a great deal about him from those many people who have kindly given me their recollections: Lord Adrian, Lord Annan, Professor Derek Beales, Lord Briggs, Professor William Brock, Professor Owen Chadwick, the late Professor John Clive, Professor John Elliott, Professor Sir John Habakkuk, Professor Sir Michael Howard, Mr Denis Mack Smith, Professor Sir John Plumb, Dr Robert Robson, Dr A. L. Rowse, Lord Runciman, the Hon. Sir Steven Runciman, Mr Raleigh Trevelyan and Dame Veronica Wedgwood.

I am grateful to the following individuals and institutions for allowing me to consult and quote from materials in their possession or of which they hold the copyright: Mr G. M. Trevelyan, Mrs Mary Moorman, the Trustees of the Trevelyan Family Papers, the Master and Fellows of Trinity College, Cambridge, and the Editors of the *Cambridge Review*. I should also like to thank the staff of the University Library, Cambridge; the Bodleian Library, Oxford; the University of London Library; the University of Birmingham Library; the University of Sussex Library; the University of Reading Library; the University of Durham Library; the Robinson Library, University of Newcastle upon Tyne; King's College Library, Cambridge; the Churchill Archives Centre, Churchill College, Cambridge; Trinity College Library, Cambridge; Cambridge City Library; the House of Lords Record Office; the Public Record Office; the British Library; the Liddell Hart Centre for Military Archives, King's College, London; the New York Public Library; the Rare Book and Manuscript Library, Columbia University; the Harry Ransome Humanities Research Center, University of Texas at Austin; the Bentley Historical Library, University of Michigan; the Houghton Library, Harvard University; the Queen's University Archives, Kingston, Canada; and the Bertrand Russell Archives, MacMaster University, Hamilton, Canada. For particular suggestions, references and items of information, I thank Professor Derek Beales, Professor Alan Brinkley, Dr David Butler, Lord Crawford, Mr Oliver Everett, Mr John Fuggles, Dr Patrick Higgins, Professor William C. Lubenow, Mr Andrew MacLennan, Dr H. C. G. Matthew, Dr John Morrill, Dr Jonathan Parry, Dr David Reynolds, Mr Kenneth Rose, Dr Miles Taylor and Sir Keith Thomas.

But these are not the only debts of gratitude I have accumulated during the course of writing this book. It is a pleasure to thank Richard Williams, Claire Kudera, Takemi Ueno, Ian McBride, Donald Firsching, Bruce Smith and James Tueller for their research assistance, both at the beginning and at the very end of this project. I am most grateful to the American Council of Learned Societies for awarding me a Fellowship for the academic year 1990–91, which enabled me to complete the research for this book, and to begin writing it. I owe a particular debt to Trevelyan's daughter, Mrs Mary Moorman, for her hospitality, for her reminiscences, and for making available to me those of her father's letters which are still in her possession. I am no less grateful to Dr Robert Robson, of Trinity College, Cambridge, who kindly read this book in typescript, made many helpful suggestions, and saved me from innumerable errors. My agent, Mike Shaw, played his customary part with his customary skills, but deserves much more than just customary thanks. And it has been a pleasure to work for a second time with Stuart Proffitt, my editor and friend at Harper-Collins, who has been an unfailing source of strength, wisdom, encouragement, and constructive criticism, and who has lavished endless time and trouble on this book from beginning to end.

But once again, my most heartfelt thanks are due to my wife, Linda Colley – even though that phrase 'once again' carries with it connotations of the routine and the commonplace which in her case are wholly and misleadingly inappropriate. She first suggested this project to me, and her own study of Sir Lewis Namier has been both model and inspiration throughout.[13] She has read and commented on the manuscript as a whole, which has been immeasurably improved as a result. And she has tolerated, with the patience born of a long decade's experience, the self-indulgent self-absorption which my writing inevitably brings with it. No one has ever described this unendearing condition better than Virginia Woolf, an author whom, as it happens, G. M. Trevelyan greatly disliked. But, along with the dedication, these words of hers express, more eloquently than any of mine, the full extent of my loving gratitude:

> When a person's thick to the lips in finishing a book . . . it's no use pretending that they have bodies and souls so far as the rest of the world is concerned. They turn the sickle side of the moon to [the] world: the globe to the other . . . One of these days our moons shall shine broad in each other's faces.[14]

D.N.C.

New Haven
16 February 1992

I
THE LIFE AND THE MAN

The Trevelyans are a very old family. All families, we must suppose, are equally old . . . but an 'old family', I take it, can trace an ascent far back in the catalogue of gentry. That much the Trevelyans can do.

G. M. TREVELYAN, Sir George Otto Trevelyan:
A Memoir (1932), p. 1.

We are all moles – though of course we must all go on driving our little tunnels as straight as we can and with all our strength, until the mole-catcher come. But if we are moles in vision, the best of us become gods in spirit.

G. M. Trevelyan to Sir George Otto Trevelyan,
25 December 1898.

When the first extravagances of early youth were over, he had asked three things of life: that he might enjoy domestic happiness beside a populous hearth; that he might prove himself honourable and high-minded in all the relations of life; and that he might do something lasting for the liberties and for the welfare of his country.

G. M. TREVELYAN, Lord Grey of the
Reform Bill (1920), p. 369.

The Central Saloon at Wallington: 'My boy', Sir George Otto Trevelyan told the young Steven Runciman, on showing it to him for the first time, 'man has not achieved anything more beautiful than this.'

THE CENTRAL SALOON at Wallington Hall, Northumberland, is one of the most remarkable rooms in any English country house. During the early 1850s, John Dobson, the Tyneside architect, roofed over what had previously been an open courtyard, and the great hall thus created was distinctively decorated by the Trevelyan family and their Pre-Raphaelite friends.[1] On the lower pilasters of the inner courtyard are paintings of flowers: foxgloves, columbines and lilies among them. In the spaces between the arches are William Bell Scott's eight scenes of Northumberland history, from Roman times to the nineteenth century. And on the spandrels above are portrait medallions of famous Northumbrians, including the Emperor Hadrian, Bishop Nicholas Ridley, Admiral Collingwood, Earl Grey, George Stephenson, Sir Walter Calverley Trevelyan, and Sir Charles Edward Trevelyan. Here, set out in arresting visual form, are the influences that moulded the life and work of George Macaulay Trevelyan: the sense of family pride and dynastic distinction; the commitment to public service and creative endeavour; the love of individual liberty and personal freedom; the belief in ordered progress and rational reform; and the delight in nature and the countryside. All his life, Wallington meant more to Trevelyan than any other home. 'How my thoughts turn', he wrote to his father from Italy in June 1918, 'to the grey stone house and tall dreaming trees.'[2]

I

The best and briefest description of Trevelyan's forbears has been provided by his kinsman Humphrey:

The literature about the Trevelyans of Wallington sometimes gives the impression that they emerged by a special procreative act of

Providence from the Evangelical families known as the Clapham
Sect. They were, in fact, by Nettlecombe out of Clapham, and their
remarkable qualities were the endowment as much of the one as of
the other.[3]

Put less allusively, and more prosaically, this means that Trevelyan,
like his youthful friend and near contemporary Bertrand Russell,
belonged to two separate but overlapping aristocracies of late-
nineteenth-century Britain: the aristocracy of privileged birth, and the
aristocracy of exceptional talent.[4] The Trevelyans were an authenti-
cally ancient family, and the senior branch had been established
Cornish gentry since late medieval times (not for nothing is the name
correctly pronounced 'Trevilian' or 'Trevilyan').[5] Indeed, their origins
were so remote that the family coat of arms includes a horse rising
from the waves, commemorating the legendary first Trevelyan, who is
said to have swum his steed from St Michael's Mount to the Cornish
mainland for a wager, while the other knights of King Arthur's court
were drowned. Even if there was no truth in this account, it encouraged
Trevelyans to believe that the history of their family went back almost
as far as the history of their country.[6]

By the thirteenth century they were established on the Fowey estuary
in Cornwall; in the mid-fifteenth century Sir John Trevelyan married
an heiress of the Raleighs; and in the mid-sixteenth century the family,
while retaining its lands in Devon and Cornwall, migrated to
Nettlecombe in Somerset. Two hundred years later the Trevelyans
inherited the estate of Wallington in Northumberland, which came to
them from the Blacketts, a family of Newcastle industrialists, who had
bought their way into the landed gentry, but later became extinct
in the male line.[7] This much-augmented inheritance was eventually
presided over by Sir Walter Calverley Trevelyan, sixth baronet, who
held the title from 1846 to 1879, and whose first wife, Lady Pauline,
was responsible for arranging the decoration of the central saloon at
Wallington. On Sir Walter's death the estates were divided: the West
Country properties stayed with the senior branch; but the Wallington
estate – which amounted to 22,000 acres worth £15,000 a year – passed
to a cousin, Sir Charles Edward Trevelyan, who in 1834 had married
Macaulay's sister Hannah, and had himself been created a baronet in
1874.[8] Sir Charles died in 1886, and the estate was inherited by his
only son, George Otto Trevelyan, who thus became the second
baronet. George Macaulay Trevelyan was his third and youngest child.

As a member of the aristocracy of birth, Trevelyan came from what his elder brother Charles once described as a 'governing family'. Indeed, Trevelyans had been governing England, and governing India, for generations. As with many gentry families, it was the younger sons and distant relatives who had taken the boat east of Suez. For much of the nineteenth century they were engaged in military service, and ten Trevelyans lost their lives in the carnage of the Indian Mutiny.[9] Perhaps this was why later generations turned to less risky professions, such as Sir Ernest John Trevelyan, who was Judge of the Calcutta High Court from 1885–1898, and subsequently Reader in Indian Law at Oxford University.[10] And with the end of the Raj already in sight, Humphrey Trevelyan joined the Indian civil service in 1929. On Indian independence he transferred to the diplomatic service, eventually becoming Ambassador to Moscow and, on his retirement, Chairman of the Trustees of the British Museum. He was the most outstanding British diplomat of his generation, and ended his career a peer and a Knight of the Garter, distinctions unique in modern times for a man of his profession. Even by the most exacting Trevelyan standards, he had done extremely well.[11]

For two yet more distinguished members of the family – Trevelyan's grandfather and great-uncle – India was only part of their political and professional lives. Lord Macaulay was a member of the Supreme Council of India from 1834–8, and was responsible for important reforms of the legal and educational systems. On his return to England he was briefly Secretary of War from 1839–41, and Paymaster-General from 1846–7. While Macaulay was a politician who sometimes masqueraded as a proconsul, his brother-in-law, Sir Charles Edward Trevelyan, was a 'statesman in disguise': a civil servant so zealous and determined that he seemed more like a politician than an administrator. His early years were spent in junior posts in the Indian civil service, and he was later Governor of Madras (1859–60) and Financial Member of the Governor-General's Council (1862–5).[12] From 1840 until 1859 he was Assistant Secretary to the Treasury, and was responsible, among other things, for the public works programme which the government instituted in the aftermath of the Irish potato famine. He was also the co-author of the Northcote–Trevelyan report on the civil service, which recommended the abolition of patronage and the introduction of entry by 'open competition'; and he was a lifelong opponent of the purchase system in the British army. Trollope satirized him as Sir

Gregory Hardlines, in *The Three Clerks* (1858). Trevelyan thought Sir Charles 'a great man', 'the best of us'.[13]

His father and brother moved with equal ease in the worlds of government and public affairs. Sir George Otto held ministerial office in every Gladstone administration, and was on terms of intimacy with the foremost Liberal leaders of the day: John Morley, James Bryce, Sir William Harcourt, Lord Rosebery and Lord Spencer among an older generation; Campbell-Bannerman, Sir Edward Grey and H. H. Asquith among the younger men. And as the author of a widely read book on England and the American Revolution, he was almost as well known and well connected in the United States, numbering Theodore Roosevelt, Henry James, John Hay, Elihu Root and Henry Cabot Lodge among his closest friends.[14] Trevelyan's elder brother Charles was virtually predestined to carry on the family tradition in politics in the next generation. He began his public career as Private Secretary to Lord Houghton when he was Lord Lieutenant of Ireland, went on a round-the-world cruise with Sidney and Beatrice Webb in preparation for parliamentary life, and became an MP before he was 30. He obtained junior office in the Liberal Government in 1908, was Secretary of Education in the two Labour administrations of 1924 and 1931, and from 1930 until 1949 he was Lord Lieutenant of Northumberland.[15]

By the standards of our own time, this was an astonishingly privileged and patrician background for an historian, and Trevelyan grew up confident that his place in the social hierarchy was very near the summit. And with social security went financial ease: Trevelyan never needed to earn his living. Of course, he was a younger son, but his parents left him well provided for, and in 1928 he inherited a house and small estate at Hallington, near Wallington, from a distant relative. Those were the sort of distant relatives he had.[16] As G. M. Young perceptively remarked, Trevelyan's work was 'the fruit of leisure, of freedom, of independence': indeed, one of the reasons why he so valued liberty, and celebrated it so eloquently in his writings, was that he had enjoyed it all his life. But freedom and independence carried with them an obligation, as Trevelyan explained to his brother Charles in 1905:

> No Trevelyan ever sucks up either to the press or the chiefs or 'the right people'. The world has given us money enough to enable us to do what we think right: we thank it for that, and ask no more of it, but to be allowed to serve.[17]

Trevelyans were neither trimmers nor wobblers: having formed their opinions, they were expected to maintain them forthrightly and fearlessly, regardless of what the majority might think. In 1829, the young Charles Trevelyan endured much opprobrium because he denounced his superior at Delhi, Sir Edward Colebrooke, for taking bribes, and as Governor of Madras he was so intransigent in his opposition to a proposed income tax that he had to be recalled to London. In the next generation, Sir George Otto Trevelyan twice resigned from Gladstone's Cabinets: once in protest against the education reforms of 1870, and later because he disapproved – for a time – of his leader's conversion to Home Rule.[18] Trevelyan's elder brother Charles was no less independent-minded. He quit his junior post in the Liberal Government in 1914 in protest against the war, and left the Labour administration in 1930 because he disapproved of his colleagues' indifference to higher education. In the same way, Trevelyan himself spoke out against Italy's invasion of Tripoli in 1911, and in favour of a détente with Mussolini in 1938, regardless of the fact that the first was much disapproved of in Rome, and the second in London. 'Fierce honesty' was a characteristic which everyone noticed who met him, and most – though not quite all – admired.[19]

In understanding Trevelyan the historian, it is essential to remember that it was from this Olympian perspective that he viewed the past. For Trevelyan, history was not something which had happened long ago, which left behind decaying evidential residues, which was written about in the mouldering pages of learned quarterlies, and which provided professional academics with a means of livelihood. On the contrary, history was something which his forbears *had made*, which his family was still making, and which was thus an integral part of the fabric of his own life. The history of the nation was but the history of the Trevelyans writ large. And this gave him an astonishing sense of intimacy with past figures, whom he treated not as historical characters, but as personal acquaintances, as social equals and as close contemporaries. He spoke of 'Johnny Russell' and 'Pam' as if he had visited them only yesterday, and A. L. Rowse remembers him once exploding, 'Billy Pitt, damn his eyes!'[20] This sense of personal involvement with an historical past which was also his family's past gives much of the vividness, the immediacy and the conviction to Trevelyan's work. He wrote history as an insider.

Indeed, it was precisely because he was an insider that he obtained access to documents that would have been unavailable to less well-connected scholars. When working on the first of his Garibaldi volumes, Trevelyan was able to consult French military material housed in the *Archives Historiques de la Guerre* in Paris, thanks to the personal intercession of the Foreign Secretary, Sir Edward Grey.[21] One of the most original parts of a later volume lay in the account of British foreign policy, based on Lord John Russell's correspondence, which Trevelyan had been able to see because the Hon. Rollo Russell was 'an old family friend of my father and me'. And when writing *England Under Queen Anne*, he enjoyed privileged access to the papers of the great Whig families which would have been denied to an historian of humbler origins.[22] For someone of Trevelyan's background and generation, family papers were still to be found in family homes, not in the impersonal deposits of county record offices. On his father's death, in 1928, he himself inherited a large collection of manuscripts: Macaulay's journals, which he gave to Trinity College; Fox's correspondence, which he eventually donated to the British Museum; and Sir George Otto's letters, which he used as the basis of his personal memoir of his father.[23]

The second aristocracy to which Trevelyan belonged was the aristocracy of exceptional talent. Through the Macaulay connection, the Trevelyans were related to the extensively intermarrying cousinhood of high-minded, middle-class, Evangelical families, including the Wilberforces, Darwins, Wedgwoods, Butlers, Keyneses, Thorntons, Stephens and Haldanes, which together produced a disproportionately large number of eminent men and women, and who collectively formed a remarkably stable and influential intelligentsia.[24] They moved easily between the worlds of learning, literature, and public affairs. They were a formidable presence in Cambridge (in Oxford rather less so), and in the home and Indian civil services, and they provided the backbone of the great Victorian and Edwardian periodicals. They believed in hard work, academic excellence, public duty, competitive examinations, intellectual integrity and unostentatious living. They had little time for London society or conventional high politics, but exerted influence indirectly through their writings and their public works. From the days of the Clapham Sect, they had no doubt of their right to mould intelligent public opinion.[25]

Of course, many of these people might have come to know each other even if there had been no family links: they were as much a freemasonry as an aristocracy.[26] But the ties of kinship helped to bring them together, and so to strengthen their sense of clan identity and public mission. In this, Trevelyan himself conformed exactly to type, as is well illustrated by his relationship with the composer Ralph Vaughan Williams. Trevelyan himself was not at all musical; but they were undergraduates at Trinity together, where Vaughan Williams also read history, and they remained lifelong friends. Indeed, Vaughan Williams's efforts to trace – and to adorn – a 'national' style in music certainly owed something to the influence of Trevelyan's histories.[27] But in addition, Vaughan Williams was both a Darwin and a Wedgwood on his mother's side, and his first wife was Adeline Fisher. One of Adeline's sisters, Florence Fisher, married the historian Frederic William Maitland, who was a great influence on Trevelyan at Cambridge, while her brother was H. A. L. Fisher, historian, Minister of Education, President of the British Academy and another of Trevelyan's closest friends. 'What a splendid life,' Trevelyan wrote, on learning of Fisher's death, 'what noble works accomplished! No life of our time is to me more admirable. And no one's friendship did I value more.'[28]

Trevelyan's links with the intellectual aristocracy were further consolidated when he married Janet Penrose Ward in 1904. As the daughter of Mrs Humphry Ward, her credentials were impeccable: indeed, in terms of distinguished forbears, she could more than hold her own with the Trevelyans. For she was also the granddaughter of Thomas Arnold, Headmaster of Rugby, and niece of Matthew Arnold, the poet and critic. Inevitably, a favourite pastime for George and Janet was playing what Bertrand Russell once described as 'the game of great-uncles', when they half-jokingly, half-seriously, tried to decide whose relatives had been the more eminent.[29] Among Janet's more distant kin were W. E. Forster, Gladstone's Minister of Education, and Dame Emily Penrose, successively Principal of Bedford, Holloway and Somerville Colleges. And there was a closer connection with a much more illustrious clan. One of Janet's aunts, Julia, married Leonard Huxley, the son of T. H. Huxley; and their children included Julian Huxley, the scientist, and Aldous Huxley, the novelist, who were thus Trevelyan's cousins by marriage.

In addition to tying the Trevelyans even more closely into the intellectual aristocracy, Janet Trevelyan was a remarkable woman in her own right. She was always known as 'the clever child' of the family, and from an early age was renowned for the force of her intellect and the independence of her spirit. Julian Huxley was much impressed by the fact that at sixteen, she was already reading Carlyle and keeping a diary. Between the ages of 17 and 21 she translated Jülicher's *Commentary on the New Testament* from German into English, a mammoth undertaking which ran to 635 pages.[30] She was devoted to the Italians, was a member of the British-Italian League, a founding impulse behind the creation of the British Institute of Florence, and the author of *A Short History of the Italian People* (1920). She also wrote a biography of her mother, and it was from her that she inherited the great public cause of her life: the creation and preservation of play centres for children in London. From 1929 to 1936 she successfully campaigned to raise money to save the Foundling Hospital site, now known as Coram's Fields, from the developer, so that it might be used as a children's playground. She was a tireless and resourceful fund raiser, and in recognition of these endeavours was made a Companion of Honour in 1936.[31]

Janet Penrose Ward was thus an ideal Trevelyan wife: well connected, independent-minded, public-spirited, and more than averagely intelligent. All Trevelyan women were expected to conform to these exacting standards, and many of them did. Pauline, Lady Trevelyan wrote for the *Edinburgh Review* and *The Scotsman*, as well as organizing the decoration of the central saloon at Wallington. And Trevelyan's elder brother Charles married Mary Bell, the half-sister of Gertrude Bell, who was herself no less formidable. During the Second World War, James Lees-Milne visited Mary Trevelyan at Wallington, and his account vividly captures the intimidating effect of a Trevelyan lady in full sail:

> She is authoritarian, slightly deaf, and wears pince nez ... The two daughters are abrupt and rather terrifying. After dinner, I am worn out, and long for bed. But no. We have general knowledge questions. Lady Trevelyan puts the questions one after another with lightning rapidity. I am amazed and impressed by her mental agility, and indeed by that of the daughters, who with pursed lips shout forth unhesitating answers like a spray of machine-gun bullets. All most alarming to a tired stranger. At the end of the 'game', for that is what they call this prep school examination, they award marks. Every single member of the family gets 100 out of 100 ... I get 0 ... Deeply humiliated, I receive condolences from the Trevelyans, and assurances I shall no doubt do better next time.

'I make an inward vow', he unsurprisingly concluded, 'that there never will be a next time.'[32]

To the social assurance derived from belonging to the aristocracy
of birth the Trevelyans thus added the intellectual assurance derived
from belonging to the aristocracy of merit, with the result that their
sense of dynastic identity and family pride was very highly developed.[33]
Sir George Otto Trevelyan wrote a biography of Lord Macaulay;
Trevelyan in turn produced a life of Sir George Otto; and more recent
generations have continued to write about their forbears. According
to A. L. Rowse, the family was 'apt to think that there were Trevelyans
– and then the rest of the human race.' When Steven Runciman visited
Wallington for the first time just after the Armistice, he was taken into
the central saloon by Sir George Otto Trevelyan, who announced,
without a trace of vanity, false modesty or embarrassment: 'My boy,
man has not achieved anything more beautiful than this.' And how
appropriate it seemed that in the next generation, Lord Macaulay's
diverse accomplishments were shared out in equal measure between
his three great-nephews: Charles, the politician; Robert, the poet; and
George, the historian. A French lady, new to London life, met all three
brothers at a party. 'Tell me,' she asked, 'are these Trevelyans a sect,
like the Wesleyans?'[34]

According to Beatrice Webb, Charles Trevelyan, who inherited the
baronetcy and the Wallington estate on his father's death in 1928,
was 'a man who has had every endowment – social position, wealth,
intelligence, an independent outlook, good looks and good manners.'
But despite these inestimable advantages, and despite the early promise
of his career, he achieved much less than was hoped for him. As a young
Liberal, he tended to hector and shout people down in argument, and
was too tactless in his criticism of the party leadership.[35] During the
interwar years he failed to establish close relations with the Labour
leaders, and became blindly obsessed with the virtues of Soviet Russia.
He resigned too easily from office, and in 1937 was expelled from the
Labour Party, along with Stafford Cripps, for his support of the Popular Front. He was also notoriously mean, and throughout his life
behaved as though he was trying to get twenty-one shillings out of
every pound. When appointed Lord Lieutenant of Northumberland
he refused to go to the expense of purchasing the requisite uniform,
and when some delegates from the TUC visited Wallington in 1932
he took the greatest delight in making a total of £8 15s 0d from selling
them copies of his guidebook to the house. Nor were these his
only eccentricities. As Lord Lieutenant, he was known to walk the
moors in a state of total nudity, and well into his seventies he

Sir George Otto Trevelyan, Caroline, and sons (*from left*) Charles, George, and Robert, on the steps of Wallington, the family home.

fathered a bastard – much to his youngest brother's disapproval.[36]

Trevelyan's other brother, Bob, was even more wayward, though he was widely loved by his extensive circle of friends. Despite parental disapproval, he spent his life writing undistinguished poetry and unproduced plays, which he published at his own expense. Desmond MacCarthy remained a lifelong admirer, but although Bob's verses were technically competent, they were repetitive, unoriginal and seemed to most people to be a pale imitation of Robert Bridges. In 1912–13 he accompanied E. M. Forster on his first visit to India, and they remained good friends thereafter.[37] Of the three brothers, he had most to do with Bloomsbury, and regularly figured in Virginia Woolf's diaries. And he was on very good terms with Bernard Berenson, whom he used to visit regularly at *I Tatti*, and whose English he helped to improve. He was often described as a 'child of nature', and as being 'engagingly undignified': both descriptions were apt. His conversation was rambling, confused and often incoherent, while his personal habits were the despair of his friends. He rarely washed, his dress and demeanour were uncouth, his table manners were appalling, and he was excessively fond of nude bathing. On one visit to *I Tatti*, he dried himself after taking a dip by walking up and down, to the consternation of a visitor who found '*une espèce de sauvage tout nu qui se promène de long en large comme si c'était la chose la plus naturelle du monde.*'[38]

Of the three brothers, who in their youth were known as 'the Trevvies', it was soon clear to shrewd observers like Beatrice Webb that George Trevelyan was gifted with 'far greater talent and power of concentrated work'.[39] He was more creative than Bob, had greater staying power than Charles, and had better judgment than either of them. He was not without his faults and foibles, but of the three brothers he was the one most likely to carry dynastic distinction on into the next generation. From an early age, Trevelyan had it instilled into him that he came from a family of remarkable ability, and he seems to have found this heavy burden of parental expectation more stimulating than daunting. And he clearly hoped that distinction might descend into his own children. His elder son, Theodore, was given the middle name Macaulay and was widely regarded as a boy of exceptional charm and promise. But in 1911 he died of appendicitis at the age of four and a half, and Trevelyan was devastated. As he explained to William Roscoe Thayer, Theodore 'was a swift spirit, full of joy and intelligence, and if his zeal for "Horatius", which he knew by heart, was any proof, he might have followed in our family way.' One of the reasons why Trevelyan made such a cult of his dead son was that he mourned him as the lost bearer of the family flame.[40]

II

But this was the only great personal unhappiness in an otherwise fulfilled and successful life.[41] Trevelyan had been born in 1876 at Welcombe, his mother's house near Stratford-upon-Avon, and his upbringing and education were conventionally upper class. Among his earliest recollections were the woods in Phoenix Park, where his father lived in his official residence as Chief Secretary for Ireland. In 1885 he was sent to Wixenford, a private school on the borders of Berkshire and Hampshire, and four years later to Harrow. In October 1893 Trevelyan went up to Trinity College, Cambridge, where Macaulay, his father, and his two brothers had been before him. He became a Scholar during his second year and, despite a breakdown brought on by overwork, obtained a First in the Historical Tripos in 1896.[42] He was sure by then that the writing of history would be his 'task in life', and resolved that a Fellowship at Trinity was the best base from which to begin it. With the encouragement of Maitland and Acton, he began research into the Peasants' Rising of 1381, and was duly rewarded with a Fellowship at Trinity in 1898 – the first ever given by the College in history, G. P. Gooch having been turned down the year before. This gave him the opportunity to convert his Fellowship dissertation into a book, which appeared, under the Longman imprint, as *England in the Age of Wycliffe*, in 1899.[43]

Thus far, Trevelyan's career was indistinguishable from that of any aspiring professional historian. His thesis was completed, his first book was out, he was giving lectures on modern European history, and the road to a conventional academic career in Cambridge was open to him. But in 1903 he resigned his Fellowship at Trinity, left Cambridge for London, and in the following year married Janet Penrose Ward. They settled down at a house in Cheyne Gardens in Chelsea, and Trevelyan threw himself into the political and literary society of the metropolis. He helped to found and edit a progressive journal called the *Independent Review*. He taught and lectured at the Working Men's College in Great Ormond Street. And although he had no ambitions to enter public life, he was well known in Liberal political circles. But then, as always, it was his writing which was the main concern. In 1904 he produced *England Under the Stuarts*, a textbook for the Methuen series edited by Sir Charles Oman. Then came a study of George Meredith's verse, which was later followed by an edition of his poetry. But the great work of these years was the Garibaldi trilogy, which appeared between 1907 and 1911. And just before the First World War broke out, this was followed by a biography of John Bright, and a collection of essays entitled *Clio: A Muse*.

In 1914, the pattern of his life once more changed abruptly – as it did for millions of others. After much agonized debate, Trevelyan decided that he must support Britain's declaration of war. At the end of the year, he visited Serbia, with the aim of strengthening that nation's resistance to the Central Powers, and in March 1915 he went on a tour to the United States, where he put the British case in a series of lectures. But despite his defective eyesight, which meant he was unfit for military service, Trevelyan was determined to get to the front, and in the autumn of 1915 he became Commandant of the first British Red Cross ambulance unit to be sent to Italy. His two fellow officers were his friends Geoffrey Winthrop Young and Philip Noel-Baker, and for the next three and a half years they served on the mountainous front northwest of Venice, between Isonzo and Piave, transporting wounded soldiers to hospitals behind the lines. Although he never mentioned it, Trevelyan was conspicuously brave, and insisted on sharing with his drivers many of the most dangerous tasks under fire. In the closing stages of the war, he was honoured by both the Italian and the British Governments, and on his return to England wrote a self-effacing account of his experiences entitled *Scenes From Italy's War*.[44]

When he returned home late in 1918, Trevelyan had little desire to resume his life in London and so moved out to Berkhamsted – partly so as to enjoy the peace of the countryside, and partly because of the excellent schooling it provided for his two surviving children, Mary, who had been born in 1905, and Humphry, who had followed in 1909.[45] As soon as his account of Italy and the First World War was completed, he returned to the biography of *Lord Grey of the Reform Bill* on which he had begun work in 1913, and which eventually appeared in 1920. There was also a final book on Italy before the advent of Mussolini cooled Trevelyan's Mediterranean passion: *Manin and the Venetian Revolution of 1848*, published in 1923. But by then he had turned his attention exclusively to his own country, with *British History in the Nineteeth Century*, which appeared in 1922, and his one-volume *History of England*, four years later. In 1928 both Trevelyan's parents died within a few months of each other, and his elder brother Charles inherited the Wallington estate and the baronetcy. Meanwhile, thanks to the bequest from his distant relative, Trevelyan established himself nearby at Hallington Hall, where in future years he was to spend his Easter, Christmas and summer vacations.[46]

The reason these visits were so intermittent was that he had just returned to academe, having accepted the Regius Chair of Modern History at Cambridge in July 1927, following the death of Professor J. B. Bury. His great-uncle had refused the post, but Trevelyan was 'proud as a peacock' to hold it.[47] He resumed his Fellowship at Trinity and made the house at Garden Corner, leased from Caius College, his residence during term time. In his early years as Regius Professor, he completed his most ambitious work, *England Under Queen Anne*, in three volumes: *Blenheim* in 1930, *Ramillies and the Union with Scotland* in 1932, and *The Peace and the Protestant Succession* in 1934. During the same decade, he also published two biographical works: a brief but revealing memoir of his father, and the official life of Viscount Grey of Fallodon. And in 1938 he produced a short study of the Glorious Revolution of 1688, to mark its three hundred and fiftieth anniversary. In recognition of his position as Britain's premier historian, Trevelyan had been appointed to the Order of Merit in 1930. By the end of that decade, he was looking forward to retiring from his chair, and planned to spend the rest of his life at Hallington, writing books for as long as he was able.

But in 1940 two unexpected events occurred which changed the course of his life again. J. J. Thompson, the Master of Trinity, died suddenly; and Winston Churchill became Prime Minister. The Fellows wanted the Mastership held in abeyance for the duration of the war. But, like the Regius Chair, it was a Crown appointment, and Churchill would brook no delay in filling it. Trevelyan was the obvious candidate, and despite his genuine reluctance, was eventually prevailed upon to accept. It was, he told his daughter, the 'one thing' his father had 'most wanted for him', and it restored 'an element of *romance* in life to me'.[48] As he put it in his *Autobiography*, it made 'my life as happy as anyone's can be during the fall of European civilization.' Despite the straitened circumstances of wartime, he presided with dignity over the Fellowship, helped secure the acquisition of Newton's Library for the College in 1943, and was tireless in extending hospitality to visiting American dignitaries. When he reached seventy, the retiring age introduced in 1926, the Fellows unanimously extended his term of office for the longest period allowed by the College statutes, and it was not until 1951 that he and Janet finally left the Lodge.[49]

Despite the burdens of the office, Trevelyan had continued to write, and in 1944, he had produced his most sensationally successful work, the *English Social History*. He also completed *A History of Trinity College*, and his own, unself-revealing *Autobiography*, which was published in 1949. In 1953, he was invited by the Council of Trinity College to deliver the Clark Lectures at Cambridge, which were subsequently published as *A Layman's Love of Letters*. It was his swansong on the Cambridge podium. 'The lecture room', E. M. Forster appreciatively recalled, 'was filled not only by his contemporaries, but by the young, and it remained full to the end of the course.'[50] Thereafter, he divided his time between Cambridge and Northumberland, and helped nurse Janet through a long and debilitating illness, from which she died in 1956. In his last years, Trevelyan returned to the writers who had meant most to him in his youth. He compiled anthologies of Meredith and Carlyle, and it was fitting that his last important published piece was an article for *The Times* in December 1959, marking the centenary of Macaulay's death.[51]

In the last decades of his life, Trevelyan was generally regarded as 'the most eminent historian of his time', and this was well reflected in the public recognition he received. He accumulated thirteen honorary doctorates from British, American and European universities – and they were given out much less frequently in his day than in ours. In 1946, he became High Steward of the Borough of Cambridge, as Macaulay had been before him, and in succession to Lord Keynes.[52] In the following year, he was elected President of the Historical Association, and in 1951, he served as President of the English Association. By then, he had become the first historian ever to be made a Fellow of the Royal Society, under the special statute which enabled men of great merit who were not scientists to be elected. He also became Chancellor of Durham University, in succession to Lord Londonderry, at a time when to elect an academic and a commoner to such a position was almost unheard of.[53] And in 1955, he was presented with a festschrift, *Studies in Social History*, edited by J. H. Plumb – another honour less commonplace then than now.

When Trevelyan's autobiography appeared, he had been described by Sir Robert Ensor as 'the greatest English historian now living', and by V. H. Galbraith as 'probably the most widely read historian in the world: perhaps in the history of the world'. On his eightieth birthday, in 1956, these tributes were paid again in the press and by the BBC, and a new illustrated edition of the *History of England* was issued.[54] From Cambridge, an appeal was launched in the columns of *The Times* to found a series of lectureships in his honour. The signatories were Herbert Butterfield, Sir Arthur Bryant, Sir George Clark, Sir John Neale, Lord Percy of Newcastle and Sir Winston Churchill. In their letter, they described Trevelyan as 'one of our foremost national figures', who was, like Lord Macaulay before him, 'the accredited interpreter to his age of the English past.' He attended the first series of lectures, given in 1958 by A. L. Rowse, an unforgettable sight, 'in a gown grown bottle-green with age, swathed in an overcoat which . . . had belonged to his father, brown muffler, grim moustache, steel spectacles, to a warm outburst of welcome.'[55] It was almost his last public appearance. There was a final honour in 1961, when he became, in the company of Winston Churchill, one of the first Companions of Literature. He died in the following year, and his will was proved at £157,765.[56]

Thus briefly described, Trevelyan's career was – as Gladstone said of Macaulay's – an 'extraordinarily full life of sustained exertion', a 'high table-land without depressions', with 'success so uniform as to be almost monotonous'. For more than fifty years, he had trodden what he once sceptically described as 'the primrose path of progress and fame'.[57] He never applied for a job he did not get: indeed, with the exception of his Trinity Fellowship, he never applied for a job at all. And the positions which he refused were arguably as distinguished as those which he accepted: the Directorship of the London School of Economics, a Readership in Modern History at Cambridge, and the Presidency of the British Academy. In 1945, he withdrew his name from the final short list of three which had been drawn up for the Governor-Generalship of Canada.[58] And although he accepted the Mastership of Trinity, he refused to take the title which by then customarily went with the office. He set out his reasons, with characteristic directness, in a letter to his daughter, Mary. Janet, he explained, did not want to be Lady Trevelyan. Moreover, there had already been one Sir George in the family, and the addition of another might be confusing. And in any case, Trevelyan had already got the OM, which his father had had before him, and that was the only honour seriously worth having.[59]

Whether he ever turned down a peerage remains unclear. Trevelyan tradition holds that he did, and by the 1930s there was definitely talk in Establishment circles about his being ennobled. Nor is it difficult to imagine such an offer being made by Baldwin or Churchill. But his father had refused a peerage from Asquith in 1908, and in the light of his own remarks at the time of the Trinity Mastership it seems highly unlikely that Trevelyan would have been tempted. Since the days of the Parliament Act, Lloyd George and Maundy Gregory, the peerage had become much debased, and in any case, Cambridge men of Trevelyan's background and generation – like Vaughan Williams and E. M. Forster – only accepted honours which came after their name, but not before it.[60] On the other hand, there is no firm evidence that Trevelyan was ever offered a peerage; the opportunity of following his great-uncle into the Lords might well have tempted him; and he certainly encouraged E. D. Adrian, his successor as Master of Trinity, to accept the peerage that he was offered in December 1954.[61] So the evidence is inconclusive.

Either way, it should be clear that Trevelyan lived and moved in a world very different from that of the average professional historian of today. For nearly half a century, he enjoyed a unique position of cultural authority which derived as much from his range of contacts and connections throughout the British Establishment as from his unchallenged position as a public educator. He was related to many of the central figures in English academic and intellectual life, including Sir Leslie Stephen and F. D. Maurice among an older generation, Sir Walter Morley Fletcher and Sir Geoffrey Keynes among his near contemporaries, and Dorothy Hodgkin and David Butler among a younger generation. Indeed, the ramifications of the intellectual aristocracy were so extensive and pervasive that Trevelyan could boast close or distant connections with *every* Master of Trinity this century except the present incumbent: Montagu Butler and Sir J. J. Thompson before him, and Lord Adrian, Lord Butler, Sir Alan Hodgkin, and Sir Andrew Huxley who followed him into the Lodge.

In the same way, Trevelyan enjoyed 'from his boyhood upwards the intimacy of men in power', and had friends or relatives in every British Cabinet – whatever its political complexion – until 1955. A. J. Balfour was a relative by marriage, he met Asquith and Ramsay MacDonald socially in the years before 1914, and Lloyd George later published one of Trevelyan's letters from Serbia in his *War Memoirs*.[62] He was well acquainted with Liberals like Sir John Simon, Sir Edward Grey and Walter Runciman; with Conservatives like Lord Halifax and Lord Stanhope; and with Labour figures like Arthur Ponsonby and Hugh Dalton. One friend and fellow Harrovian, Stanley Baldwin, appointed Trevelyan Regius Professor of Modern History at Cambridge. Another, Winston Churchill, made him Master of Trinity. And the precise details of that appointment were handled by a young man named John Colville, who later claimed – perhaps rather self-aggrandizingly – that he had brought about Trevelyan's acceptance by letting it be made known that if he refused, a much less appropriate person such as Professor Lindemann might be appointed instead.[63] Like Trevelyan, Colville had been educated at Harrow and Trinity (where he had read history), and he was the grandson of the Marquess of Crewe, who had himself been a colleague of Charles Trevelyan's in the prewar Liberal Governments.

Indeed, Harrow and Trinity only widened still further the impressive range of Trevelyan's contacts and connections. When he went up to Trinity in the autumn of 1893, sixty-eight out of the 105 MPs from Cambridge were from Trinity, the highest number from any Oxbridge college, accounting for one MP in ten. At the same time, one-third of Gladstone's last Cabinet was composed of Trinity men, including Sir William Harcourt, Earl Spencer, and Trevelyan's own father. One more of them, Sir Henry Campbell-Bannerman, would go on to be Prime Minister, following another Trinity man, A. J. Balfour, and witnessing the election to Parliament of a third, Stanley Baldwin.[64] Forty years on, it seemed as though little had changed. In February 1940, Trevelyan wrote to *The Times*, pointing out 'how many of the most vital interests of this country in this year of crisis are committed to Old Harrovians', including seven senior ministers, the Chief Whip, the Chief of the Imperial General Staff, and the King's private secretary. 'Such a list', Trevelyan concluded, 'would be creditable even for Oxford or Cambridge: for a school of five hundred to six hundred boys, it is something very much more.'[65]

An even tinier élite to which Trevelyan belonged was the Cambridge Apostles, and this again was something of a dynastic attachment. His father had been elected in 1859, his brother Bob in 1893, and Trevelyan himself two years later. Sir George had been elected in a vintage decade, and his contemporaries were still a force in Trevelyan's early life.[66] They included Edward Bowen, who was Trevelyan's housemaster at Harrow, and author of the school's songs; Oscar Browning, who had taught history at Eton, and was a Fellow of King's when Trevelyan was an undergraduate; Henry Sidgwick, who was a Fellow of Trinity from 1859–69, and again from 1885 to 1900, and sometime Professor of Moral Philosophy; and Montagu Butler, who had been Headmaster of Harrow between 1859 and 1886, and was Master of Trinity from 1886 to 1918.[67] And Trevelyan's own generation was scarcely less distinguished or influential, including as it did G. H. Hardy, the mathematician; Desmond MacCarthy, the literary critic; Eddie Marsh, later private secretary to Winston Churchill; and the philosophers Bertrand Russell and G. E. Moore. And in the next decade, newly elected Apostles included Lytton Strachey, John Maynard Keynes, Leonard Woolf, Rupert Brooke, and E. M. Forster.[68]

By this time, Trevelyan had resigned his Fellowship at Trinity, and moved to London. When he did so, he ceased to be an active participant in the affairs of the Society, and became instead an 'Angel'. But as with most Apostles, his loyalty to the Society and to its members remained lifelong. He attended the annual London dinners, and in 1935 made a 'most eloquent eulogy' on the jurist Sir Frederick Pollock, the senior member of the Society, who had recently celebrated his ninetieth birthday.[69] By that time Trevelyan was back in Cambridge as Regius Professor, and certainly attended some of the regular Saturday night meetings. Then, as in his own day, a disproportionate number of undergraduate members were drawn from Trinity: Alan Hodgkin, Denis Robertson, Victor Rothschild – and Anthony Blunt and Guy Burgess. During the late 1930s, Trevelyan went out of his way to help Burgess find a job, and according to Andrew Boyle it was Trevelyan's personal intervention with Cecil Graves, the Deputy Director-General and a personal friend, that eventually secured for Burgess a position with the BBC.[70] (There is no record of his reaction to Burgess's later career, but it is not difficult to imagine what he must have thought.) Trevelyan's last Apostolic appearance was in 1951, when the Society gave a dinner to celebrate his seventy-fifth birthday.

There was one yet smaller club to which Trevelyan belonged, and that was the Order of Merit. Like the Apostles, his membership was a compound of family connection and individual accomplishment. It was established in 1902 by King Edward VII, and one of its purposes was to recognize outstanding creative achievement in the arts, the sciences and the humanities. From the time of its inception, Trevelyan regarded it as the 'highest honour in the state', and when Sir George Otto became an OM in 1911, his son's delight knew no bounds. The appointment, he told his father, 'stamps your life as a recognized success as well as a real one.' It was, he went on, 'a very great honour, and the only very great "honour".'[71] Within two years of Sir George Otto's death, Trevelyan himself was appointed, and to this day they remain the only father and son both to have been members of the Order. (They were also both Honorary Fellows of Oriel College, Oxford.) But while Sir George Otto had reached the appropriately venerable age of 73 when his achievements were thus recognized, Trevelyan was, for a humanist, quite astonishingly young: a mere fifty-four. He had, as he confided to his brother, always hoped to be made an OM: but even he had not expected 'to get it for many years'.[72]

Well before the end of his life, Trevelyan was the senior member of the Order, and by that time, a remarkably large number of his friends and colleagues had joined him there: Vaughan Williams in 1935, H. A. L. Fisher in 1937, and Gilbert Murray in 1941.[73] In 1946, Lord Keynes was appointed, but he died before being able to receive the award. In 1949 and 1951 came two more Cambridge Apostles: Bertrand Russell and G. E. Moore. And after Trevelyan's death, there was G. P. Gooch in 1963 and E. M. Forster in 1969, both in the last years of their lives. To these humanists should be added the scientists whom Trevelyan knew at Trinity: J. J. Thompson (1912), Lord Rutherford (1925) and Lord Adrian (1942). Although technically in the gift of the sovereign, the means by which appointments are made to this Order remain shrouded in secrecy: 'some young woman', Trevelyan once told Stanley Baldwin, 'might write a Ph. D. thesis on it.' But there is consultation between members, and Trevelyan definitely had a hand in the appointment of H. A. L. Fisher in 1937.[74] Moreover, he soon became so senior a figure that his words must have carried disproportionate weight. In John Gross's felicitous phrase, there was in Britain, during the first fifty years of this century, an 'Order of Merit culture', largely liberal in tone, and Trevelyan, like his father, was at the very centre of it.[75]

Among these worlds within worlds of what we would now call the British Establishment, Trevelyan was effortlessly at ease and at home. He took it for granted that he belonged there, and his life was one long vindication of that presumption. But what made Trevelyan an even more significant figure was that this high standing in official circles was paralleled by his unrivalled popularity with the general public, as his books sold in massive numbers for more than half a century. The Garibaldi trilogy established him as the best-selling historian of his generation, and by the outbreak of the Second World War, *England Under the Stuarts* was in its seventeenth edition. By 1949 *British History in the Nineteenth Century* had sold 68,000 copies and the *History of England* 200,000. But even these astonishing figures were eclipsed by the *English Social History*. Within a year, it had sold 100,000 copies, and by the early 1950s sales had exceeded half a million.[76] There had been nothing like it since Macaulay – a precedent of which Trevelyan was well and happily aware. Nor do these statistics give any accurate impression of the total audience that Trevelyan reached: for many of his books were bought by libraries and used in schools and must have been read many times over. The tributes paid him in his later years – that he had done more to promote interest in history than any other man alive – were wholly deserved.[77]

Most of Trevelyan's books appeared under the Longman imprint, thereby perpetuating into the third generation the 'remarkable' connection between a dynasty of authors and a dynasty of publishers.[78] The firm was founded by Thomas Longman in 1724, and by the early nineteenth century its authors included Wordsworth, Coleridge and Southey. By mid-century, Longman had established a reputation for publishing improving books of high educational quality, which were equally well suited to the home or the school or the library, and its authors included such luminaries as Buckle, Lecky and Froude. But its brightest jewel was Macaulay, whose *History of England* proved a sensational success. Volumes three and four were published in December 1855, and within ten weeks 26,200 copies had been sold. In March the following year, Longman sent him £20,000 as an interim payment for his royalties, and the cheque was 'preserved by the firm as a curiosity in the history of publishing.' When he ventured into print, Sir George Otto naturally turned to Longman, and in 1897, when Trevelyan wanted to publish *England in the Age of Wycliffe*, he automatically followed suit. Thereafter, he may well have brought other authors Longman's way, since by the interwar years it also published G. P. Gooch, G. N. Clark, R. W. Seton-Watson, the Webbs and the Hammonds. In 1924, the company celebrated its bicentenary, and it was Trevelyan who proposed the toast to 'Literature and Science'.

The climax of this relationship came during the Second World War, when the Longman offices in Paternoster Row were bombed, their entire stock was destroyed, and the famous Macaulay cheque was apparently lost. Longman immediately set about reprinting all Trevelyan's books and, despite wartime shortages, did its utmost to obtain sufficient paper to ensure that enough copies of the *Social History* were printed. In July 1944, Trevelyan sent Robert Longman this letter of encouragement and appreciation:

> Here I sit in Cambridge in perfect safety, while you in London are bearing the weight of the second Battle of Britain in the last stage of the victorious war ... I have been connected with your firm for forty-five years, and have published fifteen out of my twenty books with you. My father and great-uncle published with you ever since the 1820s. Never once has there been any misunderstanding between the members of my family and the members of your firm. Never once have your people failed to produce our books up to the best standards of the time. And now you are producing my latest work under fire courageously borne by men and women alike.[79]

In May 1946, by which time the *English Social History* was an established bestseller, Macaulay's cheque was found, and it was sent to Trevelyan along with his own very substantial royalty payment. Nine years later, Longman published his festschrift, *Studies in Social History*, and at the presentation dinner Trevelyan paid his last tribute to the firm: 'There is nothing in my life as an historian that has been a greater source of pride and advantage to me than my co-operation with Longmans, a tradition in my family of more than a century and a quarter.'[80]

The Longman connection was central to Trevelyan: it reinforced his sense of dynastic identity, and it was the means by which he reached his principal public audience. But his links with *The Times* were almost as important in consolidating his position as national historian and public teacher. Before the First World War, most of Trevelyan's journalism had appeared in such Liberal periodicals as the *Independent Review* and the *Nation*. But he was already using the correspondence columns of *The Times* as a way of attracting public support for his preservationist endeavours, and this he continued to do for the rest of his life. During the interwar years, he became an indefatigable letter writer, on a wide range of subjects of general public concern: London statues, BBC pronunciation, Cambridge customs, George II's command of English, the number of Old Harrovians in the government and the German invasion of Holland in May 1940.[81] And he also wrote many generous obituary letters about friends and colleagues, such as Sir Walter Morley Fletcher, whom he had known as a Fellow of Trinity; Miss Mary

Cropper, a Westmorland poet; and Robert Somervell, his former schoolmaster at Harrow. Such writings in *The Times* helped to establish Trevelyan's identity in the public mind as the historian who helped to mould and influence informed opinion.[82]

By this time, he was also contributing lengthy articles on historical topics and current events: Sir Walter Scott, the Union with Scotland, the centenary of the passing of the Great Reform Act, the Silver Jubilee, and the Coronation.[83] His books were prominently and favourably reviewed, and were once described as a 'public benefaction'. When he published his memoir of his father, it occasioned a laudatory leading article entitled 'Three Generations'. And every major event in Trevelyan's life was greeted with editorial comment: the publication of the *History of England*; the award of the OM; his appointment as Master of Trinity; and his election to the Chancellorship of Durham. His obituary notice glowingly described him as 'a great Englishman', and there was a final, appreciative leading article.[84] Among twentieth-century historians, Trevelyan was unique in receiving such sustained and respectful attention from *The Times*. And he was equally loyal in return: in understanding his well-disposed attitude towards the foreign policy of the National Government during the 1930s, this close connection should certainly be borne in mind.[85]

The third medium whereby Trevelyan reached out to a large audience, and in so doing further impressed his image on his times, was the BBC. Under the dictatorial leadership of Sir John Reith, and with the strong support of Stanley Baldwin, the BBC was a self-appointed agent of cultural decency and self-improvement, and stood in the forefront of the interwar battle against the irresponsible press lords. In 1923 Trevelyan's elder brother Charles was a member of the Sykes Committee, which recommended that broadcasting should be a public corporation and a public service rather than be left to private enterprise.[86] And between 1935 and 1939 two of Trevelyan's closest friends, H. A. L. Fisher and R. C. Norman were, respectively, a member and the Chairman of the Board of Governors. In 1929 Trevelyan made his broadcasting debut by delivering the third in a series of 'National Lectures', on 'The Parliamentary Union of England and Scotland'. During the next twenty years, he broadcast on a variety of topics: on 'The Nature and Function of History', on 'Roman Britain', on 'Thomas Carlyle as an Historian', and – predictably – on 'Macaulay and the Sense of Optimism'. And in 1948 he took part, with Lord David Cecil, Bertrand Russell and Christopher Dawson, in a discussion of 'Ideas and Beliefs of the Victorians'.[87] By such broadcasts his position as the national historian and public educator was only further enhanced.

By virtue of his name, his ancestry, his illustrious relatives, his splendid offices, his links with Westminster and Whitehall, his prolific publications, his prodigious sales, his journalism and his broadcasting, and his public presence, Trevelyan acquired, during the course of his long life, a position of cultural authority which rivalled that of his great-uncle a century before, and which no historian since his time has come close to equalling. He was Britain's unofficial Historian Laureate, the Hereditary Keeper of the Nation's Collective Memory, combining – in terms of a later generation of practitioners – the popular appeal of Sir Arthur Bryant, Sir John Plumb, A. J. P. Taylor and Dame Veronica Wedgwood with the Establishment connections of Lord Blake, Lord Briggs, Lord Bullock and Professor Owen Chadwick. 'I am sure', Trevelyan had written at the outset of his career, 'writing history is the only thing I am really good at, and certainly the only thing I care about.' Half a century later, nothing had changed. He had, he told Charles, made his mistakes. But 'the one thing I was never a fool about was my task in life, and ... I have done what I set out to do.'[88]

III

The formative influences on Trevelyan's mind were those appropriate to someone of his family, his class and his generation. Pre-eminent among them was that of his great-uncle, as mediated by his own father. Sir George Otto Trevelyan had been born at Rothley Temple in Leicestershire, which had also been Macaulay's birthplace, and he was already ten years old when the first volume of his uncle's *History of England* appeared. One of his earliest recollections dated back to 1843, when Macaulay told him that he was going to spend five more years collecting material to write his great work, which the little boy assumed meant 'buying the very best pens and plenty of blue and white foolscap paper.'[89] Macaulay never married, but was on very close terms with his sister and her husband, and he treated the young George Otto more like a son than a nephew. In 1876, the year of Trevelyan's birth, George Otto produced his biography of Macaulay, which his son always maintained was 'much the best thing any person named

Trevelyan ever wrote.' And because of Sir George's exceptionally long life – he survived to the age of ninety – his 'Uncle Tom' remained a real presence and a vital force for Trevelyan until he was over fifty.[90]

But it was in Trevelyan's formative years that he had most come under Macaulay's influence. When a small boy at Wallington, his mother had read to him from the famous third chapter of the *History of England*, describing the social and economic condition of the country in 1685. Before he entered Harrow, Trevelyan had avidly devoured the *History* for himself, and also his father's biography – and rereading these works remained a regular ritual throughout his life.[91] As an undergraduate at Trinity, he was obliged to attend chapel, which meant he walked past his great-uncle's statue near the entrance every day. By then, however, the tide had turned against Macaulay, and he was no longer the admired authority that he had been during the last decades of his life. His exuberant, mid-Victorian optimism seemed inappropriate in the very different era of *fin-de-siècle* uncertainty. To the new school of professional scholars, much influenced by Teutonic ideas of 'scientific' history, Macaulay's style was as suspect as his sources. While he was a Cambridge undergraduate, Trevelyan was told by Sir John Seeley, the then Regius Professor, that Macaulay was a charlatan – an insult which he neither forgave nor forgot. And one of the reasons why he was so delighted at his father's OM in 1911 was that it publicly recognized 'literary history in the Macaulay tradition'.[92]

All his life, Trevelyan loyally defended Macaulay's history and his approach to history writing. In the years before 1914, he felt especially embattled on his great-uncle's behalf: hence his famous riposte to J. B. Bury's inaugural lecture at Cambridge, which had claimed that history was 'a science, no more and no less'.[93] After the First World War, and the general discrediting of all things German, Trevelyan delightedly told his father that 'we have lived through the anti-Macaulay period'. But even as late as 1932, in his biography of Sir George Otto, he was still denouncing intellectuals 'who were jealously indignant of Macaulay's great fame.'[94] In private, and sometimes in public, Trevelyan was prepared to admit Macaulay's faults. He recognized that he was 'biassed, pugnacious, often impatient', and that he possessed 'an inherent over-certainty of temper, flattered by the easy victories of his youth.' And his 'prejudices and his mistakes' were correspondingly glaring: his lack of training in historical research, his incorrect deductions from the evidence he had used, his weakness in understanding human motivation, and his uneven treatment of the Church and the gentry in his third chapter. And Trevelyan also thought Macaulay's faith in progress, however justified in his own lifetime, had not been borne out by twentieth-century events.[95]

But all this paled into insignificance beside what was to him the genius of Macaulay's gifts: his stupendous erudition, his incomparable prose, his narrative verve, his skill in construction, and the apparently effortless ease with which one subject flowed into another. He brought to bear on his writings an unusually well-stocked mind, and the rich experience of his varied career. He was, Trevelyan insisted, often much more fair-minded than his anti-Whig detractors asserted, and he was the first real social historian, who was as interested in the lives of ordinary people as in the deeds of the high and mighty. And in writing serious history that was in its day 'as popular as the most popular works of fiction', he made the study of the past an integral element in the public life of Victorian England.[96] In his turn, Sir George Otto had upheld and celebrated this tradition, and Trevelyan was determined to carry it on into the third generation. All his life, Trevelyan held to Macaulay's view of history: that it was a branch of literature no less than of scholarship; that it should be an essential part of the national culture of its time; and that it was for the general, well-educated public that he himself – and, he had once hoped, Theodore after him – had a duty and a calling to write.

All Trevelyan's history was written, as one reviewer critically observed, as if he had 'a bust of Lord Macaulay upon his desk'. His early books, especially *England in the Age of Wycliffe*, read in their more exuberant moments like a parody of his great-uncle's style, and Trevelyan had to work long and hard to break himself of that habit. 'I always read Ruskin while I am writing,' he told Bob, 'to prevent falling into Macaulayese.'[97] In his textbook accounts of the seventeenth and nineteenth centuries, Trevelyan began with panoramic sections surveying the social scene, which clearly owed much to Macaulay's third chapter. One of the reasons he wrote *England Under Queen Anne* was to take up the account at the death of William III, which was where Macaulay's unfinished *History* had left off. The *English Social History* was another tribute to Macaulay's pioneering interest in seeing the past as peopled by 'a fair field, full of folk'.[98] As the unofficial Historian Laureate of his generation, Trevelyan saw himself as following in Macaulay's footsteps. And throughout his life, he constantly wondered how Macaulay might have responded to contemporary developments, such as the decline of the Whigs, and the Government of India Act of 1935.[99]

Oddly enough, the second figure who most deeply influenced Trevelyan's mind and outlook was another Victorian who had had no time whatsoever for Macaulay, and that was Thomas Carlyle. To Carlyle, Macaulay was a 'vulgar' man, 'intrinsically common', 'a managing ironmaster with a vigorous talent for business', whose mind was 'the sublime of commonplace', and whose ideas were devoid of 'the slightest tincture of greatness or originality or any kind of superior merit.'[100] But as with Macaulay, so with Carlyle, it was the mediative influence of Trevelyan's father which was crucial. For Carlyle was quite won over by the personality revealed in Sir George Otto's biography of his uncle, and sent him a generous letter, fulsomely praising both the *Life* and the man, which the author proudly printed in later editions, and which Trevelyan published again in his memoir of his father. Thus began a close friendship between the two men. Carlyle was one of those who put Sir George up for election to the Athenaeum, and although himself eighty-two, went down in person to vote. And they often went for long walks together on Hampstead Heath, talking and arguing about history and literature. On one occasion, Carlyle held forth for two hours on the Elder Pitt, a monologue which Sir George Otto remembered as 'the best talk he ever heard from the mouth of man'.[101]

Carlyle died in 1881, but during the next twenty years, while Trevelyan was at his most impressionable, he remained a cult figure. 'When I was a young man in the nineties,' Trevelyan recalled over half a century later, 'the long red row of Chapman and Hall's six-and-thirty slim volumes of his works, well bound, well printed, two shillings each, still occupied shelf room in many a household.'[102] Trevelyan began to read Carlyle seriously at Cambridge, and he was overwhelmed by what he found. He thought there was no work more 'sage' about the past than *On Heroes and Hero-Worship*, no writing more 'sage' about the 1830s and 1840s than *Past and Present* (by 'sage' he meant 'full of the most important truths'), while he regarded *Sartor Resartus* as 'the greatest book in the world'. One of the earliest things he got into print was in defence and in praise of Carlyle: poet and historian, genius and hero.[103] He taught *Heroes and Hero-Worship* at the Working Men's College, and acclaimed C. H. Firth's edition of Carlyle's *Letters and Speeches of Cromwell*. And it can hardly be coincidence that Trevelyan's London house was very close to where Carlyle himself had lived during his last years, as 'the Sage of Chelsea'. Trevelyan later became a trustee

of this historic property, and although Carlyle went out of fashion after
1914, Trevelyan continued to read him appreciatively, to write and
speak in his defence, and to lament the fact that he had now joined
the ranks of the 'great unread'.[104]

The Carlyle whom Trevelyan admired was the preacher and prophet
of his early years. He thought *Sartor* provided 'a moral pattern of life
and an ideal attitude to the universe.' He regarded *The French Revolution* as Carlyle's 'greatest history', which gave, in its 'sharp, living,
memorable pictures of the scenes and actors in that strange drama', an
unparalleled display of human insight and sympathy. He was moved
by Carlyle's indictment, in *Past and Present*, of the 'machine age' of the
1830s and 1840s, and by his hostility to the 'utilitarian "profit and
loss" philosophers'.[105] And he believed Carlyle's *Cromwell* was the first
book to do the Lord Protector full justice, by convincingly depicting
him as a Puritan zealot. There were, Trevelyan admitted, difficulties
with all these books: they were often one-sided, they lacked interest
in institutions and, by the time of *Cromwell*, Carlyle's preoccupation
with heroes was degenerating into an unhealthy obsession with despots.
In his later books he spewed forth prejudice – against negroes, against
Jews, against parliamentary democracy. The elderly Carlyle, the
Carlyle of the *Latter-Day Pamphlets* and *Frederick the Great*, was not
at all to Trevelyan's taste, a misanthropic authoritarian, hostile to
parliamentary government, a 'Prussian' in politics, besotted with
dictators, and wedded to an amoral 'doctrine of force'.[106]

But there can be no doubt that the early Carlyle influenced Trevelyan
profoundly. There was his high sense of moral purpose, embodied in
the Stakhanovite injunction 'Produce! Produce!', an injunction which
Trevelyan heeded all his life. 'When you read Carlyle', he once wrote,
'you feel you will never give in.' His early admiration for the French
Revolution clearly owed much to Carlyle, as did his portrait of Cromwell
in *England Under the Stuarts*. He shared with Carlyle a hatred of all that
industry and machinery did to the spiritual and physical environment,
and a delight in writing about battles and warfare. He owed to Carlyle,
at least as much as to Macaulay, an interest in 'social life', and a
belief that history was 'the essence of innumerable biographies'.[107]
And he recognized one transcendent gift that Carlyle possessed which
Macaulay lacked: his 'unrivalled instinct for the detection of men's
innermost motives', his capacity 'to write history from the inside of
the actors.' Above all, Carlyle was unsurpassed in 'his imaginative grasp
of persons, situations and events', and this essentially poetic sense of

the past – 'tender as Shakespeare in his loving pity for all men' – touched a responsive chord in Trevelyan's own nature. For like Carlyle, Trevelyan had boundless sympathy and compassion for 'the individual men and women of the poor, struggling human race.'[108]

Like Carlyle again, Trevelyan regarded hero-worship as 'a noble doctrine'. In the 1900s, he regretted that 'heroes are now forbidden in history', and much of his work may be seen as an attempt to over-turn that view.[109] Indeed, no major historian has ever produced so many books in an essentially biographical mode. Unlike Carlyle's, Trevelyan's heroes were on the side of liberty and freedom rather than of tyranny and despotism, but they were heroes, nonetheless. He wrote to praise great men, not to bury them. That was quintessentially true of Garibaldi, whom Trevelyan depicted as part poet, part man of action, and also of Marlborough, who dominates the volumes of *England Under Queen Anne*. But it was also the case with the biographies of John Bright, of Lord Grey of the Reform Bill, of Grey of Fallodon, and of the study of Manin in 1848. And in many of his books of English history, Trevelyan's prose took wing when describing the imperishable achievements of great men and women: King Alfred, William of Wykeham, the Black Prince, Queen Elizabeth I, William III and the Elder Pitt. As Sir George Clark perceptively remarked, Trevelyan 'lived by admiration', and there can be no doubt that that was, in many ways, a Carlylean legacy.[110]

It can hardly be coincidence that the third figure who most influenced Trevelyan regarded Carlyle as 'the greatest of the Britons of his time', and that was George Meredith.[111] But Meredith was a full generation younger than Carlyle, and during the 1890s and 1900s, when his reputation was at its peak, Trevelyan was one of his most ardent disciples and 'devoted sectary'. He devoured Meredith's novels and poetry while a Cambridge undergraduate, began to correspond with him around 1900, and paid regular pilgrimages to Flint Cottage, one of which was memorably described by Desmond MacCarthy.[112] In 1906, Trevelyan published *The Poetry and Philosophy of George Meredith*, the only book he ever wrote about a living person. Two years later, he contributed an eightieth-birthday tribute in the *Nation*, and in 1912 he produced a complete edition of Meredith's poetry, with extensive explanatory notes. By the interwar years, Meredith was no longer fashionable. But Trevelyan wrote an appreciative essay in 1928, the centenary of Meredith's birth, and later gave Siegfried Sassoon much help in his biographical study. Towards the end of his life, he much regretted that Meredith's poems were out of print, and sought to remedy that by publishing a new anthology.[113]

According to Trevelyan, Meredith was not only the 'head of English letters': he was also a 'philosopher and teacher' whose poetry offered the best guide to 'right living'. Like Wordsworth, he loved the English countryside, and believed that man was at his best when communing with nature. But he was the first poet of nature to assimilate Darwin's theories of evolution, and thus to convey a sense of man's kinship with the earth from which it was now known he had sprung.[114] He recognized that all good things must pass away, with only death and oblivion to follow, but believed it was incumbent on all men and women to be 'fully alive' – to be hopeful, vigorous, courageous, thoughtful, and loving. He was an optimist; he was 'youth's poet'; he believed that 'the value of life depends on serviceableness to comrades and successors.' In one guise, Meredith's rare gifts of poetical inspiration, intellectual power, and fertile imagination gave him 'a deep insight into the recesses of the human mind'. In another, his celebration of the ordinariness of normal character made him 'the poet of common sense, the inspired prophet of sanity'.[115] And it was this combination of visionary ideals with practical wisdom that so captivated Trevelyan and his generation.

In thus analysing Meredith's philosophy, Trevelyan also showed a sympathetic appreciation of his political beliefs. In domestic matters, Meredith was an advanced Liberal.[116] He opposed British involvement in the Boer War. He believed in democracy and education, and in the emancipation of women. And he had no time for the idle, pleasure-loving, irresponsible rich. All this was music to Trevelyan's ears, as was Meredith's passionate belief in freedom when it came to European politics. Like Trevelyan, he admired the French Revolution, but regretted that it had led to the Terror and to Napoleon. Like Trevelyan, he feared the military might and efficiency of the Germans. And like Trevelyan, he regarded Italian unification as 'the main historical fact of the nineteenth century', retained an 'abiding faith in the spirit of the Italian nation', and constantly preached the cause of Anglo-Italian co-operation. At the same time, Meredith was also possessed by a 'passionate patriotism'. He constantly urged that the nation must rearm in the face of the German threat. He believed that the English were 'history's blood royal', and that if Britain fell, 'mankind would breathe a harsher air'.[117] These, again, were opinions which Trevelyan fully shared: indeed, he was himself to use both these phrases in his historical writings.[118]

But it was in his books on Italy that Meredith's influence on Trevelyan was most significant.[119] Meredith paid his first visit in 1861, and five years later was sent back by the *Morning Post* as their special correspondent, to be with the Italian forces in the last phase of their war with Austria. By this time, he had completed a novel, *Vittoria*, which described the earlier Italian uprising against the Austrians in 1848. Although Trevelyan was less captivated by Meredith's novels than by his poems, he was profoundly impressed by this work. He thought the character of the Italian revolution was better evoked 'than in any history'; that it provided 'a detailed and accurate analysis of a people and a period'; that the description of Mazzini was 'an example of perfect historical portraiture inspired by the highest poetic gifts'; and that the result was 'a great prose poem on an epic moment in human affairs'.[120] When Trevelyan came to write his Garibaldi books, which he did immediately on completing his study of Meredith, he not only relied on much that Meredith had written: he hoped to produce a work of similar poetry and power.

Macaulay, Carlyle and Meredith were the three figures to whom Trevelyan owed most: but they were also part of a greater, all-consuming passion for English poetry and English literature. Among Trevelyan's earliest memories were visits to the theatre at Stratford to see Shakespeare, learning Macaulay's *Lays of Ancient Rome*, and thrilling to Scott's historical romances. At Harrow, he read Shakespeare, Milton, Shelley and Keats, and wrote a prize essay on Tennyson.[121] By this time, he had also read all of the great English novelists and was writing his own poetry. At Cambridge, he explored Swinburne and Browning in addition to Meredith and Carlyle, and it was only there that he decided that history, not poetry, must be his vocation. But the passion for literature never left him. He learned thousands of lines of poetry, and would disconcertingly interrupt guests at dinner with his recitations. He regularly reread the classic novels he had discovered in his youth. And he never wavered from his belief that history and literature were inseparable: no historian could write about the English past ignorant of what novelists and poets had said; and no critic could write about literature if he was unaware of the circumstances in which it had been created.[122]

Trevelyan's feeling for literature was, as Noël Annan has explained, essentially nineteenth-century. He thought about what he had read, but his primary response was emotional rather than cerebral. He was moved by poetry and prose, by the sound and rhythm of the words: they struck at his heart rather than his head: 'inner truth' was 'felt', not thought. And his taste in literature reflected this: there was little writing that was done in the twentieth century by which he was impressed. He once asserted that 'all novelists since Conrad are cads', on another occasion claimed never to have heard of Proust.[123] In the same way, Trevelyan regarded literary critics as men of letters, who simply and selflessly sought to convey the greatness of the author about whom they were writing. He himself had been brought up on A. C. Bradley and Harley Granville-Barker. In his own generation, he delighted in the writings of Desmond MacCarthy and Basil Willey. And among the younger men, he thought highly of Lord David Cecil and John Dover Wilson.[124] But he had no time for the vitriolic denunciations of F. R. Leavis, and would have been dismayed and bewildered by deconstruction and post-structuralism. What, he would surely have asked, did any of this arcane academic games-playing have to do with encouraging among the general reading public an appreciation of great poetry and prose?

This abiding devotion to English literature is apparent in everything that Trevelyan wrote. In volume after volume of his works on English history, he celebrated the writings of Piers Plowman and Chaucer, Shakespeare and Milton, Jane Austen and Dickens, Wordsworth and Keats. And in his more polemical writings, he constantly urged the need to reunify the study of history and literature.[125] More generally, Trevelyan was correct in his claim that 'love of poetry has affected the character, and in places the style, of my historical writings, and in part dictated my choice of subjects.' In support of this, he instanced Garibaldi, 'because his life seemed to me the most poetical of all true stories', and Grey of Fallodon, with whom he shared a common devotion to Wordsworth, and whose own life, personality and fate were a prose poem in themselves.[126] At an even deeper level, Trevelyan held an essentially poetic view of the past: a recognition of the transience and the tragedy of human life, which brought with it a boundless compassion for men and women, trapped in time and circumstance. Never did he forget, and never did he allow his reader to forget, that here on this earth, here in this place, previous generations had lived and died, and that the same fate awaited all those who came after them.

In *A Layman's Love of Letters*, Trevelyan talked with unusual candour about the writers who had meant most to him. 'I have now', he observed, 'for seventy-two years, lived and had my being in English literature, particularly English poetry.' He spoke of Matthew Arnold's criticism of Byron, Shelley, Coleridge and Gray. He discussed Kipling and Browning. He lectured on Housman, Wordsworth, and other poets of nature. He mentioned historical fiction and history as litera- ture. He analysed the Border ballads and Walter Scott. And he paid a last tribute to Meredith. Each individual, Trevelyan insisted, must 'discover by experiment what are his own tastes, irrespective of the fashion of the hour.'[127] For literature was not an intellectual con- undrum, to be solved by certain rules. It was 'joy, joy in our innermost heart. It is a passion like love, or it is nothing.' It was 'our greatest national inheritance', and he concluded with a ringing plea to young people to make the most of it:

> What an immense and variegated landscape is stretched around you for your delight. It is all free for you to search, of infinite variety in its appeal, from comic prose to the highest poetry, all the ages of England, and all the moods of her most remarkable men set down in words inspired. It is all of it your heritage. Search it and enjoy it. It has been to me a great part of the value of life, and may it be the same to you.[128]

Like many members of the late nineteenth-century intelligentsia, Trevelyan's passion for poetry meant he had little time for organized religion, despite the fact that his grandfather, Sir Charles Edward Trevelyan, was a devout Evangelical, and that his father held to a 'broad but severe Protestant religion'. Even as a schoolboy, he was already hostile to the 'papist trash' of Catholic religious imagery, and he later claimed that he had ceased to be an Evengelical at the age of 13, 'on discovering that Genesis I was untrue, as Darwin had, I was informed, proved it to be.' Having read Ernest Renan's *Vie de Jesus* in 1893, he became a militant agnostic, and when he visited France in 1899, he was appalled to find it such a 'pit of clericalism'.[129] One of the reasons why he left Cambridge was that he thought 'a definitely agnostic atmosphere' was 'essential to my free development of work and life.' In the pages of the *Independent Review* he attacked the unthink- ing manner in which most educated Englishmen went to church, more as a social ritual than for spiritual guidance. And in a paper read to the Heretics' Club in Cambridge, he urged that both Christians and agnostics should learn to be more tolerant of each other. 'Outside Our Father's house', he concluded, 'are many mansions.'[130]

So militant was Trevelyan's agnosticism in these years that, for a time, it threatened to get in the way of his making an appropriate marriage. In 1899, he fell in love with Hester Lyttelton, who would have been a perfect match. She was descended from a titled but not grand family, and of her brothers one went on to be a cabinet minister, another to be Chief of the Imperial General Staff, a third to be a bishop, and a fourth to be Headmaster of Eton.[131] But both sets of parents considered that the children were too young, and for such a devout Anglican dynasty there can be no doubt that George's militant unbelief was a fatal drawback. In 1904, Hester married Cyril Alington, who later became Headmaster of Eton. Trevelyan soon recovered from the rebuff, but initially, Mrs Humphry Ward was equally displeased when her daughter took up with a man 'so wholly non-Christian', who 'looks forward to a civil marriage'.[132] Eventually George and Janet had their way and were married in Oxford, where a perfunctory ceremony in the Registry Office was followed by a secular service in Manchester College Chapel. 'Of course', Lady Trevelyan later wrote to Bob and his wife, 'there was nothing in the least doctrinal, but it was very high-toned and "ethical",' all allusions to the Deity being qualified by the words 'If Thou existest'.[133]

Thereafter, Trevelyan's disapproval of Catholics and Anglo-Catholics seems never to have lessened. Among historical figures, he never appreciated Cardinal Newman, and among contemporaries, he disliked Hilaire Belloc as much as Belloc disliked him. As the self-appointed champion of 'Catholic history', Belloc regarded Trevelyan as 'a typical product of the highly anti-Catholic English universities and governing class.' Unlike Trevelyan, he believed that the Reformation had been a terrible mistake, and the Civil War and execution of Charles I a disaster. And he denounced Trevelyan's Whiggish treatment of Charles II, of 1688, and of James II. Between 1925 and 1931, Belloc began producing a multivolume *History of England*, no doubt intended as a Catholic corrective to Trevelyan's own survey.[134] But it never sold very well and fizzled out at 1612. Belloc's hostility was thus a compound of genuine doctrinal difference, aggravated by envy. For while Trevelyan enjoyed unrivalled public standing and popular success, Belloc was tied to the treadmill of hack journalism, and his serious work suffered accordingly. Trevelyan was not alone in regarding him as prejudiced in his views and inaccurate in his scholarship. Indeed, on one occasion, he even called him a 'liar'. Always beware, he warned the young Arthur Bryant, of 'the whole tribe of Jacobite and Catholic writers.'[135]

Although Trevelyan had no time for priests or Anglo-Catholics, his general attitude to religion began to mellow during the interwar years. In part, this was because he came to recognize that his own innermost thoughts had always been, in their way, concerned with 'the spiritual nature of things'.[136] As an adolescent, he explained to Mary in 1926, he had been in a 'state of spiritual unrest, of mingled joy and melancholy, seeking guidance and a religion, but finding I must make one (or find one) for myself, with the help of preachers, poets and heroes of my own choosing.' And he was also prepared to admit that this quest for 'spiritual values' was not one which everyone felt obliged or able to make. 'I was . . .' he went on, 'too impatient with other people who adopted orthodox religions ready made for them: I know now that all cannot be "seekers" for religion or ways of life of their own.' As he later explained to Hilton Young, there were many people, especially among the less advantaged, for whom faith was clearly a great comfort: 'I sympathize with their desire for the old religions, though not needing them myself.'[137]

During the same period, Trevelyan came to take an increasingly well-disposed view of the Church of England. In part this was because in 1930 his daughter, Mary, married John Moorman, an Anglican clergyman with a scholarly interest in ecclesiastical history, who later became Bishop of Ripon. The fact that Moorman liked the countryside undoubtedly helped commend him to his prospective father-in-law. But as Trevelyan explained in a letter to Bob, he genuinely liked him:

> He . . . belongs as much to the academic as to the clerical world. His views are liberal-minded, and I have talked about religion and history with him with much agreement, and no feeling of barrier such as I should feel with a narrow-minded parson or an Anglo-Catholic. He is a fine walker, and has walked his fifty miles.[138]

Perhaps this also helps to explain why Trevelyan warmed to ecclesiastical statesmen like Temple, Davidson and Hensley Henson. In 1935, he told Mary that the Church of England now seemed to him '"liberal" in the best sense of the word, which it used often to be much less when I was young.' And at about the same time, he began to read the Bible systematically, getting through two chapters a night until he died.[139] Thus mellowed, he was no longer the 'muscular agnostic' of his youth, but now described himself as an 'Anglican agnostic'. 'I am', he insisted, 'a flying buttress of the Church; I support it, but from the outside.'[140]

Even so, when the possibility arose that he might become Master of Trinity, Trevelyan was not entirely easy in his mind. He would be the first holder of the office not to be a practising Christian, and would be expected to attend chapel regularly on Sundays. Accordingly, he summoned two senior Fellows, and for forty-five minutes gave them an account of his changing religious beliefs. Having concluded his narrative, he added, without a pause: 'So where can I buy a surplice?' He dutifully attended chapel, read the lesson on special occasions, and preached one sermon, on 'Religion and Poetry'. His theme was predictable: 'the vague but powerful intuition which many of us feel about life and the universe', an intuition which might most appropriately be labelled religious, and which the great poets had done most to express.[141] In his later years, Trevelyan seems to have mellowed still further, and was delighted when Dom David Knowles, a Benedictine monk, eventually succeeded him in the Regius chair. And, despite what he knew of Trevelyan's earlier views on Roman Catholicism, the admiration was very soon reciprocated.[142] But the old agnostic was not entirely vanquished. As an OM, he attended the Coronation of Queen Elizabeth II. There was, he felt, 'too much Church of England stuff'.

IV

Given the class and the generation to which he belonged, it was not altogether surprising that Trevelyan began life as a militant agnostic. But although a member of the intellectual aristocracy, he also had little time for those who thought of themselves as intellectuals. In part, this was because he did not care for their cliques or organizations. At the time he was elected to the Apostles, the Society was greatly under the influence of G. E. Moore, and Trevelyan had little sympathy with the emphasis placed on personal relationships and intellectual speculation.[143] One of the reasons why he resigned his Trinity Fellowship was that he thought the atmosphere in Cambridge too parochial and too hypercritical, and that it would be much easier for him to write books if he went away. In 1910, he refused to join a newly formed Academy of Letters, because he disapproved of literary societies handing out prizes and medals.[144] At almost the same time, he denounced 'the fatuous dons who compose the so-called British Academy', and

asked H. A. L. Fisher not to put his name forward for election. He
eventually became a Fellow in 1925, but sternly declined to be President, on the grounds that he had better things to do with his time and
his talents.[145]

But much worse than this, to Trevelyan's mind, was the behaviour
of the most influential and self-regarding literary coterie of his time:
the Bloomsbury Group. His brother Bob got on well with them, and
many of Bloomsbury's most distinguished members were distant relatives, Cambridge contemporaries, or fellow Apostles. For one of their
number, Trevelyan came to feel the very greatest admiration, and that
was John Maynard Keynes. He thought well of Keynes's intellect, and
regarded his judgement of men and events as generally sound. After the
First World War they were at one in their disapproval of the Treaty
of Versailles; both were involved with the affairs of the *Nation*, Keynes
as Chairman of the board, Trevelyan as a contributor; and they collab-
orated in the early 1930s in attempts to help Jewish academics suffering
under the Hitler regime.[146] In what to Trevelyan seemed a very un-
Bloomsbury-like way, Keynes was possessed of 'an immense disinterestedness and public spirit', as Bursar of King's, as founder of
the Cambridge Arts Theatre, and in his work for successive British
governments. He was flattered to follow Keynes as High Steward of
the Borough of Cambridge, and when Roy Harrod came to write
Keynes's authorized biography, Trevelyan gave him all the assistance
and encouragement he could.[147]

For Trevelyan, Keynes was the Bloomsbury exception who very
much proved the rule. He also had a certain amount of time for
Leonard Woolf, to whom he gave early advice about walking in
Northumberland and with whom he maintained an intermittent correspondence thereafter. And although Woolf found Trevelyan's literary
tastes incorrigibly philistine, he wrote a generous review of the *History
of England* and later composed a warm and affectionate memoir.[148]
But Trevelyan never warmed to Virginia, whom he thought 'a horrid
woman', and regarded the rest of Bloomsbury as 'a dreadful lot'. He
thought their morals disgraceful, their influence pernicious and their
lack of public spirit utterly reprehensible. Many of them were scions
of the intellectual aristocracy, and it has rightly been suggested that
their sceptical, mocking, rebellious tone was a reaction against 'their
fathers' too-blameless characters.' But for Trevelyan, who accepted
these stern Victorian conventions wholeheartedly, except in matters
of religion, this was deplorable.[149] And this emerges clearly in his

uncertain relations both with one of Bloomsbury's formative influences, and with one of its brightest ornaments: Bertrand Russell and
Lytton Strachey.

Initially, Trevelyan's relations with Russell were close and cordial.
They were near contemporaries (Russell was born in 1872), and they
came from very much the same privileged stable: both patricians, both
Whigs, both Trinity men, both Apostles, both possessed of first-class
minds and first-class prospects.[150] During the years before 1914, they
saw a great deal of each other: they went on walking holidays in
England and in Italy, they regularly met in London, Russell reviewed
the first Garibaldi book very favourably in the *Edinburgh Review*, and
at some point Trevelyan helped Russell financially.[151] But already their
different philosophies of life were beginning to emerge. Trevelyan
disapproved of Russell's amorous adventures and regretted the breakdown of his first marriage, while Russell, for his part, thought Trevelyan's attitude to such matters insufferably Victorian. He once told
Russell that Trevelyans never made matrimonial mistakes. 'They wait',
he said, 'until they are thirty, and then marry a girl with both sense
and money.' As Russell later remarked, despite some difficult times,
he never regretted that he had disregarded this prescription.[152]

Then, in 1914, they fell out over Britain's entry into the First World
War. After much agonizing, Trevelyan came down in favour, while
Russell was so vehemently opposed that he was deprived of his Trinity
Lectureship and was later sent to prison. In 1915 Trevelyan asked
Russell to repay the money he owed him, and by the interwar years
their relations were very distant. They do not seem to have met, and
Russell spent a great deal of time in America. Trevelyan can hardly
have approved of Russell's pot-boiling books, his trivial articles for the
Hearst press, and his still stormy (and much-publicized) private life.[153]
And it is not difficult to imagine what he must have thought about
Russell's widely disseminated views on morals and on education. By
this time, Trevelyan was convinced that he was 'an ass', 'a bloody
fool', a man without political judgement or common sense, who was
incapable of adjusting his early beliefs to the changing world.[154] In
1949 Russell was described in one newspaper as 'a teacher who has
been teaching people all your life how to live.' 'I hope', Trevelyan
wrote to him, in evident disbelief, 'you are satisfied with the results of
your efforts.'[155]

But just as the First World War had divided them, so the Second
World War brought about something of a personal reconciliation. As

Master of Trinity, Trevelyan was instrumental in rescuing Russell from the treadmill of American lectures and journalism, by bringing him back to a five-year Lectureship in the College in 1944. Russell was delighted, stayed in Newton's rooms, and found 'George Trevy ... much mellowed, very friendly and nice.' And as Russell became more respectable and more responsible, with the OM, the Nobel Prize for Literature and the appearance of his *History of Western Philosophy*, Trevelyan seems to have warmed to him again.[156] But he remained wary nevertheless. In April 1956 Russell was scheduled to broadcast an eightieth-birthday tribute to Trevelyan at ten in the evening. After making a very brief speech, Trevelyan rushed home from the celebratory dinner at Trinity to hear it, 'because you never can tell'. In fact, it was an admirable appreciation of Trevelyan's life and work, interspersed with recollections of their years together before the First World War. 'Your talk on the wireless last night', Trevelyan wrote to Russell, 'was a fine synopsis of our lifelong friendship, and gave me the greatest pleasure. I thought it could not have been better done.'[157]

Although Trevelyan thought Russell lacking in judgement and common sense, he never doubted the brilliance of his mind; he may grudgingly have admired the steadfastness with which he adhered to his original beliefs; and the final exchange seems to have been genuine on both sides. No such generous feelings influenced his attitude towards Lytton Strachey, despite the fact that their two families had much in common. The Trevelyans and the Stracheys were both West Country landed dynasties. Both had acquired baronetcies, both had provided Indian administrators across the centuries, and both had close connections with the intellectual aristocracy.[158] When Strachey went up to Trinity to read history in the autumn of 1899, Trevelyan was already established as a Fellow, and Strachey's election to the Apostles in 1902 was a further link between them. But in an earlier generation Sir Charles Edward Trevelyan had found Lytton's father, Colonel Richard Strachey, to be clever but wayward, and in need of 'an experienced and sagacious man always over him to keep the effusions of his genius within bounds.' Much the same could be said of Trevelyan's attitude to Lytton.[159]

After their initial meeting, Strachey regularly went to breakfast with Trevelyan and they went on lengthy walks and cycle rides together, when Trevelyan held forth on a variety of subjects. But Strachey gradually began to tire of what he regarded as Trevelyan's heavy-handed, patronizing and avuncular kindness. 'He is very – I think too – earnest,'

Lytton wrote to his mother, and that remained his opinion of Trevelyan for the rest of his life.[160] Nor did his election to the Apostles bring them any closer together. Strachey's concerns with homosexual relationships and with ethical and metaphysical speculation were of little interest to Trevelyan, while his desire to mock and to shock appalled him. But Strachey soon established himself, in succession to G. E. Moore, as the dominant influence in the Society. According to Bertrand Russell, there was a 'long drawn out battle between George Trevelyan and Lytton Strachey . . . in which Lytton Strachey was on the whole victorious.' How far the Society was in fact thus riven remains debateable. But for all his lifelong loyalty to it, Trevelyan had always disliked the other-worldly pretensions of some of the Apostles. And Russell was correct to observe that after Keynes was elected in 1903, there was a period when 'homosexual relations among the members were for a time common'.[161]

But there were other reasons why the two men did not get on. In 1901, Strachey obtained only a Second Class in Part One of the Historical Tripos. Despite this, he was elected to a Scholarship at Trinity. But in what was ostensibly a letter of congratulation, Trevelyan took pains to point out Strachey's scholarly and – by implication – personal shortcomings:

> We (that is to say the College) have elected you to do credit to us, and . . . this really lays an obligation on you to do us proud. You must get a First now. To do that, you will have to work reasonably hard, and fill up a lot of weak places, or rather vacuums . . . Your answers are all essays – clever essays to cover a good deal of ignorance. Please regard yourself as married to the College and to History – and bigamy has its duties as well as its privileges.[162]

It is not difficult to imagine what Strachey must have thought of this well-meaning but heavy-handed missive. Yet in observing that Lytton wrote 'clever essays to cover a good deal of ignorance', Trevelyan put his finger on the technique which he was to employ throughout his life. It never commended itself to Trevelyan, and he was probably not surprised when Strachey only obtained another Second in 1903. This made it almost certain that he would not obtain a Trinity Fellowship. But it may have been more than coincidence that Strachey's examiner was R. Vere Lawrence, a man who at that time was very much under Trevelyan's influence.[163]

Perhaps it was not surprising that Strachey wrote a barbed account of Trevelyan's wedding ('The happy pair are to lead the Simple Life and will go to Oxford in a special train'), and thought the Garibaldi books 'tiresomely told'.[164] During the First World War, relations were further strained, as they found themselves on different sides, with Strachey taking up a militantly pacifist position. Nevertheless, Trevelyan's response to Lytton's two most famous books was, in his private letters, decidedly appreciative. In August 1918 he read *Eminent Victorians* 'at one long sitting in the train across North Italy', with 'the most intense pleasure, approval and admiration.' He thought the portraits of Gordon, Manning and Florence Nightingale admirably done, and it was only family loyalty which inclined him to argue that Arnold alone did 'not have full justice done to him'. But he did not 'think the book "cynical"'. He congratulated Strachey on his 'judgement', his 'real historical sense', and concluded that he had 'found a method of writing about history which suits you admirably, and I hope you will pursue it.' Nor was he any less enthusiastic about the biography of Victoria. 'I suspect you are tired of hearing how good *Queen Victoria* is,' he wrote in May 1921, 'but I should like to say to you, much as I like the last book, I think it beats it a lot.'[165]

But as this last sentence implies, Trevelyan had in fact been appalled by the supercilious and dismissive tone of *Eminent Victorians*. He hated its zestful iconoclasm and self-conscious irreverence, thought its impressionistic approach the height of scholarly irresponsibility, and disliked the unsympathetic treatment of his subjects' private lives. Trevelyan believed in great men and women, and he was enraged that Lytton cut them down to size in such a sneering and dishonest manner. By the time Strachey came to write his biography of Victoria, his own attitude had mellowed somewhat, which explains why Trevelyan found it more congenial. And *Elizabeth and Essex*, published in 1928, was even more measured in tone. Trevelyan's letter to Strachey reveals his true feelings about Lytton's earlier books:

> It is much your greatest work, and its success bears out my theory against your own – or what used to be your own. You used to tell me that your strength was satire and satire alone, so you must choose people whom you did not much like in order to satirise them – like the Victorians ... I thought that argument bad then, and now the time gives proof of it. Your best book has been written about people to whom you are spiritually akin, far more akin than to the Victorians. And it is not a piece of satire, but a piece of life.[166]

As if to return the compliment, Strachey found Trevelyan's *England Under Queen Anne* 'very good and instructive'. But if Trevelyan thought that Lytton had mellowed for good, he was soon to be disappointed, for in 1931 he produced *Portraits in Miniature*, a much more barbed piece of writing, which contained a series of brief essays on 'Six English Historians'. The tone was Lytton at his most deflating, and in the course of one of them he described the death of Professor E. A. Freeman thus: 'the professor had gone pop in Spain'.[167] As Strachey recorded with glee in a letter to Roger Fry, Trevelyan was outraged:

> Virginia [Woolf] had just met Lord Esher who told her that he had just met George Trevelyan who was foaming at the mouth with rage – 'Really! I should never have believed that a writer of Lytton Strachey's standing would use an expression like that – "went pop!"'
> So some effect has been produced, which is something.

Perhaps it is not surprising that when Strachey died in 1932, Trevelyan's letter of condolence to his sister was distinctly lukewarm. He spoke of Lytton's 'rare talents' – a phrase which was decidedly double-edged – and left it at that.[168]

In retrospect, Trevelyan much regretted that he had not spoken out against Strachey at the time.[169] For he was certain that Lytton had poisoned history, traduced the Victorians, and created a fashion for 'cheap . . . nasty . . . absurd one-volume biographies' designed to meet the contemporary demand for sensational literature.[170] But after Lytton's death, he spoke his mind more freely. In 1944, he delivered an address in Scotland in honour of his old friend John Buchan. One of the reasons Trevelyan had admired Buchan was that he 'despised literary coteries', and avoided 'the squabbles and narrowness to which "intellectuals" of all periods are too prone.' But in addition, he thought him a much better biographer than the author of *Eminent Victorians*: 'Unlike Lytton Strachey, he began by finding out all that was known on the subject and then wrote a biography that gave a faithful picture, both of the man and his times.'[171] And in his Clark Lectures, Trevelyan decried the twentieth-century fashion – inaugurated by Strachey – for 'debunking', and proceeded in turn to debunk two of the debunkers: Raymond Mortimer on Kipling, and E. M. Forster on Sir Walter Scott.[172]

But Trevelyan's hostility to Strachey and Bloomsbury was also the product of personal anxiety springing from family pride. For he was descended from an eminent Victorian who might have been a prime target of Bloomsbury debunking. In *Portraits in Miniature*, Lytton had already dismissed Macaulay for his 'coarse texture of mind – a metallic style – an itch for the obvious and the emphatic – a middle-class Victorian complacency'.[173] But it was not only his public writings which were at risk from Lytton's stiletto: it was also his private life. For Macaulay had never married, had never been known to have had any love affairs, and had written letters to his sisters, Hannah and Margaret, so ardent and affectionate as to seem almost incestuous. When Sydney Roberts, the Secretary of Cambridge University Press, suggested that they might be published, he was amazed at the vehemency of Trevelyan's reaction: 'Over my dead body!' he replied. 'I'm not going to have those Bloomsbury people laughing at my great-uncle.'[174] Even though he had given them to Trinity, Trevelyan kept a firm hold on the use made of Macaulay's papers during his lifetime, only granting access to responsible scholars like Arthur Bryant, Richmond Croom Beatty and John Clive.[175]

'As to "intellectuals"', ... Trevelyan wrote to his daughter during the middle of the Second World War, 'one of the greatest disappointments of my life has been the decadence of that class (if you can call it a class), of which I first became aware when Lytton Strachey came up to Cambridge.'[176] As a statement of his innermost feelings, there can be little doubt that this was correct. Of course, he did not dislike all writers, all academics, all historians. But he expected them to be of 'broad and sympathetic understanding' and to conform to the same high standards of private morality and public responsibility that he set for himself.[177] For those who did, his loyalty and admiration were unbounded. His tribute to H. A. L. Fisher has already been quoted. Even more revealing is his glowing appreciation of John Lawrence and Barbara Hammond, written at almost the same time:

> I admire and love the two Hammonds immensely. They are very rare examples of real saintliness of character combined with intellectual and scholarly power and service to the public in the rough ways of the world's arena, and all savoured with great good sense.[178]

The contrast to Lytton and Bloomsbury could hardly have been more explicitly drawn.

V

Although for most of his life he was a famous public figure, Trevelyan was also a very private man. True to his late Victorian upbringing, he kept his feelings to himself, and expected other people to do the same.[179] Indeed, he was an extremely difficult man to get to know, and it is not clear that anyone ever knew him really well. There was, as Sir John Habakkuk has observed, 'something about him which inhibited speculation about his personality.' Among his relatives who have left published reminiscences of him in old age, Trevelyan emerges as recognizably the same person – 'a figure hewn in the rock on a grand scale, by which we lesser mortals cannot hope to be measured.'[180] Nor do the evocations of him by others give much away: among those who have set down their recollections of him in print, neither J. H. Plumb nor A. L. Rowse seems to have known him all that well. Both draw attention to his 'bleak surface', to his 'guarded heart', and to the 'impersonal front' he presented to the world. And late in Trevelyan's life, a Longman publicity officer harshly but correctly described him as being 'in anecdotage and newsworthiness' a 'somewhat arid proposition'.[181]

The most vivid picture of Trevelyan as a young man comes from the diary of Beatrice Webb, who stayed with the family for Christmas 1895, and described him with uncommon insight:

> The younger brother is a youth of great promise. Tall and graceful, with a sensitive face, small intellectual head, dark rich colouring, expressive eyes, a keen conversationalist and sympathetic companion, he would be a singularly attractive youth if he were not so uncannily self-possessed and self-controlled. He is bringing himself up to be a great man, is precise and methodical in all his ways, ascetic and regular in his habits, eating according to rule, 'exercising' according to rule, going to bed according to rule, and neither smoking, tea or coffee drinking, nor touching alcohol. Sport he indulges in with the deliberate object of cultivating the barbarian in himself, fearing the scholar's overwork and hypochondria. He is always analysing his powers, and carefully considering how he can make the best of himself. In intellectual parts, he is brilliant, with a wonderful memory, keen analytic power, and a vivid style. In his philosophy of life, he is, at present, commonplace, but then he is young – only nineteen![182]

In later years, Beatrice was more succinct: she thought him 'a consummate prig', who lived 'a strenuous and conscientious life' and displayed 'considerable talent'. By the time he came to write his *Autobiography*, this was a verdict with which Trevelyan himself had come to agree.[183]

Essentially the same character is revealed in a remarkable table which exists in the papers of John Tressider Sheppard, who was elected an Apostle in 1902, the same year as Lytton Strachey, was a central figure in the affairs of the Society for the next half-century, and was Provost of King's from 1933 to 1954.[184] Twelve Apostles, elected in the years between 1886 and 1902, including G. E. Moore, Desmond MacCarthy, Strachey and Sheppard, and the two Trevelyan brothers, were classified – it is not clear by whom – according to ten different characteristics, and were awarded points on a scale of one to twenty. Trevelyan scored very low marks – much lower than his brother Bob – for perception, humour and personality. He came in the middle range for common sense, conversation, manners, intellect and charm. And he scored very high marks only for temper and affection. The headings and the rankings may tell us more about Apostolic attitudes than about Trevelyan. But the analysis of Strachey (low in common sense, temper and personality, and high in conversation and humour) seems well observed, and the young Trevelyan who emerges from these rankings is also instantly recognizable.

One of the reasons why Trevelyan seemed so intimidating as a young man was that from an early age he knew his calling was to be history, and for the whole of his life, he single-mindedly devoted himself to his talent and to his task. 'I enjoy enormously', he wrote to Charles in 1898, on the appearance of his first book, 'the feeling of having my career and having my future in my hands. I am very eager for the fray.' In 1904, he told Charles he had made 'a cold and careful calculation', that if he was to be 'a considerable historian' he had 'six years at the most to play with': the very years in which the Garibaldi books duly appeared.[185] In 1911, he turned down the Readership for which he was being sounded out at Cambridge, and his reasons for doing so are instructive: 'The question now is whether I am going to be a person who wrote three amusing books about Garibaldi, and then trailed off, or whether I am to go on writing first-rate books.' He was determined to do the latter, and one of the reasons why he was so distressed by the Great War was that it took him away from his writing. 'With four or five of the best working years of my life taken out for this war,' he fretfully told his father in 1917, 'I shall have to hurry up with what is left of it afterwards.'[186]

Like his grandfather, Sir Charles, Trevelyan drove himself astonishingly hard all his life, possessed, as H. A. L. Fisher once observed, of 'that ardour and persistency of purpose without which no great things are done.' 'I believe', he told Desmond MacCarthy in 1901, 'in methodical work at some carefully chosen subject.' 'I must discipline myself again . . .' he wrote forty years later, 'I have been living too much for pleasure.'[187] But neither pleasure nor leisure had any place in his scheme of things. For half a century there was scarcely a time when he did not have a book on hand, as well as several essays and reviews. He did all his research himself, corrected his own proofs, and made his indexes. Although only a fragment of it has survived, it is clear that his correspondence was enormous, and until he became Master of Trinity it was all done by hand. As John Burrow has perceptively remarked, Trevelyan's was 'a character inadequately warmed by self-indulgence.'[188] In his stamina, in his iron self-discipline, and in his physical robustness, no less than in his immense output, Trevelyan showed himself a true child of the Victorian era. As Chancellor of Durham, when nearly eighty, he would not admit that heavy rain was a reason why an academic procession should not take place in the open air.[189]

The combination of hard work and ferocious honesty made Trevelyan, especially in his early years, an intimidating man, and although he had a large circle of acquaintances he did not make friends easily. He spoke too directly, with no thought for other people's feelings, and they understandably resented such devastating candour. At Harrow, where he was 'wrapped up in literary and historical imaginings', Trevelyan admitted that he was, in social terms, 'a misfit'. At Cambridge, G. E. Moore invited him on several reading parties during the vacations, but found him extremely difficult to get on with.[190] In 1912, there was a mix-up in London with William Rothenstein, who offered to make a drawing of Trevelyan, which he abruptly refused on the grounds that he could not afford to buy it. But Rothenstein had intended it as a gift and a mark of appreciation, and was much hurt at such curt dismissal. Trevelyan was sincerely contrite. But it took some time to sort things out. And in the interwar years, Steven Runciman remembers Trevelyan furiously berating Raymond Mortimer at the dinner table, when he had the temerity to suggest that the 'Glorious Revolution' was not entirely a 'good thing'. 'As a youth', Trevelyan recalled, 'I was very much a fool about personal relations, and grew to wisdom very slowly by experience.' It was not an experience which others always enjoyed.[191]

In the same way, his relationships with his own children do not seem to have been particularly warm. As in most upper-class households, the children were brought up by nannies while their parents were busy with their good books and their good works; in addition, Trevelyan spent a great deal of time away, travelling and researching in Europe. And after the death of Theodore, both parents seem to have made a cult of him in a manner which can only have harmed his surviving siblings: making annual expeditions to the grave and weeping ostentatiously over their lost dauphin.[192] The inevitable result was that both Mary and Humphry were made to feel that they were disappointments compared with the apotheosized Theodore, and Lord Trevelyan believes that 'a degree of estrangement of the son from the father and the daughter from the mother was the consequence.'[193] Only in later life, when he could treat them as adults, do Trevelyan's relations with his children seem to have eased. He took pride in Humphry's election to a Fellowship at King's in 1947. And his letters to Mary were open and candid, rightly treating her as a fellow historian of high intelligence. But they remain curiously distant and unwarm.[194]

Trevelyan appeared all the more forbidding because he was in so many ways a patrician puritan. Like most members of his family, he was not much blessed by a sense of humour. He possessed a boisterous, schoolboyish, late-Victorian sense of 'fun', but had no capacity for laughing at himself, and in the entire corpus of his major works, there are no jokes.[195] History, like life, was far too serious a business for that. And, like the Victorians again, he had no small talk. He was totally uninterested in gossip or personalities, and if he had nothing to say, he said nothing. Especially for the young, these long, brooding, seemingly interminable silences were a daunting experience. Nor did he indulge himself or his family in the vulgar creature comforts of the middle classes. In his youth, life at Wallington was spartan: Beatrice Webb remembered it was impossible to get an early-morning cup of tea. After his marriage, Trevelyan continued to live 'an austerely intellectual life style'. And his own home at Hallington was not for the fastidious or the faint-hearted: the food was bad, there was no wine, the cider was sour, the beds were hard, the hot water was lukewarm, the rooms were draughty, and there was lino on the floor. Trevelyan did not mind: he probably never noticed.[196]

In himself, he was the most untidy of mortals – though not quite in the same league of dishevelment as his brother Bob. By the 1900s, his clothes were already the despair of his friends. His mother begged him to dress better: to no avail. He simply instructed his Cambridge tailor

to 'send me a blue suit, the same measure and exactly like the last.'[197]
He cultivated what is now known as 'designer stubble' long before it
became fashionable to do so, and his hair was tended less often than
it should have been. During the Second World War, James Lees-Milne
accompanied Trevelyan to Blickling, on National Trust business. He
found the old man to be 'very uncouth in his dress and person', and
was taken aback to observe Trevelyan removing his dentures, and
cleaning them.[198] When he was a junior Fellow at Trinity, about to
be married, John Elliott was asked by Trevelyan which of his books
he would like as a present. He asked for *England Under Queen Anne*,
which Trevelyan duly brought into College one morning, wrapped in
a brown paper bag. But he was so unkempt that Elliott's bedmaker
mistook Trinity's former Master for a tramp.

When Trevelyan went on a lecture tour to the United States during
the First World War, Henry James correctly described him to a friend
as being 'of great ability and virtue, great general literary accomplishments, etc., but perhaps of rather limited grace.' He was, James went
on, 'full of substance and knowledge and intelligence', but was 'without
great outward ornament'. As Owen Chadwick has observed, Trevelyan
was in most ways a 'wholly unostentatious man'.[199] His conversation,
between the silences, was abrupt and barking in manner. He was a
poor speaker with an unmellifluous voice – harsh, rasping and grating.
Although he was assiduous in his attention to the social duties of the
Trinity Mastership, junior members seem to have found visits to the
Lodge something of an ordeal. For all these reasons, he was probably
well advised to withdraw his name from the short list for the Governor-
Generalship of Canada: however attentively he would have carried out
the job in other ways, he would not have been a success on the social
side. For all his great qualities, it is difficult to believe that the Canadians would have warmed to a man once described by George Kitson
Clark as resembling 'a very distinguished, but slightly dilapidated bird
of prey'.[200]

Yet despite these forbidding characteristics, even his critics admitted
that Trevelyan possessed many of the attributes of greatness. Beneath
the stern exterior lay a deeply ardent and emotional nature, not easily,
and not always, held in check. As with Macaulay, there were passionate
feelings pent up. He was famous for his crackling laugh, known as
'Trevvy hitting it for six', and when he laughed in Trinity Great Court
Leonard Woolf claimed he could be heard in Clare and St John's.[201]
He was also easily moved, especially by poetry or literature: there are

many who remember him suddenly breaking down, in heaving sobs and profuse tears, as he recited Wordsworth or Meredith. And as this suggests, he was the most unselfconscious of men, quite unaware of the impact of his personality or his reputation on other people. As Master of Trinity, he insisted on interviewing scholarship candidates in history. But he never could understand why so many of them seemed overwhelmed when he introduced himself by saying, 'Hello, I'm Trevelyan, I'm the Master,.' And at Hallington, after dinner, the guests were often invited to play a game of rhymed historical 'consequences', which was prefaced by their host remarking that Lord Acton had been no good at it, but Asquith had been a master. It was, Lord Trevelyan recalled, an observation which, quite unintentionally, 'struck terror into the less historically endowed of the party.'[202]

He was also genuinely modest and completely without self-importance. True, he never forgot he was a Trevelyan, and he never doubted that he possessed '*distinction* of mind'.[203] But he was totally without vanity or pomposity and sincerely believed that while he had talent, he was no genius, no hero. He freely admitted that he had been born with 'the most extraordinary advantages', and that he had had 'the most extraordinary good luck in life.'[204] Although he worked astonishingly hard, it never occurred to him that there was anything particularly meritorious in that, and he was the last person to draw attention to the fact: he just got on with it. And while his range of friends and connections was exceptionally wide, he never dropped names, with the result that many people in Cambridge never seem to have had the least idea how well connected he was, or how much good he did, in the world outside. He was devoid of snobbery, indifferent to titles, and in all his letters there is not a trace of the anti-Semitism so characteristic of his class.

At the same time, Trevelyan was exceptionally public-spirited, a phrase which his admirers use again and again when describing him, and rightly so, for he was a child of what Stefan Collini has accurately described as the Victorian 'culture of altruism'. As Trevelyan once observed to his brother Charles, 'we inherit the moral stamina produced in grandpapa by religion or otherwise, and apply it straight off to our infidel sense of duty.'[205] The books he wrote, the causes he espoused, the positions he accepted: all was done out of this iron sense of public obligation. For Trevelyan, the world was divided into two sorts of person: those who fulfilled their public responsibilities, and those who did not. His admiration for the first was as boundless as his

Trevelyan

contempt for the second. Along with this public-spiritedness gradually came a certain kind of high-principled tolerance. Trevelyan was too vehement in his views to be tolerant by temperament, but since he passionately valued liberty and freedom, he always felt bound to respect the other person's opinion. Especially in later life, if someone expressed a view which contradicted his, one of his favourite responses was to say, 'If that's what you think, you're quite right to say so', which, as Harry Williams recalled, was 'a combination of intensity and tolerance which left you in no doubt about his estimate of your opinion.'[206]

Trevelyan was also the most generous of men: the only one of the three brothers, as Beatrice Webb observed, 'who has given handsomely to the public causes in which he believed.'[207] As a conservationist, he was one of the first great benefactors of the National Trust, giving freely of his time and his money. And as an historian, he was no less generous. His admiration for such contemporaries as Gilbert Murray, G. P. Gooch and H. A. L. Fisher was genuine and lifelong. He encouraged young scholars like Arthur Bryant, Steven Runciman, Veronica Wedgwood, A. L. Rowse, H. J. Habakkuk and J. H. Plumb. There are many letters from lesser figures thanking him for the help and assistance he had given them.[208] No man of his generation can have had more books dedicated to him, ranging from John Buchan's *Augustus* to Siegfried Sassoon's study of Meredith.[209] And his generosity extended to those whom he had little cause to like. He helped obtain the chair of modern history at Manchester for Lewis Namier, despite Namier's contempt for his work; and in Cambridge he was a consistent supporter of Herbert Butterfield, even though he had written *The Whig Interpretation of History*. Even to such critics Trevelyan was a singularly magnanimous man.[210]

All this is the more remarkable because he was much afflicted by a deep strain of melancholy, which pervades all of his writings, even his many books with what he liked to call 'happy endings'. His prose is conspicuously devoid of the bounce, the jauntiness, the ebullience and the confidence of Macaulay's. Even in the 1900s, Bertrand Russell noted that there was about him 'an air of settled gloom', and as the years went by, his gloom only increased.[211] To the personal tragedy of Theodore's death was added the eclipse of the aristocracy and the spoliation of the countryside. The demise of the Liberal Party in England, and the advent of Fascism in Italy, destroyed the very foundations of the liberal, rational, optimistic world in which he had been brought up. And he regarded the First and Second World Wars as total calamities, which had wrecked European civilization as he knew and loved it. 'George is cheerful in company,' Bob wrote to Bertrand Russell in 1941, 'but often sinks into gloom when alone. He feels the world he cares for is at an end.' At almost the same time, Harold Nicolson visited him at Trinity, and his account conveys the same elegiac mood:

> We adjourn for port and coffee to the combination room. I sit next to George Trevelyan, the Master. I look round, upon the mahogany and silver, upon the Madeira and port, upon the old butler with his stately efficiency. 'It is much the same', I say to him. 'Civilization', he replies, 'is always recognizable.'[212]

For fifty years Trevelyan brooded not just upon the past, but upon the unfolding drama of current affairs in the light of the past. He found little in what he saw to cheer him, but unlike many disillusioned and disenchanted patricians, he never succumbed to bitterness or resentment or obscurantism. He might no longer be in sympathy with the world, but he continued to do his duty by it. It would have never occurred to him to do anything else. By his last decades, his youthful priggishness and ferocious honesty had mellowed into 'a character of noble simplicity, just, generous, affectionate, unselfish, and throughout true to an exacting code of honour and service.' He came to regret the harsh things he had said in his youth.[213] Unlike most academics, he was conspicuously devoid of envy, a virtue which is in no sense diminished by the fact that he had singularly little to envy anyone else for. His loyalty and integrity were plain for all to see. He was utterly without malice or pretence. As Trevelyan wrote of Sir Edward Grey, so it might have been said of him: 'at the close of his life, all who were sensitive to the touch of greatness felt it in his presence.'[214]

Two brief, late vignettes of Trevelyan vividly convey the sort of person that Beatrice Webb's youthful zealot had become. The first is by Father Harry Williams, remembering a meeting of the Trinity College Council almost at the end of Trevelyan's Mastership:

> The future of a particular Fellow was being discussed, and it looked as if Trevelyan had sunk into a senile doze. Proposals which were less than generous were gradually gaining acceptance round the table. But Trevelyan wasn't asleep. For at this point he suddenly thundered out: 'Is this a College, or a bloody institution?' The proposals were at once dropped, and considerably more generous ones adopted.[215]

And the second is by George Lyttelton, who encountered him at Trinity high table in March 1956:

> Old George Trevelyan was in hall. He is rather deaf, and sat for the most part eying his plate with a sort of aloof and brooding ferocity – a look as of thunder asleep, but ready. And once or twice it flashed and rumbled finely, e.g. at the recollection of the way in which *The Times* treated Abraham Lincoln at the beginning of the Civil War. Isn't that grand – unappeasable wrath at injustice, however ancient?

'I believe', Lyttelton concluded, 'if someone had recalled how Ulysses outwitted Ajax over the armour of Achilles, we should have had another cloud burst.'[216]

Trevelyan's last years tested to the full his essential nobility of temperament: widowed, half-blind, increasingly infirm, he awaited the end patiently, and without self-pity or fear. 'After fifty-two years of perfect companionship,' he wrote to Arthur Bryant, 'it seems unnecessary to have to go on alone. My father and mother after sixty years' marriage died within six months of each other. I wish I had that luck. But I am content to take what comes.'[217] At Hallington, where he could no longer walk, he would sit for hours in the pale Northumberland sunlight. At Cambridge, many friends came to read to him, from Trinity, from King's and from Christ's. And he consoled himself by reciting vast quantities of the poetry he had learned as a youth. Towards the end, John Clive went to visit him, and never forgot the 'very old and distinguished figure, the last of the great Whig historians, full of years, of kindness, and silence, and dignity.' A month or two before he died, his kinsman Humphrey saw him for the last time. 'I am sorry to hear, sir,' he remarked, 'that you have been unwell.' Trevelyan replied: 'I am eighty-six; it is time I was off.'[218] And so, very soon, he was.

VI

Fifteen years earlier, Trevelyan had observed that 'historians, scholars and literary men who have led uneventful and happy lives, seldom afford good subjects for biography', and he did his best to ensure that his own life should not be subjected to such scholarly scrutiny.[219] In part this arose out of a genuine feeling of reticence about himself: he no more wanted people prying into his privacy than Bloomsbury prying into Macaulay's. And in part it came from a genuine belief that his life was singularly devoid of interest. For as Trevelyan himself recognized, what mattered most about him are the books he wrote, the circumstances in which he wrote them, and the kind of historian he was. In 1909, on the death of George Meredith, he had written these words to the American historian William Roscoe Thayer:

> Of a great author, if taken in full old age, far more lives on than any other kind of man. His best self lives on in his books. But . . . he was as wonderful as his books – and very like them.[220]

The same may fairly be said of Trevelyan himself.

II

THE LIBERAL
INTERNATIONALIST

An epoch in which some portion of mankind, whether by a few men of genius or by common impulse, achieved new and wonderful things, is more important than one in which custom was unchanged and achievement barbarous.

G. M. TREVELYAN, 'The Latest View of History',
Independent Review, I (1903–4), p. 409.

By the way, I have nothing whatever to do with Italy under the present regime. I will say nothing against it in public – it is not our business. But I don't like it.

G. M. Trevelyan to R. W. Seton-Watson,
20 February 1928.

It is a wonderful evening, and the Master and Mrs Trevelyan take me for a walk down the limes and on to the Fellows' Garden beyond. George Trevelyan tells me that Gladstone told his father that they should always be grateful for living in the great age of Liberalism. 'Other generations, my dear Trevelyan, will be less fortunate.' But who could have conceived that any generation would have suffered as we have done?

N. NICOLSON (ed.), *Harold Nicolson:
Diaries and Letters 1939–1945* (1967),
p. 188, entry for 16 October 1941.

The Wren Library, Trinity College, Cambridge: Trevelyan believed that Trinity was 'the most beautiful of all settings for superlative powers of mind', something he had better cause than most to know.

THE WREN LIBRARY of Trinity College, Cambridge, is one of England's most splendid monuments to the cosmopolitan spirit of Renaissance humanism and classical learning.[1] The sonorous grandeur of the completed design, the cloistered colonnade of the lower level, the Tuscan pillars, the Ionic columns and the Doric frieze recall the Forum in Rome, the Theatre of Marcellus by Serlio and Sansovino's library at Venice. And the Grinling Gibbons carvings, the busts of Newton and Bacon, the full-size statue of Lord Byron and the figures of Divinity, Law, Physic and Mathematics which surmount the balustraded parapet proclaim the vigorous unity of European culture and the confident pre-eminence of Continental thought. To this assured civilization and splendid inheritance – secular, liberal, optimistic, progressive, internationalist – George Macaulay Trevelyan belonged as much by inclination as by ancestry, as much by desire as by descent. It was this world, and these values, that he intended to celebrate, to uphold and to illuminate in his historical writings. And it was the seemingly irrevocable self-destruction of this birthright as a result of the First World War which formed the greatest public sorrow of his life and times, a destabilizing catastrophe from which he never fully recovered.

I

In the light of his much-prized family background, it is almost impossible to imagine that the young Trevelyan could have espoused any political creed other than that of late-nineteenth-century Liberalism. His great-uncle, Lord Macaulay, and his grandfather, Sir Charles Trevelyan, were both reformers by instinct and inclination: in Britain and also in India, the constitution, education, the civil service and the financial system were restructured and overhauled thanks to their zealous endeavours. As a young MP, Macaulay made his name with a series of brilliant speeches in favour of the Great Reform Bill, and in the 1840s was the chief architect of educational reform in India. His brother-in-law, Sir Charles Trevelyan, was the joint author of the Northcote-Trevelyan report, which urged the reform of the civil service, so that recruitment might be by competition based on merit, rather than by connection based on patronage; and he was also responsible for the fundamental reordering of the Indian financial administration. Both men believed passionately in progress and in improvement, and sought to modify the antiquated structure of British and imperial government so as to bring it into step with the tenor of the times. But they were not just political reformers: they were moral crusaders, in a righteous rage to get things done – and to get things changed.[2]

An even more potent influence on Trevelyan's political outlook was the public career of his own father, Sir George Otto. He first entered parliament in 1865, as MP for the local constituency of Tynemouth, immediately attached himself to the radical wing of the Liberal Party and was appointed to the junior office of Civil Lord of the Admiralty in Gladstone's first administration. Although he resigned over the Education Bill, he was an ardent supporter of the other great reforms of the years 1868–74, and was later appointed Chief Secretary for Ireland in the aftermath of the assassination of Lord Frederick Cavendish in 1881. He briefly flirted with Liberal Unionism at the time of Home Rule, but soon returned to the Gladstonian fold, and was Secretary of State for Scotland in the GOM's last administration. He retired from public life in 1897, and thereafter devoted himself to his multivolume history of the American Revolution.[3] But as befitted a close friend of Harcourt, Rosebery, Morley and Bryce, he remained staunch in his Liberal beliefs, he opposed British aggression in the Boer War, he revelled in the party's great electoral triumph of 1906, and he was one of the names on Asquith's list of five hundred possible peers which was drawn up at the height of the Parliament Bill crisis.[4]

Inevitably, the burden of family pride and political expectation devolved in the next generation on Trevelyan's elder brother, Charles, whose social conscience and high sense of public duty made him uneasy in his enjoyment of the privileges to which he was born.[5] He was elected to Parliament in 1899 as Liberal MP for the Elland division of Northumberland, and – perhaps rather surprisingly – supported the Liberal imperialists over the Boer War. But on domestic matters he soon established a reputation as a radical and a progressive, with a strong commitment to the taxation of land values and to social reform. He was a close friend of the Webbs, with whom he had been on a round-the-world tour, and a member of the Rainbow Circle and of the London School Board. But despite these impeccably Liberal credentials and connections, his tactless criticisms of his party leaders, his intemperate attacks on his party's policy, and his general demeanour of impatient and insensitive puritanism meant that office was a long time in coming, and it was only in October 1908, when his friend Walter Runciman was appointed President of the Board of Education, that Trevelyan at last obtained junior preferment, as Parliamentary Under Secretary.[6]

With such a family background, it is not surprising that, in G. P. Gooch's words, George Trevelyan 'inherited what may be broadly described as the liberal creed with its robust confidence that the world could definitely be improved by bold thinking and constructive statesmanship.' He later claimed that he was 'a strong Liberal' at the age of four, met Gladstone at his father's dinner table, and proudly remembered that at the general election of 1892 he was the only boy at Harrow who owned up to being a supporter of the GOM.[7] As an undergraduate at Cambridge, he was a Secretary of the Liberal Club, and spoke in favour of social reform and Church disestablishment at the Union. He was on the very closest terms politically with his elder brother, campaigned actively for the Liberals at general elections, and donated generously to party funds. He was vehemently opposed to Tariff Reform and regarded the Conservative Party as increasingly materialistic and corrupt. 'Mammon is his god,' he remarked of the new brand of Tory MP, 'and he is not even a gentleman.' He welcomed old-age pensions and the People's Budget, supported the People's Suffrage Federation, and wholeheartedly backed the government in its battle against the House of Lords.[8] 'We live', he wrote to Charles towards the end of 1910, in confident and optimistic mood on the occasion of his brother's fortieth birthday, 'in a world with a great future before it', adding, significantly, 'of which we are a part.'[9]

It is worth investigating four aspects of the young Trevelyan's Liberal activism in more detail. The first was his close involvement in the London Working Men's College, then located in Great Ormond Street, which had been founded by F. D. Maurice in 1854.[10] Trevelyan became a regular teacher there in October 1899, and was soon lecturing on 'Charles I and the Civil War', 'The English and French Revolutions', and 'The Unification and Freedom of Italy'. It was an experience he found wholly satisfying. He loved working in a place 'still pervaded by an atmosphere of the Liberal Victorian culture of men like Tom Hughes, Ruskin, Westlake and Ludlow.' He enjoyed the close fellowship between the instructors and the instructed, and relished teaching pupils drawn from a much wider social background than that of Cambridge undergraduates.[11] He persuaded Francis Cornford and G. P. Gooch to offer their services; he organized week-end visits to Trinity for members of the College; and he worked hard to raise money for the building fund. For Trevelyan, such labours – part social, part educational – best embodied his liberal, high-minded ideal of putting history in the service of 'the people'. Indeed, he later claimed that at the time of the Boer War, it had only been his London teaching that had kept him sane.

The second aspect of Trevelyan's Liberal activism was his contribution to *The Heart of The Empire*, a book edited by C. F. G. Masterman, which appeared in 1901, at the height of Liberal divisions over the Boer War.[12] Its subtitle was *Discussions of Problems of Modern City Life in England*, and it was published by T. Fisher Unwin, Richard Cobden's son-in-law and an ardent pro-Boer. Its contributors included some of the most distinguished young Liberals of their time – Masterman himself, G. P. Gooch, Noel Buxton, and A. C. Pigou – and they wrote on such pressing social problems as housing, education, temperance reform, and imperialism.[13] Trevelyan himself produced the title, and wrote the final chapter, 'Past and Future', in which he unequivocally nailed his colours to the Liberal mast. 'The spirit of laissez-faire,' he insisted, 'once the salvation, is now the bane of England', since the natural process of the unregulated modern economy was 'towards evil rather than good.' What was needed, he went on, was 'more interference by the state', so as to curb 'the free play of great material interests.' But as long as the Conservatives remained in power, no such reform was possible. For they were 'the enemy': corrupt and inept, in thrall to the brewers and the jingoists, and indifferent to matters of social injustice. To Trevelyan, the Tories were thus 'almost wholly a force for evil.'[14] The book sold well, was soon reprinted, and played a modest part in the post-Boer War Liberal revival.

Trevelyan's third area of Liberal activism was his support for the *Independent Review*, which he helped to found in late 1902, as 'an intellectual Liberal monthly', devoted to promoting 'liberalism and progress and peace.'[15] Its message was essentially the same as *The Heart of The Empire*, it was strongly critical of the 'reactionary' Balfour government, and its contributors included such Liberal intellectuals as H. A. L. Fisher, Roger Fry, Desmond MacCarthy, Arthur Ponsonby, Sidney Webb and C. R. Buxton. Trevelyan gave generously of his time and his financial support; he corresponded with such contributors as Leonard Woolf, Bertrand Russell and Thomas Sturge Moore; and he wrote a wide range of reviews and articles on such subjects as religion, nature, poetry, Oliver Cromwell and Henry Sidgwick.[16] Wherever possible, he took pains to draw out the contemporary significance of historical events. When discussing a book on Gerrard Winstanley, the seventeenth-century land reformer, he noted that Britain was 'more snobbish and has worse land laws than any other country in Europe.'[17] And in two reviews of books about nineteenth-century Britain, he advanced an interpretation of the years from 1780 to 1830 that in its language rivals E. P. Thompson at his most righteously outraged. Britain in this period, Trevelyan insisted, was 'not a free country'. As a result of what he called 'Tory persecution', liberties and freedoms had been suppressed, and all that was left was 'a system of hypocrisy and tyranny'.[18]

Perhaps inevitably, Trevelyan's final field of active Liberal endeavour was in the realm of foreign affairs. Like his father, like John Bright and like Gladstone, he was a Liberal internationalist: he hated despotism, loved liberty and freedom, believed strongly in non-intervention in European affairs, and vehemently disapproved of imperial dominion over other nations and races. As he wrote to John Maynard Keynes in 1905: 'We have been so long accustomed to "think in nationalities" that we have lost the idea of international changes and international parties which seemed quite natural to our grandfathers.'[19] He disliked the militant imperialism of Joseph Chamberlain's colonial policy, was revolted by the jingoism, the flag-waving and the lack of conciliation associated with the Boer War, and protested in a letter to *The Times* against the terrible conditions in the British concentration camps.[20] He was convinced that the government misunderstood the Boers (especially the strength of their religious beliefs) and feared that Britain would become another 'Austria in Italy' – an oppressive imperialist power. 'The mother of freedom', Trevelyan wrote despairingly to Charles late in 1901, 'has become the Austria of the twentieth century.'[21]

In more optimistic vein, Trevelyan welcomed the Russian revolution of 1905 with great but guarded enthusiasm. 'However many generations it may take,' he observed with what now seems well-judged

prescience, 'Russia will be free some day.' But despite his delight that
a blow had been struck against Tsarist despotism, he doubted whether
the country 'would produce a man as attractive as Garibaldi to lead
them', and predicted that the struggle might well go on for fifty or
one hundred years, 'just as happened in Italy'.[22] In 1907 he protested
to *The Times* about the deportation of the revolutionary leaders to exile
in Siberia, untried and unconvicted; and he was active in raising money
for the Russian Exiles Relief Fund, of which he was Treasurer, organizing concerts and sales of goods. Three years later, he protested against
the partition and occupation of Persia by Britain and Russia, once
again writing to *The Times* and lobbying Walter Runciman, his closest
friend in the Cabinet. He was much opposed to the idea of further
Russian imperial expansion; he feared that the agreement would bring
'discredit to the good name of England' and be a 'setback to the moral
element in our foreign policy'; and he felt sure that the end result
would be the same as in Egypt – permanent British occupation.[23]

In the years immediately before 1914, Trevelyan was also drawn
into the politics and propaganda of Balkan independence. And he had
no doubt which side he was on. As a friend of Italy, he did not like
Austria-Hungary, and in the tradition of Bright and Gladstone, he
regarded the Turkish Empire as evil, corrupt, despotic and intolerant.
Along with Masterman, Ponsonby, the Buxton brothers and Ramsay
MacDonald, he was an active member of the Balkans Committee,
strongly supported Serbia in its war against Turkey, but was much
distressed by the later clash between Serbia and Bulgaria.[24] In the
summer of 1913 Trevelyan visited Serbia at the invitation of its government and army, in his capacity as a member of the Serbian Relief Fund,
and later published several accounts of his experiences. He acclaimed
the 'national revival – moral, civic and military', which had taken place
during the last decade, and rejoiced in the 'democratic and independent' spirit of the Serbian people and the Serbian army. And as with
the Russian revolution of 1905, it was the Italian analogy which most
struck and cheered him. For Serbia, he believed, was 'now engaged in
a war of liberation [for the South Slavs] similar to that undertaken by
Piedmont for the other Italian provinces.' And he had no doubt that,
in accordance with its 'traditional role', it was England's duty to show
'sympathy with such movements'.[25]

As Trevelyan later admitted in his autobiography, 'until the war of
1914, I was a keen Liberal politician.'[26] Indeed, that was something
of an understatement. Earnest, high-minded, determined to do good,

morally upstanding and beyond reproach, devoid of a sense of irony or humour, convinced of the righteousness of his cause and eager to denounce his opponents in fiercely critical terms: thus described, the young Trevelyan embodied the New Liberalism with positively prig-gish ardour. And that was certainly the impression conveyed by H. G. Wells when, in *The New Machiavelli*, published in 1910, he wickedly parodied Charles and George Trevelyan as the Crampton brothers. To Wells, they were smug, self-satisfied, respectable, but unendurably boring, and quite devoid of human warmth or feeling. The elder brother, Willie, is the politician, 'rich and very important in Rock-shire', who eventually becomes Post Master General in the Liberal government. But it was on his younger brother, Edward, that Wells poured most of his scorn. His voice is 'strained' and 'unmusical'. He 'magisterially' rebukes those who do not agree with him. He is at work 'upon the seventh volume of his monumental life of Kosciusco'. And as a result, he has 'become one of those unimaginative men of letters who are the glory of latter-day England.' Not surprisingly, Trevelyan had no time for Wells, whom he later dismissed as 'a little cad'.[27]

Although by the 1900s Trevelyan had definitely decided that his real vocation lay in writing rather than in politics, and in history rather than literature, there can be no doubting the strength of his Liberal partisanship in the years which extended from his undergraduate days at Trinity to the outbreak of the First World War. As we have seen, one of the main reasons why he left Cambridge for London in 1903 was so that he could write the sort of history he wanted to write in a freer and less hypercritical atmosphere. But it is also true, as Owen Chadwick has pointed out, that Trevelyan was eager 'to engage in Liberal politics, to electioneer, to assist with clubs or with unions, to aid the Working Men's College, to be at the centre of the literary world.'[28] History may have been his first priority, but at this stage in his life it was informed by, and inseparable from, his deeply held Liberal convictions. In his choice of historical subjects, no less than in his treatment of them, Trevelyan's progressive political opinions were a significant influence. For his aim was to write and to promote what he described in 1911 as 'the cause of literary and Liberal history'. How did he set about doing it?[29]

II

The greatest historical achievement of Trevelyan's prewar Liberal years was his Garibaldi trilogy, which he published between 1907 and 1911. There were good liberal and historical reasons why he should have been drawn to an Italian subject. Many Englishmen regarded the Roman Republic and the Italian city states as the foremost precursors of modern British democracy. Ever since the Renaissance, it was to Italy that upper-class Englishmen had gone to complete their education on the Grand Tour. During the nineteenth century, the links between England and Italy had been particularly close.[30] Liberal Italian patriots had fled to London in the aftermath of the failed revolution of 1848. Among British politicians, Lord John Russell and Gladstone had been proud to proclaim themselves friends of Italian freedom, and poets and writers like Swinburne, Byron, Keats, Shelley, Meredith, the Brownings, Tennyson and Ruskin had felt what Trevelyan later described as 'the unrivalled appeal to the imagination which Italy, of all lands, can make'. The result was that many guides, travelogues and histories had been published about Italy in English, and Trevelyan's Garibaldi books discernibly echo the literary conventions of this genre, with their veneration of the city and civilization of Rome, and their hatred of the decadent and despotic Catholic Church.[31]

But there were also strong family reasons why Trevelyan was drawn to recent Italian history. His father, like most Whigs and Liberals of his generation, regarded Garibaldi as the greatest champion of freedom he had known, and in 1867 he had even gone to Italy in the hope of joining Garibaldi's Redshirts for their attack on Rome. He was unsuccessful, but always looked back on this adventure as 'the greatest romance of my life'.[32] And Garibaldi's connections with Northumberland were particularly close. In March 1854, en route from America to Italy, he had been rapturously received in Newcastle, and had been presented with a sword and a telescope which had been bought with subscriptions made by the working men of Tyneside.[33] Thereafter, Garibaldi remained very much a local hero, and it was as such that he was saluted by William Bell Scott in the last of his paintings which adorn the central hall at Wallington. Entitled *Iron and Coal*, it is a celebration of the industrial might of Newcastle and the skilful vigour of its workers. In the bottom right-hand corner is a newspaper – probably the *Northern Daily Express* – ostensibly for 11 March 1861. And the headline, clearly visible, reads: 'Garibaldi in Italy. Struggles for Freedom. Triumphant Entry into Naples.'[34]

In Trevelyan's own generation, the Italian connection remained very close. As a lifelong friend of Bernard Berenson's, his brother Bob spent more time in Italy than in any other foreign country. In 1895, Trevelyan himself crossed the Alps for the first time, 'and fell in love with Italy then and there.' Two years later, his father took him up to the heights of the Janiculum and told him the story of Garibaldi's ill-fated defence of the Roman Republic.[35] And Trevelyan's wife fully shared her husband's attachment to the 'land of lands': indeed, in 1930 she gave the annual Italian Lecture to the British Academy. But this was not the only way in which Trevelyan's marriage strengthened his ties with Italy. In 1904, Bernard Pares gave him a copy of Garibaldi's *Autobiography* as a wedding present. It was this gift, later described by Richard Pares as 'one of the most momentous wedding presents in literary history', which finally kindled Trevelyan's historical curiosity into flame.[36]

The resulting trilogy – something 'original and solid', as he described it to H. A. L. Fisher – was neither a comprehensive account of Garibaldi's life and times, nor a full-scale history of the Risorgimento.[37] Trevelyan's concern was to isolate the central episodes of Garibaldi's life which he believed were also crucial in the establishment of Italian freedom and the making of the Italian nation as a liberal, constitutional monarchy. The first book dealt with Garibaldi's heroic but unsuccessful defence of the short-lived Roman Republic which had been proclaimed in February 1849; with its brutal overthrow at the hands of the French, the Austrians, the Spanish and the Neopolitans; with Garibaldi's ill-fated love for Anita; and with his retreat, escape and exile. The second described Garibaldi's return to Italy in 1854, the war between Austria and France, the landing of the thousand at Marsala in 1860, the capture of Palermo, and the forging of the uneasy but essential alliance between Garibaldi and Cavour. The final volume recounted the invasion of the Papal States by the army of Piedmont, Garibaldi's gradual progress through the Italian mainland, his entry into Naples, his brilliant victory at the Battle of the Volturno, and his retirement to Caprera, his life's work successfully accomplished.

Trevelyan was in his thirties when he wrote the Garibaldi trilogy, and the books are suffused with the buoyancy and confidence of undisillusioned youth, as well as with many of its ardent simplicities. For he had no doubt that the Risorgimento was a latter-day morality tale, a battle between good and evil in which virtue eventually triumphed.

The villains of the story were painted in the most sombre colours. The Catholic Church under Pope Gregory XVI and Pope Pius IX was dismissed as 'the most ancient and terrible theocracy in the western world.' The repressive regime of Ferdinand II, King of Naples and Sicily, was likened to 'Turkish barbarism' – from Trevelyan's pen a particularly damning term of reproach.[38] And the Austrians and the French (at least before 1859) were little better. On the other side were the Italian patriots, 'thousands of obscure men and women', who cared 'more for the idea of their country than for their own comfort and interest' and who responded nobly to 'the appeal of the great simple passions' of liberty and nationhood.[39] And they were inspired by a trinity of incomparable leaders: Mazzini the prophet, Cavour the statesman, and Garibaldi the soldier, the poet as man of action, the Carlylean hero incarnate.[40]

This, at least, was how Trevelyan depicted Garibaldi – as 'the most poetically-minded of the world's famous warriors', who 'believed in Italy as the saints believed in God.' He was the 'man of destiny' who lived 'the most romantic life that history records', and who possessed 'all the distinctive qualities of the hero, in their highest possible degree, and in their very simplest form.'[41] He was selfless and incorruptible, humane and generous, courageous and indomitable. He was the champion of the oppressed, a fighter against desperate odds, a matchless leader of men who inspired his devoted followers to sublime deeds of which they did not believe themselves capable. And when he retired to Caprera he took with him 'the adoration of his countrymen whom he had freed, and the applause of the world whose heart he had made to throb.'[42] For Trevelyan, Garibaldi was the great man in history par excellence, by whose glorious achievements he measured subsequent revolutionary leaders in Russia and Serbia. As H. A. L. Fisher later remarked, 'a youth of generous aspirations who prepares himself to take a part in the public life of his country is never at a loss for a hero.' He was describing Macaulay's view of Sir James Mackintosh: but the words apply equally well to Trevelyan's opinion of Garibaldi.[43]

As one reviewer perceptively noted, Trevelyan's trilogy told 'a story that will not be read by any Liberal without emotion.'[44] For he did not present the Risorgimento as the inevitable outcome of long-term impersonal forces, nor as the accidental by-product of squalid and selfish political manoeuvrings. On the contrary, he treated it as an epic drama, a transcendent romance, possessed of 'all the elements whereby history becomes inspiring, instructive and dramatic'. In the miraculous course of Italy's national awakening, Trevelyan believed that 'fervid liberalism struggled with obscurantism for the possession of the world.'[45] Clerical reaction, despotic government and imperial oppression were defeated, while secular progress, personal liberty and national independence triumphed. And so did international amity – partly because of England's sympathetic involvement, partly because Garibaldi himself 'was far above base racial pride, and regarded all men as brothers', and partly because 'all Europe was watching this poet's daydream enact itself into the world of living men.' The result was that in Trevelyan's hands, 'the story of Italian freedom' was raised 'to a pinnacle of history far above common nationalist struggle' and became 'a part of the imperishable and international poetry of the European races.'[46]

Appropriately enough, the publication of the first Garibaldi volume in 1907 coincided with the centenary of its hero's birth, and once again his matchless deeds as the creator of the Italian nation were widely celebrated, both in England and in Italy. In July of that year, the Duke of Sutherland arranged a great meeting at Stafford House at which Trevelyan was one of the speakers.[47] The appearance of the last volume in 1911 coincided with the fiftieth anniversary of the final establishment of the Italian nation. To celebrate this, Trevelyan wrote in *The Times* extolling the achievements of the Italians since unification, and in the conclusion of the last Garibaldi book, developed the same theme even more magniloquently:

> Nothing is more remarkable – though to believers in nationality and ordered liberty nothing is more natural – than the stability of the Italian kingdom ... The building is as safe as any in Europe ... The power of this great national movement has fortunately been directed only to securing Italian liberty, and not to the oppression of others ... The result has been the unstained purity and idealism of patriotic emotion there.[48]

Not surprisingly, the Garibaldi trilogy meant that Trevelyan himself became 'quite a hero in Italy': in the words of one Foreign Office man, he was very much *'persona gratissima'*.[49]

But while his epic drama of a wholly successful Risorgimento was enthusiastically read by the Italian public, it was clear from the very outset that Trevelyan's interpretation did not entirely convince. For his account of Italy's noble past seemed belied by Italy's present – and very different – condition. It presumed that all the major difficulties and disagreements had been finally settled with the creation of the Italian state. Yet by the early twentieth century, there was widespread criticism of the political structure by conservatives, republicans, socialists and Marxists.[50] Its picture of purity, idealism and patriotism was so difficult to reconcile with the sordid intrigues, the corrupt politicians and the comic-opera kings of the 1900s that one reviewer had the temerity to ask whether Trevelyan actually knew anything about contemporary Italy at all.[51] And since the Italy of Trevelyan's time had clearly fallen some way below the heroic level of events that had characterized the Garibaldian epic, this inevitably raised doubts as to whether the Risorgimento had been as successful, as sublime and as unsullied as Trevelyan had so lyrically contended.

Indeed, a careful reading of the Garibaldi books suggests that Trevelyan had his doubts too. On occasions, he was prepared to admit that the Risorgimento had proceeded too rapidly, that the accumulated evils of two thousand years of misgovernment and three centuries of foreign occupation had not all been eradicated, and that the politicians who now ruled in Italy were but a pale shadow of the great men who had gone before.[52] In his epilogue to W. J. Stillman's *The Unification of Italy*, published in 1909, he expressed these views more forcefully: the country was deeply divided between the prosperous industrial north and the impoverished agrarian south, the system of taxation was inequitable and in urgent need of reform, the civil service was incompetent or corrupt, and too much money was being spent on armaments. And there was no longer any 'great statesman' in charge of Italy's affairs, no one of the stature of Mazzini or Cavour. Instead, there was only Giolitti, whom Trevelyan dismissed as nothing more than a manipulator of parliaments and electorates.[53]

Nor were these doubts about Italy confined to the domestic sphere. Since Trevelyan distrusted and disliked the very idea of one country wielding dominion over another, one of the greatest virtues of the new Italian nation had been its complete lack of imperialistic design on the territories and freedom of others. Internationally, as well as domestically, it was a truly liberal regime. Nor was this surprising. After all, the Italians had only obtained their freedom and their unity by throwing off the yoke of foreign overlordship: it was thus entirely right that they should not seek to oppress others as they themselves had for so long been oppressed. But in 1911, under Giolitti, the Italians set off in search of an empire, and shelled and invaded Tripoli. Trevelyan was both devastated and disgusted. 'These Tripoli horrors', he wrote in anguish to his brother Robert, 'and the whole folly of the war discourage me terribly. I don't think I shall have the heart to go to Italy again for many years . . . The action of the degenerate Italians of today', he went on, 'in going to conquer another race at the expense of European peace takes the heart out of me as far as my books are concerned.'[54]

As if this was not bad enough, the Italians justified their action by pointing to England. 'The worst of it is,' Trevelyan wrote to H. A. L. Fisher, 'it is the would-be imitation of *us* – to appear to be a great power – that has misled them.'[55] He sent a letter to *The Times* which was unsparingly even-handed in its condemnation. The 'indiscriminate massacre of Arabs' by Italians seeking an empire was unforgivable; but as the greatest imperial power in the world, the British were 'in no position to scold them for imitating ourselves.' And in his introduction to *English Songs of Italian Freedom*, published later that year, Trevelyan reiterated his views. He continued to insist that the Risorgimento was 'a tale which will for ever remain among the most inspiring of the legends of the human race.' But he admitted that Italy had, 'of her own accord thrown away the one inestimable advantage that she has hitherto had over the other Great Powers, of being the conqueror of no other race, and mistress only in her own house.' The cruellest irony of all was that the Italian warship which had bombarded Tripoli was named *Garibaldi*. 'It is not hard', Trevelyan concluded, 'to guess what the namesake of that ship would have thought of this attack upon the liberty of others.'[56]

III

Trevelyan's Italian histories written in the years before the First World War must also be seen in their English context. For the Garibaldi volumes, appearing as they did in 1907, 1909 and 1911, caused something of a sensation in Liberal circles. Gilbert Murray felt they made 'a permanent difference to one's outlook', while C. R. Buxton thought they showed Trevelyan had chosen 'a really usefuller life than the political.'[57] They caught the contemporary political mood of reforming optimism in ways that have never been better described than by Sir John Plumb:

The year in which Trevelyan wrote *Garibaldi's Defence of the Roman Republic* was 1906, and it was published in 1907. These were the years of the greatest Liberal victory in English politics for a generation. The intellectual world responded to the optimism of the politicians. Here was the manifest triumph of that long nineteenth-century tradition of liberal humanism; the final defeat of obscurantism was at hand. It was one of those rare moments in history in which the atmosphere of life is lyrical and charged with hope, when man seems his own master, his destiny secure.[58]

As Trevelyan observed in his first volume, there were occasions in history 'when new principles of government are being formed', and when, as a result, 'men are moved by appeals to the imagination'.[59] To British Liberals, the years from 1906 to 1911 were just such an occasion and the Garibaldian epic provided just such an appeal. Thus regarded, the Garibaldi trilogy was to the 'New Liberalism' what Macaulay's *History of England* had been to the era of the Great Exhibition: it provided historical justification for the prevailing optimism of the times, a precedent of which Trevelyan could hardly have been unaware.

More precisely, the Garibaldi books taught English Liberals a series of important lessons. They showed how the British public had come to idealize Garibaldi as a model of gallantry and chivalry, and how through him they had come to view the Risorgimento in admiring terms as a liberal protest against tyranny and reaction.[60] They showed how the success of the Italian revolution, and Garibaldi's triumphant visit to England in 1864, had helped to strengthen the movement for democracy at home, which culminated in the Second Reform Act of 1867. They described one of the great Victorian epics of nation-building and state creation at the very time when the Liberals were engaged in what turned out to be the last such experiment: the making of the Union of South Africa. And in comparing the peaceful character of the state created by Cavour to the blood-and-iron imperialism of Bismarck's new Reich, they provided historical validation for the growing anxiety in Liberal circles about the rampant militarism of a unified Germany. 'If . . . the example of Cavour had been preferred to that of Bismarck as the model for the patriots and statesmen of modern Europe,' Trevelyan argued, 'the whole world would now be a better place than it is.'[61]

Having done with Garibaldi, Trevelyan turned from an Italian man of war to an English man of peace, whom he admired no less ardently:

John Bright.[62] As with Garibaldi, there were strong family connections. Trevelyan's father, when first he entered the Commons, had
regarded Bright as his hero and mentor, and Trevelyan drew extensively on Sir George's recollections when writing his book, which
enabled him 'to speak with personal intimacy of events that occurred
ten years before I was born.' Trevelyan's mother, Caroline Philips,
was directly descended from one of the great Manchester mercantile
dynasties, whose support had been so essential for Bright and Cobden
in their crusade against the Corn Laws. Her uncle, Mark Philips, was
one of the first post-Reform Act MPs for Manchester, a Unitarian, a
wealthy manufacturer and a great admirer of Free Trade. And her
father, Robert Needham Philips, was no less wedded to Lancashire,
its economy and its politics, and was himself later MP for Bury. Both
appeared briefly in the biography of Bright, and one of the reasons
why Trevelyan evokes the world of the Manchester School so vividly
was because it was an integral part of his own family history on his
mother's side.[63]

As with the Garibaldi trilogy, the timing was once again perfect:
Trevelyan was asked to write the biography by Bright's son in 1908,
he began work on it three years later, and it was published in 1913.
With the exception of Gladstone himself (already memorialized in
three volumes by John Morley), no figure in the history of nineteenth-
century Liberalism enjoyed so high a reputation among his successors
in the early twentieth century as did Bright. 'I shall', Trevelyan
observed, 'be very glad to take to Bright, and do it during several years
of what will be an heroic age of our English politics, fought out by so
many of the men I know and live among, on behalf of Bright's own
principles.' Unusually for the biography of a Victorian worthy, Trevelyan
wrote it in only one volume, and this partly explains why it sold so
well.[64] It was widely read – and admired – by Liberal men in public
life: Sir Cecil Spring-Rice, John Morley and Asquith himself. And it
was, as Trevelyan later admitted, very much biassed against Bright's
opponents, especially Peel and his handling of the Corn Law crisis.
'The Tories', Trevelyan noted with evident pleasure, 'don't like the
book'; and, he added revealingly, 'it would be a bad book if they did.'[65]

Trevelyan's attitude towards Bright was very similar to his attitude
towards Garibaldi: one of almost unqualified admiration. Even as a
boy, he had admired him. 'What a brave man he was', Trevelyan had
written on Bright's death in 1889, 'to uphold the peace policy almost
alone, in the face of nearly all England; but now it is evident to all

how right he was.'[66] Accordingly, in his biography, he set out to
portray Bright's 'deep and tender humanity of disposition', his honesty
and his incorruptibility, his 'righteousness and good sense', and most
of all his 'moral ascendancy'. He depicted 'the Quaker side of his life,
which was the real secret of it all', and despite his own belligerent
agnosticism, did full and sympathetic justice to Bright's 'religious
feeling'.[67] And he saluted Bright for the courageous stand he had taken
in opposing Britain's involvement in the Crimean War, observing that
'to attack the justice and wisdom of a popular war while it is still in
progress requires more courage than any other act.' For Trevelyan,
what was most exemplary about Bright was thus the remarkable combination of 'his tender selfless motives and his fearless strength', a combination which made him, like Garibaldi, a 'rare example of the hero as
politician'.[68]

Appropriately enough, Trevelyan argued that nineteenth-century
Liberalism was very much Bright's creation and Bright's achievement.
His attacks on the Corn Laws and the Crimean War were the first
great moral political crusades, bringing 'new aims, new methods, new
spirit' into English public life. And his demands for an extension of
the franchise, for a diminution in the privileges of the Church and the
aristocracy, and for legislation to remedy grievances in Ireland, were
all aimed at bringing 'the working man into the political arena'. In
this, Trevelyan argued, Bright triumphantly succeeded, for with the
death of Palmerston, Gladstone 'reconstituted the Liberal Party, no
longer as a Whig Party, but as a Party of progress and democracy,
sworn to carry Bright's programme into effect.'[69] The result was the
passing of the Second Reform Act, the 'withdrawal of England from
European entanglements', and the extensive legislation of Gladstone's
first ministry of 1868–74. The 'mountains of prejudice' which had for
so long barred the pathway to reform had been conquered, and the
institutions of Bright's country were 'remodelled almost after his own
heart'.[70]

Thus described, Bright was depicted by Trevelyan as a central figure
in the making of Victorian England. But Trevelyan was also determined to show that the circumstances of Bright's life, and the causes
for which he had fought, retained their relevance more than a generation after his death. The industrialized Manchester in which Bright
grew up witnessed 'a marked retrogression in the physical and moral
state of the people', and seemingly unbridgeable 'social divisions
between rich and poor'. 'In spite of much subsequent reform',

Trevelyan observed, this was still 'a fundamental evil of our own age.'[71] In the same way, Bright himself had been a vehement campaigner against the Game Laws, against the landed monopoly of great estates, against aristocratic privilege and against the House of Lords' veto. Yet in many ways, this 'democratic crusade against the privileged orders', this 'tussle of the British democracy with the aristocracy in possession' remained unresolved, even after the passing of the 'People's Budget' and the Parliament Act. And at a time when the proponents of Tariff Reform seemed set to capture the Conservative Party, it was well to set out again Bright's arguments for Free Trade, formulated in opposition to the Corn Laws: namely that it was better for prosperity at home, and for expanding exports abroad.[72]

In foreign and imperial affairs, Trevelyan contended, the continuing relevance of Bright's philosophy was even more marked. For Bright was the Liberal internationalist par excellence: hostile to European entanglements, to the doctrine of the balance of power, and to imperial aggression and aggrandisement. Trevelyan's account of Bright's courageous and high-minded campaign against the Crimean War was the most deeply felt part of the book, and its contemporary significance for Liberals who had opposed British aggression at the time of the Boer War was clear. 'I was surprised', Lord Bryce wrote to A. V. Diccy, 'to find myself so much in agreement with John Bright's views about the Crimean War, which has long seemed to me a blunder only less bad than the South African War.'[73] And A. G. Porritt, in reviewing the book for an American scholarly journal, made the same point. As Trevelyan's account had shown, 'Bright opposed the Crimean War because it was foolish as well as because it was wicked.' 'His example', Porritt continued, making the obvious connection, 'doubtless fortified Sir Henry Campbell-Bannerman, Mr Asquith and Mr Lloyd George, when in 1900 they opposed the Boer War, and had to meet attacks and undergo unpopularity similar to that meted out to Bright and Cobden in 1855 and 1856.'[74]

But Bright's high-minded internationalism had continued long after the Crimean War was over, and was presented by Trevelyan as a touchstone for early-twentieth-century Liberals. In 1882, Bright had resigned from Gladstone's government in protest against the bombardment of Alexandria by the British – an action which Trevelyan, who had been so mortified by the Italian attack on Tripoli, was not alone in retrospectively admiring. Bright had also been extremely hostile to that 'chamber of horrors euphemistically termed [the] "integrity of the

Ottoman Empire"' – as were Trevelyan and other like-minded Liberals, who were so concerned with the liberation of the Balkan states.
And Bright was 'vigilantly critical' of British rule in India, in favour of
decentralization in government and the admission of native Indians
to the Council, both of which proposals had been embodied in the
Morley-Minto reforms of 1911 and which, as Trevelyan observed,
'may be carried yet further in time to come.'[75]

Put more positively, Bright's prime international objective was the
promotion of peace, a subject of particular interest (and concern) in
1913. Bright believed, as did Trevelyan, that the best antidote to a
belligerent foreign policy was to lessen the aristocratic role in government, and to do so by giving more power and influence to the enfran-
chised working classes. And the fact that there had been no major
European conflagration since the Crimea, while at the same time the
'weight of the working man in our political system' had greatly
increased, suggested that this optimistic view had been borne out by
events.[76] But even so, the international horizon was clearly darkening.
Bright had disliked 'extravagant armaments' and 'provocative foreign
policy': he had not lived long enough to see the Kaiser in full spate.
Bright had regarded the doctrine of the 'balance of power', of British
involvement in the affairs of Europe, as a 'foul idol', and it had been
a measure of his success that both Gladstone and Salisbury had heeded
his words. But Trevelyan could not but wonder 'whether or not in our
own day the idol has been refurbished'. As he himself remarked, in
what soon turned out to be an ominously prescient sentence, war would
bring 'an end of "Victorian prosperity" and of much else besides.'[77]

Like Garibaldi, therefore, the Bright biography was very much a
Liberal tract for the times.[78] But by 1913 the times were very different
from the glad, confident morning of 1906, the 'heroic age' which
Trevelyan himself had observed in 1908, or even the parliamentary
triumph of 1910–11, as the Liberal government found itself increasingly bogged down with Irish Home Rule, Welsh Church Disestablishment, widespread domestic unrest, growing international tensions and
an unprecedented arms race with Germany. And so, as the vigour and
reforming zeal of Asquith's government faltered, it was timely to
remind the Liberals of the great issues which had been triumphantly
fought out in the past, and also of the unfinished battles which still
needed to be won. To that extent, Trevelyan's life of Bright was a
work of historically based encouragement to the increasingly embattled
Liberal governments. As John Morley told Trevelyan, the book was

not just a portrait of a 'sagacious, honest, manful, noble' figure: it was also 'a great service to good causes, in days not very good.'[79]

The Bright biography must also be understood against the background of a series of financial scandals (of which Marconi was only the most famous) and the widespread allegations of corruption in the bestowal of honours that bedevilled the Liberal government in the years immediately before the First World War, causing high-minded men like Charles Trevelyan much anxiety.[80] In eloquent contrast to these sordid contemporary intrigues, Trevelyan depicted Bright as a decent, consistent, disinterested paragon, who was honourable in all his dealings, who was beyond reproach in his business affairs, and who neither sought nor accepted honours. According to Trevelyan, he was 'the symbol of an honest man in politics', who with Gladstone had 'done most to exalt public life above the material level.'[81] In thus celebrating Bright in Carlylean terms, as 'the hero as politician', Trevelyan's biography may also be read as a gesture of reproach to a party and a government which had increasingly fallen away from the high Victorian standards of rectitude in public life – standards which Bright himself had exemplified so powerfully.

IV

By 1914, it seems clear that the Liberalism to which Trevelyan had been so ardently committed – in both its Italian and British guises – was no longer as uncorrupt, confident, creative or successful as it had seemed less than a decade before. To his great regret, Italy had ceased to live up to those high-minded precepts of domestic and international decency which he believed to have been the essence of the Risorgimento spirit. And by comparison with the life and times of John Bright, the Liberal Party in Britain seemed corrupted, divided and to have lost its way. At the same time, Trevelyan's own circumstances, previously so happy and so hopeful, turned suddenly sour. The death of Theodore in 1911 almost exactly coincided with the demise of the *Independent Review*,[82] and he was simultaneously much distressed by the lack of progress in his brother's political career. Despite continued lobbying by his father, Charles was still in the same junior post at the Board of Education in 1914 that he had been in six years before. It was, Trevelyan concluded, 'a life's tragedy before which there is nothing to be done.'[83] So disenchanted had he become that in 1912, when he met Ramsay MacDonald for the first time, he concluded that he had 'more sense' than 'all the government put together'. And in the next year, he told Arthur Ponsonby that 'our present discontents' could only be blamed on 'the silly old government'.[84]

Then came the First World War. Even before all the armies of the great powers were fully mobilized, Trevelyan feared that 'millions of people are going to be killed in this senseless business', and his initial response – as befitted the biographer of Bright – was one of outright opposition to British involvement in this Continental quarrel. Along with most Liberal intellectuals he joined the British Neutrality Committee, signed their letter to *The Times* in early August, and supported his brother's resignation from the government 'heart and soul'. Such a display of loyalty to conscience and conviction had, he urged, 'raised the level of public life'.[85] But as soon as Germany invaded Belgium, Trevelyan's position changed abruptly. Under these circumstances – the rape of a small, neutral nation by a militarist aggressor which threatened to dominate the whole of Europe – the views of John Bright were neither right nor relevant. 'Frankly,' Trevelyan wrote on 13 August, 'I am not going in for any pacific or antiwar movements till the war is won to such a degree that I think peace ought to be made ... The present awful struggle', he went on, 'is to save England, Belgium and France from the Junkers, and to save our island civilization with its delicate economic fabric, from collapse.'[86]

For the duration of the conflict, Trevelyan was 'very pro-war', and 'all for going on till we win'. He was convinced that the Kaiser represented a greater threat than had Napoleon a century before, and feared that unless the Germans could be expelled from France and Belgium, then 'civilization as we know it is done for.'[87] By thus going over 'bag and baggage' to the 'war party', Trevelyan found himself taking the same side as his father, but placed himself in opposition to both his brothers. Inevitably, this deep family split caused all the Trevelyans the greatest regret, distress and embarrassment. 'It grieves me deeply', Trevelyan wrote to Charles, 'and indeed makes me quite ill, not to be able to help and sympathize in anything you are doing at this juncture.' As for Charles, the only thing he personally minded about the war was the disagreement with his brother, whose intelligence, judgement and advice he had previously so admired. But now, Charles lamented, 'he, like the rest, wants to hate the Germans.' For a time, Charles hoped that his brother and his father would 'slide back'. But this was not to be. Trevelyan's relations with his elder brother remained cordial. But their old Liberal political camaraderie, and their shared sense of public mission, was gone for ever.[88]

Nor were these personal difficulties confined to his immediate family, for by deciding to support Britain's involvement in the war Trevelyan had also cut himself off from many of his closest friends among the Liberal intellegentsia. L. T. Hobhouse, Gilbert Murray and the Hammonds took the same view of the matter as he did. But Arthur Ponsonby, Bertrand Russell and E. D. Morrel remained true to their original convictions.[89] In the company of Charles Trevelyan, they all became conscientious objectors, tireless campaigners for peace via the Union of Democratic Control, and eventually members of the Labour Party. Along this route Trevelyan steadfastly refused to go. But as he explained to Bertrand Russell, in an attempt to make up after they had walked the whole length of the Strand quarrelling violently, he felt 'very deeply, so far as I can feel anything personal in this public cataclysm, that at a certain point, I abandoned the men I most admire, and joined the war party.' It was a generous, perhaps even a guilt-ridden, olive branch to which Russell apparently replied in kindly terms.[90] But their days of close friendship and political agreement were over.

To make matters worse, it was now not at all clear what Trevelyan himself should do. Once hostilities commenced, he was, on his own admission, 'a fish out of water, for in fact I have nothing in the world that I am any good at, except writing history, and till civilization is partially resumed, it is an art useless to anybody.' He wrote a pamphlet urging support for Serbia, and in December 1914, encouraged by Sir Edward Grey, he paid a two-month unofficial visit to the Balkans, with R. W. Seton-Watson, on behalf of the Serbian Relief Fund.[91] They were much impressed at 'the heroic resistance of the Serbian army', but greatly feared that they would be overwhelmed by Austria-Hungary. Through letters to the Foreign Office (some of which were circulated to the Cabinet) and in the correspondence columns of The Times and other newspapers, they urged that Britain must send 'further material support to our small but redoubtable ally', who deserved 'all the help that England can spare'.[92] And in the spring of 1915, Trevelyan went to the United States, to talk on behalf of the Serbian Relief Fund. According to the British Ambassador, Sir Cecil Spring-Rice, the visit was a great success, the more so since 'his intense conviction as to the necessity and justice of the war is all the more striking, because of his own views a short while ago.'[93]

But Trevelyan's greatest anxiety was, predictably, that Italy might enter the war on the side of the Triple Alliance, as by treaty she was pledged to do. He was greatly relieved when the Italians stayed neutral in 1914, and was positively jubilant when they came in on the side of the entente in May 1915. 'Italy's soul has won,' he wrote triumphantly. 'Italy that our grandfathers loved and aided has come alive again, and she is fighting with us and for us.' Initially, he thought of going to Rome, in a private capacity but with Foreign Office approval, to promote closer contact between England and Italy and to write propaganda articles in favour of Britain's new ally.[94] On second thoughts, he decided to volunteer for action on the Italian front. Contrary to popular rumour, Trevelyan was neither a pacifist nor a conscientious objector. But he was 38 years old, and was judged unfit for military service on the grounds of defective eyesight. Only by agreeing to take charge of a Red Cross ambulance unit did he eventually get to the front. Appropriately enough, he carried with him a handkerchief that had once belonged to Garibaldi, for luck. He needed it, for he was often under fire, worked massively long hours, and won the affection and admiration of the men whom he commanded.[95]

Throughout his period of active service, Trevelyan remained in close touch with the British authorities, and later described his experiences in *Scenes From Italy's War*, a book which was much more than just another conventional account of life at the front,[96] for it also sought to explain, in essentially historical terms, why Italy had entered the war and what it had been fighting for. Trevelyan was convinced that Italy would never have sided with Germany and Austria, partly because of the abiding claims of Anglo-Italian friendship, and partly because of 'her political liberty and her instincts for humanity and justice.' More positively, he believed that it was the people, rather than parliament, who had decided that Italy must join the struggle on the side of the entente, and that they had done so by a display of spontaneous patriotic sentiment similar to that which had carried Garibaldi to glory and Italy to unity in 1860. From the same Risorgimento perspective, Trevelyan saw the war itself as the last great battle for Italian nationhood, the final struggle to fling off the Teutonic yoke of German financial infiltration and Austro-Hungarian imperialism. By winning back the unredeemed lands on the northeast frontier, Italian nationhood, hitherto incomplete, was finally and fully achieved in this

'Fourth war of the Risorgimento'. 'These great events,' Trevelyan
believed, had made Italy 'in the moral sense.' And he had been
delighted to observe that the spirit of Garibaldi had been appreciatively
invoked by this new generation of Italian patriots.[97]

In his first historical disquisition on the country's affairs just after
the war, 'Englishmen and Italians: Some Aspects of Their Relations
Past and Present', Trevelyan repeated and extended these views, dwelling nostalgically on 'the long line of friendships between Italian patriots and influential English men and women' as they had existed and
developed since the Renaissance, but especially in the century after
1815. In cultural terms, he believed that England owed Italy a debt
that could never be repaid. And in political terms, he reiterated his
view that it was the close connections between the two peoples which
had helped bring about the Risorgimento and ensure Italy's partici-
pation on the side of the Allies during the war. He paid predictable
homage to Byron and Swinburne, Ruskin and Meredith, Tennyson and
Browning. He praised a succession of far-sighted English politicians –
Charles James Fox, Lord Grey, Lord John Russell, Lord Palmerston
and Gladstone   for their devotion to Italy's – and freedom's – cause.
And he restated the argument that it was from Britain that liberal Italy
had learned about constitutional monarchy. 'In politics', he insisted,
'modern Italy under Cavour went to school in England.'[98]

But in this lecture, Trevelyan was as much concerned with the present and the future of Anglo-Italian relations as with the past. For he
had no doubt that the links which had previously bound his two favourite nations together, to their mutual advantage, were now becoming
much weakened.[99] The dethroning of the classics and the demise
of the Grand Tour meant that Englishmen – and especially English
politicians – did not know Italy as well as their Victorian forbears had
done, and the fact that Italian liberals no longer sought refuge
in Britain as they had in the mid-Victorian years meant that this decline in knowledge was becoming a reciprocal process. Once again,
Trevelyan was speaking with the traditional voice of the liberal internationalist. 'Linguistic ignorance and racial isolation' were, he warned,
Britain's 'greatest national dangers in the new era opened out by
the war.' In the aftermath of Versailles, England could no longer stand
apart from Europe, even if most of its inhabitants were untrained to
mix with their Continental neighbours. For, he concluded, 'since the
war, we are, whether we like it or not, a part of the Continent.'[100]

V

But in the aftermath of war and victory, it was Italy, rather than England, which caused Trevelyan the greater anxiety, as its subsequent conduct – both at home and abroad – once more failed to live up to his liberal and heroic interpretation of its history. In the postwar settlement at Versailles, Italy demanded far more than those parts of the defunct Austro-Hungarian Empire to which it had a strong and widely recognized claim. With an acquisitiveness which matched that of Britain and France, the Italians sought large areas of Serbia and Austria, and were later to claim parts of Greece and Corfu. In private, Trevelyan greatly lamented that the Italians were in a 'highly irrational and most regrettable mood'. But publicly, he still sprang to their defence, again writing to the newspapers along familiar lines.[101] For Britain, he reminded his audience, was the greatest imperial power in the world, and had just acquired as League of Nations mandates large parts of the German and Turkish Empires. As such, the British were 'in no position to lecture Italy' for committing similar acts of imperial aggression. But his brother Charles dismissed this as special pleading, as 'the most beastly jingoism on behalf of the Italians', and Trevelyan himself was clearly very uneasy.[102]

Then, in October 1922, came Mussolini, whose new Fascist regime spelt the abrupt end of Italian liberalism as Trevelyan had known, loved and celebrated it. In Italy itself a few scholars such as Benedetto Croce continued to uphold the traditional liberal interpretation throughout the 1920s and 1930s.[103] But the very success of the Duce implied that they, like Trevelyan, had completely misunderstood the nature both of Italian liberalism and of Italian history. For if the Italians were truly as freedom-loving as Trevelyan had constantly insisted, and if their nation state had been such a model of democratic and constitutional propriety, then how could Mussolini's authoritarian regime ever have come to pass? Even more disconcerting was the argument developed by apologists for the Duce, such as Giovanni Gentile, the philosopher, and Gioacchino Volpe, the historian, that it was Fascism rather than liberalism which was the true heir to the Risorgimento. And there was certainly something to be said for this: for had not Trevelyan remarked that Garibaldi himself 'believed that an honest dictatorship was the best means of carrying out the democratic will in times of crisis'?[104] Either way, the dramatic rise of Fascism suggested that in some fundamental sense Trevelyan had misread the Italian past and the Italian people.

Inevitably, Trevelyan's response to these postwar developments was anguished and unhappy. In his Sidney Ball Memorial Lecture of 1923, he explored 'The Historical Causes of the Present State of Affairs in Italy', and visibly struggled to make sense of the contemporary politics of a country which he loved, already in the grip of a system which he hated, yet unwilling to condemn its people root and branch. He was concerned to address two simple questions. Why had parliamentary government failed in Italy? And why had Mussolini's Fascism succeeded? Part of the answer, Trevelyan suggested, was that the Italians lacked the 'obscure, inherited instinct' of the British for constitutional government. Between 1860 and 1914, parliament had become increasingly discredited, liberals and conservatives ignobly squabbled over the sweets of office, and the bureaucracy became ever more corrupt. And after the First World War, the rise of socialism, and then of Bolshevism, meant that parliamentary government was rendered quite ineffectual and the way was open for Mussolini's march on Rome. For Trevelyan, the problem with the Italians was that

> Their social and political history had unfitted them for expressing themselves by means of a general election. It is, in my view, very unfortunate that the Italians fail to express the national will at the polling booth, but it is not at all unnatural ... In England, a general election is a moral earthquake ... But in Italy a general election is the sum of a number of obscure intrigues.[105]

Put more positively, Trevelyan suggested that Italian politics, although undeniably democratic, had from the time of the medieval city states operated in an essentially noninstitutionalized way. The national will was expressed, not via the ballot box, but by 'a concourse of citizens in each city'. Such gatherings, Trevelyan believed, had been the very essence of the Risorgimento movement, and had also propelled Italy into the First World War on the side of the Allies, even when parliament had been distinctly unenthusiastic. But the difficulty with such a tradition of direct democracy was that ever since Julius Caesar 'the Italians as a race have always had a leaning towards a dictator as the surest means of expressing the popular will'.[106] In that tradition, Trevelyan freely admitted, came Manin and Garibaldi. And in that tradition also came Mussolini, whose march on Rome was yet another example of direct democracy in action. Trevelyan even went so far as to label the Duce 'a man of genius', a 'very sincere patriot', who had brought his country peace, security and economic revival. But he was not entirely at ease with this analysis. Under this new regime, he feared 'the curtailment of liberty', and the intimidation of the press and political parties, and warned that 'the chief thing that the Italian character lacks is more moral courage in world affairs.'[107]

This was a much more sombre picture of the Italian past – and of the Italian future – than that which Trevelyan had painted with such inspired optimism only fifteen years before in the Garibaldi books. And this was also true of his last major work of Italian history, which appeared in the same year: *Manin and the Venetian Revolution of 1848*. It was intended as a companion to his Garibaldi trilogy, and was the result of many visits to Venice and of his close contacts with Venetian intellectuals during the war. It developed more fully Trevelyan's belief that it was the civic life of Italy which provided the key to the country's politics and its unification.[108] But although it caught very well the greatly changed mood of postwar disenchantment, it was not 'much of a popular success' in the way that the Garibaldi volumes had been. In part, this was because the tortured complexity of Manin's character and the labyrinthine intricacy of Venetian politics did not easily lend themselves to the grand and epic treatment which Trevelyan had lavished so much more plausibly on Garibaldi. Perhaps, too, his depiction of Manin's Venetian regime as 'a dictatorship based on popular confidence and affection' seemed a little too much like Mussolini for comfort.[109]

Either way, the book was much less optimistic in tone than his earlier Italian histories. In *Garibaldi's Defence of the Roman Republic*, Trevelyan had depicted the events of 1848–9 from an essentially Italian perspective, as the ill-fated but heroic prelude to the great drama of the Risorgimento and the ultimate triumph of Italian liberalism. Tragedy there may have been: yet it was soon followed by redemption. But in *Manin and the Venetian Revolution*, he was much more preoccupied with the darker European perspective. He insisted that 1848 was 'an ill year for the future of mankind.' In 'negative terms', it was 'one of the governing dates in modern history.' 'The failure of the Continental liberals', he went on, 'to establish some measure of free government and national self-expression at the time when Europe was ripe for such a change, was a disaster on the grand scale', leading instead to the military despotisms in Russia, Prussia and Austria, and ultimately to the conflagration of the First World War itself.[110] From the perspective of the early 1920s, it was 1914 rather than 1860 which had been implicit in 1848. And so, while the youthful, ardent Trevelyan of *Garibaldi* had been most concerned with the success of liberal hopes, the sadder and wiser Trevelyan of *Manin* was more preoccupied with their disappointment.

In the years that followed, Trevelyan cut away from Italian history altogether, and his surviving correspondence from the 1920s and 1930s records his growing disenchantment with Mussolini's regime. In 1923 he feared 'the breakdown of free government' and observed with sorrow and anger 'the breach growing month by month between the Fascists and the liberal friends of England in Italy.' Two years later, he deplored the murderings and beatings which Mussolini's regime condoned: 'I am done with the Fascists altogether,' he wrote to Charles, adding, regretfully, that 'Italy isn't'.[111] In 1926, he likened the Fascists to the Jacobins, and described Mussolini as a 'European nuisance' who had 'to do something hysterical once a month' to feed the appetite of his party. Trevelyan's visits, which had previously been almost every year, became less frequent, for (as he later explained) 'Fascism was abhorrent to me, because it set out to abolish the easy, kindly temperament of the Italian people that I loved', and sought instead 'to drill and bully [them] into second-rate Germans.' In 1939 he went for what he thought would probably be his last visit. 'How different', he wrote to Charles, with sadness and resignation, 'are the circumstances from my very first visit with papa and mama in 1897.'[112]

But within a year there was worse to come: the ultimate disaster of the Second World War, in which Italy abandoned its historic links with Britain and ranged itself alongside the Germans. In the *Spectator* he wrote an anguished piece entitled 'June Tenth', the day that Italy had declared war on Britain. 'To some of us older men,' he began, 'this is the bitterest day we have yet known in all our lives.' And to his daughter, Mary, he was even more succinctly desolate: all he could say was that 'things have got past writing about'. In despair and protest, he sent back the medals which the Italian Government had awarded him during the First World War.[113] But an even lower point was reached when in 1944 British troops led the invasion of Italy, and did terrible damage to the countryside, the cities and many great works of art. It was a dreadful, mocking ruin of those great liberal hopes for Italy with which Trevelyan had started out. 'I did not forsee', he later recalled, 'that I should ever write books about [Italy's] liberation, and live to witness her great misfortune.' Did he, perhaps, recall some lines he had written in *The Poetry and Philosophy of George Meredith*: 'the most maddening of all forms of tragedy' was 'the growing up of evil where good was planted'?[114]

VI

For a late-Victorian liberal like Trevelyan, the snuffing out of Italian freedom and democracy was only one part – albeit perhaps the most regretted – of the greater tragedy of the First World War. As he later recalled in his *Autobiography*, 'the war of 1914–1918 enlarged and saddened my mind.' And so, indeed, it did. On the very last day of August 1914, he predicted that European war would bring 'the ship-wreck of civilization'.[115] The metaphor was different from Sir Edward Grey's more celebrated remark about the lamps going out all over Europe, but the message was essentially the same: the freedom-loving, internationalist world that was to Trevelyan the very embodiment of civilization was doomed. Although he never wavered from his belief that Prussian militarism and Austrian imperialism must be defeated and that Britain must fight on to victory, he had no doubt that this conflict was an 'all-embracing central catastrophe' which had brought about 'the greatest destruction of life and wealth in the recorded history of mankind.' 'We are at present', he observed in his Creighton Lecture for 1919 on 'The War and the European Revolution in Relation to History', 'no better than a company of antediluvians, who have survived the fire-deluge, sitting dazed among the ruins of the world we knew.'[116]

For Trevelyan, the most that could be said in favour of the war was that his own family had suffered no immediate loss; that Britain – and Italy – had emerged victorious; and that it had led to the destruction of the four great eastern autocracies which, like all good Liberals, he had so vehemently detested. He initially welcomed the overthrow of the Russian monarchy as 'the greatest event since the French Revolution', and he was no less delighted at the declaration of war by the United States on the side of the Allies, and at the defeat of Prussian militarism, the break-up of Austria-Hungary and the dismemberment of the Turkish Empire, all of which seemed to portend a 'new age of liberty and moral force' and democratic freedom.[117] In the short run, at least, it seemed as though the mid-nineteenth-century liberal revolutionaries had been accorded a posthumous triumph and that the turning point of 1848, which had so stubbornly refused to turn then, had finally done so seventy years later. 'I believe democracy is on the march now, all along the line,' Trevelyan told his mother. 'The world's great age begins anew.' The 'despotisms of the *ancien régime* in Central and Eastern Europe' had at last been overthrown, and this held out the prospect that a 'new era', a 'bold adventure', in European history might begin.[118]

But it soon became clear that the 'bold adventure' was going to turn out disastrously. For the last thing ushered in by the 'delayed revolutions' of 1917, 1918 and 1919 was the long hoped for, liberal millenium. Instead, they brought 'a doubtful and perplexing future', characterized by 'extreme and chaotic violence', with Europe 'starving and falling rapidly into anarchy'.[119] 'Why the dull Steppes ever spawned such a race of pitiful rascals as the Russians', he wrote in enraged despondency to Charles in February 1918, 'I don't know. If it wasn't for the Anglo-Saxons, it would be a good planet to get off. But there is Us and the US.' Yet within a year, even this comforting illusion of transatlantic amity was shattered. 'I am alarmed by the movement against the League of Nations in America,' Trevelyan wrote to his father exactly twelve months later. 'If the Senate throws out the League of Nations Treaty, there will be Bolshevism and war all over Europe for a generation to come, while America smugly retires into her shell.'[120]

It was an ominously acute prediction. The Treaty was duly thrown out; Bolshevism duly triumphed; and America duly retired. In 1921, Trevelyan told John Buchan that he could 'see no way out for public affairs', and in the years which followed he could only lament 'the appalling mess we have made of this planet.'[121] To Fascism in Italy was added Communism in Russia, Nazism in Germany and a host of authoritarian regimes spread across the Continent. And American isolationism only made things worse. For Woodrow Wilson, once the great white hope of liberal Europeans, Trevelyan had nothing but scorn: 'I absolutely hate him now,' he wrote to his mother in February 1920.[122] 'The outcome of the War of 1914–18', he sombrely observed in a new conclusion to *British History in the Nineteenth Century and After*, published in 1937, 'has been to destroy liberty, democracy and parliaments in the greater part of Europe.' The Garibaldian world of liberty and freedom had vanished, and for Trevelyan, the result was devastating. As he later recalled in his *Autobiography*, the First World

War had freed him 'from too easy an historical optimism.' But that was not emancipation: it was disillusion.[123]

Put another way, this meant the destruction of the old Liberal creed of progress, improvement and reform. After 1919, it was no longer possible for men like Trevelyan to believe in 'a world with a great future before it', in which they themselves would play a great part. The old creed of 'liberalism and progress and peace', was dead, and it was no longer possible to maintain a 'robust confidence that the world could definitely be improved by bold thinking and constructive statesmanship.' 'It is curiously different', Trevelyan wrote to his mother in 1921, 'living before the war and after it. The certainty of permanence has gone.'[124] And so, for Trevelyan, had the certainty of progress. Never again was he to write with the ardent optimism that pervades the pages of the Garibaldi books. The opening of the first volume contains a magniloquent evocation of Rome, 'the heart of Europe and the living chronicle of man's long march to civilization.' But after the war, it was clear to Trevelyan that that march was halted, if not ended, and he never wrote like that again. Indeed, these words, used by Trevelyan of his father apply in considerable measure to himself:

> He regarded the war as the most unmitigated calamity, and fully realized that it made an end of the civilization to which he belonged ... The grey dawn of peace showed that the landmarks he knew had vanished in the night, and he was too old to join in the search for their successors.[125]

One of the most conspicuous landmarks which had vanished was the Liberal Party: the party of Bright, of Gladstone, and of his own father and brother; the party which Trevelyan himself had regarded in his youth as a permanent and beneficent feature of the British political landscape. Initially, he continued to support Asquith's government because it was waging a war in which he himself believed, and he later backed Lloyd George as the man most likely to bring about victory. But he had no doubts that the war had effectively broken the party, and that without the working-class vote it had no future. By 1918 he was equally disenchanted with Lloyd George and Asquith, and in 1926 he resigned the Presidency of his local Liberal Association.[126] Trevelyan was convinced that the demise of the Liberal Party was a 'catastrophe', and the return of his old friend, Walter Runciman, to high office on the formation of the National Government in 1931 brought him small comfort. Six years later he wrote Liberalism's obituary in his revised edition of *British History in the Nineteenth Century and After*. As a result of the First World War, he noted, 'the Liberal Party was rent and destroyed, and has never recovered importance, for the Labour Party in later elections step by step took its place.'[127]

But it was not just the demise of the Liberal Party as a political institution that caused Trevelyan distress: it was also the disappearance from British public life of the traditional liberal intelligentsia, those men like Morley, Bryce, Haldane and Trevelyan's own father, who in their generation had moved with effortless ease and assured authority between literature and politics, history and public affairs. That was the world in which Trevelyan was brought up, and in which he himself had lived and moved and had his being in the years from the turn of the century to the First World War. Yet as his own family experience had so poignantly shown, the First World War had been bitterly divisive. And by the interwar years, the liberal intelligentsia had effectively disappeared. In his memoir of his father published in 1931 Trevelyan saluted him as 'a bygone type': 'the literary man who was also a politician, the politician and literary man who was also an historian.'[128] By then, indeed, there were few such figures left: Trevelyan himself, H. A. L. Fisher, and one or two others. But their direct political influence was much less than that of the generation before them. In 1938, Trevelyan and Fisher published books simultaneously, and were the recipients of a leading article in *The Times*. But however respectful its treatment of them, it made it clear that they were the survivors of a vanished world: 'If before the war the Liberal had much to be thankful for, it has been a sorry world for him ever since.'[129]

VII

Sometime in the early years of the twentieth century, possibly 1904, the young George Macaulay Trevelyan wrote a letter to the even younger John Maynard Keynes, offering advice as from one Apostle to another about the future career which the latter should adopt. 'I keep hearing from different people', Trevelyan reported, 'that you have made up your mind to go into the civil service.' Surely, he went on, this was not a good idea. 'Do let me beg you', he continued, 'to keep an open mind.' More constructively, Trevelyan urged that Keynes should take risks: from the secure base provided by his Cambridge Fellowship, he should make his reputation at the bar, and then go into politics. Of course, Keynes did no such thing, and as a result Trevelyan's letter is invariably quoted as a classic example of historians' lack of wisdom in making predictions. But the later part of it has received rather less attention. 'It is', Trevelyan opined, 'on such choices, made in early youth, that the fate of the country in the future ultimately depends.' And he concluded with a sentence more perceptive and prescient than even he could then have known: 'Our supply of liberal aristocrats is running dry.'[130]

Much of Trevelyan's early life can usefully be understood in the light of that remark. Before 1914, his public activities and his historical writings were, for the most part, a deliberate and highly successful attempt to deny and defy that trend in British political and intellectual life which he had discerned with such evident regret. But ironically the remainder of his career merely bore out its essential truth, as Trevelyan's own liberalism ran dry in its turn. Perhaps this would have happened anyway, as Trevelyan became older, sadder and mellower. But there can be no doubting the depressing and distressing impact of public affairs. What hope was there in British politics, when the party of Bright and Gladstone was all but defunct? And while, on the Continent, 'new nations and new principles of government' were indeed being formed after 1918, they were as alien to Trevelyan as they would have been to Garibaldi himself. Under these circumstances, Trevelyan's outlook became less radically optimistic, more meditatively conservative. 'G. M. T. has been moving to the right,' J. L. Hammond told his wife in the summer of 1922. 'Is it the war that has changed him? I suppose so.'[131]

Nevertheless, the liberal attitudes which Trevelyan had embraced so ardently and so wholeheartedly in his youth never fully deserted him. One of the reasons for his concern to preserve the countryside in the interwar years was that he hoped it might provide a haven of refuge for the toiling masses of the cities, about whose plight he had written so eloquently in The Heart of The Empire. In 1926 he deplored the General Strike on the grounds that the government and the coal owners had behaved disgracefully towards the miners. 'I care much more', he wrote to his brother in 1934, when explaining his dislike of the Labour Party, 'about individual freedom as the precondition of good civilization than about anything else in politics and society.'[132] In July 1945 he was so disenchanted with Winston Churchill's belligerent electioneering broadcasts that he was prepared to welcome 'a Labour government as probably the lesser of two evils.' At least, he went on, they would be able to nationalize the mines, and reach some sort of accommodation with Russia. And as late as 1950 he still described himself, in a letter to his brother Charles, as 'a moderate man and a Liberal.'[133]

But it was in foreign affairs that his liberalism and his moderation endured most strongly. His love of Italy – or rather of the Italian people – remained to the end. In 1935 he was 'more anxious for the fall of Fascism than for anything else.' But he deplored Britain's policy towards Mussolini after the Duce had invaded Abyssinia. Trevelyan hoped that sanctions would work, feared they would not, and deeply regretted that the British had not been prepared to back up their threats with force. The government, he believed, should either have fought or left Italy alone. Instead, the result of imposing ineffectual sanctions had been wholly regrettable. It had enabled Mussolini to claim a victory; it had turned the Italian people against Britain; and it had driven the Duce into the arms of the Führer.[134] Three years later, when Britain publicly recognized Mussolini's conquest of Abyssinia, Trevelyan spoke out in the columns of *The Times*, deploring, in familiar terms, the 'righteous indignation' of those who had protested against this diplomatic settlement. He freely admitted that Italy's conduct had been indefensible. But what right had the British, of all nations, who had 'over a long period of time effected the violent seizure of an enormous portion of the globe', to censure other countries for military aggression and imperial acquisitiveness?[135]

Throughout the Second World War, Trevelyan remained indefatigable in championing the cause of Italian freedom. In May 1940, at the behest of the Foreign Secretary, Lord Halifax, he broadcast to the Italian people, 'as an old friend of Italy, who has never ceased to be her friend', urging them not to enter the war on the side of Germany. He recalled the great days of Garibaldi, his own early visits, his later work for the Red Cross, and the close alliance between England and Italy, which had defeated German aggression once before. The arguments, he insisted, were the same in 1940 as they had been in 1915: Germany must be stopped.[136] It was all in vain. But still Trevelyan did not abandon the Italians. In the tradition of his earlier work for the Russians and the Serbs, he served as the Vice President of the Friends of Free Italy, which later became the British-Italian Society. He protested at the internment of Italian political refugees who had fled to Britain, like their nineteenth-century forbears, in search of liberty and safety. He broadcast again on the fall of Mussolini. He urged that no precipitate action should be taken, in any postwar settlement, in depriving Italy of the port of Trieste. And he never wavered in his belief that there was 'another Italy below the surface of Fascist-Nazi oppression which will emerge when victory is won.'[137]

In 1947, Trevelyan paid what turned out to be his last visit to Italy and, despite the deprivations of postwar austerity, he greatly enjoyed it. It was, he told his brother, 'an immense pleasure to feel the weight of oppression gone, and to find Italians all rejoicing in it and talking freely again.'[138] Despite everything that had happened to Italy since 1870, Trevelyan remained convinced that his hero would never have espoused militarism, imperialism or Fascism. 'Garibaldi', he told Gilbert Murray on his return, 'never contemplated, nor would, I think, have tolerated, any suggestion that Italians should bear rule over other people.' Of course Italy's history had in many ways been a disappointment since the heady and heroic days of the Risorgimento. But, Trevelyan still insisted, none of 'these developments, and still less Fascism, can be laid at Garibaldi's door at all.' 'During the last war', he triumphantly concluded, 'the memory and name of Garibaldi was used by the Resistance Movement and the anti-Fascists as their rallying word.' Ten years later, it was wholly appropriate that Trevelyan was made an Honorary Member of the Institute for the History of the Risorgimento, and he never lost his faith in the Italian people, in Italian history, and in Italian liberty.[139]

To the end of his life, Trevelyan also remained equivocal and uncertain about the British Empire, which he always thought a far more formidable instrument of aggression and domination than any of Italy's colonizing endeavours, which seemed small-scale by comparison. One of the reasons why he withdrew his name from the short list for the Governor-Generalship of Canada in 1945 may have been that he still had real moral qualms about accepting even an essentially ornamental proconsular role. Two years later he rejoiced at the independence of India, and he might have rejoiced even more had he known that one of the prime architects of that independence, another Harrow and Trinity man, Jawaharlal Nehru, had avidly read the Garibaldi books as they had originally appeared, and had there and then conceived the ambition of waging his own 'gallant fight for freedom', of liberating India as Garibaldi had liberated Italy.[140] And in 1956, Trevelyan was so outraged at the British invasion of Egypt at the time of the Suez crisis that he vowed he would never vote Conservative again. So far as is known, he never did. John Bright, to say nothing of Garibaldi, would surely have approved.

III

THE WHIG
CONSTITUTIONALIST

The tradition of the [Whig] party started from the solid achievement of the destruction of Stuart despotism. This, to the Whigs, was the central event of history ... Whiggism ... always remained a unique British product ... Vague modern hopes of liberty for all mankind blend with a hearty English pride in ourselves, as the pioneers who had long ago hewn out the path still to be traversed by less favoured nations.

G. M. TREVELYAN, *Lord Grey of the Reform Bill* (1920), p. 31.

I write as an Englishman not as a Whig.

G. M. Trevelyan to Arthur Bryant, 18 October 1934.

Germany and England must learn to 'tolerate' ... each other's form of government. Dictatorship and democracy must live side by side in peace, or civilization is doomed. For this end I believe Englishmen would do well to remember that the Nazi form of government is in large measure the outcome of Allied and British injustice at Versailles in 1919.

G. M. Trevelyan to *The Times*, 10 August 1937.

Grey Street, Newcastle: the column at the north end honours the street's epony-mous earl, described by Trevelyan as a 'patrician thoroughbred', whose career went 'far to ennoble the annals of English stagecraft' between 1800 and 1829, and who was 'the man of the hour' from 1830 to 1832.

GREY STREET, Newcastle upon Tyne, is probably the most magnificent urban thoroughfare in provincial England. Along its stately curve, and up its gentle gradient, an unrivalled sequence of neo-classical buildings unfolds, which culminates, at the north end, in a splendid monument to the street's eponymous earl.[1] For in the company of George Stephenson, Charles, second Earl Grey was Northumberland's most celebrated nineteenth-century son. From the top of his column, Grey looks down on the people beneath, the very embodiment of paternal concern, patrician statesmanship and aristocratic disinterestedness. And at the base, an eloquent inscription celebrates his lifelong advocacy of peace, records his 'fearless and consistent' championing of 'civil and religious liberty', and acclaims him as the architect of the Great Reform Act of 1832. In the opinion of the Whigs, Lord Grey stood 'high in the ranks of British statesmen', and for no one was this more true than his fellow north-countryman George Macaulay Trevelyan, who was eventually to be his biographer.[2] 'I had been brought up at home', Trevelyan later recalled, 'on a somewhat exuberantly Whig tradition', and to the end of his life, he retained a Whiggish predilection for 'those bits of history that have clear-cut, happy endings.'[3]

I

Given Trevelyan's ancestry and his upbringing, it could hardly have been otherwise. In a minor sort of way, Wallington itself was a quintessentially Whig house. An important phase in its rebuilding, at the hands of Sir William Blackett, was begun in 1688, the year of the Glorious Revolution.[4] The extensive alterations carried out during the first part of the eighteenth century were by Daniel Garnett, who had begun his career in the household of Lord Burlington. And the

Pre-Raphaelite paintings in the central saloon provided a panoramic view of English history as an unfolding Whiggish drama of continuity and change, reform and progress, with one great scene following another in ordered sequence.[5] In the library were Macaulay's books, vigorously annotated in his own hand, and also some of the letters of Charles James Fox, which had passed to Sir George Otto Trevelyan. And in the study was the desk at which Macaulay wrote his *History of England*, as well as the writing table used by Sir George Otto when working on his *History of the American Revolution*.

It was Macaulay's belief that the Whigs had always stood for 'civil freedom, religious toleration, civilization and social improvement', and as someone who was 'proud to be a member' of the party, he had good cause to know.[6] As an undergraduate at Cambridge he had been a Tory, but by the mid-1820s he had wholeheartedly embraced the creed of Whiggery. He wrote a succession of dazzling essays in the *Edinburgh Review*, the prime organ of the Whig intelligentsia, and made his name as a public figure with his impassioned speeches in support of the Great Reform Bill. He was eagerly taken up by Whig society and became a regular habitué of Holland House, where he mixed easily with the men and women who had known Charles James Fox. And his *History of England* was an unashamedly Whiggish account of the seventeenth century, celebrating progress, improvement, toleration and reform, the great events of 1688 and the reign of William III. For Macaulay, the Glorious Revolution was 'the least violent the most beneficent' of all such constitutional convulsions, which explained Britain's subsequent happy progress and its unrivalled influence throughout the world.[7] And the nation's avoidance of revolution in 1848 – the very year in which the first volume of his *History* appeared – offered the ultimate vindication of the wisdom of the Great Reform Act.

Although he was a radical in politics, Trevelyan's father, Sir George Otto, was impeccably Whiggish in his social contacts and in his historical writings. When he moved to London in 1865, he at once gravitated towards Brooks's and Holland House, and it was his experiences there which enabled him to evoke so vividly the world of traditional Whiggery when he came to write his *History of the Early Years of Charles James Fox*. His biography of his uncle was another work of Whiggish – and family – piety: indeed, it was only because Trevelyan was born shortly after his father had completed it that he was given Macaulay as his middle name.[8] Sir George Otto's final work of scholarship was his *History of the American Revolution*, which he was writing as Trevelyan grew up, and which may have influenced him even more than the works of his great-uncle. He told the story of how a great rebellion against a tyrannical monarch led to the making of a new nation. He sympathized with the revolutionaries, and found it difficult to see the point of view of their opponents. He saw moral virtue as being on the side of the revolution and of those English Whigs who supported it. And he believed that it was precisely because of its moral virtue that the American Revolution actually triumphed.[9]

Appropriately enough, Trevelyan's first book, his revised Trinity Fellowship dissertation, *England in the Age of Wycliffe*, was in some ways the most Whiggish piece of history he ever wrote. He had read Stubbs at Harrow, and was much influenced by the Bishop's Whiggish views of medieval England. At Cambridge, he was inspired and encouraged by the Liberal and Catholic Lord Acton to look for great issues and their moral significance. And Trevelyan believed he had found them in the fourteenth century, which he regarded as 'the meeting point of the medieval and the modern worlds', the one 'sick almost to death', the other 'forming in the greatest minds of the day.'[10] He drew approving attention to an important series of constitutional developments: the early efforts made by the 'Good Parliament of 1376' to turn out ministers, to claim the prerogative of impeachment, to grant and withhold taxes, and to make itself responsible for the affairs of the nation. He described at length, and with outraged relish, the many shortcomings of a medieval Church which enjoyed 'all the prestige of a thousand years' prescriptive rights over man's minds': the danger that its doctrines and its institutions presented to the state and to individual freedom; its swollen endowments, its unacceptable wealth and its exemption from taxation; the worldliness and avarice of its bishops; the abuses of pluralism and simony; and the corrupt and conservative friars.[11]

This provided the background for three movements of dissent and protest which Trevelyan set out to evoke and explain. The first was the subversive doctrines adumbrated in opposition to the Church by John Wycliffe. In essence, Wycliffe stood 'for England against Rome, for the State against the Church'. He rejected the authority of the Pope, believed that the Church's endowments should be secularized, dismissed the doctrine of transubstantiation, and took his stand on the authority of the Bible rather than that of the priests or the sacraments. The second movement was the Peasants' Revolt of 1381, described by Trevelyan as the 'most spontaneous and general uprising of the working classes that ever took place in England'.[12] It was directed against the great landlords and the Church, and the aim was to secure the personal and economic freedom of the peasantry from their feudal obligations. And the third was the fluctuating fortunes of late-medieval Lollardy, until it was subsumed in the broader demand for religious reform in England in the 1520s. Trevelyan was eager to 'put the Lollards in their right place', and for him that meant equating them with 'the rise among the English of an indigenous Protestantism.'[13]

In the short run, Trevelyan admitted, none of these new movements accomplished much. The parliamentary initiatives which were won in the 1370s were soon lost. The religious reforms urged by Wycliffe were not implemented in his lifetime or for a century after. The Peasants' Revolt was easily suppressed. And for most of its history, the appeal and importance of Lollardy was decidedly limited. But in the long run, Trevelyan insisted, and in retrospect, these were seminal developments in the history of the English nation. The claims made by the House of Commons provided the precedents for 'the establishment of the liberties of England in the seventeenth century.' The reforms of the Church urged by Wycliffe and the Lollards were eventually carried out in the Tudor reformation, by the Crown and Parliament acting through the bishops. And although the Peasants' Rising was put down, it was a significant 'sign of national energy', which not only showed the degree of 'independence and self-respect in the medieval peasant', but also helped explain why 'in England there was a continuous spirit of resistance to tyranny.' As Trevelyan made plain at the outset, 'Only in the light of later history do we perceive in full that the age of Wycliffe holds a great place in the progress of our country, that its efforts were not futile, and that its great men did not live in vain.'[14]

Of all Trevelyan's history books, this was undoubtedly the most present-minded, with the result, as one reviewer pointed out, that it made 'the lights too high, and the shadows too deep.'[15] The author was too fierce in his partisanship for Wycliffe and for the cause of what he thought was personal freedom. He judged and condemned the medieval Church by the very different standards of a much later age, and his account of parliamentary proceedings read more like the seventeenth or the nineteenth century than the fourteenth. He was too concerned to show the ways in which English attitudes and experience already differed from the Continent. And the book was littered with vivid but misleading comparisons between the medieval world and

more recent times. The Parliament of 1376 was likened to that of
1640. John of Gaunt was compared with a modern American 'political
boss', who cut 'big deals' in the Privy Council. The gathering of the
Lollards at St Giles's Fields in 1414 was thought to resemble the
Chartist demonstrations of 1848. And there were frequent comparisons
between the Peasants' Rising of 1381 and the French Revolution
of 1789.[16] As another reviewer remarked, the whole book showed
Trevelyan's 'strong disposition to interpret the problems of the past
by the party politics of the present'. Indeed, it was his belief that
the author seemed unable to distinguish between 'the Barons of the
fourteenth century and the Whigs of the seventeenth or the Radicals
of the nineteenth.'[17]

These classic Whig themes of religious toleration and constitutional
progress, combined with the first signs and portents of England's rise
to greatness as a world power, were explored more fully in Trevelyan's
next work, *England Under the Stuarts*. He had been lecturing on the
seventeenth century to the Working Men's College, and was asked to
write the book by Sir Charles Oman, as part of a new *History of England*
which he was editing for Methuen. The seventeenth century was the
cradle of Whiggery, and Trevelyan produced a textbook remarkable
for its verve, brio and high spirits. For he had no doubt that he was
dealing with one of the central episodes in the evolution, not just of
his own country, but of modern European civilization. Germany had
given the world her Reformation, and France her Revolution: but it
was seventeenth-century England which pioneered a new system of
limited monarchy and parliamentary government, which combined freedom with efficiency and liberty with strength. In so doing, Trevelyan
insisted, England's achievement ran contrary to the general trend
of the times. Across the length and breadth of Europe, Catholic reaction and military despotism were almost everywhere in the ascendant.
It was the unique accomplishment of the English that during these
otherwise unpropitious decades they established and safeguarded the
principles of individual freedom and religious toleration.[18]

But until almost the very end of the century, it was not clear that
these principles would triumph. Until 1640, religious freedom and
parliamentary independence were under constant attack from the
Stuarts, who 'left their indelibly negative impression upon England.'
James I was hostile to Puritans and to Parliament, and foolishly sought
the friendship of Catholic powers, especially Spain. And Charles I,
aided and abetted by Laud, sought to establish his personal rule and

'play the tyrant'. Only because of the 'prolonged, heroic and unselfish action by the representatives of English country gentlemen' in Parliament, those Puritan squires 'not wholly unlike the Evangelical cliques of the early nineteeth century', were these royal ambitions successfully opposed.[19] By 1640, the threat of 'undisguised absolutism' and of 'military despotism' was so great that the nation as a whole had become 'thoroughly aroused'. And the resulting Civil War was 'the decisive event in English history'. It was neither a battle of classes (like the French Revolution), nor a conflict of two regions (like the American Civil War). It was a war about ideas; it witnessed 'the triumph of parliamentary institutions'; and the execution of the King proclaimed 'the slow emancipation of the mind from the shackles of custom and ancient reverence.' And so the point was reached at which 'our island had cut free from the political history of the Continent.'[20]

Trevelyan much admired 'the moral splendour of our great rebellion and our Civil War', but he found the interregnum less easy to write about, since 'the rule of kings was dead, and Parliament failed to establish its new claim to obedience.' Like all Whigs, he was not altogether at ease in dealing with Oliver Cromwell. Following Carlyle, he recognized the Lord Protector's Puritan zeal and acknowledged that he had defended 'the civil liberties of England from royalist reconquest.'[21] But he disliked his authoritarian attitudes, and also his treatment of the Irish. Nor was Trevelyan much interested in the Restoration, which seemed to him little more than the prologue to what he called 'the second Stuart despotism'. Both Charles II and James II sought to rule England on the basis of Catholic faith, a standing army, and an alliance with France; and it was to oppose these retrograde developments that the Whig Party came into being. Its supporters were in favour of religious toleration and parliamentary sovereignty, and it was these principles that were successfully enshrined in the 'Glorious Revolution' of 1688. Limited monarchy, party government and freedom of worship were now established, and after the accession of William III England became the linchpin in the alliance against the overweening and intolerant despotism of Louis XIV. By 1714, thanks largely to the zeal of the Whigs and the heroic generalship of Marlborough, 'the persecuting Catholic despotism of France' was beaten, and 'the tolerant Protestant constitution of England' emerged triumphant.[22]

In the course of his pages, Trevelyan showed a certain imaginative sympathy with the losers of England's seventeenth-century history: the

Stuarts, the Cavaliers, and the Tory Party of Harley and Bolingbroke. Nor should this be surprising, since his Nettlecombe forbears had been staunch royalists.[23] But his own feelings were clearly engaged on the other side. This was, after all, the century which Macaulay, S. R. Gardiner and C. H. Firth had made their own, and although he placed more emphasis on the religious content of Puritanism than had his great-uncle, and stressed the growth of party rather than the Cabinet as the major constitutional innovation which followed the Restoration, his interpretation was fundamentally the same as that of his forbears among the great Whig historians.[24] There were more allusions to the French Revolution, and the book contained disparaging remarks about 'dull Germans', 'Continental pedants' and the 'barbarous and unprovoked persecutions' of Louis XIV. In writing about 'military despotism', Trevelyan deliberately drew the comparison with Czarist Russia, and must have had contemporary Germany and Austria-Hungary in mind as well. And in his conclusion, he took pains to stress that he was telling a story with a happy ending:

> At a time when the Continent was falling a prey to despots, the English under the Stuarts had achieved their emancipation from monarchical tyranny by the act of the national will; in an age of bigotry, their own divisions had forced them into religious toleration against their real wish; while personal liberty and some measure of free speech and writing had been brought about by the balance of two great parties. Never perhaps in any century have such rapid advances been made towards freedom.[25]

Trevelyan's final work of prewar Whiggery was his biography of the second Lord Grey, which he was invited to undertake while he was working on his life of John Bright. There had been nothing written on Grey for nearly seventy years, and he accepted the invitation with alacrity. 'I was born and bred to write about Grey and the Reform Bill,' he told his parents.[26] In fact, only three chapters were completed before the First World War broke out, most of the book was written after the Armistice, and it was not published until 1920. Despite this lengthy delay – no other work ever took Trevelyan so long – he regarded it as a labour of love. It was another story with a happy ending: the 'glorious summer' of 1832 coming after 'a long winter of discontent and repression'. The Greys were Northumberland neighbours, and Trevelyan later recalled his visits to Howick, where 'its happy family life, its beech woods and its sea cones, seemed much the

same in 1920 as in 1820.'[27] He regarded the book as being 'the best
way now left of doing Fox justice', by showing that 'it was he who
made the Reform Bill possible.' And in his speeches and in his letters,
the young Thomas Babington Macaulay had left an unforgettable picture of the great parliamentary drama of 1830–32, which Trevelyan
now thirsted to recreate.

But in addition, Trevelyan himself had long been attracted to the
period. It gave him the chance to study the impact of the French
Revolution on British political life. He regarded the years from 1780
to 1830 as one of the greatest eras of English creative accomplishment:
the novels of Jane Austen; the paintings of Joseph Wright, Constable
and Turner; and the poetry of Wordsworth, Coleridge, Keats,
Byron and Shelley. Yet at the same time, Trevelyan was much intrigued
– and much outraged – that this was, in political terms, a period of
almost unrelieved 'Tory reaction'. He had already sketched out this
interpretation in a series of essays in the *Independent Review*, and in
1905 Beatrice Webb recorded that he was writing 'a history of England, 1790–1810, which is to be a glorification of Fox and rehabili-
tation of the French Revolution', and would, she thought, probably
turn out to be 'a modernized replica' of his father's work.[28] While he
worked on Garibaldi and John Bright, Trevelyan put this project aside.
But it re-emerged and was subsumed in the life of Grey. For although
cast in the form of a biography, Trevelyan admitted that his book was
'really a history of the reform movement from the French Revolution
to 1832', with most emphasis laid on the very beginning and the very
end.[29]

In writing about the 1790s, Trevelyan ground several Whig axes.
He praised Charles James Fox in extravagant terms, as a 'kind, grand,
human creature', who brought 'Shakespearian' qualities to public life,
and argued that it was only because he kept the Whig Party intact and
independent that Grey was able to carry reform forty years later. He
insisted that Fox and Grey had been correct to welcome the French
Revolution, and contended that the British Government should also
have been more sympathetic, instead of allying with the Slavic and
Teutonic despotisms to snuff out the cause of freedom on the Continent. He described Grey's proposals for parliamentary reform, made
in 1793 and 1797, and urged that the passing of the Fourth Reform
Act in 1918 showed that it was 'no longer possible to argue that engage-
ment in a great war renders parliamentary reform unsafe.'[30] And he
depicted the Younger Pitt in the darkest of colours, as an alarmist,

repressive tyrant, who gagged the press, suspended Habeas Corpus, restricted expressions of free opinion, allowed imprisonment without trial, and ushered in forty long years of 'Tory reaction'. 'The difficulty', Trevelyan wrote in July 1914, 'is not to seem too partisan in telling the purely domestic history of the 1790s. Pitt was really such a mean cad, and the world doesn't know it, and thinks it a "Whig tradition". But it will have to get accustomed to the truth about him again.'[31]

Trevelyan had little to say about the period from 1800 to 1830, except to note that in 1806 Pitt 'took the best way of defending his reputation. He died', and to denounce Perceval, Castlereagh, and the Six Acts that were passed in the aftermath of Peterloo. But it was only with the drama of the Reform Bill itself that his account once again caught fire. He believed that the widespread displays of popular protest between 1829 and 1832 signified 'a prodigious national revulsion against all that had happened in England in the last forty years.'[32] And in dealing with this crisis, he had no doubt that the Whigs displayed supreme gifts of statesmanship. In framing the measure as he did, Grey judged the prevailing mood perfectly: it was the least the country would accept, and the most that Parliament would swallow. And in dealing with a divided Cabinet, a hostile House of Lords and an increasingly irascible King, he scarcely put a foot wrong. For Trevelyan had no doubt that the stakes had been of the very highest. Without such a measure, he was certain there would have been civil war. But the triumphant passing of the Act ensured that 'extravagant Toryism' was vanquished, that Parliament was once again made responsible to the people, and that for the rest of the century, reform, not revolution, was the British way of doing things. By 1920, the contemporary moral was plain:

> In an age when the law of perpetual and rapid change is accepted as inevitable, and the difficulty is to obtain progress without violence, there may be profit in the story of a statesman who, after a period of long stagnation and all too rigid conservatism, initiated in our country a yet longer period of orderly democratic progress, and at the critical moment of the transition averted civil war and saved the state from entering on the vicious cycle of revolution and reaction.[33]

Trevelyan believed that it was thanks to 'those liberal-minded aristocrats, peculiar to our island', who were prepared 'to act boldly on behalf of the people', that the 'political traditions and instincts' of the English had come to 'differ profoundly from those of Germany, of

France, and even of America.'[34] He admitted the Whigs had made their mistakes: over the Regency Bill, by their association with the Prince of Wales, and as a result of their secession from Parliament in 1797. Nor was Grey without his faults: too ambitious during his early years and too lethargic a leader in the 1810s and 1820s. But Trevelyan's essential admiration for Grey and his fellow Whigs was clear. 'No party', he observed, 'was ever better worth joining', and the passing of the Great Reform Act was 'the greatest and most glorious campaign in the one hundred and fifty years of its history.' He did not mention that Grey was fundamentally a shallow man, who could be envious, self-righteous and vindictive. Instead, he depicted him as a 'patrician thoroughbred', of 'singularly pure reputation', whose career went 'far to ennoble the annals of English statecraft' between 1800 and 1829, and who was 'the man of the hour' from 1830 to 1832.[35]

Naturally, those who did not share Trevelyan's Whiggish preference for 'the cause of progress' were unconvinced by this highly partisan interpretation.[36] One reviewer regretted his 'zealous advocacy of the virtues of the Whigs and his condemnation of their opponents', and dismissed his claim that the passing of the Fourth Reform Act in 1918 proved that Pitt could have carried moderate parliamentary reform in the 1790s as totally unconvincing.[37] Another summarized the book as 'an indictment of Tory administration during the era in which Grey lived . . . conceived in the unmeasured violence of a political antagonist.' Indeed, he thought the general effect was 'to make the tradition of Burke and Pitt, of Castlereagh, Canning and Wellington, appear contemptible rather than intelligible.'[38] Throughout this book, Trevelyan was conspicuously lacking in imaginative sympathy with the Whigs' opponents, was too much aware of the final achievements of Victorian constitutional development, and failed to rid his mind of the unhappy nineteenth-century histories of most of the great nations of Europe. He was no doubt sincere in his determination 'not to seem too partisan': but he had not succeeded. *Grey of the Reform Bill* was very much a work in the 'Whig tradition'.

These three early books ranged from the fourteenth to the nineteenth century. And they were very different in method and form: a revised Fellowship dissertation, a commissioned textbook and an authorized biography. But they displayed common Whig attitudes. They were concerned with central episodes in the making and remaking of English national identity, when a new and better future was struggling for mastery with a corrupt and obscurantist past. They

were preoccupied with popular protest and discontent, with opposition
to tyranny and oppression – whether from the medieval Church, the
Stuart monarchs, successive Tory governments or Continental despots
– and they celebrated progress and reform, freedom and liberty. They
pointed up the growing divergence between England's history and that
of the Continent, while at the same time making frequent comparisons
with the French Revolution, which the young Trevelyan clearly
regarded in a more favourable light than his great-uncle. They
acclaimed 'the English genius for improvization, for ordered liberty,
and for self-help in a crisis', and they took it for granted that England
was 'a country where men love to be led by their superiors in rank and
fortune.'[39] In short, each book provided only a partial picture of a very
complex historical situation. As Trevelyan remarked in *England in the
Age of Wycliffe*: 'True wisdom does not always ... consist in universal
sympathy and tolerance. The world is moved in the first instance by
those who see one side of a question only.' And it was as the merest
afterthought that he added: 'although the services of those who see
both are indispensable for effecting a settlement.'[40]

II

Lord Grey of the Reform Bill was primarily written during the years
1918–19. But the interpretational framework had clearly been
established by the autumn of 1914. For during the interwar years,
Trevelyan's Whiggism became significantly less partisan, less belligerent, less intransigent. The First World War had undermined his belief
in continuity, progress and reform, and had also, as he later admitted,
'helped to free me from some party prejudices' and 'prepared me to
write English history with a more realistic and less partisan outlook.'[41]
Events in Russia since 1917 led him to reconsider his attitudes towards
revolution (and to monarchs), and thereafter he took a much less fav
ourable view of 1789.[42] And although he recognized that the advent
of a Labour government showed 'the flexible old machinery of the
constitution swallowing yet another bloodless revolution', he was
clearly unhappy about the new world of mass democracy ushered in
by the Fourth Reform Act. The sight of a Buxton and a Trevelyan in
the Cabinet certainly carried on 'the "continuity" of English public
life.' But this was scant recompense for the demise of the Liberals. In

the twentieth century, it seemed as though history no longer had endings that were either clear cut or happy.[43]

But it was also that as Trevelyan got older, and as he read more and thought more, he became a more reflective and open-minded historian. The new work of Keith Feiling and Sir William Holdsworth persuaded him that there was more to be said for the Tories than he had previously allowed. His admiration for Conservative historians like John Buchan and Arthur Bryant was a further sign of the broadening of his historical sympathies. They had, he noted on one occasion, 'practically unWhigged me, without wholly Toryfying me.'[44] As a result, he came to see that *both* political parties deserved some of the credit for Britain's progress, and he was prepared to admit that his earlier accounts of England from 1660 to 1714, and from 1780 to 1830, were too one-sided. During the interwar years Trevelyan's main achievement was that, like Lord Macaulay in an earlier generation, he enlarged the Whig interpretation of history from one that was the restricted property of a party to one that was subscribed to by the nation as a whole.[45] The events of 1914–18 had only reinforced his belief that the British were 'history's blood royal', with 'the greatest record of ordered progress in the world', 'broadening down from precedent to precedent.' But it was the nation as a whole which now concerned him, not just the Whigs. And it was the writing of their 'unpartisan national history' which was now his objective.[46]

This was vividly illustrated by the revised version of *England Under the Stuarts*, which he published in 1925.[47] Apart from updating the bibliography, and the pruning of some youthful stylistic excesses, the alterations were relatively few. But they were very significant. He revised some sections of constitutional history in the light of the more favourable view of the monarchy's case put forward by Holdsworth in the sixth volume of his *History of English Law*. He rewrote the account of the execution of Charles I, excised the phrase about 'the slow emancipation of the mind from the shackles of custom and ancient reverence', and instead described the beheading of the King as 'a mistake and a crime'.[48] And after reading Keith Feiling's *History of the Tory Party, 1640–1714*, he softened his remarks about the followers of Harley and Bolingbroke. In the first edition he had dismissed the Tory Party's behaviour in the years 1697–1701 as 'ungrateful, violent and stupid'. He now described it, in more measured terms, as 'unwise'. And in subsequent pages, he modified his earlier condemnation of the Tories for being unwilling and uneager to wage war against the

French.[49] As a result, the book was much more sympathetic to monarchs and conservatives than the first edition had been twenty years before.

The same shift of emphasis and broadening of sympathies is apparent in *British History in the Nineteenth Century*, which Trevelyan published in 1922, another textbook which covered the years 1782 to 1901. It was clearly developed from his earlier work for the biographies of John Bright and Earl Grey, and some of his prewar opinions continued very much in evidence. He remained convinced that the early years of the reign of George III, culminating in the American Revolution, had been 'disastrous'. He still thought well of the Whig aristocracy, and especially of Charles James Fox: 'the first democratic leader and orator of modern England'. He continued to believe that the passing of the Great Reform Act, for which the Whigs had been prepared by fate, was the central event in modern British history. He had not modified his view that the support which Britain gave to the Turkish Empire for so much of the nineteenth century was profoundly mistaken. His admiration for Bright – and for Gladstone – was undiminished, and his attitude towards Joseph Chamberlain remained distinctly lukewarm. As befitted a former 'New Liberal', he seemed especially well disposed towards the Fabians. And he still believed that Britain's victory at Waterloo had ushered in 'a hundred years of progress in liberty and high civilization.'[50]

But compared with Trevelyan's previous writings on the period, it was the book's even-handedness which most stood out. He lavished fulsome praise on the Younger Pitt, describing him as 'the last great statesman of the eighteenth and the first of the nineteenth century.' He admitted that the 'conservative reaction' after the French Revolution 'was certainly inevitable', and 'may have been desirable'. He noted that 'the honour of beating Napoleon fell as clearly to the Tories as the honour of beating Louis XIV had fallen to the Whigs.' He paid tribute to Wellington, not only for his greatness as a soldier, but for his hatred of militarism. He pointed out that Grey's Cabinet of 1830 contained former Tories as well as Whigs, which meant that the Great Reform Act was passed by 'the heirs of Fox' with the 'help of allies from the ranks of Pitt.'[51] He was much more generous to Peel than he had been in his biography of Bright, praising him for his liberal attitudes, and for 'seeking to preserve British institutions by respect for public opinion and by careful thought for the general interest.' He even wrote appreciatively of Palmerston, who 'magnificently mirrored' the qualities of his own countrymen; of Disraeli, who 'educated' his party anew to the cause of democracy and reform; and of Salisbury, who 'stood for character, principle and tradition', and 'maintained public life on a high level.'[52]

All this enabled Trevelyan to write Britain's national history with a tolerant and imaginative comprehensiveness that he had never displayed before. The essence of the passing of the Great Reform Act was that 'the nation' had asserted and defined itself, and in each successive extension of the franchise, in 1867, 1884 and 1918, Trevelyan believed that 'the nation was defined afresh'. And along with this broadened sense of the British political community went a heightened appreciation of the 'national character'. He wrote feelingly about 'British common sense and good nature', and about 'British idiosyncracy and prejudice'. He believed in 'the national instinct for fair play', and British 'good humour'.[53] He thought their nineteenth-century history demonstrated 'the genius of the English people for politics.' And he had no doubt that by the end of her reign, the apotheosized Queen Victoria had become both 'the representative of the public life of the nation in its non-political aspects', and 'the symbol of all that was mighty and lasting in the life of England and of the races associated with England in Empire.'[54]

Put another way, this meant that Trevelyan was more than ever the celebrant of English exceptionalism. For the history of nineteenth-century Britain was one of 'continuous growth', in stark contrast to developments on the Continent. 'Political self-government, central and local, was an English invention', and Britain's parliamentary system was 'the envy of "less happier lands"'.[55] There was, he noted with evident relief, 'no analogy in our own experience' to the events of 1789. Other nations might have revolutions, but the British regarded them as something alien, 'to study, classify and explain'. The passing of the Great Reform Act meant that 'England was not involved in the vicious cycle of continual revolution and reaction, and that our political life kept its Anglo-Saxon moorings.' The disturbances across the Channel in 1848 engendered 'satisfaction in the thought that we were not as other nations', who had failed to discover 'our secret of combining liberty with order'. But for Trevelyan, the real sadness of 1848 was not that the revolutions had happened, but that they had not succeeded. For if they had, the development of 'the military despotisms of Central Europe' might have been prevented, and the First World War averted.[56]

As these remarks imply, *British History in the Nineteenth Century* was also significant in that it articulated Trevelyan's growing disenchantment with what he described in the introduction as 'the strange world in which we live today'. Several reviewers noticed that more than half the book was devoted to the years before 1832, that the coverage thereafter was distinctly scrappy and uneven, and that apart from Peel's ministry of 1841–6, and Gladstone's reforms of 1868–74, he had little interest in subsequent events.[57] At some point in Britain's late-nineteenth-century history, Trevelyan lost his Whiggish confidence in ordered progress and continuing reform. He clearly disliked the new style of politics inaugurated by Joseph Chamberlain: the 'wire pulling' of the caucus and the jingoism of the new imperialism. He regretted that under a democracy, 'there is no provision for the training of a class of statesmen'. And he made this revealing comment about the declining quality of public life: 'In the seventeenth century, Members of Parliament quoted from the Bible; in the eighteenth and nineteenth centuries from the classics; in the twentieth century from nothing at all.' As he admitted to his parents, the later sections of the book had been 'a great trouble to write'. He had 'to observe a kind of neutrality.' He could not 'say freely all I think and feel.'[58]

In *British History in the Nineteenth Century* Trevelyan established the substantially modified Whig approach he was to adopt in his most important pieces of interwar history writing. His confidence in inevitable and indefinite progress, even within Britain itself, had been much weakened. His belief in Britain's exceptionalism had been greatly reinforced. And his political partisanship had been transmuted into a broader, more sympathetic appreciation of what he liked to call 'Englishry'. As a result, the book was much more widely welcomed than his biography of Lord Grey had been. One reviewer noted Trevelyan's concern with 'the organic unity of our national history'. Another observed that he 'never failed to understand the case of his opponents, or to give their views a proper weight', and that he wrote 'like a judge and not like an advocate.'[59] And Élie Halévy praised him for his 'quiet and high-minded impartiality'. But the most suggestive review came from Gerald Hurst, who remarked that Trevelyan had now written two textbooks on two centuries of British history, which led him to wonder whether there might be, 'at a future date, a continuous popular history from his brilliant pen.' Such a work, he predicted, 'would be a national possession.' Trevelyan was soon to prove him right.[60]

In his *Autobiography*, Trevelyan noted that it was the success of this second textbook, and the encouragement of Robert Longman, his publisher, which persuaded him to attempt soon after a one-volume *History of England*. But in fact he had been toying with the idea of such a book ever since the First World War. In June 1917 he was already thinking about how he should occupy himself once peace returned, and the 'main competitors' in his mind were an account of *England Under Queen Anne*, and a full-scale *History of England*. In 'this age of democracy and patriotism', he felt 'strongly drawn' to 'write the History of England, as I feel it, for the people.' Having cleared his mind 'of some party prejudices', he felt as though he had 'a conception of the development of English history, liberal but purely English, and embracing the other elements.'[61] Once he had finished his biography of Grey, his nineteenth-century textbook, and his study of Manin and Venice, it was to this project that he turned. In 1924, he was invited to deliver the Lowell Lectures at Harvard University, which gave him the opportunity to try out an early version. Even by his standards, he worked with astonishing speed, and the book was completed and published in 1926.

The last comparable one-volume effort had been J. R. Green's *Short History of the English People*, which had first been published as long ago as 1874, and Trevelyan was determined to write a book which would serve his own time and generation at least as successfully. He covered the two millenia of history which separated pre-Roman Britain from the First World War, and he wrote about Wales, Scotland and Ireland as well as England, and about the British Empire as well as the British Isles. His chief concern was with political events and developments, but he also described the lives of ordinary people, and evoked the environment in which they lived. As Leonard Woolf observed, Trevelyan's England was 'complex and kaleidoscopic': 'a composite entity in which hills and streams, living people, and a political State coalesce.'[62] But the basic outline was simplicity itself. The centuries before the early Tudors were very largely a prologue, as the nation gradually came into being, and established its own identity, 'based on peculiar characteristics, laws and institutions'. Only since the reign of Elizabeth had the English taken their rightful place among the comity of nations and made their special contribution to civilization.[63] That, in essence, was the story Trevelyan sought to unfold. And in so doing, he was obliged to set out, more explicitly than ever before, what he regarded as the essential themes of his country's history.

The first was the unique nature of the British constitution, which was itself the product of British insularity and British character. 'In answer to the instincts and temperament of her people', Trevelyan declared, the English had 'evolved in the course of centuries a system which reconciled three things that other nations have often found incompatible – executive efficiency, popular control, and personal freedom.' And the key to this was Parliament: 'the natural outcome, through long centuries, of the common sense and good nature of the English people.'[64] It was in the Middle Ages, Trevelyan insisted, that Parliament first recognizably came into being, and the rejection of Richard II in 1399 was very like the overthrow of James II in 1688. Its power and prestige was greatly enhanced under the early Tudors, and by the end of the seventeenth century it had finally and irrevocably wrested power from the Crown, and 'established human freedom on a practical basis.' The two-party system, Cabinet government, and the office of Prime Minister gradually evolved, and all survived the misguided attempt by George III to impose his 'personal government'. With the passing of the Great Reform Act, 'the nation was thenceforth master in its own house', and the way was open to later, and orderly, extensions of the franchise. There may have been 'no logic' in the process of 'bit by bit enfranchisement'; but there were 'great practical advantages to the life of the nation in the very graduality of an uninterrupted movement towards democratic control.'[65]

Trevelyan believed that 'the complex forms and free spirit of English government' persisted 'from century to century, with continuity in change.' But although it was Parliament which won, defended, and defined English freedom, the development of liberty was as much a sacred as a secular matter. For in England the growth of parliamentary supremacy went hand in hand with the growth of religious toleration. By the fourteenth century, the cosmopolitan but corrupted medieval Church was the object of widespread criticism, which gave rise to the demand that the state should exert authority over it. 'Every important aspect of the English reformation', Trevelyan believed, was thus 'of native origins.'[66] By 1530, 'the full-blown spirit of English nationalism' would no longer submit to papal authority, and so Henry VIII drove through the Reformation with the sanction and support of Parliament. This 'great revolution' freed 'the English Church and State from the bonds of Rome', and under Elizabeth a national Protestant Church was established. But the rise of Puritanism made it increasingly difficult to force all Englishmen to worship at the same altar. Just as the Glorious Revolution of 1688 established secular liberties, so the Act of

Toleration passed in the following year effectively introduced freedom of worship. And although there remained certain restrictions on Roman Catholics and Dissenters, these were gradually abolished during the nineteenth century.[67]

But these singular internal developments, Trevelyan believed, could only be understood in a Continental context. The Roman occupation left little lasting legacy, and the successive waves of Nordic invaders left a maritime inheritance which was only to be entered into many centuries later. From the Norman Conquest to the 1450s, England was subordinated to 'French feudal civilization', and it was only with the ending of the Hundred Years War, and the advent of the Tudors, that the obsessive desire to reconquer France was given up, and that England began to distance itself from the Continent. Because 'English freedom was rooted in insular peculiarities', the nation required, for the full maturing of its institutions, 'a period of isolation from European influence and dangers'. And during the next four centuries that was precisely what it enjoyed: 'from Tudor times onwards, England treated European politics simply as a means of ensuring her own security from invasion.'[68] For much of the time, this meant leaving the Europeans alone. But from the reign of Elizabeth onwards, it also meant that England was occasionally obliged to take the lead when the rise of a new Continental despotism threatened both Continental and national security. Against Philip II, against Louis XIV, against Napoleon and against the Kaiser, it was the English who were the most resourceful and resilient adversaries, thereby rescuing from tyrannical rule the very Continent on which they had, for the most part, turned their backs.

The nation which so successfully and so beneficially detached itself from the Continent did not become introspective and isolationist. Instead, England entered 'upon the wider spaces of her destiny'. The love of far horizons and the delight in maritime adventure, were the legacy of the Scandinavian invaders, and it was as a seafaring nation, 'at once insular and oceanic', that Trevelyan believed 'English civilization was fused into its modern form.'[69] Henry VIII was the father of the British navy, and it was he who established a 'heretical sea power on the flank of the great Continental despotisms.' It was sea power which enabled the English to establish their colonies, to 'plant the flag of liberty beyond the ocean', and eventually to become the centre of a great world empire.[70] And it was also sea power which enabled them to defeat a succession of would-be Continental tyrants. Francis Drake was the prototypical naval hero. Both Marlborough and Chatham knew how to co-ordinate battle by land and sea, and their victories propelled their country to 'the acknowledged leadership of the world, in arms, colonies, commerce, in political and religious freedom, and in intellectual vigour.' And how appropriate it was that Nelson remained 'the best loved name in English ears.'[71]

These, for Trevelyan, were the essential themes in England's history – a history which was not only separate from, but also superior to, that of other European nations. The early establishment and continual importance of Parliament 'raised the political history of Britain into a sphere apart from the political life of the Continent.' During the sixteenth and seventeenth centuries, 'Britain alone of the great nation states successfully . . . turned back the tide of despotism, and elaborated a system by which a debating chamber of elected persons could successfully govern an Empire in peace and war.' After 1688, 'English institutions for the first time became an example to the world, though they remained something of a mystery, and were very imperfectly understood.'[72] During the eighteenth century, the British 'looked with contempt on French, Italian and Germans, as people enslaved by priests, kings and nobles, unlike your freeborn Englishmen.' Between 1789 and 1914, the British successfully accommodated their parliamentary system to modern circumstances, and exported it to their Empire, while other nations went through bloody revolutions. And in the twentieth century, parliamentary institutions elsewhere 'have withered like waterless plants', while in Britain they had survived, unchallenged, triumphant and universally admired.[73]

As Trevelyan freely admitted, he had provided a national history which was liberal and Protestant in approach, which preferred 'the forces of progress' to 'mere obscurantism', which showed a particularly warm appreciation of the contribution and achievements of the traditional landed classes, and which retained a lingering belief in 'the destiny of Britain'.[74] But while in all these ways it was a recognizably Whig production, most reviewers were rightly impressed by the book's 'fairness and sincerity', its 'largeness of view', and the 'reasonableness and broad temper of his general attitude to his great theme.'[75] Never before had Trevelyan written with such imaginative sympathy – for the medieval Church, for Roman Catholics and for Jacobites; for Mary Tudor, for Charles I and even for George III. In writing this book, his intention had been to evoke and to explain – and perhaps to reinforce – the continuity and the community of British national life and British national identity, and to celebrate 'the fundamentally kind and tolerant nature of our English world.' To his delight, he received ample reassurance from Tory friends like John Buchan that he had succeeded.[76] And so he had. For the consensual patriotism of his history was perfectly suited to the emollient Toryism of the age of Baldwin.

A reviewer of *British History in the Nineteenth Century* had remarked that the First World War had 'diminished our expectations and increased our self-satisfaction', and there were certainly indications of this in Trevelyan's larger work. One American vehemently objected to its 'ardently national' approach, and to its 'insular sense of superiority'.[77] Considering the unhappy state of many European countries by the mid-1920s, a certain amount of quiet pride and grateful relief was understandable. In any case, it was the diminished expectations which stood out more emphatically than the complacency. For it was not just that the book flagged as it neared the twentieth century; that the epilogue covering the years 1901–18 was perfunctory; or that Trevelyan described the First World War as 'the greatest catastrophe of modern times'.[78] It was also that the book as a whole was conspicuously lacking in the robust and boisterous confidence of Macaulay, and was pervaded by an increasing sense of melancholy and doubt. Although Trevelyan believed in progress, he disliked many of its results. He accepted democracy, but only did so reluctantly. He recognized revolutions were sometimes beneficial, yet regretted the brutal and violent form they often took. The final words of his history were thus an expression of uncertainty and perplexity, and were a long way from the resounding and confident perorations of his prewar books: 'Of the future, the historian can see no more than others. He can only point like a showman to the things of the past, with their manifold and mysterious message.'[79]

Once Trevelyan had completed the first of his great wartime projects, he immediately turned to the second: a history of England during the reign of Queen Anne. He was attracted to it for many reasons. Lord Macaulay's account had been left unfinished at exactly this point, and 'the idea of taking up the tale where my great-uncle's history had broken off' was 'a fancy at the back of my consciousness.' As a Cambridge undergraduate, Trevelyan's special period had been the War of Spanish Succession, he had visited the Blenheim battlefield in 1895. By then he was already resolved to write about Queen Anne.[80] As a northcountryman, he had long been drawn to Scottish history, and this book gave him ample opportunity to indulge his interest in, and knowledge of, the Borders. And for an historian who enjoyed writing about battles, this was a period of unsurpassed fascination: 'I like drums and trumpets', he explained to Bob, 'provided they were blown a good hundred years or more ago!' Above all, such a 'full-dress history', conceived on the grandest possible scale – Trevelyan anticipated it would take him ten years and four volumes – seemed an appropriate venture for a man at the peak of his powers and the head of his profession. For his aim was to produce 'the chief historical work of my life', which might have a 'permanent place among histories in the future.'[81]

As with his three books of prewar Whiggery, Trevelyan was dealing with an era in his country's history which furnished 'no parochial theme': for once again, he was writing about a pivotal period of transition, in which a new world was slowly but victoriously struggling against the old. The Stuart century had been a time of rebellion and revolution, of civil war and regicide, of gunpowder, treason and plot. By contrast, the eighteenth century was marked by 'humanity, moderation and co-operation'. But when Anne came to the throne in 1702, this happy outcome 'was not yet certain'.[82] Deeply rooted differences – over religion, foreign policy and the succession – had to be resolved, and the constitutional innovations implicit in 1688 – limited monarchy, Cabinet government, and the two-party system – had to be recognized and worked out. Thanks to the 'prudently compromising' statesmanship that characterized the Queen's reign, these outstanding problems were successfully settled, and the way was open for the 'moderate courses' of Walpolean Whiggism, when England pioneered 'the great art of letting your neighbour alone.'[83] How Trevelyan's attitude had shifted since the angry young Whig who wrote *England in the Age of Wycliffe*. Then he had been on the side of the progressives and subversives. Now his concern was with the men who could see both sides of a question, who had smoothed an age of strife into an era of stability.

One essential element of this protracted, post-Revolutionary settlement was the Union with Scotland carried in 1707. Trevelyan had no doubt that this was an 'act of wise imperial initiative', which reconciled 'the two peoples on terms of equality and justice', and so was 'one of the greatest and happiest facts in our island history'.[84] Of course, there were short-run difficulties and discontents, but in the longer term, its impact was wholly – and mutually – beneficial. By uniting the two countries, the Protestant succession was assured. By releasing Scotland from 'poverty and isolation', it ushered in that country's golden age of Burns and Scott. And it enabled the Scots to play a major part in overseas expansion, thereby making the British Empire much greater than any English Empire would ever have been without them. As Trevelyan had observed before, in his BBC National Lecture of 1929, the Union of England and Scotland was the central episode in the making of modern Britain, and a lasting monument to the virtues of 'compromise and concession'. No wonder there had been a service of thanksgiving attended by Queen Anne: for the 'greatest of all the victories with which God had blessed her reign.'[85]

These momentous domestic developments had appropriately momentous international consequences. As in Elizabeth's time, and as would happen again with Napoleon and the Kaiser, Britain was the 'chief agent' in opposing the 'pride and world-ambition of a despot', and in determining to keep the Low Countries free from hostile occupation. On land, the Duke of Marlborough produced a succession of sensational victories, which humbled the once proud army of Louis XIV, and at sea Britain established itself as the pre-eminent naval power in the world, 'on a basis whence no enemy has been able to dislodge it.'[86] Underlying these military triumphs, and making them possible, was a financial and commercial strength which France could not rival, and which the Dutch, worn down by invasion and occupation, could no longer equal. The result was that at the Treaty of Utrecht of 1713, Britain stood forth as the greatest power in the world, with fewer rivals than in 1815 or 1919. A freedom-loving nation, savouring liberty and relishing independence, had for the first time proved itself 'superior to despotism'. 'In Anne's reign', Trevelyan later wrote, 'it seemed to me Britain attained by sea and land her modern place in the world.'[87]

The individual who deserved most of the credit for this astonishing transformation in Britain's fortunes was John Churchill, first Duke of Marlborough, whose personality, achievements and failings dominated all three volumes. He was too devious and too secretive a character to be a larger-than-life hero in the Garibaldi mould. But Trevelyan had no doubt that as a military commander, as a British politician and as a European statesman, Marlborough was the saviour of his country's freedom, and the arbiter of the Continent's destinies. Yet in describing the Duke in such adulatory terms, Trevelyan was setting himself against his own family tradition. For Macaulay had been 'duped' by contemporary Tory propaganda into depicting the Duke as a 'villain of genius', a man of 'avarice, meanness and treachery'. Trevelyan admitted Marlborough's 'proneness for double-dealing', and criticized his reluctance to make peace once the war had been won.[88] But he also believed that reparation should be done to him for Macaulay's savage caricature. As he explained to Mary:

> I am getting very fond of Marlborough, for all his faults. He was *humane*, he was wise, he was not passion's slave or party's or fanaticism's, and he served his country and his age with all his incomparable armoury of genius and temper till he had completed his work, and ushered in the age of toleration and of reason – he himself being the most tolerant and reasonable of men.[89]

Significantly, Trevelyan described Marlborough as a 'Moderate Tory', and these words applied with equal appropriateness to the other central characters who moved 'England forward on the tide of destiny' during Anne's reign. First among them was the Queen herself, who preferred ministries of a nonpartisan complexion and who was inspired by the ideals of 'moderation, good sense and humanity, for which the Stuart line had not always been conspicuous.' During the early years of her reign, she threw her support wholeheartedly behind Marlborough and his two closest colleagues: Harley and Godolphin. As Speaker of the Commons and then Secretary of State, Harley manipulated Parliament behind the scenes, and was described by Trevelyan as 'a public servant and a moderator', while as Lord Treasurer, Godolphin raised the necessary funds, and was 'much more a public servant than a party politician.'[90] Between 1702 and 1708, these three 'Tories without zeal' governed the country and prosecuted the war on moderate, nonpartisan lines. As such, they 'represented the national feeling', and upheld 'the great traditions of patriotic government'. For Trevelyan, it was both fitting and appropriate that Louis XIV was 'beaten by a coalition ministry of moderates.' And they were the men in the story he admired most. 'I am', he told Mary, 'getting more of a Harleyite and a Marlburian than a true-blue Whig.'[91]

But it was not just the moderates to whom Trevelyan was well disposed in his account: his tolerance extended to fierce partisans – and on both sides of the political divide. He gave the Tories full credit for passing the Act of Settlement in 1701, which fixed the reversion of the Crown after the death of Anne on Hanover, to the exclusion of James II's Catholic son. And he paid tribute to their zeal in approving the European alliances which were the essential prelude to the renewed war with Louis. 'On both issues', he concluded, 'the Tories of 1701

did what the interests of the country required.' Of course, the Whigs
were more eager in their support of the war once it had broken out,
but they were 'useless' as peacemakers once victory had been secured,
and it fell to the Tories to negotiate the Treaty of Utrecht.[92] In the
course of so doing, Bolingbroke let down Britain's allies, especially the
Dutch, but Trevelyan had no doubt the peace was 'a great achievement'. Then it was the turn of the Whigs again: for while the Tory
leadership flirted with Jacobitism, it was they who secured the Hanoverian succession. In short, both parties contributed much to British
political life during these years. Just as the Whigs 'answered to something persistent in the national mind and character', so the Tories
'expressed the other aspect of England's needs and ideas.' Indeed, by
now Trevelyan had come to believe that each party was necessary
for the other's wellbeing: 'Where there are no effective Tories', he
concluded, 'there can be no proper Whigs.'[93]

For Trevelyan, the essential theme of the nation's history during
the reign of Queen Anne was the victory of tolerance and moderation,
humanity and good sense, and as British institutions were gradually
moulded in the image of British character, these became the hallmarks
of the country's political tradition:

> The establishment of liberty was not the result of the complete tri-
> umph of any one party in the state. It was the result of the balance
> of political parties and religious sects, compelled to tolerate one
> another, until toleration became a habit of the national mind. Even
> the long Whig supremacy that was the outcome and sequel to the
> reign of Anne, was conditional on a vigilant maintenance of insti-
> tutions in Church and State that were specially dear to the Tories,
> and a constant respect for the latent power of political opponents,
> who were fellow subjects and brother Englishmen.[94]

Throughout these three volumes, he wrote as a 'fellow subject' and
'brother Englishman', and he did so with a patriotic pride in which
affection and admiration were equally mingled:

> What men that little rustic England could breed! A nation of five
> and a half millions, that had Wren for its architect, Newton for its
> scientist, Locke for its philosopher, Bentley for its scholar, Pope for
> its poet, Addison for its essayist, Bolingbroke for its orator, Swift for
> its pamphleteer, and Marlborough to win its battles, had the recipe
> for genius![95]

As with so many of his books, Trevelyan was exceptionally lucky in the timing of the publication of *England Under Queen Anne*. His second volume, which celebrated national compromise, patriotic coalition, and nonpartisan collaboration, came out the year after a National Government had been established to deal with the financial crisis of 1931. And by the time his last volume appeared, the advent of Nazi government in Germany gave added force to his celebration of British decency and democracy. Indeed, his comments in that book on the demise of parliamentary institutions, on the destruction of 'liberty of press and person', and on the 'permanent suppression' of all opposition, can only be read as a rebuke to Hitler and Mussolini. No wonder Trevelyan was attracted by the continuities of British history. For the successful establishment of the Hanoverian regime not only registered 'the triumph of English liberty and law': it also set upon the throne a family whose direct descendants were still there – unlike most other European dynasties.[96] 'Even after the war', he later recalled, 'the reign of Queen Anne and the history of England up to the end of Victoria's reign, still seemed to me, when I came to write about them, to be stories with a happy ending.' But the caveat about his own times was as revealing as the affirmation about the centuries which had gone before.[97]

III

The publication of these books established a new identity for Trevelyan in the interwar public mind. He was no longer seen as the Liberal partisan or the Whig polemicist: instead, he had become the *'national historian'*. Not for nothing did each of his three greatest works have the word 'England' or 'British' in their title. Indeed, it was this same solemn, national identity which, during the 1930s, Trevelyan constantly urged the young Arthur Bryant to grow into. He hoped that Bryant's Toryism was 'broadening into Englishry, as I hope my Whiggery has to some extent so broadened in the course of years.'[98] In April 1938 Bryant wrote a piece for 'Our Notebook' in the *Illustrated London News*, in which he compared two different types of liberalism. The first was the partisan tradition, which ran from 1688 and 1832 to the Liberal welfare reforms of the 1900s. The second was the deliberate cultivation of a tolerant, open mind, especially towards those who did not share one's own beliefs. Trevelyan's comment on this piece was revealing: 'I think I have, taught by the last war and advanced years, moved out of the one into the other.'[99] No longer did he defend the wisdom of intolerance, as he had done in *England in the Age of Wycliffe*.

It was in his new identity as the 'national historian' that Trevelyan was involved in a series of public occasions in the years between the wars, the first of which was his Romanes Lecture at Oxford. It was given in 1926, on the very same day that the General Strike was called off, and was entitled 'The Two-Party System in English Political History'. At a time when it seemed possible that this was being abandoned for a three-party system, Trevelyan refused to 'speak of the twentieth century', adding, with what Élie Halévy called 'a fine touch of Whiggish pride and aloofness' that it was 'a period I have never studied.'[100] But for the earlier centuries, he treated the subject with conspicuous even-handedness, recognizing that it was in the ebb and flow of party warfare, rather than the isolated achievements of the Whigs, that British history had been made, and Britain's liberties won. The continuity of parties, from the late seventeenth to the late nineteenth centuries was, he insisted, 'a great fact in English history.' But serious research on the subject was only just beginning, and the 'proper study of the party system' would take us 'far beyond the four walls of Westminster', and would encompass constituency politics, the press, religion, the relation of landlord and tenant, employer and employed. In short, Trevelyan believed that the history of party should be broadly conceived, and as such would amount to 'a new method of approach to English history as a whole.'[101]

Ever since 1688, Trevelyan argued, 'party' had been the essence of British parliamentary government, without which the English would not have managed their unique historical achievement of combining efficiency with freedom, a successful state with personal liberty. The bond of party introduced discipline into the legislature and the executive and so helped to ensure that the nation's affairs were properly conducted. But the party system, parliamentary government and personal freedom were 'not an inevitable stage of progress, certain to be reached by every nation in turn, but a peculiar form of polity, not easily worked with success.' Having refused to speak of the twentieth century, Trevelyan then listed many other countries where, in his own time, such a system had failed to survive. In France, there had been parliamentary government for fifty years, 'but she still finds it a difficult system under which to raise the necessary taxes.' In Italy, it had been abandoned, 'together with freedom of speech, press and person.' Russia had 'not yet brought herself to attempt it.' In Spain and Greece, parliamentary institutions were 'little more than camouflage of very different realities.' And Germany was 'trying it for the first time in her history; we wish her good fortune.'[102]

Having paid his tribute to the uniqueness and wisdom of Britain's system of government, Trevelyan sought to sketch out the evolution of party from 1688 to 1832. He noted the extreme violence of two-party rivalry during the reigns of William and Anne. He suggested that under Walpole 'the Whigs definitely took their stand on moderation, latitudinarianism, and freedom of thought and speech', and that it was in this period that 'the excellent and difficult habit of leaving other people alone became the custom of the country.' He urged the need for more research into the Tories, during their long period of 'hibernation' between 1715 and 1760, and drew attention to their 'innate respect for law and order, even when administered by their rivals.'[103] From 1760, assisted by George III, the Tory Party returned to power, and ruled the land until 1830. While the Whigs neglected finance, and preached peace with France, Pitt the Younger broadened the base and scope of Toryism, as Peel was to do in a later generation, and Lord Liverpool's administration won the war against Napoleon. Thus described, British history was the work of the Tories no less than the Whigs. 'No one party', Trevelyan concluded, 'can cover all the ground. Hence the necessity for a two-party system.'[104]

In 1932 it was one hundred years since the passing of the Great Reform Act, and it was appropriately commemorated in Newcastle, where a further inscription was added to Earl Grey's monument: 'After a century of civil peace, the people renew their gratitude to the author of the Great Reform Act.' In the City Hall there was a public meeting, attended by the men and women of Tyneside, and the platform was crowded by the Grey family from Howick, their relations and friends, of whom Trevelyan was one.[105] It was, he recalled, a 'memorable occasion', which 'bore witness to the persistent historical traditions of England.' Grey of Fallodon, who had carried the family tradition of public service into the new century, made an appropriately felicitous speech. But the 'most unexpected and most applauded of the orations' came from old Lord Halifax, another member of the 'Grey connection', whose father, Charles Wood, had been a junior minister at the time of the Reform Bill crisis and had married Mary Grey. Halifax was over eighty, but 'his mental vigour was out of all proportion to his bodily strength.' For that night, Trevelyan later recalled, 'the fires of the Reform Bill came to life again', as Halifax 'perorated and gesticulated', and Charles, Earl Grey 'held on to his coat-tails . . . lest he should fall off the platform.'

For *The Times* Trevelyan wrote two extended articles, which took a broader and less partisan perspective of the events of 1829–32 than he had done in his biography of Earl Grey.[106] 'In our domestic history', Trevelyan opined, '1832 is the next great landmark after 1688.' The Great Reform Act 'saved the land from revolution and civil strife, and made possible the quiet progress of the Victorian era.' Like the Revolution of 1688, 'the Reform Bill was a great Conservative as well as a great Liberal measure', and it was sponsored by a Cabinet which included not only Whigs, but also former Tories like Palmerston, Melbourne, Graham and Stanley, who recognized that the political system must be drastically adjusted to take account of the social and economic changes associated with the Industrial Revolution. And they composed a perfectly judged measure. 'It was', Trevelyan observed, 'a bull's eye of legislative marksmanship, when an inch more to the right or left would have been fatal.' As a result, 'a change that in any other lands or in an earlier England would have caused bloodshed and the breaking up of laws had been carried like any other Act of Parliament.' It was, Trevelyan concluded, even-handedly, 'an affair of which Englishmen of all classes and parties may be proud, and it was a characteristically English business from beginning to end.'

In the course of his essay, Trevelyan noted that the Crown now enjoyed 'greater security and prestige than it had when worn by the sons of George III', and as the national historian he wielded his pen on behalf of the monarchy, on the occasion of George V's Silver Jubilee in 1935, when he wrote the lead article for *The Times* commemorative edition.[107] Compared with the easy certainties of the Victorian age, the present seemed 'a tumbled world, subject to recurrent waves of distress and fear.' But throughout this 'riot of change', the monarchy, the system of parliamentary government and the British Empire remained 'a bulwark of freedom in evil days', amidst 'the crash of other Empires and the destruction of other liberties'. How well, Trevelyan went on, all this testified to 'the adaptability of our flexible constitution to meet sudden extreme dangers and great permanent changes of circumstance.' And the monarchy had not only survived as an emblem of stability in this rapidly dissolving world: its importance had actually increased. For since the Statute of Westminster had been passed, which effectively made the great dominions autonomous, the Crown was now 'the sole legal and symbolic link of the whole British Empire.'

In the same article, Trevelyan also suggested that Britain itself had seen much careful, consensual progress during the twenty-five years of the King's reign. The Liberal Party had declined, but Labour had taken its place, which meant that 'modern England therefore stands committed to a continuation of the two-party system under new auspices.' Equally remarkable was the way in which 'Conservative statesmen, to whom the principal charge of the country has fallen', had adopted 'what would formerly have been regarded as ultra-Liberal views': in giving independence to Southern Ireland and Egypt, in helping India along the road to self-government, and in providing a 'system of social services' even more 'extensive and elaborate' than that which the Liberals had established before 1914. At the same time, modern inventions, especially the wireless, were making 'the whole island a single community, increasingly conscious of itself as such'. This might be unspectacular progress; but it was progress, nevertheless. As he put it in a letter to Mary: 'We are not so gay, perhaps not so great, a people as in Victoria's Jubilees: but I don't think we are a worse one – we are certainly less insolent.'[108]

The climax of these Silver Jubilee celebrations was the presentation of loyal addresses by both Houses of Parliament in Westminster Hall. The King's reply took a broad, philosophical view of the occasion. 'Beneath these rafters of medieval oak, the silent witnesses of historic tragedies and pageants,' he reminded his audience, 'we celebrate the present under the spell of the past. It is', he went on, 'to me a source of pride and thankfulness that the perfect harmony of our parliamentary system with our constitutional monarchy has survived the shocks that have in recent years destroyed other empires and other liberties.' And the explanation was clear: 'The complex forms and balanced spirit of our constitution were not the discovery of a single era, still less of a single party or of a single person. They are the slow accretion of centuries, the outcome of patience, tradition, and experience, constantly finding channels old and new for the impulse towards liberty, justice, and social improvement inherent in our people down the ages.' And this was not just true of Britain, but of the Empire as well: 'In these days, when fear and preparation for war are again astir in the world, let us be thankful that quiet government and peace prevail over so large a part of the earth's surface, and that under our flag of freedom, so many millions eat their daily bread, in far distant lands and climates, with none to make them afraid.'[109]

These were 'admirable Whig sentiments', expressed in the most eirenic and placatory language. In the words of Joseph M. Hernon, they showed that the Whig interpretation had by this time become 'the accepted, popular consciousness of British history'.[110] Appropriately enough, it was Trevelyan, the one historian of his generation most responsible for that development, who had written the speech, with the exception of the sentence in which he spoke about Queen Mary, which the King inserted himself. Trevelyan told very few people, explaining to his daughter that 'It spoils it if the world knows who wrote the King's speech – especially on such an occasion.' As a token of royal appreciation, Trevelyan was sent a rather bizarre set of gifts, including a photograph of Their Majesties, a signed copy of *The King's Book*, and a gramophone record of George V's Jubilee speeches.[111] How times had changed – and how the Trevelyans had changed – since 1871, when Sir George Otto had written his savagely critical anonymous pamphlet, attacking the alleged riches of Queen Victoria, entitled *What Does She Do With It?* By the interwar years, Trevelyan was a firm and fervent monarchist: Regius Professor, member of the Order of Merit, and speechwriter to the King. As he had written in *Grey of the Reform Bill*, 'Monarchy in the reign of George III was very different from monarchy in the reign of George V.'[112]

Inevitably, he was much concerned as the drama of the Abdication unfolded during 1936. 'When a man at his time of life becomes "infatuated",' Trevelyan wrote to Mary in mid-November, 'and the woman is selfish, she may make him do anything. It is strange that having accepted the greatest position in the world, he should be unwilling to sacrifice his personal happiness to it.' And after it was all over, he was sure that the country was well rid of Edward VIII. As he explained to Mary: 'Getting George [VI] instead of the nervous and unreliable Edward is a great gain in more ways than the marital. My cabinet minister friends, two of them, tell me they had doubted whether he (Edward) would take the kingship at all, he disliked it so. If he had not disliked the office, he would not have given it up for Mrs Simpson.'[113] And he expressed the same opinion, with an additional and characteristic swipe at the intelligentsia, in a letter to Arthur Bryant: 'We have escaped a great danger. He had some fine qualities, but he was unsuited to be King, and he did not want to be King. We should never have had a proper monarchy under him. And a stand has been made against the view that sexual licence is a natural right of man, a doctrine which half our literary and intellectual leaders have been preaching for the last forty years. I feared they might have converted the country, but clearly they haven't.'[114]

As an OM, Trevelyan attended the Coronation of King George VI and Queen Elizabeth, by which he was deeply impressed: 'No ceremony on earth could equal it for splendour, history, religion, and Englishry, all blent into a unique thing . . . The King in golden robes and a large crown holding the two sceptres was like a medieval king. The Queen was the most moving thing in it all, and Queen Mary next – and the King the finest.' And once again he wrote eloquently for *The Times* explaining what the monarchy now meant to the nation and the Empire.[115] By retiring from politics, the Crown was able to enjoy the benefits of 'influence and high symbolism.' For Trevelyan believed that 'the new English democracy is in love with the Crown': radicalism had withered away; 'the modern Labour Party has no quarrel with the English monarchy'; and 'the Crown is the one symbol that all classes and parties can without reservation accept.' But as well as uniting the nation, the monarch was now 'the sole symbol of the unity of the Empire', and how splendid Trevelyan felt it was 'to have a personal object for common loyalty who is not a party man, still less a dictator.'

The year after the Coronation of George VI was the two hundred and fiftieth anniversary of the Glorious Revolution, and Trevelyan agreed to write a brief account of it for the Home University Library.[116] He still regarded it as 'one of the most amazing stories in the world', which 'never grows old to me', and when he returned to Cambridge as Regius Professor he had chosen – or, by nice coincidence, been allotted – 1688 as his telephone number. In his *Autobiography*, he modestly described the book as being 'a final clearance' of his work on seventeenth-century history, and there can be no doubt that the interpretation he put forward was a kind of retrospective prelude to *England Under Queen Anne*. For the true glory of the revolution – unlike many political convulsions – lay in its moderation, and in its long-lasting effects. It was a 'sensible' revolution because it was without bloodshed and because it opened up for future generations 'the way of escape from violence'. It was a conservative revolution, because its objective, successfully accomplished, was to uphold the law against a law-breaking, would-be despot of a monarch. It was a national revolution, because it was the combined work of Whigs and Tories, who in a brief moment of patriotic compromise and prudent common sense sank their differences, and established limited monarchy, individual freedom, and religious toleration. And it was a beneficent revolution because it led to 'the chaining up of fanaticism alike in politics and religion', and enabled the English to learn 'the difficult art of leaving one another alone.' Unlike 1789, 1688 'reconciled more than it divided.'[117]

When writing about the Glorious Revolution, Trevelyan felt the touch of his great-uncle on his shoulder, even more than with *England Under Queen Anne*. He noted in the bibliography that 'Macaulay's personal bias requires a great deal of correction', but he had increasingly come to share his hostile view of the French Revolution and also his interpretation of 1688 which, by giving England 'strength as well as freedom', was the foundation stone of its later greatness.[118] As he explained to Bob:

> I kept off the 'high lights' purposely, partly because there is not room to develop them over so small a canvas, partly not to rival Macaulay, because it would be a failure as rivalry, and I was anxious to strike a different note from Macaulay, to secure confidence for my general views, which as you see are not really very different from Macaulay's after all! For on the big impersonal issues he was right.[119]

But there was one significant difference in these two accounts, and that was the circumstances in which they appeared. Macaulay's history was first published in 1848; Trevelyan's came out in the month of Munich. And it must surely have been with Hitler and Mussolini in mind that he concluded his book with this warning: 'the system of government by discussion has its disadvantages . . . in face of absolutist governments of a new and more formidable type than those of Europe of the *ancien régime*.' How, he seemed to be asking, would 'the better elements usually found in English political culture – humanity, decency and common sense' fare against *that*?

IV

Both as an historian and as a public man Trevelyan's interwar Whiggery was thus much modified: in domestic terms, it was increasingly consensual and nonpartisan; and internationally, it stressed more than ever the unique British virtues of liberty, stability and order, which once again seemed so little in evidence on the Continent – especially in the case of Germany. Although Trevelyan had visited that country as an undergraduate, and although he spoke the language, he knew virtually 'nothing' about Germany, had few friends there, never wrote about it, and disliked the 'German character', particularly 'the crassness that expects other people to be always on their side over everything, or else to be regarded as hostile.' Indeed, he was so put off by its tradition of Bismarckian militarism that he underestimated the German contribution to European civilization, and especially to historical inquiry (although in *England Under the Stuarts* he did praise Ranke's *History of England, Principally in the Seventeenth Century* as 'one of the great histories of our country, too much neglected').[120] But he could not ignore Germany's dominating and disruptive presence on the international scene. How, as a Whig historian, did Trevelyan respond to this Continental challenger, the most vigorous and threatening embodiment of 'military despotism'?

Even as a Whig historian of modified views, Trevelyan recognized that the war against the Kaiser was another example of Britain taking 'the leading part in resistance to the world dominion of a single state', as it had previously done against Philip II, Louis XIV and Napoleon. And after his initial hesitations in August 1914, Trevelyan had no doubt that the war against the Kaiser's Germany was just: more just, indeed, than the war against Revolutionary France. For then, Britain had allied with the clerical despotisms of Prussia and Austria to crush liberty, whereas during the First World War, Britain was in alliance with the liberal democracies of France, Italy and the USA against the military despotisms of the Central Powers.[121] But the darker side for Trevelyan of this much-preferred alignment was that the peace treaties made in 1919, when the politicians felt obliged to give in to popular and vindictive clamour, were far less generous and far less wise than the settlements of 1713, 1763 and 1815, when British statesmen had been free of democratic constraints, and had negotiated treaties which were more magnanimous, more statesmanlike – and thus more successful.

In 1815, at the Congress of Vienna, the aim of Castlereagh and Wellington had been 'security not revenge'. 'Popular passions' may have been 'at blood heat' in England, but they wielded no influence over the peacemaking progress. The dismemberment of France was prevented; most of the country's colonies were returned; and there was only a moderate indemnity. And in the same way, the East Indian empire of Java and Sumatra was restored to Holland. The result,

according to Trevelyan, of this 'generous and wise' settlement, was
that 'it prevented a war of revenge by France, and it gave security to
the British Empire for a hundred years.'[122] He wrote these words in
British History in the Nineteenth Century, published in 1922, and the
implied criticism of the Versailles settlement of only three years before
was plain. He made the same point in his *History of England*, published
four years later, where he once again acclaimed the 'justice and
even leniency to the conquered' displayed by Wellington and
Castlereagh.[123] And in *England Under Queen Anne*, his description of
the Treaty of Utrecht as 'a Peace which proved in the working more
satisfactory than any other that has ended a general European conflict
in modern times' was another indirect rebuke to the bungled efforts
of 1918–19.[124]

Ten years further on, when Trevelyan wrote an epilogue to *British
History in the Nineteenth Century*, he was unsparing in his criticisms of
the settlement of 1919. The treaty was made, he insisted, 'in a passing
mood so little representative of England's usual good sense and good
nature.' And it was democracy which was essentially to blame. Asquith
and his supporters, who stood for moderation, were vanquished in the
general election of 1918, which Lloyd George, the darling of the press
and the voters, won on a platform which could be summed up in one
word: 'vengeance'. The great object of the treaty, Trevelyan insisted,
should have been to enable Germany 'to survive as a peaceful democracy.' Instead, 'the German nation was humiliated': union with Austria
was forbidden; so was membership of the League of Nations; as regards
reparations, 'she was treated in a manner so fantastic as to help ruin
her without benefiting her creditors'; and 'all her colonies were taken
away.' To Trevelyan, this was the crowning folly, utterly without justification or historical precedent: 'At the end of all previous wars, the
defeated enemies of England had always retained, or received back,
some at least of their colonies.'[125]

From the time that the details of the treaty became known, Trevelyan
believed that a terrible mistake had been made and a great opportunity
missed. For he had no doubt that Germany's grievances against it, and
against the allies who had imposed it, were legitimate. As a result, he
was throughout the interwar years a staunch supporter of appeasement.
But to his regret, this was not a policy which interwar British governments pursued with any conviction or success. He was sure that it
was because of Britain's failure to appease the Weimar Republic that
democracy in Germany had been fatally undermined. Vindictive peace

Trevelyan as a prim and priggish young Fellow of Trinity in the early 1900s: not surprisingly, Lytton Strachey found him 'very – I think too – earnest'.

Trevelyan as Commandant of the first British Red Cross Ambulance Unit to be sent to Italy: 'We have been so accustomed', he wrote to his father, 'for generations to look at the victims of great historical catastrophes through a historic telescope from our study chairs that to find oneself at the other end of the telescope is disconcerting.'

Three generations: Sir George Otto Trevelyan, George, and Theo, 1910. Theo's death, in the following year, was the greatest private tragedy of Trevelyan's life: 'There was to have been', he wrote to his father, 'another generation – or so at least my fancy had it.'

Trevelyan believed that walking was the best means whereby a man might regain possession of his own soul, by rejoining him in sacred union with nature.

The three brothers on the moors, sometime after the Second World War: Charles, Bob and George 'Tell me', a lady once asked, having met all of them at the same party, 'are these Trevelyans a sect, like Wesleyans?'

Trevelyan with King George VI and Queen Elizabeth at the Quatercentenary celebrations of Trinity College in 1948: 'It was clear to all the world', Trevelyan later wrote in his *Autobiography*, 'that England had survived the war.'

treaties invariably lead to a demand for a war of revenge among the vanquished, and it was on that programme that Hitler came to power in 1933. Yet to Trevelyan, this made it more necessary, not less, that Germany must be appeased. The only hope, he believed, lay in 'going patiently on, trying to be friendly wherever we can.' As late as 1938, he remained convinced that it would be statesmanlike and sensible to return some of Germany's colonies.[126]

This does not mean that Trevelyan liked or trusted Hitler: on the contrary, he regarded him from the very beginning as a tyrant and a menace. Time and again, he denounced 'this appalling German return to savagery', 'the terrible shadow of Nazi terror', this 'government by murder', this 'most dreadful form of government in history, which has crushed all that is good in Germany, and threatens to crush all that is good everywhere else, and believes in cruelty and lies.' 'It is', he told his daughter, 'a *moral* issue, like all the things in history that most interest me.'[127] And Trevelyan had no doubts as to which side he was on. He hated the Germans for seeking to eradicate 'Christianity and all other forms of independent culture', and – in an allusion to Matthew Arnold – he hoped that 'Hebraism and Hellenism' would draw closer together 'in a common resistance to this new barbarism.' And from 1933 onwards he was very active, in the company of J. J. Thompson, Lord Rutherford and William Beveridge, in the affairs of what became known as the Academic Assistance Council, which helped German Jewish academics who were dismissed from their jobs by Hitler. It was dreamed up when Beveridge visited Trevelyan for a weekend in Cambridge in May 1933, and eventually it helped more than a thousand émigré scholars.[128]

Until early in 1935 Trevelyan adhered to the widespread view that the appeasement of Germany, accompanied by some form of agreed disarmament, carried out under the auspices of the League of Nations, was the best hope for securing world peace. And since this was what the National Government claimed to be doing in the first years of its existence, he was inclined to approve. 'Our government policy to Germany', he thought in May 1935, 'on the whole not bad.'[129] But once Hitler's aggressive intentions became clear with the reoccupation of the Rhineland in the spring of 1936, and once an alliance with Mussolini became a distinct possibility, Trevelyan was soon convinced that British policy must change. He was certain that 'we must make up some of the leeway in armament – especially as Germany is again armed to the teeth.' 'In the presence of Mussolini and Hitler', he had no doubt that 'we must bring our air and naval force up to the measure of safety in such a world.' 'Hating Hitler and Mussolini and believing in the League of Nations' was not, he concluded, 'in itself a policy, though many people seem to think so.'[130]

From 1935 until 1939 Trevelyan believed that the only hope of dealing with Hitler (and Mussolini) was through a policy of appeasement pursued from a position of strength. He was sure that force was the only thing that the dictators understood.[131] He was convinced that Britain should not threaten to use it unless it possessed the armaments to make such threats realistic. And he had no doubt that 'if you possess a quarter of the world, you must either be prepared to defend it, or give it up when dealing with people like Hitler or Mussolini.' In short, he believed that 'the only chance of being able to preserve peace with Hitler and Mussolini – except by abject surrender and suicide – is to give them some cause to fear us.' Indeed, one of the reasons why he had so little time for the Labour Party was that for most of the 1930s it was so hostile to any talk of war that it opposed rearmament and conscription.[132] By late 1935 Trevelyan was clear that rearmament was essential. And that was an opinion which he shared with another man who held an essentially Whiggish view of the past, and of Britain's place within it: Winston Churchill.

Of course, Trevelyan and Churchill had much in common. They were both patricians by birth and by outlook, came from 'governing families', and were on cordial, but never intimate, terms all their lives. They were near contemporaries at Harrow, where they were taught English and history by the same schoolmasters, Robert Somervell and Townsend Warner, and they shared a lifelong attachment to literature and to the past. As young men, they had been equally captivated by the heroic figure of Garibaldi, whose biography Churchill had planned to write a decade before Trevelyan took up the idea.[133] Both were ardent New Liberals, and Charles Trevelyan was a junior minister when Churchill was President of the Board of Trade and Home Secretary. At that time, Trevelyan believed that Churchill and Lloyd George were 'the very pulse' of the government 'machine', and thought 'their personal alliance' a 'great piece of luck' for the cause of Liberal social reform.[134] But both Trevelyan and Churchill found the First World War a deeply disturbing experience, which swept away many familiar landmarks, and as a result both became increasingly conservative during the 1920s and 1930s.

Trevelyan greatly admired Churchill as an historian, for he regarded him, in the company of G. M. Young and John Buchan, as one of the few men 'writing sense about history that gets read'. But during the 1930s they became rivals for public attention, as Trevelyan's history of *England Under Queen Anne* came out at almost the same time as Churchill's biography of Marlborough. As a result, the Blenheim archives were closed to Trevelyan, who had to make do instead with the fifty volumes of transcripts that Archdeacon Coxe had placed in the British Museum during the nineteenth century.[135] Moreover, Churchill's pious and partisan account of his great ancestor led him to denounce Macaulay as a 'liar', as 'the prince of literary rogues', for his unflattering portrait of the great Duke in his *History*, which provoked Trevelyan, who was no less inclined to family piety, to spring to his great-uncle's defence in the *Times Literary Supplement*. And as Trevelyan himself admitted, his own books probably sold less well than they might otherwise have done, because they were in direct competition with Churchill's volumes: 'people can't always be reading about the Marlborough wars,' he later recalled, 'and of course, everybody wanted to read Winston.'[136]

But these were relatively minor quibbles, and Trevelyan went out of his way to praise the biography, both in public and in private, and to give Churchill all possible assistance.[137] He read the proofs of every volume, made corrections and suggestions, and lent Churchill an autograph letter of 1680 from the young John Churchill to the young Prince William of Orange, which was reproduced in the first volume of Winston's biography.[138] In his letter to the *TLS*, Trevelyan took pains to stress his 'great admiration' for the work, and his 'earnest hope for its popularity and success.' He was especially impressed by Churchill's handling of the politics and the battle scenes, and told Mary that it was 'a wondrous work of scholarship and insight as well as authorship'.[139] And he readily admitted that Macaulay's hostile picture of Marlborough was 'the worst thing in his *History*', and expressed himself in full agreement with Churchill's portrayal of the great Duke, as well as with his general interpretation of domestic and European politics. Indeed, his only real criticism of the work was that it was too long, too detailed, and thus might not reach as broad an audience as it deserved to do. And so he urged Churchill, when he turned to his next task, which he hoped might be a biography of Napoleon, to complete it in not more than two volumes – assuming, of course, he was 'not back in office at some call of England's'.[140]

This sentence may be taken as implying that Trevelyan was also a

supporter of Churchill's political crusades during the 1930s. Indeed, it
has been argued by Sir John Plumb that Churchill was 'the one public
figure' for whom Trevelyan 'had an almost uncritical admiration
throughout his life', and that, in the company of Anthony Eden and
Duff Cooper, they were both equally hostile to appeasement.[141] This
is an appealing picture – of the last great Whig statesman and the last
great Whig historian, standing shoulder to shoulder against the foreign
policy pursued by the National Government. But the evidence does
not bear it out. In the autumn of 1914 Trevelyan had been outraged
by what he regarded as Churchill's concealment, as First Lord of the
Admiralty, of the sinking of the battleship HMS *Audacious* by the
Germans. The episode had, he told his father, 'gone far to shatter my
belief in him.'[142] For the next fifteen years, the documents are regret-
tably silent. But it seems likely that Trevelyan would have had little
enthusiasm for some of Churchill's more extravagant military enter-
prises: the defence of Antwerp, the forcing of the Dardanelles, the
sending of troops to Russia to fight the Bolsheviks, and the Chanak
episode. And it seems even more probable that Trevelyan would have
had little time for those buccaneers who comprised Churchill's
interwar entourage: Birkenhead, Beaverbrook, Bracken and Boothby,
who were so lacking in what Trevelyan called 'spiritual values'.

   In fact, from 1931 to 1939, Trevelyan was a firm supporter of the
policies and the personnel of the National Government. Among cabinet ministers, the men he knew best and most admired were all
appeasers: Sir John Simon, who was Foreign Secretary from 1931 to
1935; Walter Runciman, who was President of the Board of Trade
between 1931 and 1937 and was sent to Prague in the following year
as an 'independent mediator' between the Czechoslovak Government
and the Sudeten German party; and Lord Halifax, the Foreign Secretary between 1938 and 1940. He thought Stanley Baldwin the kindest
Prime Minister since Charles James Fox (than which there could be
no higher praise), and from the moment Neville Chamberlain took
over, Trevelyan 'always believed' in him.[143] In addition, he was a
close friend of the Secretary to the Cabinet, Sir Maurice Hankey,
who regarded Churchill as a 'cad', and was in strong sympathy with
Geoffrey Dawson, the editor of *The Times* and another firm supporter
of the National Government.[144] In November 1935, Trevelyan told
his daughter that the National Government had 'done more for this
country than any since the war.' And a year later, he informed W. M.
Crook that he was 'not any longer political', adding that 'insofar as

every citizen has some politics, I am a supporter of the National Government.'[145]

From none of its members would Trevelyan have received favourable accounts of Churchill's politics or personality. And Trevelyan himself clearly shared the widespread view that Churchill was a man of unstable character and deeply suspect judgment. This was particularly marked in the case of India. 'If TBM had been born one hundred years later', Trevelyan told Sir John Simon, who between 1927 and 1930 chaired a Statutory Commission which recommended further advance in India towards self-government, he was sure his great-uncle's thoughts on the subject would be 'in a direction that would not be very far from yours.'[146] He shared the views of his kinsman, the young Humphrey Trevelyan, who had recently joined the Indian civil service, that the reforms eventually embodied in the Government of India Act of 1935 were 'the least bad, probably of a number of bad courses – Churchill's being probably the worst.'[147] And at the height of Churchill's intransigent and alarmist opposition to that measure, Trevelyan made this suggestion to Baldwin: 'Why do you not propitiate Winston by erecting a statue to Marlborough at the public expense?' 'I suppose', he added, 'this is a joke, but no country but ours would not have a statue to such a man.'[148]

Throughout the 1930s, Trevelyan was equally at odds with Churchill on the subject of appeasement. As the diplomatic crisis unfolded in 1938, culminating in the Munich settlement, he was 'wholly on Chamberlain's side', could not 'understand how any pacifist or peace lover can be anything else', and was disgusted and alarmed by 'the war-whoop, for it is nothing else, rising in the press and the country'.[149] He was convinced that Germany, Italy and Japan could beat Britain and France, partly because they were better armed and partly because Britain had so few allies. 'For all Winston's vague talk about a "Grand Alliance"', Trevelyan was convinced that 'Poland, Hungary and Yugoslavia will remain neutral'.[150] But his most vehement and comprehensive denunciation of Churchill came in May, in this letter to Mary:

> I believe Churchill to be wrong again – as he was over India, the King business, and Ireland the other day. He is always striking with immense emphasis the wrong nail on the head. These small states are not willing to fight our battle against Germany. Calling on them to do so in the name of the League of Nations will no longer help . . .
> The idea of England binding up all the small neutrals who

surround Germany and are at her mercy, binding them all up in an
armed league against her is a sheer impossibility . . . The attempt
will only precipitate war, which we may yet avoid. Churchill can only
think in military terms. He never could think in other terms – e.g.
his recent utterances about the Irish ports. And, in military terms,
he is always thinking wrong.[151]

Despite their common love of language and shared sense of history, this
was an issue on which Trevelyan and Churchill were totally at odds. To
be sure, Trevelyan did not approve of what Hitler was doing and want-
ing. And he would certainly 'go with the country if war comes.' But since
Britain lacked adequate forces and adequate friends, he was convinced it
would be wrong to have 'English civilization destroyed' by deciding 'to
fight for Bohemia'. Under these circumstances, he had no doubt that
it was right to give way to Hitler, and in the aftermath of the Munich
settlement, he expressed himself 'more grateful to Neville than to any
statesman in my lifetime'. And having heard the details of the settlement
from Walter Runciman, Trevelyan was convinced that the terms were
the best that could have been got, short of going to war.[152] Nor was he
sure that the subsequent British guarantee of Poland was altogether wise.
Times had certainly changed since the late summer of 1914. Then his
brother Charles had wanted peace, while Trevelyan had joined the war
party. But now it was Charles who was much more eager for military
intervention. 'This time', Trevelyan told Mary, 'I am the pacifist and
CPT the jingo – within limits.'[153]

V

But those limits were very soon reached, and when war finally broke
out in earnest in early 1940, Trevelyan had no doubt which side he
was on. 'I don't think the Allies is the cause of God', he told Mary
early in March. 'But I fear the other side is the side of the Devil.' But
he was also in no doubt that Germany alone was not to blame. For
Britain and France and America 'in different ways have had our share
in *raising* the Devil from 1919 onwards' – partly because of the foolish
vindictiveness of the Versailles Treaty, partly by imposing sanctions
against Italy, which drove the Duce into the embrace of the Führer,
and partly because of what he now recognized had been a failure to

rearm satisfactorily. 'The combination of defying great enemy powers without arming as they were armed', he told Bob in July 1940, 'has been a hideous and fatal folly.'[154] Reluctance to spend more on defence may have been 'an earnest of our desire for peace – but alas we started rearming too late, and did not put enough beef into it when we did start.' 'If we had really armed two years before', he added in July, 'we should not be in this mess.' But as it was, 'We and the world with us, are being punished, this time with terrible severity, for the old, incorrigible English fault of not adapting policy to armaments or armaments to policy.' And Trevelyan had no doubt that this was a state of affairs for which 'all parties are to blame'.[155]

Inevitably, this led him to a greater appreciation of Churchill's achievements – both before and during the war. 'The late government and Baldwin's government', he told Charles in June 1940, 'have let us down shockingly over rearmament.' 'We have all', he went on, 'been great fools.' But, he added, 'the present government seems good – barring one or two weak spots. The Labour people seem particularly good.'[156] In July 1940, at the editor's invitation, Trevelyan wrote an article for the *Sunday Times*, setting Britain's perilous position in historical perspective. This was, he insisted, 'a war to prevent the complete triumph of evil.' 'It is', he went on, 'more true than ever before in our history that we must conquer or die.' The Napoleonic Wars afforded the best precedent: 'Pitt's stiff upper lip, Nelson's ardour, Wellington's imperturbable calm'. 'Our greatest asset', he continued, 'is our national character; it is now to be put to its extreme test, and I believe that it will ring true.' And he ended with a peroration scarcely less eloquent than Churchill's 'finest hour' speech of a month before:

> That in 1940 the British Empire stood 'alone' in the breach, may yet be looked upon in happier days as the proudest service we ever did the world in all our long, historic testimony for freedom.[157]

Three months later, when Churchill appointed Trevelyan Master of Trinity, he sent the Prime Minister a reply in which recollection and appreciation were felicitously mingled:

> I am touched by your kindness and fortified by your good opinion. In your great way, and in my small way, we have been called to unexpected destinies, since the time when, as your junior at Harrow, I admired from a distance the driving force of your great character, which is now our nation's great support.[158]

In response to a letter of congratulation from Eddie Marsh, Trevelyan wrote in a similar vein: 'You may certainly take great credit for your belief in *him* all along. The country has for very good reason come round to your view.'[159] And so, to some extent, had Trevelyan himself. In a postscript to *British History in the Nineteenth Century and After*, he admitted, when surveying the 1930s, that 'we were, nearly all of us, blind and foolish.' And he managed another ringing peroration:

> Only after the fall of France in 1940, when friend and foe had given us up for lost, did the moral strength of Britain and the Empire appear in full . . . symbolized by the leadership of Winston Churchill. The ultra-pacifist people, who had chosen to be still half-armed when the fight was forced upon them, were undismayed in 'the hour when the earth's foundations fled', and put up such a fight on sea and air and land that the name of Britain became a banner to rally the forces of freedom all the world over.[160]

Or, as he put it more succinctly, in a later letter to Mary 'Baldwin and Chamberlain and the "appeasers", including to a considerable extent *ourselves*', had been wrong, while 'dire events' had 'proved . . . Winston right.'[161]

Nevertheless, he remained, throughout the war, something of a sceptic. In May 1940, he recognized that 'if the Labour people want Churchill, I suppose they will have him.' But like most people in the know, Trevelyan did not think it at all a good idea. 'I have grave fears about him', he told Mary, 'but Halifax and Chamberlain may be able to look after him.' And he added, significantly, 'Chamberlain has behaved nobly.' At the end of the year, he was not much impressed by the Prime Minister's Christmas reshuffle. He thought the new appointments were 'bad': Margesson was lacking in judgement, and 'the stupidest type of politician', while Eden was 'not fitted for the FO'.[162] Although he recognized that he was 'a great parliamentarian', Trevelyan also felt that 'lapses of taste are an essential part of Churchill, the price we pay for him.' He thought the Prime Minister's 'optimism' was 'subjective and temperamental', especially in regard to the bombing of Germany, which Trevelyan thoroughly detested.[163] He was sure that Churchill was wrong over Greece, because his 'obstinacy is sometimes a blessing, sometimes a curse.' He did not like the 'belligerent' tone of the Prime Minister's first election broadcast in the spring of 1945. And he was not sure that the Conservatives would benefit by the widespread feeling of 'excited gratitude' towards the man who had won the war.[164]

Once he had moved into the Master's Lodge and completed the *English Social History*, Trevelyan began to write a history of Trinity College. It was exactly fifty years since he had first gone up as a freshman, and his aim in producing the book was to provide 'notes on the buildings and history of the College' for the use of 'Trinity men, old or young, who know as little about Trinity now as I did when I came up in 1893 and, looking round at the Great Court and the Cloisters, wished that someone would tell me something about them.'[165] In one guise, it was the supreme example of Whig history: an unfolding account of progress, improvement and reform, in which religious toleration was gradually extended, and academic excellence was increasingly attained, culminating in Trevelyan himself who, as Master of the College, was both the guardian and embodiment of Trinity traditions. He wrote of Trinity as a 'national institution', which trained men for 'public service', and as 'the most beautiful of all settings for superlative powers of mind.' He dwelt at length on its close royal connections, noted that Lord Grey of the Reform Act had been an undergraduate there, stressed that the College system was deeply rooted 'in the life of England', and urged how this gave 'Oxford and Cambridge a unique character in the world.'[166]

But to the extent that this was a Whig history of his College, it was very much in Trevelyan's later consensual, nonpartisan mode. He dealt fair-mindedly with religious and academic controversies – except, perhaps, when it came to the Oxford Movement. He stressed the periods of stagnation and decline in the College's history, especially during the early-eighteenth-century era of the Whig ascendancy, when 'Trinity was 'unworthy of its past and of its future'.[167] He celebrated scientists like Newton, J. J. Thompson and Rutherford with as much zeal as he wrote about Byron, Macaulay and Tennyson. He expressed some slight concern that the 'literary, classical and liberally religious atmosphere' of the Trinity in which his father and Leslie Stephen had been undergraduates was being replaced by Fellows who 'were now, first and foremost specialists'. And his remarks on the periodic 'purges' of Fellows, which took place at times of abrupt political change between the sixteenth and the eighteenth centuries, must have been written with the more recent, and more terrible, experience of Nazi Germany in mind.[168]

Trevelyan's history of Trinity effectively ended in 1918, with the death of Montagu Butler. But shortly after the war ended there was one last public ceremony, one final anniversary, which gave Trevelyan as much satisfaction and comfort as anything could in those bleak austerity-ridden years. In June 1947 a further page was added to the history of Trinity when the College celebrated the fourth centenary of its foundation by Henry VIII. King George VI and Queen Elizabeth drove across the Great Court to the Lodge in an open car, just as Victoria and Prince Albert had driven in a horsed carriage one hundred years before. As Trevelyan later recalled in his *Autobiography*, it was a moment of thankfulness. For as the trumpets sounded above the Great Gate, proclaiming the entry of the King and Queen, 'it was clear to all the world that England and Trinity had survived the war.'[169] 'Survived' rather than 'triumphed' was for Trevelyan the operative word. As he had written to Hilton Young on VE Day, 'I like stories with good ends to them, like 1745–6 or 1939–45.'[170] But there was a world of difference between 'good ends' and the 'happy endings' of an earlier era.

VI

In the aftermath of war, Trevelyan's opinions about Churchill remained ambivalent almost to the end, as admiration was still tinged with disapproval. He preferred to see Labour in government in 1945 rather than the Conservatives, and thereafter he remained unconvinced that Churchill's return to power would be in the best interests of the country. In 1948, he sat between Churchill and Smuts at lunch, after the latter had been installed as Chancellor of Cambridge, following the death of Stanley Baldwin. 'Smuts was far the most trained intellect of the two', he reported to his daughter, 'and to me the more attractive.'[171] And at heart, Trevelyan stood by his earlier opinions, remaining a Chamberlainite and a man of Munich. In 1952, Viscount Simon produced his autobiography, *Retrospect*, which contained a determined defence of his conduct over India and as Foreign Secretary between 1931 and 1935, and a cogent justification of Munich and appeasement. 'I find my political opinions singularly like yours all through,' Trevelyan wrote to him:

> I certainly agree with you about Munich. Personally, I was perhaps a little too much inclined to 'appeasement'; but I have always held that appeasement would only be effective if accompanied by rearmament. I resigned from the League of Nations Union when the branch

here passed at the same meeting two resolutions: (1) in favour of resisting Mussolini; (2) against the very small rearmament the government was proposing. Could human folly go further?[172]

Nevertheless, with the passing of the years, Trevelyan's view of Churchill's character and achievements gradually mellowed. He recognized that he was one of the titanic historical personalities of his time, and urged Churchill's doctor, Lord Moran, to keep a diary, on the grounds that posterity would want to know as much as possible about him.[173] In 1946 Trevelyan presented Churchill with the autograph letter of his illustrious ancestor that had been used as an illustration in the first volume of Marlborough, and he was 'honoured' by Churchill's signature to the letter in The Times calling for funds to establish the Trevelyan Lectures at Cambridge University ten years later.[174] And he welcomed the appearance of Churchill's History of the English-Speaking Peoples, for the last revisions of which, Churchill had, incidentally, reread Trevelyan's History of England. The grounds for his approval were the same as for all his works: the time would come, Trevelyan told Churchill, when the public 'will stop reading us professional historians, but not you.'[175]

Yet ironically enough, it was the appearance of the Alanbrooke diaries, edited by Arthur Bryant, which more than anything convinced Trevelyan of Churchill's authentic greatness. They were published in 1956–7, at a time when any criticism of Churchill seemed almost heretical. But they showed that his relations with the Chiefs of Staff had often been stormy and acrimonious, and that Churchill himself was not always the infallibly magnanimous hero of popular patriotic myth. To Churchill's most ardent admirers, they were ill-timed and unwarranted criticism. But to Trevelyan they were important historical evidence, from which Churchill emerged as being more credible, more human and more admirable than the venerated icon he had by then become:

So far from lowering my estimate of Winston, the book, to me, has raised it. He was not very considerate of his advisers in the matter of taking counsel at two o'clock in the morning etc., but the great impression left on me by the facts of the book is this: he asked for advice, and very often took it, sometimes contrary to what he had first thought himself. This habit of taking counsel, combined with his own personal qualities, is what won the war. Napoleon fell because he could never take counsel. His Marshals were only his servants, whereas Winston treated his generals as his advisers.[176]

Trevelyan was over eighty when he wrote this, and his eyesight was by then so poor that the book had been read to him. But the shrewdness and insight of these remarks shows that he had not lost his touch in the interpreting of historical evidence.

Nor were his Whiggish instincts entirely dormant. In February 1948 he wrote to *The Times* protesting – in vain, as it turned out – against the proposed abolition of the university seats in the House of Commons. It was, he said, 'a time honoured peculiarity of our constitution, more than three centuries old', and it had enabled great men to sit in Parliament, from Isaac Newton to H. A. L. Fisher. It was, Trevelyan concluded, 'possible to sacrifice too much to the desire for absolute uniformity everywhere and in everything.'[177] Four years later, he edited and introduced a selection of cartoons by John Doyle about the reign of William IV. Once again, he wrote a stirring and zestful account of the passing of the Great Reform Bill. But he was no longer the partisan biographer he had been more than thirty years before. For the older and more even-handed Trevelyan, the main attraction of Doyle's caricatures was that they were devoid of the brutal malice of Gillray and Cruickshank, and were 'kindly, humorous, and not in the least partisan' in their depiction of the Whig and Tory leaders.[178] Indeed, by this time, he had even come to regard Pitt the Younger as 'the greatest of British Prime Ministers', a view that would have been unthinkable in the days of his youth.[179]

Nevertheless, by the postwar years, Trevelyan was widely regarded – and had come to regard himself – as 'the last Whig historian in the world', and it was in this guise that he attended the dinner at Christ's College, held in 1955, to celebrate the presentation of his festschrift, *Studies in Social History*.[180] In his after-dinner speech, Trevelyan quoted Gibbon's famous dictum that history was 'little more than the register of the crimes, follies and misfortunes of mankind.' As a young man at Harrow, he had resolutely denied this and, however much the unprecedented horrors of the twentieth century suggested that it was a valid dictum, Trevelyan still retained his Whiggish beliefs in progress and in England's destiny. 'We must add', he concluded, 'that history is also the register of the splendour of man and his occasional good fortune, of which our island has had more than its share.'[181] Thirty years before, in his British Academy Lecture on the Whig historians, H. A. L. Fisher had described Macaulay's hero, Sir James Mackintosh, in words which sum up Trevelyan with equal appropriateness. He was, Fisher observed, 'a Whig who began life as a firebrand and ended as a sage.'[182]

IV

THE RURAL ELEGIST

Shooting . . . was a fine sport, and helped to inspire the class that then set the mode in everything . . . with an intimate love and knowledge of woodland, hedgerow and moor, and a strong preference for country over town life, which is too seldom found in the leaders of fashion in any age or land.

G. M. TREVELYAN, *British History in the Nineteenth Century (1782–1901)* (1923), p. 168.

The sudden destruction of rural life, which never was more prosperous than it was fifty years ago; the substitution of life in 'great cities' for life in large towns; the rapid diffusion of the vulgarity bred in those great cities into every corner of our island by locomotion and the cheap press, has destroyed all that was characteristic of Old England.

G. M. TREVELYAN, 'The White Peril', *Nineteenth Century*, L (1901), p. 1045.

His strength, integrity, simplicity, his steadfastness in any purpose or policy once formed, and his perfect naturalness in every relation of life . . . flowed from the same wellsprings of old English rural life which inspired him as a countryman, a naturalist and an author . . . His heart was not in the streets or in the council chambers but in the woods and beside the streams: and his books have taught many where and how the best joys of life in England are to be found.

G. M. TREVELYAN, *Grey of Fallodon* (1937), pp. vii, 363.

From the Tyne to the Tweed, the Northumbrian coastline bears visible witness to its violent and contentious past, as the castles of Dunstanburgh and Bamburgh rise arrogantly out of the sea in ruined and brooding grandeur.

'Northumberland', Trevelyan once observed, 'throws over us, not a melancholy, but a meditative spell.'

THE NORTHUMBERLAND countryside is wild, rugged, un-manicured, and as historically resonant as it is matchlessly beautiful.[1] Here the Romans constructed their great defensive barrier of Hadrian's Wall; here the Vikings sacked the Monastery of Lindisfarne in AD 793; here, across the medieval centuries, the English fought the Scots for possession of the Border Marches; and here were plotted a succession of abortive uprisings, beginning with the Pilgrimage of Grace in 1536 and ending with the Jacobite Rebellion of 1715.[2] From the Tyne to the Tweed, the Northumbrian coastline bears visible witness to this violent and contentious past, as the castles of Dunstanburgh and Bamburgh rise arrogantly out of the sea in ruined and brooding grandeur. To the west lie brown-green hills, desolate upland moors, ancient and modern border forests, and the fertile valleys of the North and South Tyne. And towards the Scottish border, springing almost from the banks of the Tweed, rise the loftier, rounded Cheviots, silently changing colour as sunshine and cloud and rain and snow sweep over them. George Macaulay Trevelyan adored this county and this country more than any other: its dramatic past, its magnificent vistas, its animals, its birds, its trees, its flowers and its big, pale blue sky. 'Northumberland', he once observed, 'throws over us, not a melancholy, but a meditative spell', and in turn, that spell was cast over all his historical writings.[3]

I

As a product of the late-Victorian landowning classes, Trevelyan was inevitably drawn to nature and to country pursuits. The moors and mountains of Northumberland were visible from the windows of Wallington, and no high walls or screens of trees separated the house and its grounds from the neighbouring countryside. Capability Brown had been born nearby, was educated at the estate village of Cambo, and made the ornamental lake at Rothley. The grounds at Wallington had been landscaped in the style of Charles Bridgeman, the flower gardens were full of exotics, collected since the time of Sir Walter Trevelyan, and Sir George Otto had constructed a large conservatory in 1908 in which he grew enormous fuchsias, geraniums and bougainvillaea. One of the earlier owners of Wallington, Sir John Fenwick, was a breeder of horses; another, Sir Walter Blackett, reared Bedlington terriers; and a third, Sir Walter Calverley Trevelyan, produced prize cattle. Sir John Trevelyan, the fourth baronet, was a close friend of Thomas Bewick, the engraver and naturalist, and his son, another Sir John Trevelyan, was one of the first members of the Royal Horticultural Society. Like many country houses, Wallington possessed watercolours by J. M. W. Turner of local scenes, and cases of stuffed birds, fossils and bones. And on the lower pilasters of the central hall were those delicate paintings of flowers, commissioned or undertaken by Pauline, Lady Trevelyan.[4]

In his outlook and his recreations, Trevelyan was a classic product of this privileged rural environment. Among his earliest and happiest recollections were 'the blue sky and racing cloud of a west wind day across the moorlands.' As a boy, he read Wordsworth and Ruskin, and soon began to recognize the importance of natural beauty for man's spiritual life. He regarded botany and geology as the only serious forms of science: scholars like Darwin and Huxley, to both of whom he was related, were men after his own heart. And he was an enthusiastic shot, although less accomplished than his brother Charles.[5] He disapproved of slaughtering reared pheasant, and like any good Liberal resented the closure of moors and forests for the exclusive use of Edwardian shooting parties. But he listed shooting in *Who's Who* as one of his recreations, regularly bagged wild pheasant and hares at Wallington, and as Master of Trinity during the years of wartime austerity and deprivation thought nothing of going out into the Cambridge country-side with a gun, 'shooting for the pot' – especially if a royal visitor or other distinguished personage was expected for a meal.[6] It was as a countryman that Trevelyan was brought up, as a countryman that he viewed the world – and as a countryman that he wrote his histories.

But it was not just as a member of the aristocracy of birth that Trevelyan came into direct contact with nature: it was also because of his close connections with the aristocracy of talent. Members of the mid-Victorian intelligentsia, increasingly uncertain in their Christian convictions, turned instead to the innocent and reposeful countryside for spiritual inspiration and transcendental excitement. One of Henry Sidgwick's most attractive books was entitled *Walking Essays*. Leslie Stephen was President of the Alpine Club, the greatest walker and mountaineer of his generation, and although ordained a clergyman, came to prefer the ethics of Wordsworth to those of Jesus Christ. And James Bryce opposed the closure of grouse moors and deer forests in Scotland because he believed 'the grandeur and the loveliness of the mountains and glens and the silence of the moorlands lying open under the eye of heaven' should be available for everybody, 'stirring their nature and touching their imagination.'[7] These men were among the closest friends of Sir George Otto Trevelyan and, like him, they all came to believe that walking long distances in the countryside was the essential path to mystical experience, to mental ecstasy and to spiritual enlightenment. They lifted up their eyes unto the hills, from whence duly came their help.

In large part as a result, Trevelyan's own passion for walking was such that Leonard Woolf once dubbed him a 'Muscular agnostic'. Ever since his Harrow days, when his housemaster, Edward Bowen, had told him 'O boy, you can never walk less than twenty-five miles on an off day', he had delighted in tramping long distances in the country.[8] And at Cambridge, he found like-minded spirits among his Liberal friends. In the Easter vacation of 1895 he went with Vaughan Williams, Ralph Wedgwood and G. E. Moore on a reading party to Seatoller in Borrowdale at the foot of Honister Pass.[9] Aside from their shared interest in history, one of the reasons for his friendship with G. P. Gooch was that they went for a weekly walk together in term time. And Trevelyan formed especially close ties with Hilton and Geoffrey Young, whom he regarded as the dearest friends of his life. Both brothers were drawn to the country – Hilton to birds and Geoffrey to mountains – and Trevelyan and Geoffrey Young once walked from Cambridge to Marble Arch in twelve and three-quarter hours. And this Wordsworthian delight in walking was shared by many Liberal intellectuals of Trevelyan's generation, whom he met in Cambridge or later in London: Bertrand Russell, G. F. G. Masterman, the Buxton brothers, and J. L. and Barbara Hammond.

The most famous expression of this shared Liberal love of the countryside was the Man Hunt, loosely modelled on the Harrow game of 'hare and hounds', which was founded in 1898 by Trevelyan, Geoffrey Young, and Sidney McDougall. Every Whitsuntide, the finest flower of the new Liberal intelligentsia descended on the Lake District, usually at Seatoller, sometimes at Stool End near Langdale. They were divided into hares and hounds, and for three days they hunted each other over the fells. Trevelyan adored the game, since it enabled him to exploit his 'only athletic accomplishment of running and leaping downhill over very broken ground'. He took part in 1898–1902, 1904–14, 1919 and 1924–6, when he retired, at the age of fifty.[10] Other regular attenders in the prewar years, apart from Charles and Robert Trevelyan and Geoffrey and Hilton Young, included Herbert Samuel, Raymond Asquith, W. H. Beveridge and Hugh Dalton. Each evening, after a vigorous day's exercise, the company gathered round the fire to sing songs like 'John Peel', sometimes with new words specially written, as in 1926, when Mary Trevelyan wrote this verse, to mark her father's last hunt:

> George is an historian of the most superior sort
> He knows more facts in history than anybody ought.
> But when he comes to Lakeland, he's better things to do
> And he hunts with all the energy of thirty-one or -two.[11]

After his own beloved Northumberland, it was the Lake District that took the firmest hold on Trevelyan's affections. It was, after all, the country of Wordsworth, the supreme poet of nature, whose biography his daughter, Mary, was one day to write. Shortly before the First World War Trevelyan acquired a cottage called Robin Ghyll, in Langdale. The accommodation was spartan, but until he inherited Hallington in 1928 it was the only country home that Trevelyan possessed. Every summer he took his young family there, and they indulged in appropriately strenuous outdoor activities. Theodore Macaulay Trevelyan was buried close by, in Great Langdale Churchyard, and there in the fullness of time were placed the ashes of his parents, 'beneath the bracken and the rocks'.[12] Appropriately enough, it was in connection with the Lake District that Trevelyan first made a contribution as an active conservationist. In 1912 he wrote to *The Times*, supporting the National Trust's appeal for £4,000 to acquire the Roman fort at Ambleside, near the head of Windermere. In the following year, he again wrote in to protest at the proposed motor road over the Scafell peaks. Although he did not know it at the time, such public appeals in the cause of conservation were very much the shape of things to come.[13]

Throughout his life, Trevelyan's greatest delight was in solitary country walking: he was neither a road walker nor a mountaineer, although he was elected an honorary member of the Alpine Club in 1956.[14] There were few corners of Great Britain where he had not tramped. He knew the hills and moors of Northumberland as well as any man of his generation. He had walked extensively in Scotland and had gone the full length of Offa's Dyke. He had walked round the coast of Devon and Cornwall, 'twice or more'. On one occasion he went on a walking tour to the West Country with Bertrand Russell, himself no faintheart, who made Trevelyan promise to be content with a mere twenty-five miles a day. 'He kept his promise', Russell later recorded, 'until the last day. Then he left me, saying that now he must have a little walking.' Russell also told the story that on Trevelyan's wedding day he and his wife had journeyed by train from Oxford to Truro, whereupon Trevelyan left the train, 'saying that he could not face the whole day without a little walk', and covered the forty miles to the Lizard, where the newlyweds were due to spend the night. Trevelyan's daughter disputes the date (it was the second day of the honeymoon, not the first), but does not deny the story.[15] Even in his seventies, Trevelyan remained notorious for taking unsuspecting guests at Hallington for short strolls after lunch, which turned out to be thirty-mile hikes.[16]

For Trevelyan, the essence of these walks was not so much the physical exertion, but the solitude and the silence which went with it. As a Cambridge undergraduate, and a junior Fellow of Trinity, he had walked the moors, the Cheviots and the Border country alone, trying to decide between the competing calls of poetry and history, and searching for a set of 'spiritual values' which would mean more to him than established religion.[17] All his life, Trevelyan remained convinced that it was in the countryside that Britain's history had been made, and that it was nature which had provided the inspiration for its poetry and literature. More mystically still, Trevelyan believed that walking was the best means whereby a man might regain possession of his own soul, by rejoining him in sacred union with nature. All these feelings for the countryside – poetic, historical and religious – were eloquently set down in his earliest essay in naturalistic evocation, on the Middle Marches of Northumberland, which was published in the *Independent Review* in 1904:

In Northumberland alone both heaven and earth are seen; we walk all day on long ridges, high enough to give far views of moor and valley, and the sense of solitude above the world below ... It is the land of far horizons, where the piled or drifted shapes of gathered vapour are for ever moving along the farthest ridge of hills, like the procession of long primaeval ages that is written in tribal mounds and Roman camps and Border towers on the breast of Northumberland.[18]

Trevelyan's earliest historical writings are also suffused with this mystical love of the countryside. The opening chapter of *England Under the Stuarts* vividly evokes the outdoor pursuits of the country gentlemen, especially their delight in hunting and fowling.[19] One of the reasons why Trevelyan so warmed to John Bright was that, despite his Rochdale connections, he had been educated 'deep among moorland hills on the borders of North Lancashire and Yorkshire', and ever after loved to get away from politics, wander the northern hills and fish in Scottish streams, as he did in 1856 and again in 1870 when recovering from nervous breakdowns.[20] There was the same attraction for Trevelyan in writing about Lord Grey of the Reform Bill. Like his own family, the Greys of Howick were Northumberland landowners, and Trevelyan knew the fields and the coastline of their estate at first hand. Equally attractive to Trevelyan was Lord Althorp, another hero of the Reform Act: in manner more like a country squire than an aristocrat, forced by his sense of duty to play a part in political affairs, but really much happier tending his beeves and his turnips in Northamptonshire.[21] This tension, between the competing claims of rural quietude and public duty, was to be explored by Trevelyan again, in a more melancholy mood, in his later biography of Grey of Fallodon.

From the mid-1890s Trevelyan was also drawn to walking in Italy, and by the time he came to write the Garibaldi books he knew the whole country from the Alps to Sicily. Indeed, with the exception of England, he regarded Italy as the most glorious country in the world, and devoted some of his most lyrical passages to it in his essay on 'Walking'. On foot or on bicycle, Trevelyan had gone over the ground of Garibaldi's retreat from Rome to the Adriatic in 1849 and followed his campaigns of 1860 in Sicily.[22] On several of these energetic visits he was accompanied by Geoffrey and Hilton Young: they took many of the pictures which illustrated the Garibaldi books, and in gratitude and affection Trevelyan dedicated *Garibaldi and The Thousand* to them. In the same book, Trevelyan wrote extensively on Garibaldi's activities as the owner of the island of Caprera: the man who tended the flowers, who befriended the birds, who cultivated his vines, and who looked after the animals. One of the many reasons why Trevelyan admired Garibaldi was that he loved nature and he loved liberty: the two things about which Trevelyan himself cared most. As Owen Chadwick has rightly remarked, 'In three-quarters of Trevelyan's attitudes to liberty, you can feel the wind blowing among the hills.'[23]

The problem for Trevelyan and his Liberal friends was that by the early years of the twentieth century, the countryside and the natural world were no longer as central to British life as once they had been.[24] A succession of social investigations, from Booth's survey of London in the 1880s to C. F. G. Masterman's *The Condition of England*, published in 1909, depicted an urban population that was impoverished, undernourished and spiritually deprived. And how could it be otherwise? For the city was sordid and morally unwholesome: a place of ugliness, drink, vice, depravity and crime. And this was bound to be so, since most people who lived and worked and suffered and died there had by this time lost all touch with nature. In 1902 R. C. K. Ensor took some Manchester labourers out into the country, and noted with regret that 'none of them knew or could name forget-me-nots, daisies, dandelions, clover, pansies or lilies of the valley.' To C. F. G. Masterman, the moral was clear: 'They experience no exaltation in Nature because they are cut off from the experience of Nature.'[25] Not surprisingly, the late nineteenth and early twentieth centuries saw many attempts to reconnect the urban proletariat with its rural roots, of which the Garden City Movement and the model villages of Lever, Cadbury and Rowntree were among the most famous.

Although a countryman himself, Trevelyan was hardly unaware of the darker side of urban life. His own family background encompassed Manchester as well as Northumberland, and like many members of the Northumbrian landowning classes, his forbears had been closely – and very profitably – involved in the Industrial Revolution. The eighteenth-century elegance of Wallington Hall and park had been paid for by the Blacketts out of their coal and lead mining royalties and their real estate developments in Newcastle. The creamware dinner service which bore the family coat of arms had been given to the Reverend George Trevelyan in 1795 as a wedding present by Josiah Wedgwood. Tyneside was the birthplace of the railway, and George Stephenson was appropriately commemorated in one of the portrait medallions in the spandrels of the central hall at Wallington. John Dobson, the designer of that remarkable room, was the greatest north country architect of the early Victorian years, and was also responsible for Eldon Square, the Royal Arcade and the Central Railway Station at Newcastle.[26] And the final picture in William Bell Scott's historical tableau was a celebration of the industrial pre-eminence of Tyneside: its iron, its coal, its steam engines and its shipbuilding.

By the turn of the century, Trevelyan had come to share the prevailing Liberal view that 'the great cities' were the 'breeding and living places' of 'vulgarity and the cheap press': in short, that 'George Stephenson has ruined us.'[27] And in the first part of his concluding essay in *The Heart of The Empire*, he developed this theme more fully. Before the Industrial Revolution, he argued, life in England had been 'beautiful and instructive', whereas now it was 'ugly and trivial'. Nine-tenths of our forefathers, he went on, lived in the countryside, but now the majority of people were compelled to live where they 'can never see the earth for the pavement, or the breadth of heaven for the chimney tops.' In past times, he believed, economic activity had beautified the country: the enclosure of the fields, and the building of houses and workshops in vernacular styles. But now barbed wire had replaced the hedgerows, 'endless rows of little prisons', thrown up by the jerry builder, had superseded the country cottages, and the natural music of the birds and the streams had been overwhelmed by 'the perpetual but irregular roar of traffic.' The introduction of machinery had driven out 'the old natural school of craftsmanship and art', while the 'variegated, flaunting vulgarity of the modern town' had spelt the end of local loyalties and customs.[28]

In his contribution to *The Heart of The Empire*, Trevelyan devoted most attention to lamenting the world that had been lost. But in a complementary essay, entitled 'The White Peril', he roundly condemned the ills and iniquities of contemporary city living, and even expressed grave doubts about the future prospects of such a civilization. During the last half-century, he argued, 'a population living in country cottages and small towns' had been superseded by 'a population living a wholly artificial life in great cities.' As a result of the Industrial Revolution, the majority of British people had been divorced from nature and were now compelled to live a life 'that is in its externals like one long journey on the underground', and which was dominated and debased by the public house, the music hall and the cheap press. The result was 'intellectual, moral and spiritual degeneration': a world of 'ugliness, vulgarity, materialism, the insipid negation of everything that has been accounted good in the past history of man.' And he concluded in terms even more apocalyptic: 'All that is good in the world is threatened ... We are mortgaging the whole future of mankind.'[29]

In a subsequent letter to his brother Bob, Trevelyan expressed some embarrassment at the extravagance of the language he had employed in this piece. 'I went mad for two weeks last autumn ...' he wrote, 'and saw men as idiots walking. While in that state, I wrote an exceedingly mad article in a monthly magazine, in which a lot of truth was buried in a hopeless amount of bunkum.'[30] It was understandable that he should have blushed at the bunkum. But there can be no doubting that he was expressing the truth as he saw it. In *England Under the Stuarts*, published at almost the same time, he made essentially the same point, deploring 'the all-pervading influence of the towns', and regretting the fact that in modern times, 'what pays best is generally ugly.' As a countryman and as a Liberal, Trevelyan had no doubt that nature was good but that the town was evil. It was in the countryside, not in the city streets, that 'spiritual values' were to be sought and found. And in terms of the domestic politics of the 1900s, this meant that the task was clear: to carry through a programme of social reform which would mitigate the greatest evils of urban living and bring mankind back into harmony and communion with nature. For Trevelyan in the years before the First World War the cause of Liberalism was also the cause of natural beauty.

II

During the interwar years, Trevelyan's love of the countryside continued unabated: but it did so in a substantially changed political and social context. The demise of the Liberal Party and the break-up of the Liberal intelligentsia meant that the close connection between radical political attitudes and belief in the spiritual solace of nature had been uncoupled, and that other political parties could now appropriate this transcendentalist rural rhetoric. The 'revolution in landholding' which took place immediately after 1918, as many of the great aristocratic estates were broken up and one quarter of England was put onto the market, meant that the traditional social structure of the shires was irrevocably weakened.[31] And at the very same time, Britain's countryside was subjected to the unprecedented blight of the motor car and the charabanc, the new suburban sprawl and ribbon development, semi-detached houses and holiday bungalows. The result was a fundamental shift in the priorities of what would now be called Trevelyan's environmental politics, as he became increasingly active in the cause of rural conservation.

This new occupation was prefigured in *British History in the Nineteenth Century*, which began with a deeply felt evocation of 'the quiet old England of the eighteenth century before machines destroyed it', and provided a graphic account of the 'mainly destructive' Industrial Revolution that was much indebted to the Hammonds. Men and women, Trevelyan argued, were brutally 'uprooted from the pieties and associations of the old rural life', were divorced from nature and herded into ugly and squalid towns, and were obliged to endure 'economic misery, pauperism, starvation and class injustice'.[32] To make matters worse, 'the Industrial Revolution never came to an end': in each subsequent generation, Trevelyan insisted, 'a new economic life half obliterates a predecessor little older than itself.' Accordingly, Britain was now dominated by the ugliness of the big city and the factory and its inhabitants were brought up on a diet of daily papers, cheap magazines, novelettes, football matches and music halls. For Trevelyan, the regrettable result was

> a profound transmutation . . . towards a more mechanical and a more democratic world, the world of the great city instead of the country village, a world expressing itself more through science and journalism, and less through religion, poetry and literature.[33]

Three years later he developed this theme more fully in his *History of England*, which contained many lyrical passages of rural evocation, that anticipated the later *Social History*. 'What a place it must have been', Trevelyan observed in one of his most luxuriant but bitter-sweet paragraphs, 'that virgin woodland wilderness' of Anglo-Saxon England

> still harbouring God's plenty of all manner of beautiful birds and beasts, and still rioting in the vast wealth of trees and flowers – treasures which modern man, careless of his best inheritance, has abolished, and is still abolishing, as fast as new tools and methods of destruction can be invented.[34]

But for the time being this threat lay far in the future, and for more than half a millenium English men and women continued to appreciate, to enjoy and to enhance their natural environment. But then it had all gone irrevocably wrong. Once again, Trevelyan depicted the eighteenth century as the last – and literal – flowering of the English countryside in all its unspoiled abundance, described the Industrial Revolution as a terrible time (though having read the recent work of John Clapham, he was now more measured in his condemnation), and regretted the advent of the big city, the cheap press and 'the new half-educated democracy of all classes'.[35]

But in this more sweeping survey of national history, Trevelyan now set these developments in the broader historical perspective of man's increased command over his environment. To the extent that this meant life was no longer 'brutish and brief', Trevelyan positively welcomed these changes. But the problem, as he saw it, was that 'man's power over nature' had 'far outstripped his moral and mental development'.[36] Hence the engines of destruction unleashed in the First World War. Hence the impending ruin of the English countryside. And *The Times* was quick to draw the moral. 'One of the disturbing thoughts provoked by Mr Trevelyan', it noted in an editorial, 'is the future of natural beauty in these islands. To the historian its steady diminution is a melancholy tale.' It certainly was to Trevelyan. As he explained to his brother Bob, the writing of the most recent chapters of his history had been a cheerless and melancholy task: 'I don't understand the age we live in, and what I do understand I don't like.'[37]

These sound like the Blimpish words of a disenchanted reactionary. Yet at the very time he wrote them, Trevelyan had already begun to involve himself in the cause which was to absorb most of his public time during the interwar years and beyond: the National Trust. In the autumn of 1925 it became known that the Ashridge estate of Lord Brownlow was to be sold, which included some particularly beautiful hills, woods, commons and parkland near Berkhamsted, where at that time Trevelyan lived. It was feared that they might be sold for residential development purposes, and so an appeal was mounted by the National Trust, in which Trevelyan played the leading part.[38] He organized and addressed public meetings and persuaded another local resident, Renée Courtauld, to donate £20,000 to prime the appeal. But his greatest coup was the publication of a letter, urging that Ashridge be saved for the nation by donations to the Trust, which appeared in *The Times* on 20 October 1925 over the signatures of Stanley Baldwin, Ramsay MacDonald, the Earl of Oxford and Asquith and Lord Grey of Fallodon. With such support, £80,000 was soon raised and 1,600 acres were secured for the Trust, including the commons of Berkhamsted and Aldbury and the Ivinghoe Hills.[39]

This episode effectively marked Trevelyan's emergence as an active conservationist and as a most influential member of the National Trust. In *The Times* editorial already quoted, it was noted that while the historian might be upset at the steady diminution of Britain's natural beauty, 'its conservation, if it is to be conserved, rests with students not of the past but of the present, with the practical men who would endeavour to keep a thoughtless evolution on tolerably well-thought-out lines.'[40] One such 'practical man' was John Bailey, a quiet and retiring figure, who taught at the Working Men's College after going down from Oxford, was devoted to the countryside, and was related by marriage to H. A. L. Fisher. Trevelyan became his friend before the First World War, and in 1911 dedicated *English Songs of Italian Freedom* to him. He felt there was a 'particular propriety' in doing so, 'because the sort of attitude to literature and life that it represents, the love of poetry in particular, not as unrelated to ethics, to history, to public affairs, is the thing that binds you and me together.' This paean to 'spiritual values' might almost have been written as the manifesto of the National Trust. Two years later Bailey became its Vice-Chairman, and he was Chairman from 1922 until his death in 1931.[41]

One of the tasks which Bailey set himself during his term of office was to raise the prestige of the Trust by gaining the services of high-minded public men like Ronnie Norman, brother of the Governor of the Bank of England, and Oliver Brett, later third Viscount Esher. In the same vein, Bailey was convinced that the Trust would greatly benefit from Trevelyan's historical knowledge, his love of the countryside and his great public prestige. The conspicuous and effective part he played in the Ashridge campaign served to confirm Bailey's judgement, and in 1926 Trevelyan was duly elected to the Council of the Trust, and was immediately put on both the Estates Committee and the Executive Committee.[42] He remained on the Council until 1961, and was Vice-Chairman of the Executive Committee from 1929 to 1946. Even more importantly, he was Chairman of the Estates Committee from 1928 to 1949. As such, Trevelyan was no aristocratic ornamental, lending his name to the enterprise but doing little else. On the contrary, he was at the very heart of the Trust's affairs: indeed, in the company of Bailey, Norman and Brett, he was the controlling influence during the interwar years and beyond.[43]

As Chairman of the Estates Committee, Trevelyan was effectively responsible for the management of all National Trust properties. He assiduously attended meetings, and although opinions differ as to his qualities as a chairman, it was generally agreed that he was right on all major issues, and that his authority, wisdom and foresight were unrivalled.[44] Nor was this the full sum of his activity. Through his friendships with Stanley Baldwin (the Chairman) and John Buchan (a Trustee), he persuaded the newly established Pilgrim Trust to make substantial donations, so that the National Trust could acquire and preserve properties inland and on the coast. He ceremonially accepted gifts on behalf of the Trust: the seven-hundred-acre Longshaw estate in the Peak District in 1931, and Newtimber Hill on the South Downs six years later. In 1929 and again in 1937 he bought and donated more land to the Trust's holdings of the Ashridge estate.[45] And he was clearly of great importance when a new Chairman of the Trust had to be found in 1931 on the death of John Bailey. Trevelyan first approached his friend H. A. L. Fisher, who declined, and then settled on another north-country landowner: the Marquess of Zetland.[46]

But Trevelyan's greatest work was as a propagandist and as a benefactor. In 1929 he published an eloquent plea on behalf of the Trust entitled *Must England's Beauty Perish?*[47] He began by outlining its past history, describing its organization and explaining its work. He also pointed out that the Trust was entirely a private body, with no state support, and that its need for funds and members was extremely urgent. For while the England of Turner and Constable, Bewick and Wordsworth, had been unsurpassingly beautiful, much of it had been ruined by the first 'age of machinery', and what remained was now being destroyed at an unprecedented rate, by 'modern inventions' and the inexorable 'march of bricks and mortar'. Since the 'full development of motor traffic and its consequences', the National Trust 'has come to be regarded by lovers of nature as an ark of refuge and a bulwark in the day of trouble.' This biblical language was wholly appropriate. For as Trevelyan went on to argue, the ultimate purpose of the Trust was that it was the guardian of the nation's 'spiritual values'. What was at stake, he insisted, was 'the happiness and soul's health of the whole people.' 'Without vision', he concluded, 'the people perish, and without natural beauty, the English people will perish in the spiritual sense.'[48]

By then, and with the experience of Ashridge behind him, Trevelyan had also become much more active in the realm of conservation, especially in his beloved Lake District, where the Trust acquired over

10,000 acres during the 1920s. He regularly wrote to *The Times* urging
the need to preserve the region's increasingly beleaguered natural
beauty, and did so in letters which were invariably distinguished by
their broad historical perspective, their vivid evocation of place and
atmosphere, and their unshakeable belief in 'spiritual values'. He protested against the proposed construction of electric pylons in the Kes-
wick Valley and against a plan to build a major road into Upper Eskdale.
'To spend the ratepayers' and the taxpayers' money on such an outrage',
he concluded, 'is to be stone blind to the spiritual.'[49] He bought farms
in Langdale, near Robin Ghyll, and presented them all to the Trust. He
helped to promote the Cambridge branch of the Friends of the Lake
District. And in 1935–6 he was at the forefront of the Trust's successful
campaign to limit the amount of planting in the Lake District undertaken by the Forestry Commission. Trevelyan did not want the Fells
converted into 'German pine forest', partly because Wordsworth had
'long ago denounced the introduction of the conifer as a crime against
Nature's local bye-laws', partly because such planting threatened to wipe
out 'the old English forest trees – oak, beech, ash, elm and sycamore.'[50]

The National Trust and the Lake District claimed most of
Trevelyan's efforts as a conservationist, but not all. For there were
many other causes to which he was drawn during the interwar years.
As the scion of a great landed family, he urged that new uses be found
for country houses now that so many were being deserted by their
original owners. As a northcountryman, he urged that efforts be made
to preserve and maintain Hadrian's Wall, bought the farm next to
Housesteads Fort and gave covenants over it to the Trust, and spoke
out against the use of the Northumberland coast for bombing practice
by the RAF.[51] As Regius Professor he helped to found the Cambridge
Preservation Society, and played a major part in preserving the
unspoiled western side of the town, from Grantchester Meadows to
Madingley, from the developer. As a senior figure in the affairs of the
National Trust he was drawn into work of that kindred organization,
the Council for the Preservation of Rural England, and regularly spoke
at its annual meetings.[52] And as a famous preservationist, he lent his
support to the London green belt scheme, opposed the Land Tax Bill
of 1931 because he feared it would force owners to sell off their lands
to the dreaded jerry builder and welcomed the passing of the Town
and Country Planning Act of 1932, even though most of its provisions
were ignored through lack of money.[53]

But after the National Trust itself, the organization to which

Trevelyan devoted most of his preservationist efforts was the Youth Hostels Association, of which he became the first President in 1930. He claimed that he was no more than a figurehead, but his part was much more active.[54] As with the Trust, his name conferred great prestige on a new and uncertain organization. He was a generous benefactor, and obtained additional funds from the Carnegie Trust. He wrote letters to *The Times*, spoke at public meetings and composed rather breezy articles for its house magazine, *The Rucksack* ('now we are breakfasted, booted, and on the march . . .').[55] As he explained in a wireless address early in 1931, the intention was to help young city dwellers, especially those with limited means, to obtain 'a greater knowledge, care and love of the countryside', and to recover their long-lost rural roots. 'To be at one with nature', he argued, visitors to the country must travel on foot or on bicycle, and stay in the country for several days (and nights) at a time. The aim of the scheme was to provide cheap, spartan accommodation for such self-propelled visitors, with hostels roughly fifteen miles apart. 'The walker', Trevelyan noted, 'can get easily from one to another in a day', and added, quite unaware that most people did not possess his stamina. 'if he is energetic, he can take two in his stride.'[56]

By the early 1930s Trevelyan had thus established himself as one of the foremost activists in the battle to save the English countryside. In 1931 he gave the Rickman Godlee Lecture at London University, and took as his subject 'The Calls and Claims of Natural Beauty', in which he set down in their fullest form his views on man's relation to the natural world.[57] He began with a familiar account of the threat to the countryside and of the need for town dwellers to recover their long-severed links with nature. He stressed the importance of the countryside in inspiring the finest English poetry: Chaucer, Milton, Shakespeare and Wordsworth. He argued that as man had increasingly come to dominate his environment, so the appeal of nature was enhanced, especially in those high mountain peaks which were 'her still unconquered citadels'. And he concluded with a ringing affirmation of his belief in the countryside as the sure and certain source of 'spiritual values':

Through the loveliness of nature, through the touch of sun or rain, or the sight of the shining restlessness of the sea, we feel:

'Unworded things and old to our pained heart appeal.'

. . . This flag of beauty, hung out by the mysterious Universe, to claim the worship of the heart of man, what is it, and what does its signal mean to us? . . . Natural beauty is the ultimate spiritual appeal of the Universe, of nature, or of the God of nature, to their nursling man . . . It is the highest common denominator in the spiritual life of today.[58]

III

Trevelyan's interwar work for the National Trust confirmed his position among those we today would call 'The Great and the Good': men of high-minded concern and unassailable prestige who dutifully serve on government committees and public bodies and bring to the conduct of business a disinterested tone of superior wisdom. Immediately after the First World War he had been appointed a member of the Royal Commission to inquire into Oxford and Cambridge Universities, which was chaired by the rapidly ageing Asquith. Trevelyan played a prominent part in what he regarded as 'a tremendously big affair', assiduously visiting both universities, taking over when the Chairman fell asleep, and pushing the final recommendations in a more reformist direction by urging that more resources be given to the universities vis-à-vis the Colleges.[59] Thereafter, Trevelyan was appointed a Trustee of the National Portrait Gallery and of the British Museum (as Macaulay had been before him) and these, combined with his prominent position at the National Trust, meant that he had 'acquired interlocking directorships stretching across the cultural world' in the manner of other high-minded aristocrats such as Lord Stanhope, Lord Crawford, Lord Ilchester and Sir Evan Charteris. And as a result, Trevelyan became, during the 1920s and 1930s, a central and creative figure in the politics of cultural conservation – and thus, by extension, in the politics of Conservative culture.[60]

At this time there were three evolving and interlinked views about the tone of government, the functioning of the aristocracy, and the nature of the countryside. The first was a belief in the essential decency of the English character and English public life, as the outward and visible sign of the wholesome spiritual values of the shires. During the interwar years, decency was as much under threat as the countryside whence it derived: partly from disreputable adventurers like Lloyd George and Lord Birkenhead; partly from the irresponsible press lords. The second was the gradual shift in patrician priorities from political activism to cultural stewardship: as aristocrats ceased to be the governing class, they sought to carve out a new role for themselves as the self-appointed guardians of the national heritage. And the third was a change in perceptions of rural England as a result of the break-up of great estates, which meant that the aristocracy were no longer the exclusive owners of 'the land', but became instead the altruistic protectors of 'the countryside' on behalf of the community as a whole.[61] With each of these developments, Trevelyan was closely connected. They underscored his work for the National Trust. They eased his movement from Liberalism to Conservatism. And they brought him the friendship of three of the most significant exemplars of inter-war decency: John Buchan, Stanley Baldwin and Edward Grey.

Trevelyan's friendship with John Buchan was the oldest, and dated from before the First World War. Like Trevelyan, Buchan was devoted to the Border country and wrote beautiful descriptions of landscapes in his novels and in his historical works. Like Trevelyan again, he was possessed of a powerful historical imagination, and Trevelyan greatly admired his biographies of Montrose, Scott, Cromwell and Augustus. The two families regularly stayed with each other, and for many summers the latest Buchan 'shocker' provided the most sought-after holiday reading for the Trevelyans.[62] In 1921 Buchan became Mary Trevelyan's 'highly unorthodox' godfather (she was already sixteen), and four years later he tried to persuade Stanley Baldwin to appoint Trevelyan Regius Professor of Modern History at Oxford. Their friendship was one of the reasons why the National Trust and the Pilgrim Trust drew close together during the early 1930s, and Trevelyan regularly urged Buchan to contribute to appeals for preservationist causes.[63] When Buchan died in 1940, Trevelyan told his widow that he did not 'remember anyone whose death evoked a more enviable outburst of sorrow, love and admiration', and later he wrote a moving preface to a memorial volume.[64] Indeed, when Trevelyan was short-listed for the Governor-Generalship of Canada at the end of the Second World War, it may well have been because the Canadians were looking for someone else in the Buchan mould.

Trevelyan believed that Buchan's life of Sir Walter Scott was one of the best single-volume biographies ever written. Quite by coincidence, it was dedicated to him – and to another of Buchan's closest friends, Stanley Baldwin.[65] By then, Baldwin was one of Trevelyan's closest friends too. The demise of the Liberal Party in the early 1920s had coincided with Baldwin's rise to national prominence as the unexpected Conservative Prime Minister. And it was precisely because he projected a new brand of dutiful, conciliatory, non-partisan Toryism that Trevelyan, having despaired of the Liberals, now found safe political haven among the Conservatives. For the two men had much in common. They had both been educated at Harrow and Trinity, and, although Baldwin could not compete with Trevelyan's successes in the History Tripos, he genuinely loved the English past and English literature. He was descended from a dynasty of iron masters: but he was sincerely devoted to the English countryside, especially Worcestershire. 'To me', he observed, in one of his most famous passages, 'England is the country, and the country is England', the repository of those 'eternal values from which we must never allow ourselves to be separated.' Wearing a baggy suit, puffing his pipe, and speaking in homely, familiar tones, Stanley Baldwin seemed the very embodiment of English decency and character.[66]

To this new brand of English Conservatism, Trevelyan understandably warmed. In 1925 he had persuaded Baldwin to sign the letter on behalf of the Ashridge appeal, and in the following year he sent the Prime Minister a copy of his *History of England*. 'You will not have time even to glance at it in these troublesome times,' Trevelyan observed. 'But if ever and whenever you do, you perhaps will find in it something akin to your own philosophy of English character and history.'[67] Clearly Baldwin did, for within twelve months, he appointed Trevelyan Regius Professor of Modern History at Cambridge. Thereafter, their friendship flowered, further strengthened by Baldwin's election as Chancellor of Cambridge University on the death of Lord Balfour in 1930. Trevelyan wrote Baldwin loyal letters of encouragement at times of major political crisis, sent him copies of all his latest books, and successfully enlisted his help in preservationist causes: the countryside round Cambridge, the Malvern Hills and the Northumberland coastline.[68] As Chairman of the Pilgrim Trust and Honorary Vice President of the National Trust, Baldwin was invariably sympathetic. He also consulted Trevelyan about honours and appointments. Who, he wanted to know, among Oxford luminaries, was most deserving of the OM? (Trevelyan recommended Gilbert Murray, Sir William Holdsworth and, especially, H. A. L. Fisher, who duly received it.) Along with Lord Robert Cecil, Trevelyan thought Baldwin 'my favourite living statesman', 'the kindest Prime Minister who ever lived.'[69]

Like many people in interwar Britain, Trevelyan saw Baldwin as the man who had delivered the country out of the corrupted excesses of the Lloyd George coalition into more honourable and decent times. He spelt out his feelings in a lengthy and remarkably revealing letter to Baldwin in 1935:

> What a good Conservative Macaulay would have made if he had lived a few years longer, till the time when the Second Reform Bill came up! The thought comforts me now that I am a Conservative myself, though today Conservatism is no longer trying to ward off Democracy, but to sustain Democracy against the consequences which Macaulay prophesied would follow from its adoption – viz communistic or militaristic despotism. Whiggism and Conservatism are not opposed as fundamental principles. Indeed, I remember Arthur Balfour saying to me that he agreed with every one of Macaulay's political principles, which would somewhat have astonished most of his supporters.[70]

They remained on close terms after Baldwin's retirement. Trevelyan attended the farewell dinner given by the Athenaeum, and urged Baldwin to leave his papers to Cambridge. In 1940 Baldwin was consulted by Churchill, and recommended Trevelyan as Master of Trinity. During the war, they continued to correspond about books, appointments and honours.[71] And at the first Trinity Commemoration after Baldwin's death, Trevelyan paid him an eloquent – and perceptive – tribute:

> Stanley Baldwin was an Englishman indeed, in whom was much guile, never used for low or selfish purposes. In a world of voluble hates, he plotted to make men like, or at least tolerate, one another. Therein he had much success, within the shores of this island. He remains the most lovable of all Prime Ministers.[72]

Only one figure surpassed Stanley Baldwin in Trevelyan's interwar pantheon of the decent, the dutiful and the disinterested, and that was Sir Edward Grey, Liberal Foreign Secretary from 1905 to 1916, but now retired from public life as Viscount Grey of Fallodon. Like his kinsman, Lord Grey of the Reform Bill, Edward Grey was a Northumbrian landowner, with whom the Trevelyans had been linked across the generations in the neighbourly but not intimate fashion often characteristic of the country gentry. The young Edward Grey had first been launched into public life at the General Election of 1885, as Liberal MP for the Berwick Division of Northumberland, by Sir Charles Trevelyan, just a few months before he died. As a junior minister in the Liberal government of 1892–5, Grey had been a colleague of Sir George Otto Trevelyan's; they numbered many Liberal friends in common, including John Morley and Walter Runciman; and both later became admirers of Theodore Roosevelt. And as a Director of the North Eastern Railway, at the turn of the century, one of Grey's colleagues was the industrialist Sir Hugh Bell, whose daughter Mary married Trevelyan's elder brother Charles.

Nevertheless, during the years before the First World War, Trevelyan was too radical a Liberal to find himself much in sympathy with Grey's attitude to foreign affairs. He did not share Grey's enthusiasm for the Boer War, regretted the alliance he negotiated between Britain and Russia, was worried by rumours of secret diplomacy and military agreements, and was initially opposed to Britain's entry into the war in 1914. But thereafter, his attitude changed abruptly and fundamentally, and by the early 1920s Grey and Trevelyan had become close personal friends. It was at Trevelyan's instigation that Grey signed the letter to *The Times* appealing for funds to save the Ashridge estate, and he became a staunch supporter of the National Trust, 'in defence of the wounded beauty of all England'. At the same time, Grey was much impressed by Trevelyan's life of his forbear, and when he was installed as Chancellor of Oxford in 1929 Trevelyan was one of those whom he nominated to receive an honorary degree. Having written the life of the one famous Lord Grey, it was clearly appropriate that Trevelyan should now write about the other. Viscount Grey died in 1933 and within a year Trevelyan had agreed to undertake his life. Having completed his trilogy on *England Under Queen Anne*, it was to this biography – 'a new sort of thing for me to do' – that he turned.[73]

Like his first volume on Garibaldi, but even more so, Trevelyan conceived *Grey of Fallodon* as a tragedy: indeed, he regarded it as 'the most tragic story I have ever undertaken to write.'[74] In part, it was the personal tragedy of Grey himself, who endured misfortune, bereavement and unhappiness far beyond man's normal lot. His father died when he was twelve; he lost one brother in 1911 and another in 1922; and a much-loved nephew was killed during the First World War. His first wife, Dorothy, died in 1906, and his second wife, Pamela, in 1928. There were no children of either marriage, and so his peerage became extinct at his death. Fallodon was burned to the ground in 1917, and his cottage by the River Itchen in Hampshire was also destroyed six years later. In working so long and so devotedly for his country, Grey ruined both his health and his eyesight, so that when he finally retired in 1916, 'the bounty of nature's loveliness was spread before him, invisible.'[75] Yet so balanced was his mind and so strong and serene his nature that he 'always bore the load of his calamities' with 'almost god-like serenity'. For Trevelyan, Grey was 'the noblest human being I ever met.' And that was how he portrayed him. 'What a wonderful example', Thomas Jones observed after reading the book, 'of the noble bearing of grief.'[76]

But there was in addition the public tragedy: of the Foreign Secretary who had held office under the most trying and terrible circumstances; of the man who had always hated war, who had done his utmost to prevent it, and who regarded the outbreak of hostilities in the autumn of 1914 as the greatest calamity of his career and of his life. Modern warfare was for Grey the 'ultimate horror', because it was the inevitable outcome of 'the machine mind.' His famous remark about the lamps going out all over Europe genuinely reflected his belief – which Trevelyan himself fully shared – that 'many things' would be 'completely swept away', and that civilization as he had known it was at an end.[77] For the rest of his life, Grey continued to lament his 'failure' to keep the peace in 1914. To make matters worse, the victory of 1918 proved in many ways a Pyrrhic one, for Grey 'lived to see his hopes for the pacification of the world shattered': America's isolationism; the failure of the League of Nations; the rise of Communism, Fascism and Nazism. 'We are', Trevelyan told his daughter in May 1935, 'still involved in [Grey's] failure to appease the world.'[78]

Yet as these sad words imply, there was a further, more personal dimension to the sense of tragedy which Trevelyan felt at this time. During the years when he worked on the book, from 1934 to 1937, Trevelyan was deeply anxious about the state of Europe, and especially about events in Italy. But wherever he looked, he could see no hope. 'It is a very noble tragedy – his life, I mean – and tragedy suits me just now.' And so it was 'a great consolation to live most of the day thinking about him [Grey], instead of worrying about the impossible problem of what we ought to do about Italy.'[79] But what a change in mood and in outlook this registered. As a young Liberal, Trevelyan had written the Garibaldi books in the hope of changing the world; now he worked on the life of Grey as a means of fleeing the world. The result was a book remarkably wistful and resigned in tone. Autumnal, meditative, elegiac, and suffused by a mood of retirement near to despair, *Grey of Fallodon* is to Trevelyan something of what the Cello Concerto had been to Elgar:

> A man and what he loves and builds have but a day and then disappear; nature cares not – and renews the annual round untired. It is the old law, sad but not bitter. Only when man destroys the life and beauty of nature, there is the outrage.[80]

For Trevelyan, the very essence of Grey was that he was a countryman with 'a poetic passion for nature'. It was the Northumberland landscape that shaped his noble character and left him with a lifelong devotion to rural life. He loved his birds, especially the Fallodon ducks. He loved his rods, and wrote a book on fly-fishing. And he loved his Wordsworth. He hated 'machinery . . . a vulgarized countryside . . . telephones and cinematographs and large cities and the *Daily Mail*.'[81] Like Lord Althorp of the Reform Bill, he preferred the streams and the woods and the hills to Westminster and Whitehall. For he was a man 'wholly without ambition'. Only his devotion to his Northumberland constituents kept him in the Commons, and only his iron sense of duty kept him at the Foreign Office for eleven long and terrible years. But all of this was superficial compared with the springs of the contemplative life among the beauties of nature, to which he was abidingly drawn.[82] The result was that his mind appeared a 'great reservoir of power that seemed but half in use.' He was possessed of what J. L. Hammond described as 'marble independence', and when he died, 'something spacious and noble' went out of English life.[83] As such, Trevelyan's *Grey of Fallodon* was a requiem and a lament: not just for a man, but for a class; not just of a life, but of a whole way of living.

Although Grey had entered and remained in public life with the greatest reluctance, Trevelyan was convinced that he had acted throughout his career with unimpeachable integrity. Of course, he made his mistakes: in his approving attitude towards the Boer War, and in his adherence to the 'Relugas Compact', whereby he sought, in the company of Asquith and Haldane, to force the new Liberal Prime Minister, Campbell-Bannerman, into the House of Lords late in 1905. Nor was his conduct as Foreign Secretary without its faults, especially his lack of interest in military affairs.[84] But these were minor blemishes. Despite what his critics alleged, Trevelyan insisted that Grey was zealous in his devotion to his duties, and before 1914 never negotiated a secret treaty. And in renewing one entente with France, and establishing another with Russia, Grey ensured that Britain did not lack for allies, while at the same time avoiding formal alliances which would have limited his own freedom of manoeuvre and would only have encouraged German militarism and paranoia still further. Indeed, until the very brink of war, he sought to stay on good terms with Germany and tried to be accommodating to the Kaiser's imperial ambitions. And so, although Grey ultimately failed to keep the peace, he at least ensured that Britain went to war of its own free will, with widespread public support and powerful allies.[85]

In analysing Grey's character and career as he did, Trevelyan had no doubt that he was acting as counsel for the defence. 'It is a pleasure to all Grey's friends', Lord Crewe wrote to him in June 1935, 'to know that you are undertaking the book', and the result gave them general satisfaction.[86] Beyond any doubt, he refuted the two basic arguments made by Grey's radical critics: that he was the secretive practitioner of the 'old diplomacy'; and that his manoeuvrings had helped to bring about war rather than prevent it. Indeed, as a former radical himself, Trevelyan confessed in a footnote that in August 1914, 'we were wrong, and Grey was right.'[87] Some critics felt that Trevelyan's analysis of Grey's foreign policy did not go deep enough, and others wondered whether he was right in depicting Grey as a man who found public life abhorrent. For surely, in his frequent laments about the burdens of office, he protested altogether too much? As Trevelyan himself admitted, Grey was 'more complex in character than people knew', but in depicting him as the man who preferred Northumberland to Whitehall, he failed to do adequate justice to the curious amalgam of lethargy and energy, loyalty and obstinacy, ambition and disinterest which so often led his friends and his enemies to describe his behaviour as 'Greyish'.[88]

But it was not only the radical criticism of Grey's conduct that Trevelyan was concerned to rebut: he was equally concerned to dismiss the attacks mounted on him by Lloyd George in his *War Memoirs*. As he admitted in a letter to Lord Crewe, Trevelyan 'had occasion on a number of points ... to defend Grey against Lloyd George's wild statements'; and he told R. W. Seton-Watson that 'controversy with Lloyd George' was a 'recurring motif in the book'.[89] In particular, Trevelyan contended that Lloyd George was incorrect in claiming that Grey took office ignorant and inexperienced in foreign affairs; that he did not pull his weight on the Liberal front bench in opposition or government; that he could have prevented war in 1914 by warning Germany that summer that Britain would not tolerate the violation of Belgian neutrality; that he was personally to blame for the failure to unite the Balkan states on the side of the entente; and that he mishandled relations between the Russians and the Greeks. In each case, Trevelyan took great trouble to demonstrate the inaccuracy of Lloyd George's arguments and recollections, which he once dismissed as being 'unworthy of the great part he has played in the world's affairs.'[90]

But as well as being a critique of Lloyd George's memoirs and methods, Trevelyan's life of Grey was written unambiguously in praise of Stanley Baldwin. They were both politicians who professed to find public office a heavy burden, who loved the country and believed in 'spiritual values'; and at one point Baldwin had even considered making Grey his Foreign Secretary. When Grey's second wife died, Baldwin wrote him a letter of condolence, and he gave Trevelyan permission to publish Grey's reply. Its central passage runs as follows:

> As long as you are at the head of a Government, it will stand for what is honourable. The iron entered into my soul, when Ll.G's. Govt. after the War let down and corrupted public life at home, and destroyed our credit abroad. Ever since, it has been a relief to have public honour re-established, and you will always stand for that.[91]

In the published version, Trevelyan excised the words 'and corrupted' with the Prime Minister's agreement. But Grey's meaning was still plain: 'his sense', as Trevelyan wrote to Baldwin, 'of what we all owe you for that deliverance.'[92]

Despite its mood of retirement and withdrawal, the contemporary political resonances of *Grey of Fallodon* were thus unmistakable. Nor were they limited to the domestic sphere. For in its vindication of Grey's conduct between 1906 and 1914, it was taken by contemporaries to provide – and may, unconsciously, have been written to provide – historical validation for the foreign policy which was pursued by the National Government between 1935 and 1939. Grey had sought to maintain European peace by appeasing Germany; to ensure that, in the event of that policy failing, Britain should not lack for Continental allies; and to carry the country united into war, if the ultimate catastrophe could not be averted.[93] During the late 1930s all this had once again become government policy. In the spring of 1937, just after *Grey of Fallodon* was published, Oliver Harvey (a junior official), Sir Nevile Henderson (British Ambassador in Berlin) and Anthony Eden (the Foreign Secretary), were pondering the similarities between their own difficulties over Germany and those which Grey had faced a generation earlier. And they each admitted that it was Trevelyan's book which had enabled them to observe this resemblance.[94]

But this was not the only comparison which *Grey of Fallodon* enabled the men in power to draw. For there was a likeness of personality as well as of policy. Having read and admired the book, the Secretary to the Cabinet, Sir Maurice Hankey, was struck by the fact that 'Halifax has many of the qualities of Grey, whom he resembles from many points of view' – a north-country landowner, a strong upholder of 'spiritual values', Chancellor of Oxford University, and an appeaser of Germany.[95] It was a perceptive remark, for Trevelyan undoubtedly admired both men. And within a year Halifax actually became Foreign Secretary, which meant that Britain duly went to war a second time against Germany with its diplomatic affairs in the hands of another high-minded landowner. But by then the rustic decency of Baldwinian Conservatism was already out of date, and Halifax had no Trevelyan to safeguard his reputation for posterity.

IV

During the last, brief, uncertain years of peace, Trevelyan's gloom and apprehension only deepened still further. 'We are all, as it were, under sentence of death', he wrote to Gilbert Murray in May 1938, 'with just a very slight chance of reprieve.' But he could not bring himself to be too optimistic. Four months later he wrote to Mary Moorman, and told her that 'Grey's last word to me in August 1933 on the lawn at Fallodon was "I see no hope for the world".' To which Trevelyan now added: 'I see less today.'[96] And in October 1939, when Britain was again at war with Germany, he repeated Grey's words in a letter to his brother Bob, and continued:

> One half of me suffers horribly. The other half is detached, because the 'world' that is threatened is not my world, which died years ago. I am a mere survivor. Life has been a great gift, for which I am grateful, 'though I would gladly give it back now.[97]

Inevitably, there was more suffering to come. 'I am', he told Mary in May 1940, 'too unhappy about the war and the world to write about it.' The result, he feared, could only be 'the destruction for a long time to come of anything you can call civilization – even if we emerge victorious, or semi-victorious.'[98] And in July, he was even more apocalyptic:

> I fear we live in days when anyone of our generation who dies is lucky . . . I never had any real hope for the world after this war broke out, but it is all going even worse than I feared.[99]

But the nadir had not yet been reached. 'The world is a worse nightmare than imagination could have devised,' he wrote to Bob in August 1940. 'Every evil seems to have occurred.' In public, Trevelyan maintained 'a sober interest in all things, and a decently cheerful demeanour, as we are all most strongly bound to do'. But in private, he was so anguished that even the Mastership of Trinity brought him little comfort. 'That the crash of civilization', he told Bob, 'should have landed me here in the beautiful old Lodge, with its beautiful old world traditions . . . is a tragic-comic irony.'[100] By day, Trevelyan took refuge in literature and history: 'The past at least cannot be destroyed. It was and is as real as present and future.' By night, he dreamed of evil: 'I am quite accustomed to that now, and expect nothing else when I lie down.' To Geoffrey Dawson, he wrote that this was 'an age steadily lapsing and finally rushing into barbarism.' To Leonard Woolf he described it as 'the most tragic of all ages.' And the hardest part of it was that although the 'present nightmare' seemed 'to have so little to do with the world in which I was brought up', in fact, Trevelyan recognized that it was 'its natural child'.[101]

Like Edward Grey, Trevelyan believed that abandoning the worship of nature for the worship of the machine inexorably led to 'total tyranny' and 'total war'. And in such a conflict, the casualties inevitably included some of the familiar landmarks of his life. Holland House, where his father and great-uncle had enjoyed Whig society in its heyday, was bombed out. Hallington was requisitioned by the RAF, and Trevelyan doubted whether he would ever be able to live there again, 'certainly not in the same style.'[102] And in November 1941, it was announced that Sir Charles had made over Wallington to the National Trust, subject only to a life interest for himself. In fact negotiations had begun in 1934, and Trevelyan found himself in a peculiarly awkward position, being both his brother's executor and Chairman of the Trust's

Estates Committee. Sir Charles had always felt guilty about his wealth and had opened Wallington to the workers of Tyneside on many occasions in the past. As a socialist, he believed 'it would be better if the community owned such houses and great estates.' On his death in 1958 the Trust assumed control, and after the death of Lady Trevelyan eight years later, the house was redecorated and opened to the public.[103]

During the war, Trevelyan's preservationist labours further increased, since many properties belonging to the Youth Hostels Association and the National Trust were requisitioned by the government and many employees were called up. At the annual meetings of the YHA, he delivered a succession of exhortatory addresses, urging all members to renew their contact with Nature, 'who in her unending cycle of growth and decay and rebirth pays no regard to the feverish violence of man and his machines.'[104] At the National Trust, Trevelyan continued as Chairman of the Estates Committee and Vice-Chairman of the Executive Committee; he was also recruited to the Country House Committee and the Finance and General Purposes Committee. As such, he played a major part in securing many wartime benefactions, especially Sir Richard Acland's great gift of his Holincote and Killerton estates, and in the columns of *The Times* he defended the donor from critics who alleged that he had abandoned his hereditary responsibility as a landowner. He continued his own benefactions, giving the Trust two Lake District farms in Great Langdale amounting to 250 acres.[105] And in January 1945 he wrote an extended article in *Country Life*, once again describing the Trust's work and progress, and appealing for public support and active government sympathy in the cause of rural conservation.[106]

The years from 1938 to 1944 were thus the darkest – and some of the busiest – of Trevelyan's life. It was in this mood that he wrote and eventually published his last and most sensationally successful work: his *English Social History*.[107] It had been suggested to him, when he had completed *Grey of Fallodon*, by Robert Longman, as a companion volume to the *History of England*, in which politics and war had inevitably predominated. In earlier books, such as *England Under the Stuarts*, Trevelyan had already showed his mastery of brief, panoramic surveys of the social scene, and there was Macaulay's famous third chapter in his *History of England* which provided both a challenge and a precedent. But there were also more specific reasons why a large-scale work of social history appealed to Trevelyan at that time: for someone so disenchanted with the affairs of the world, there must have been a particular appeal in writing a 'history of the people with the politics left out'. Trevelyan's original intention was to survey the whole of English history since the time of the Romans. But the constraints of wartime made this impossible, and he confined himself to surveying the six centuries from Chaucer to Queen Victoria.[108] The book was completed in 1941 and was published in America in the following year. But it was held up in Britain because of paper shortages, and eventually appeared in the summer of 1944.[109]

Not surprisingly, the book contained scattered topical references to 'jack boots', to 'totalitarian states' and to 'military dictatorship', all of which Trevelyan regarded with evident distaste. He reaffirmed his view that 'in the wrong hands, machinery may destroy humanity.' He lamented 'the state of slavery into which academic life has fallen in countries with no ... venerable tradition of the rule of law and the liberty of the subject.' He noted with evident regret that 'one year of modern totalitarian war is more dislocating to society and more destructive of the higher branches of civilization in England than a cycle of warfare in the days of the Elder or the Younger Pitt.'[110] And he felt moved to restate the Whiggish view that 'personal freedom became universal at an early date in our country', which was 'one of the reasons for the ideological attachment of Englishmen to the very name of freedom.' They had, he insisted, always been 'proud of their liberty', and were 'quiet and orderly' in their habits. The democracy of the present day was essentially 'good-natured'. And he summed up English history in a revealingly rural metaphor: 'a continuous stream of life, with gradual change perpetually taking place.'[111]

Throughout the book, Trevelyan wrote with more feeling than ever before about what now seemed to him the mortally endangered fabric of English life: landscape and locality, flora and fauna, places and people. He described the Englishman's devotion to his horses and dogs, and developments in sheep and cattle breeding. He wrote of the trees, plants, flowers and herbs which were introduced into early-seventeenth-century England. He recalled the time when 'England was alive with game and with many birds now rare or extinct, from the Great Bustard of the downs [to] the eagle of Westmorland and Wales.' He explained the evolution of the shot-gun, from the muzzle-loading flint-and-steel gun to the more modern ejector. He evoked the 'watery, reedy solitudes' of the East Anglian Fens, with their 'innumerable oozy islands'. He wrote of Northumberland, once an 'unknown, distant, barbarous land', with its castles and peels, its bandits and shepherds, but added characteristically: 'there was always a breath of freedom blowing off the moors.'[112] He celebrated medieval English cathedrals as 'towering forests of masonry, of which the beauty and grandeur have never been rivalled either by the ancients or the moderns.' And he wrote of country houses like Montacute 'in its glory of dull gold . . . one of the most beautiful and magnificent homes in the world.'[113]

Trevelyan had no doubt that it was this pastoral civilization which had been the seed bed of all that was finest in English culture – a culture which, he insisted, had until recent times been an integral part of the lives even of ordinary people. And so he gave disproportionate space to literature, painting and architecture. Chaucer may have been a Londoner, but his poetry was shot through with the homely images of country and farm. Shakespeare's greatness was partly explained by the fact that in Tudor times, 'the forest, the field and the city were then in perfection, and all three are needed to perfect the poet.'[114] The rural scenes in *Pilgrim's Progress* were essentially the same England 'of Izaak Walton's *Angler*'. Architects like Wren and Gibbs used vernacular building materials and were particularly sensitive to the local landscape. The paintings of Turner and Constable both caught 'the unique glory of our island . . . the shifting lights and shades of sky, earth and foliage in our water-laden atmosphere.' And the strongest appeal of Tennyson's poetry lay in 'the strength, beauty and accuracy of his pictures of nature.'[115]

In his early chapters, Trevelyan depicted England in almost prelapsarian terms. 'There was none of the rigid division between rural and urban which has prevailed since the Industrial Revolution. No Englishman then was ignorant of country things, as the great majority of Englishmen are today.' The majority of the population lived in the countryside, and it was they who provided 'the nation's shield and buckler' in the form of the 'stout yeoman'. 'His independence, his hearty good nature, his skill in archery' were for Trevelyan the very essence of premodern English life. Of course, even in late medieval times, 'the new middle classes', many of them wool merchants, were already appearing 'in town and village', and they were 'often selfish enough'.[116] But their rise to pre-eminence was still a long way off. Until then, it was the landowning classes who were in charge. Their attachment to their estates was already well known, and 'foreigners were astonished at the love of the English gentry for rural life.' In its essential outlines, the social structure of England survived unaltered until the seventeenth century. 'The ordinary Englishman was not yet a townee, wholly divorced from nature.' On the contrary, 'in those days, men were much left alone with nature, with themselves, with God.'[117]

For Trevelyan, this pastoral civilization reached its apogee during the eighteenth century, an era of 'calm, broad-minded optimism', which was 'brilliant above and stable below.' As such, it was a society in 'perfectly beautiful equilibrium between man and nature', characterized by 'the balance of town and country rather than the deadweight of life in great cities, of literature rather than journalism, of arts and crafts rather than the machine.'[118] Most Englishmen still knew very little of towns, rejoiced in the close contact with nature that their country life afforded, and relished the traditions and character of their own village community. 'Buildings still added to the beauty of the land', and 'taste had not yet been vitiated by too much machine production.' Country gentlemen were concerned about their accounts and their families, attended to their estates, county business and horses, and were devoted to their gardens and their ponds 'a little more than to their books'. They lived 'a wholesome and useful life, half public, half private, wholly leisured, natural and dignified.' 'Perhaps no set of men and women since the world began', Trevelyan observed, 'enjoyed so many different sides of life, with so much zest, as the English upper classes of this period.' 'The hour', he concluded, 'was theirs, and it was golden.'[119]

But then came the Industrial Revolution, 'the most important movement in social history since the Anglo-Saxon conquest.' Trevelyan could not quite bring himself to label it a 'catastrophe', although he had no doubt that it was 'the river of life, but in the lower part of its course.' In quantitative terms, he admitted, the standard of living may have improved for some workers, but this did not outweigh the environmental deprivation and spiritual impoverishment which left 'only too little of the ancient ways.' The factory system ruined craftsmanship, and divided employers from employed. Manufacturing towns were squalid and featureless, with 'rows of mass-produced brick dwellings' built by vulgarian individualists, 'inspired by no idea beyond quick money returns.'[120] Neither the Church nor the State cared for this new proletariat, while unregulated laissez-faire meant 'liberty for the masters and repression for the men.' The result was a rootless, artificial society, in which industrial labourers became 'dissociated from the rural life of the country around.' The 'harmonious fabric of English society' was rent asunder, as England was divided between town and country, rich and poor. And the inevitable result was that 'the vitality of the village slowly declined, as the city in a hundred ways sucked away its blood and brains.'[121]

During the second half of the nineteenth century, Trevelyan insisted, the imbalance between town and country only further increased. Modern cities were 'a deadening cage for the human spirit', since 'urban and suburban life in modern England made no appeal through the eye to the imagination, as had the old village life of our island.' The 'general divorce of Englishmen from life in contact with nature', combined with the advent of nationwide elementary education, resulted in the 'mass vulgarity' of 'the new journalism', which swamped the old literate high culture with cheap sensationalism. At the same time, 'urban ways of thought and action' penetrated and absorbed 'the old rural world, obliterating its distinctive features and local variations.'[122] And the late nineteenth-century depression in agriculture accentuated still further the flight from the land. 'John Bull', Trevelyan regretted, 'was ceasing to be a countryman and a farmer; when once he was wholly urbanized or suburbanized, would he any longer be John Bull, except in the cartoons of *Punch*?' And as a result of this 'sudden catastrophe', the agriculture and aristocracy of England were both 'overthrown'. To Trevelyan, this was a 'tremendous social disaster': for 'agriculture is not merely one industry among many, but is a way of life, unique and irreplaceable in its human and spiritual values.'[123]

During the twentieth century, Trevelyan had no doubt that 'urban thought, ideas and government' had conquered the countryside almost entirely. The traditional aristocracy had largely withdrawn from the scene, since 'modern income tax and death duties' had been almost 'fatal to the whole race of landowners'. The widespread 'mechanization of life' meant there had been 'a more rapid social and economic revolution in the first forty years of the twentieth century' than ever before.[124] The submarine, the tank and the aeroplane had made wars unprecedentedly destructive. And 'the internal combustion engine' had 'ruined most of what was good in English civilization for our day, and perhaps for many days to come.' Indeed, the advent of the motor car meant that 'England bade fair to become one huge unplanned suburb.' As a result, there was an 'urgent need for the state to control the development of the whole island.' But so far, there was no sign that this was happening. Trevelyan's conclusion was sombre: '"Progress", as we of the twentieth century are better aware than our Victorian ancestors, is not always change from bad to good, or good to better.'[125]

Thus described, Trevelyan's *Social History* was permeated by 'a deep regret for the world that is fading – the world of manor houses, country pursuits, the rule of liberal and tolerant gentlemen', and by a deep apprehension of a world full of 'city-bred folk.' But the nostalgia was neither as mindless nor as ignorant as has been claimed.[126] In what seemed to be an almost subversive afterthought, Trevelyan noted that whereas the Battle of Waterloo had been won by country-bred men, the Battle of Britain had been won by town-dwellers, educated in primary and secondary schools, who were not 'and could not be the products of rural simplicity.'[127] In several places, he was critical of the state's efforts at providing a national system of education, and he rejoiced at the increased part played by women in intellectual and public life. More than once, he reminded his readers that 'merrie England' had always co-existed with 'miserable England'; that in premodern times, manual work had been 'harsh' and 'backbreaking', and the lack of medicines meant widespread disease and early death; and that in picturing the past, 'the want of comforts and luxuries we take for granted' should never be forgotten. 'Golden ages are not all of gold', he observed, perhaps thinking of those distant, halcyon Liberal years snuffed out by the First World War, 'and they never last long.'[128]

V

The sensational success of the *Social History* did little to alleviate Trevelyan's abiding sense of gloom. By this time, he was in his early seventies: it is hardly surprising that he should have been unenthusiastic about the future. 'There is', he told Mary in March 1947, 'something more fundamentally wrong than the ugliness of our great cities, though that is a part of it.'[129] The austerity of the postwar world only accentuated his melancholy: in the *Social History*, he had written with inadvertent foresight of 'our drab detail and monotony of dullness', and the fact that most of his royalties went in excess taxes cannot have helped. In 1947 the Hammonds sent Trevelyan a copy of a new edition of their *The Bleak Age*, and his disenchanted reply merely echoed the title of their book:

An age that has no culture except American films and football pools is in some respects bleaker than the one you tell of. The advent of real democracy, coinciding in time with two world wars, has done it – cooked the goose of civilization. And I doubt if Winston will make it any better if he gets in again![130]

The death of friends and relatives further increased his sadness. When Bob died in April 1951, Trevelyan told Desmond MacCarthy that 'I do not pity old people who die particularly nowadays.' And when MacCarthy himself died in the following year, Trevelyan told Bob's widow: 'It is not much privilege for old people to drag on in the present age.'[131]

But as Trevelyan had half allowed himself to hope, the postwar Labour government did not turn out to be all bad. For in addition to giving India its independence and nationalizing the mines, it showed a gratifyingly active concern for 'amenity and preservation and planning'. For all his rural rhetoric, Stanley Baldwin had done nothing, as Prime Minister, for the safeguarding of the countryside. Despite appeals, by Trevelyan among others, for the establishment of a planning authority and the creation of National Parks, there had been no effective action. In July 1945 Trevelyan wrote to *The Times*, pleading that some effort should be made by postwar governments to control 'the full tide of development', which would soon 'begin its levelling and destructive sweep over the green and pleasant parts of England which survive.'[132] A year later, after talks with Lewis Silkin, the new Minister of Town and Country Planning, and Hugh Dalton, the Chancellor of the Exchequer, he found them both 'very keen on exactly the right policy'. And policy was soon converted into action. In his second Budget, of 1946, Dalton created the National Land Fund and endowed it with £50 million, the purpose of which was to reimburse the Inland Revenue for land and houses which were offered to it in lieu of death duties, and which could then be passed directly on to the National Trust.[133]

Dalton himself was an energetic walker, a great lover of the countryside, and President of the Ramblers Association. And he was also a long-standing admirer of the National Trust, which he regarded as 'a typically British example of practical socialism in action.' As he explained to its new Chairman, Lord Crawford, he believed it had 'behind it a fine record of public service', and that it commanded 'widespread public goodwill'; he said he had always held that 'a Labour government should give it every encouragement to extend its activities.' 'That', he concluded, 'is all I am trying to do.'[134] In fact, the creation of the National Land Fund was an exceptionally imaginative gesture, since the way was now open for many more estates and great houses (and ultimately works of art as well) to pass to the Trust, where they were preserved in perpetuity for the public benefit. When in November 1947 Dalton was forced to resign, having carelessly revealed the main items of his autumn Budget to a lobby correspondent, Trevelyan wrote an eloquent and appreciative letter to *The Times* expressing 'the personal gratitude we owe to the outgoing Chancellor of the Exchequer for the practical sympathy he has shown with the cause of the preservation of the beauty of this island, for which most government departments have done less than nothing.'[135]

In the same year that Dalton resigned, a new Town and Country Planning Act was passed, which contained many provisions for the protection of the countryside, and in 1949 it was followed by the National Parks Act. Both were wide-ranging pieces of legislation, which gave the government and local authorities great powers to protect the countryside – if they chose to exert them. Under Lewis Silkin, little was done. But in 1950 Dalton returned to the government as Minister of Town and Country Planning. Trevelyan was delighted. 'He has', he told his brother Charles, 'the right ideas and sympathies about the preservation of amenities', and was 'a stronger man' than 'the incompetent Silkin'. Dalton at once declared Snowdonia, the Lake District and the Peak District to be National Parks, and vigorously supported the making of the Pennine Way.[136] In June 1950, seeking solace from the cares of office, Dalton went walking for three days in the Cheviots and spent a night at Wallington, with Sir Charles Trevelyan, whose political protégé he had been during the interwar years. They spent the evening looking at some old photographs of the Lake Hunt. 'I was there', Dalton recorded in his diary, 'in 1911, 1912 and 1913, and in each of the first two years caught George Trevelyan – a great honour.'[137]

Even after 1945 Trevelyan's preservationist activities thus continued unabated. He played a major part in the launching of the National Trust's Jubilee appeal, which was begun as soon as the war in Europe ended, donated £3,000 from the royalties of his *Social History* to help get it going, and was delighted that Dalton agreed to match what was raised, pound for pound, with a government grant.[138] He became an energetic champion of the newly formed Outward Bound

Trust, the aim of which was to teach 'character, initiative, leadership, endurance, self-help and self-dependence', as an antidote to 'the stultifying effect of permanent town and factory life', in this 'mechanical and all-too-material age.' He reaffirmed his belief that planting with conifers was wholly inappropriate for the Lake District: 'I am not afraid', he wrote to *The Times* in reply to Lord Winterton, 'of using the word "spiritual" for the nation's heritage in this region.'[139] He wrote the Foreword to *Country Code*, a booklet prepared by the National Parks Commission, and the Introduction to a history of the Youth Hostels Association. And he continued to be particularly concerned about his native Northumberland, especially the areas that had been requisitioned during the war, and the problems associated with the upkeep of Hadrian's Wall.[140]

But these were almost Trevelyan's last interventions on behalf of the cause of natural beauty. In 1949, on doctor's advice, he resigned as Chairman of the Estates Committee of the National Trust, though not before making an inadvertently memorable farewell, as Chairman of the Trust's Local Committee Conference, held in that year.[141] A young Conservative MP, William Vane, later Lord Inglewood, who had recently been recruited to the Estates Committee, set out to explain the Trust's policy regarding afforestation. In the course of his remarks, he had the temerity to suggest that the still-rumbling controversy between the Forestry Commission and the Trust about the planting of conifers was 'just too childish'. At that, Trevelyan sat bolt upright behind his Chairman's table. 'Just what do you mean by that, young man?' he barked, in his most intimidating, professor-to-undergraduate tones. 'You must know that the National Trust has played a great part in preventing the planting of conifers in the Lake District.' Two years later, Trevelyan came off the Executive Committee and the Finance and General Purposes Committee, and was made an Honorary Vice President, as Grey and Baldwin had been before him. But his work for the Trust was effectively over, and at the same time he resigned as President of the Youth Hostels Association.[142]

One opportunity remained for Trevelyan to express in public his feelings for the countryside and for the class which had once dominated it, and that was at his installation as Chancellor of Durham University in May 1950. At that time there were two campuses, and so there were two ceremonies: one in Durham itself, the other in Newcastle. To his audience 'on this bank of Tyne', Trevelyan spoke feelingly of his long, youthful, solitary walks in the hills and valleys of the Cheviots, and described the beauties of Northumberland in terms reminiscent of the essay he had written on 'The Middle Marches', half a century before:

> Ours is still the finest county of them all, with its wide, distant views of heaven and earth, the sense of ancient freedom in its strong air, its piled white clouds drifting before the west wind like the procession of the ages that is written below in tribal mounds and Roman camps and Border towns on the breast of Northumberland.

And before the Durham congregation, he lamented the decline of the old territorial aristocracy, those 'leisured and semi-leisured classes', who had 'carried on the intellect, literature, scholarship and culture of the country', but who were 'now disappearing under the pressure of taxation.'[143]

As these speeches implied, Trevelyan's preferred social order remained one in which the countryside dominated the town, and the traditional landowning class dominated the countryside. Although as a new Liberal in the years before 1914 he had supported Lloyd George's Land Campaign, he had, by the interwar years, come to regret the break-up of great estates and the decline of the aristocracy, not least because nothing better had replaced them. For as a result, the standards of public life had declined, the beauty of the countryside had been eroded and the worth of 'spiritual values' had been questioned. As Trevelyan had explained to Hilton Young back in July 1937, 'the "mixed" governments our ancestors made their ideal were really the best, though under modern economic and social conditions, they have unfortunately become impossible.' 'The difficult game', he added, 'is to find substitutes for the old aristocracy – not to be called that name.' Or, as he put it in a letter to Mary Moorman of the same month, it was a matter of finding something 'decent' to 'replace them'.[144]

In the years between the wars, and again after 1945, most of Trevelyan's public work may best be seen as an attempt to find, and to nurture, institutional substitutes for the traditional aristocracy. This was obviously so in the case of the National Trust, which became the most effective new custodian of rural beauty and 'spiritual values'. During Trevelyan's long period of influence and association, the amount of land controlled by the Trust markedly increased, as did the number of great houses in its care. And it was also from this time that a growing number of aristocrats became associated with the work of the Trust, such as Lord Zetland, Lord Crawford and Lord Wemyss.

In an almost apologetic letter to Charles, Trevelyan once described his work for the Trust as a way of atoning for the fact that he had not gone into politics.[145] But in fact the National Trust was then, as now, the pursuit of politics by other means: the attempt to ensure the survival of natural beauty and rural values after the traditional owners of the land had ceased to be able to perform those functions unaided. About this, there can be no doubt that Trevelyan cared very deeply. As he explained to Gilbert Murray in 1952, there had been two primary concerns in his life: the first was 'history and literature'; the second was 'the National Trust and country preservation'.[146]

But the aristocracy had not only been the traditional custodians of the countryside. As a privileged élite, they had also been the chief patrons of culture, just as their late nineteenth-century successors, the intellectual aristocracy, had been the leaders of learning. Trevelyan passionately believed that 'a certain amount of inequality of opportunity and leisure seems to me essential to the things I care about', by which he meant 'literature, art, imagination and free intellect'. But the levelling tendencies of the twentieth century were such that it had now become difficult 'to get a traditional aristocracy of any kind'. And so, despite his admiration for Hugh Dalton's environmental endeavours, he could not share his brother Charles's enthusiasm for the socialist millenium, 'though I fear it is an inevitable consequence of machinery and the Industrial Revolution.'[147] The best hope for the future, Trevelyan believed, lay in the universities: 'for in the universities there is at least the recognition of the value of quality, otherwise disappearing with the disappearance of all forms of aristocratic tradition.' He viewed academe as he viewed everything else, with the eyes of the countryman and the nature lover:

> The Wordsworthian joy in nature is not dimmed for me by the knowledge that I shall not possess it for ever. We come and pass and are not, but nature remains, the friend of each of us in turn.[148]

V

THE HISTORIAN
AND THE REPUTATION

The history of events is ephemeral, and for the scholar; the poetry of events is eternal, and for the multitude.

G. M. TREVELYAN, *Garibaldi and
the Making of Italy* (1911), p. 297.

I have not been an original but a traditional kind of historian. The best that can be said of me is that I tried to keep up to date a family tradition as to the relation of history to literature, in a period when the current was running strongly in the other direction, towards history exclusively 'scientific', a period, therefore, when my old-fashioned ideas and practice have had, perhaps, a certain value as counterpoise.

G. M. TREVELYAN, *An Autobiography and
Other Essays* (1949), p. 1.

We historians are fallible folk, and must be charitable to one another.

G. M. TREVELYAN, in the *Times Literary Supplement*,
19 October, 1933.

The Cambridge History Faculty Building, designed by James Stirling in his brutal, modernist phase: 'Part bunker, part factory, part greenhouse, all folly, it embodies and projects an idea of history wholly unlike that in which Trevelyan believed.'

THE BUILDING WHICH TODAY houses the Cambridge History Faculty of which George Macaulay Trevelyan was once the titular head and principal ornament, is scarcely a stone's throw from his former home in West Road. Designed by James Stirling, and constructed during the late 1960s, it dominates the Sidgwick Avenue lecture site, with its harsh, red, Accrington bricks, its superabundance of industrial glazing, its brutal angularity of form and line, its violent insensitivity to its surroundings and its brash contempt for beauty, style or art.[1] Ever since its completion, the building has been functionally suspect and aesthetically controversial. To a few admirers, it is a masterpiece, but to most observers, it is a monstrosity – Dry-as-dust implausibly clad in the leaking raiment of High-as-tech. Part bunker, part factory, part greenhouse, all folly, it embodies and projects an idea of history wholly unlike that in which Trevelyan believed. Ugly, strident, unpopular, aggressive, unwelcoming, antihumanist and anti-architecture, it seems to deny, to disown and to disavow that very different muse of history to whose service Trevelyan had dedicated and devoted his life.

I

Like his great-uncle and his father, and like such late nineteenth-century liberals as John Morley and James Bryce, Trevelyan believed that the prime purpose of history lay in its didactic public function.[2] History should be written, and history should be read, 'to instruct, enlarge and cultivate the human mind' in the responsibilities of good citizenship. Accounts of past events, past controversies, and past conflicts, enabled men and women to cultivate a 'more intelligent patriotism', by seeing 'points of view which [they] never saw before', by taking a broader perspective on the issues of party politics, and by developing the power of 'understanding great affairs and sympathizing with other men.'[3] Trevelyan further believed that individuals should study 'events gone by' so as to appreciate and acquire 'just principles and noble emotions', which were as essential for the ordinary citizen as for the professional politician. And as the story of 'individual great men', history provided 'the model and inspiration' for those lesser mortals who came after. In common with the Ancient Greeks, the Romans and the Renaissance humanists, Trevelyan believed that history was 'the basis of modern education in the humanities' and the best way of promoting civic virtue and disinterested statesmanship.[4]

At the same time, Trevelyan urged that the study of history gave a 'noble education to the mind', which made it possible for men and women to live richer, more fulfilled, more abundant lives. For great historical writing gave 'intellectual pleasure of a very high order.' It opened up new vistas in the realm of 'personal, religious and ethical ideas'. It broadened man's horizons, stimulated his mind, and lifted his spirits. It helped him to understand great literature more fully, and to enjoy art and architecture more profoundly. It enabled him to 'feel the poetry of time', to come to terms with the tragedy and the transience of the human condition, to appreciate that the past was once as real as the present, and as uncertain as the future.[5] History, in short, inculcated a special kind of reflective wisdom about human affairs and about the human predicament; and this, combined with its more public, educative function, and the regrettable decline of the classics, made it the principal element in any contemporary humane education. A person devoid of an historical background, denied the perspective of the past on the present, incapable of understanding himself in time, was, Trevelyan believed, 'not properly educated, either as a citizen or as an intellectual and imaginative being.'[6]

Since Trevelyan insisted that the purpose of history was to make the world morally and intellectually comprehensible, it followed that the prime purpose of the historian must be to write, not for his fellow professionals, but for the intelligent laity. 'If historians neglect to educate the public,' Trevelyan observed, 'if they fail to interest it intelligently in the past, then all their historical learning is useless except insofar as it educates themselves.'[7] Historians, Trevelyan believed, should write their best books, not for their fellow scholars, but for the book-reading public, not for the profession, but for the nation. And in order to appeal to this broader audience, Trevelyan argued that they must excel in three separate but connected fields. First, there was research: 'the accumulation of facts and the sifting of evidence.' Second, there was the 'imaginative or speculative' function, when the historian 'plays with the facts that he has gathered, selects and classifies them, and makes his guesses and his generalizations.' And finally there was the 'literary function': 'the exposition of the results of science and imagination in a form that will attract and educate our fellow countryman.'[8] Of each of these three facets of the historian's art and craft, Trevelyan was himself the master.

All his life, Trevelyan insisted on the primacy of original, archival research, as the only way in which historians could hope to find what they were looking for: the truth about the past. Research, he argued in 1913, was 'the day-labour that every historian must well and truly perform if he is to be a serious member of his profession.' 'The importance of research', he observed in his inaugural lecture, 'as the basis of any history worthy of the name . . . needs no proof and requires no emphasis.' From first to last, Trevelyan considered himself a research historian, and while others have disputed this claim, he was in essence correct. For he had a voracious appetite for primary source material: like Carlyle, he was his own Dry-as-Dust.[9] Early this century, when he was in Italy working on his Garibaldi books, he wrote of his experiences in one archive, where he found 'scrappy old letters, that once throbbed with the fierce life of conspiracy and war, now looking pathetically dull – except to the initiated, such as I am getting to be.' And he felt the same kind of hungry exhilaration when, twenty years later, he visited the great Whig houses in search of material for *England Under Queen Anne*. 'The sense of the continuity of English history', he recalled, 'comes over you like a charm when turning over the old letters in their original homes, with the descendant as your kind helper and host.'[10]

From the very beginning, all of Trevelyan's major books were based on careful, detailed archival research. In *England in the Age of Wycliffe* he made use of manuscripts that had recently been discovered in the Public Record Office, including a sixteenth-century chronicle by Francis Thynne, and documents relating to the trial of John of Northampton, Mayor of London from 1381 to 1383 and a partisan of John of Gaunt against Richard II. For the Garibaldi books, he ransacked public and private archives in Bologna, Rome, Genoa, Milan, Naples and Palermo. He looked at official correspondence in London and Paris, as well as the letters of Lord John Russell. He mastered a prodigious amount of secondary material, the bibliography of which amounted to fourteen pages in *Garibaldi's Defence of the Roman Republic* alone. He was an early pioneer of what would now be called oral history, interviewing some of the men who had marched with Garibaldi and obtaining letters from other eyewitnesses. And he even brought home specimens of plants from Caprera for expert identification, so that he might more knowledgeably describe the flora of the island.[11] As a result, the Garibaldi books were so weighed down with footnotes, appendixes and bibliographies that some critics found it 'all a little irksome' to the 'nonscientific reader'. Others were more appreciative, noting, quite correctly, that one of the most original features of the books was that they applied the rigorous scholarship usually associated with medieval history to 'a piece of quite modern history', a methodology which was 'as unexpected as it is invaluable.'[12]

Nor did Trevelyan's archival zeal desert him in the writing of his later works. When researching *England Under Queen Anne* he utilized a far greater range of sources than those investigated by his contemporary and competitor, Winston Churchill, in writing his life of Marlborough. The Blenheim archive was closed to him, but he was able to see Archdeacon Coxe's transcripts in the British Museum. He used private papers in the possession of the Duke of Buccleuch ('bagging another duke', as he described it to Mary), and of Earls Spencer, Stanhope and Dartmouth.[13] He consulted other manuscript collections in the British Museum, the Bodleian Library, Cambridge University Library and the Rijks-archief at the Hague. He made extensive use of the diplomatic correspondence from the French and the British Foreign Offices. And he seems to have consulted most of the available printed sources, especially the Reports of the Historical Manuscripts Commission. Nor was Trevelyan's concern with historical evidence confined to the written word: towards the end of his career, he became particularly interested in visual images. Inspired, perhaps, by Dorothy George's work on eighteenth-century caricature, he published his selection of John Doyle's cartoons of the reign of William IV, because he recognized they were a valuable historical source. And in 1951 he publicly expressed his support for the National Film Archive, partly because he recognized that the cinema was of the first importance in the cultural life of the twentieth century, and partly because he realized that film provided a unique record of important historical events.[14]

In his biographies, Trevelyan's range of sources was, inevitably, less comprehensive. But he always took pains to master the appropriate printed materials – correspondence, newspapers, parliamentary debates

– and to use as many private papers as he was able to obtain. The life of John Bright depended primarily on his own letters, journals and speeches. But Trevelyan also made extensive use of correspondence lent him by the Sturge family and by Joseph Chamberlain, and was able to draw heavily on letters already printed in the multivolume biographies of such Victorian worthies as Granville, Disraeli and Gladstone.[15] In writing his biography of Grey of the Reform Bill, Trevelyan had the free run of the family archive at Howick, and also used the Fox, Durham, Spencer and Halifax papers, all then still in private hands. He also worked on the Home Office papers in the British Museum, so as to obtain a broader picture of popular unrest, both in the 1790s, and during the Reform Bill crisis. And in *Grey of Fallodon*, Trevelyan used family papers and official correspondence, and obtained further material and recollections from many of Grey's former colleagues, including Reginald McKenna, Walter Runciman, J. A. Spender, Lord Crewe and Stanley Baldwin.[16]

Although in writing these biographies Trevelyan tried to cast his net as wide as possible, he was well aware of the limitations in his researches, of the additional constraints imposed by using manuscripts still held in private hands, and of the particular problems in writing about those who had only recently died. The life of Bright tailed off after 1880, not only because his impact on politics diminished, but also because of the rise of Home Rule, which was still a very sensitive issue in the years before the First World War – especially to those few lingering survivors from the 1880s, such as Joseph Chamberlain. In writing his biography of Grey of the Reform Bill, Trevelyan was obliged to leave out any mention of the Earl's illegitimate progeny, not out of any desire to whitewash his hero, but because old Lord Halifax, who had granted Trevelyan access to his family's papers, had read the original typescript in which Trevelyan had mentioned the fact, and was so scandalized that he insisted the passage be deleted.[17] And in dealing with Grey of Fallodon, Trevelyan had to pull his punches in the years after 1918, since so many of the protagonists were still in active politics. As he later noted, when undertaking 'the life of a person recently dead, written from papers supplied by sorrowing relatives', 'critical comment on the hero must be used with discretion.' Inevitably, this meant that such works were little more than preliminary sketches: their purpose was 'to supply material for judgement rather than to pronounce judgement.'[18]

In writing his textbooks and general surveys, Trevelyan was well aware that even this degree of original scholarship was unattainable. Except in those areas where he had done research himself, he was obliged to rely on printed secondary sources, and on the detailed work of other scholars. But he was scrupulously careful in gathering the fruits of the most recent research. In *England Under the Stuarts* he drew heavily on the work of S. R. Gardiner, but also made good use of more recent books by C. H. Firth on Cromwell and William Cunningham on the economy. *British History in the Nineteenth Century* owed much to his own biographies of Lord Grey and John Bright, as well as the prewar studies of the Hammonds on social conditions. When working on the *History of England* he read widely in the secondary literature of those centuries he did not know well. For the early period, he relied on the writings of Vinogradoff, H. M. Chadwick, Stubbs and Maitland; and he drew extensively on the work of A. F. Pollard for the Tudors, and of Basil Williams, Holland Rose and his own father for the Hanoverians. Ten years later, his reading for the *English Social History* was equally up to date. The medieval chapters utilized the most recent writings of Eileen Power, C. S. Orwin and E. E. Rich. For the Tudors and Stuarts, he had read J. U. Nef on the coal industry, R. H. Tawney on the gentry and John Saltmarsh on the disappearance of the plague. And in dealing with the Industrial Revolution, he made use of Ivy Pinchbeck on women workers, J. D. Chambers on the effects of enclosure and J. H. Clapham on the standard of living.

For Trevelyan, the second stage in the writing of history was 'the interpretation of the results of the evidence', a portmanteau description which covered a variety of activities. The most fundamental was the evaluation of the sources, the weighing of different types of evidence, one against another, and the establishment of an accurate chronology of events. Since much of Trevelyan's work was done in areas where no serious historian had ventured before, his books are full of appendixes containing detailed discussions on innumerable such technical points. What was the true extent of clerical wealth in England in the time of Wycliffe?[19] What was Garibaldi's exact route from Gibilrosa to Palermo?[20] What was the evidence that Lord Grey considered holding office under the Duke of Wellington between 1828 and 1830?[21] What was the most reliable estimate of the number of casualties at Peterloo?[22] What indications were there that Sunderland's relations with Godolphin and Marlborough deteriorated during 1708?[23] Of course, these were questions that were only of interest to the *aficionado*. But Trevelyan believed in publishing original material where he thought it important, and in making plain, for those who wished to know, why he had reached the conclusions he had where the evidence was recalcitrant or contradictory.

The trouble to which he went in getting his facts right is most vividly illustrated in his extended correspondence with the Harvard historian William Roscoe Thayer, between 1909 and 1911. During that period, Trevelyan was writing his trilogy on Garibaldi, and Thayer was completing his two-volume *Life of Cavour*. Thayer's letters have not survived, and Trevelyan's side of the correspondence is probably incomplete.[24] But his forty letters which still exist bear eloquent witness to a remarkable scholarly collaboration: open and sympathetic, yet also critical and argumentative. They exchanged archival transcripts and copies of documents. They helped each other with references. They read each other's chapters in draft. They corrected each other's proofs.[25] They tried to establish an agreed chronology for the events of 1860. They discussed endlessly the characters of Cavour and Garibaldi: the uncertain relations between the two men; their disagreement over how and when to annex Naples; their different attitudes to Victor Emmanuel.[26] 'It is really delightful', Trevelyan wrote in November 1910, returning some of Thayer's draft chapters,

> working together over the same ground as we are doing now, and with so much the same ideas of the period, and so very much the same ideals of the historian's craft and objects. The differences of our treatment and emphasis are only such as are desirable in a biographer of Cavour and Garibaldi respectively.

As he put it on another occasion: 'we agree wholly in spirit, and in nine points out of ten in detail.'[27]

But for Trevelyan, there was more to interpretation than the sorting and the sifting of the evidence. Equally important were the qualities of mind and spirit which the historian himself could bring to bear upon his material. And Trevelyan was very clear as to what those qualities were. 'He will give the best interpretation', he declared, 'who, having discovered and weighed all the important evidence available, has the largest grasp of intellect, the warmest human sympathy, the highest imaginative powers.'[28] By 'the largest grasp of intellect', he meant a broad range of historical knowledge and of worldly experience, without which there would only be narrow-minded pedantry. One reason Trevelyan disapproved of self-styled 'professional' historians was that they had no other career, no knowledge of any other life except their own. But Trevelyan believed that the more varied an historian's life, the broader the perspective he would bring to bear on his work. As he once explained to Mary:

> The literary historian, or indeed any sort of historian, ought to have a very full mind – a mind full of knowledge of many books and periods and historical personages of all ages and many countries . . . Think what Macaulay gained by the breadth of his knowledge no less than by the depth.[29]

To breadth of vision, Trevelyan insisted, must be allied warmth of human sympathy. Although Trevelyan's relations seem to have been diffident and distant at an individual level, he was possessed, like Carlyle, of boundless compassion for mankind as a whole – a poetic sense of the transience and the tragedy of the human condition, of men and women trapped by the frailty of the flesh in time and circumstance, no less in the present than in the past. He explained this feeling in a letter to Mary in 1926:

> This looking into the past that we spend so much – so very much – of our lives at, is a strange business. It is not – yet it is, that world of the Time Past. It is the romance of that which devotes us to history.[30]

And he elaborated this view at greater length in one of the most justly celebrated passages in his *Autobiography*:

> The poetry of history lies in the quasi-miraculous fact that once, on this earth, once, on this familiar spot of ground, walked other men and women, as actual as we are today, thinking their own thoughts, swayed by their own passions, but now all gone, one generation vanishing into another, gone as utterly as we ourselves shall shortly be gone, like ghosts at cockcrow.

All Trevelyan's work is shot through with this haunting, poignant sense of human insubstantiality and fallibility, the recognition that 'each historical fact is implicit with our doom'.[31]

To grasp of intellect and warmth of human sympathy Trevelyan added 'imaginative power'. 'Imagination' was a key word in Trevelyan's vocabulary, by which he meant the ability to project onself into another place, another world, another individual, by an effort of creative empathy, so that the past, now dead and gone, might be repossessed and become real and living again. For Trevelyan, there could be no history without imagination, and even a book as accomplished as A. F. Pollard's *History of England From the Accession of Edward VI to the Death of Elizabeth*, was fatally flawed because it never took wing:

> The reader ... must not expect Mr Pollard to create an appetite for historical knowledge among those who care nothing for history, for Mr Pollard is not Macaulay, and he does not work in colours. You must bring your own imagination and your own picture of the Tudor scenes. Mr Pollard will tell you what happened, and will comment on it and interpret it, but you must imagine for yourself what it looked like.[32]

But Trevelyan was a genius at 'imagining for himself what it looked like', and his books abound in memorable set pieces of imaginative re-creation: the death of the Black Prince; Shakespeare passing the gunpowder plotters in Welcombe woods; Charles I going to his execution; Marlborough chaffing at Prince Eugene's delay before Blenheim; Earl Grey beseeching the Lords to pass the Great Reform Bill; John Bright making his 'Angel of Death' speech in the Commons; and so on.[33]

Often, in Trevelyan's case, the springs of his historical imagination were released by visiting the scenes of past events: '*This* was the railway station where Garibaldi was arrested, amid *this* ruined cloister living monks once walked and talked, in *this* dark passage William the Silent was murdered.'[34] But the most famous example of the way in which his historical imagination was stirred by the visible memorials of a past time is provided by one of his earliest essays:

> The garden front of St John's College, Oxford, is beautiful to every-one; but for the lover of history its outward charm is blent with the intimate feelings of his own mind, with images of the same College as it was during the great Civil War. Given over to the use of a Court whose days of royalty were numbered, its walks and quadrangles were filled, as the end came near, with men and women learning to accept sorrow as their lot through life, the ambitious abandoning hope of power, the wealthy hardening themselves to embrace poverty, those who loved England preparing to sail for foreign shores, and lovers to be parted for ever ...
>
> The sound of the Roundhead cannon has long ago died away, but still the silence of the garden is heavy with unalterable fate, brooding

over besiegers and besieged, in such haste to destroy each other and permit only the vile to survive. St John's College is not mere stone and mortar, tastefully compiled, but an appropriate and mournful witness between those who see it now, and those by whom it once was seen. And so it is, for the reader of history, with every ruined castle and ancient church throughout the wide, mysterious lands of Europe.[35]

But there was more to Trevelyan's imagination than a vivid pictorial sense of past scenes, inspired by present locations. To him, the past was full of passions, feelings and emotions, and without his own imagination the historian could not understand them. Sometimes they were the passions, feelings and emotions of individuals: Chatham collapsing in the House of Lords; Grey of Fallodon enduring the grief and desolation of his last years. Sometimes they were the passions, feelings and emotions stirred by great events: the outbreak of the Civil War, the successful establishment of the Hanoverian succession, the repeal of the Corn Laws. But nowhere in his work was his power of imaginative empathy more brilliantly engaged than in the first volume of his Garibaldi trilogy. Here, for Trevelyan, was an epic drama: of struggle, defeat and ultimate success; of a larger-than-life character of heroic simplicities; and of a tragic, star-crossed love affair. Never before, and never again, did Trevelyan find a theme which simultaneously so captured and so liberated his imagination. As he later recalled, 'I worked like one possessed and driven by a fierce imaginative excitement. The book bears the mark of something nearer to inspiration than I have ever reached again.'[36]

The third aspect of history writing was 'the exposition of the results, which is, if you like the word, literature.' For Trevelyan never doubted that history was an art; that writing was not 'a secondary, but one of the primary tasks of the historian'; and that it was essential for the historian to take 'great and successful pains to present the results of [his] researches in an artistic form, for the instruction and pleasure of mankind.'[37] It was not just that history was the handmaid of literature: the best history, the history of Macaulay, of Carlyle, of his father, was itself literature. And Trevelyan had every intention of ensuring that his own work should belong to the same honourable tradition. But as he early on came to appreciate, Clio was a hard taskmistress. 'Style', he noted, 'is not as easily acquired as shorthand', and 'the marshalling of narrative and argument is one of the most difficult of all the arts.'

'The labour of writing and rewriting, correcting and recorrecting', he went on, 'is the due exacted by every good book from its author, even if he know from the beginning exactly what he wants to say.'[38]

In Trevelyan's case, his literary apprenticeship was the more difficult because he had, in the writings of his great-uncle, so obvious and intimidating a model. Even when working on his first book, he did his best to avoid 'falling into Macaulayese', but it proved an irresistible temptation. As he converted his Fellowship dissertation into *England in the Age of Wycliffe*, he reported to his father that 'the picturesque details and striking phrases are being dropped in here and there, like plums into a somewhat solid pudding.'[39] But as several critics recognized, the result was altogether too rich. Here, for example, is the rather metallic opening to chapter two:

> During the reigns of the later Plantagenets, one principle of the Constitution was more fully appreciated and more rigorously obeyed than in the days of the Tudor and Stuart dynasties. Not Richard the Second in the wildest fit of his insolence, or John of Gaunt in the haughtiest pride of his power, ever dared to impose unauthorized taxes on the subject without the consent of the estates of the realm.[40]

And here, dating from almost the same time, is the beginning of an article published in the *Edinburgh Review*, so unsuccessful in its contrived exuberance as to be almost out of control:

> When, after the death of Queen Anne, the clouds of oblivion began to settle down on the volcanic mountain of feuds and hatreds that for a hundred years of civil strife had been daily cast up with fire and dirt and turmoil of hell, it seemed as if nothing would ever again disturb the mists of ignorance under which the era of the Stuarts was shut off from the sympathy of succeeding generations.[41]

By the time he turned to *England Under the Stuarts*, Trevelyan had decided to take his prose in hand, and his brother Bob helped him 'to prune somewhat the exuberance of my early style', and to make it more 'chaste'. Bob had urged upon him 'the necessity of slow, careful and thoughtful work at style', and Trevelyan evidently took his words to heart. 'I don't say I have succeeded much,' he told Bob, 'but at any rate I have tried, and am trying.'[42] And he certainly improved, for although the book was written with great verve, the prose was more controlled, more measured, more evocative, and Trevelyan seems well on the way to finding his own distinctive voice. Here, for instance, is his comment on the failed rebellion of the Duke of Monmouth, in which the flowing, rather elegiac cadences of his mature style are already recognizable:

> Of Monmouth, as of Napoleon, tales were told at nightfall beneath the thatch, and his return was still expected long after he was dead. As the march of the man from Elba through the valleys of Dauphiné, so the march of King Monmouth through the lanes of Somerset is to the historian full of social as well as political significance. The record of this brief campaign is as the lifting of the curtain; behind it we can see for a moment into the old peasant life, since passed away into the streets and factories, suffering city change. In that one glance we see, not rustic torpor, but faith, idealism, vigour, love of liberty and scorn of death.[43]

Even in the Garibaldi books, there still remained more than a touch of Macaulay's 'forcible, stabbing style, driven home with illustration and antithesis', especially in his first volume, where Trevelyan denounced the misgovernment of the papal states, and the corruption of the Catholic Church. But by the time he undertook his *History of England*, a growing mastery of the art of managing words, combined with the need to make every sentence tell, helped to simplify his style without weakening his gift for the memorable phrase – as in this account of Sir Robert Walpole:

> Great Parliamentarian though he was, he never valued his ascendancy in Parliament at more than it was actually worth, and always calculated the effect upon public opinion of everything that he did or decided to leave undone. With a very small army, and no effective police, the British State might at this period have been defined as an aristocracy tempered by rioting.[44]

By the early 1930s, when he was writing *England Under Queen Anne*, Trevelyan was at the peak of his literary powers, and stylistically they remain the most beautiful of his books. Whether describing the intricacies of British politics, the complexities of European diplomacy or the climax of a Marlborough battle, there is a lucid and assured authority to the prose, which moves the reader forward from one scene to another with seemingly effortless ease.

To this mature clarity of exposition, when describing men and events, Trevelyan added unrivalled powers of evocation, when describing buildings and places, landscape and nature. His essay on 'The Middle Marches' was a notable early example, and it was Northumberland which, thirty years later, again inspired this haunting opening to *Grey of Fallodon*:

> Fallodon has no rare and particular beauty. It is merely a piece of unspoilt English countryside – wood, field and running stream. But there is a tang of the North about it; the west wind blows through it straight off the neighbouring moors, and the sea is visible from the garden through a much-loved gap in the trees. The whole region gains dignity from the great presences of the Cheviot and the Ocean. Eastward, beyond two miles of level fields across which [Grey] so often strode, lie the tufted dunes, the reefs of tide-washed rock, and the bays of hard sand; on that lonely shore he would lie, by the hour, watching the oystercatchers, turnstones and dunlin, or the woodcock immigrants landing tired from their voyage.[45]

And the same mood, and the same mastery, later pervades the *Social History*, as in this description of rural England on the eve of the Industrial Revolution:

> Indoors and out, it was a lovely land. Man's work still added more than it took away from the beauty of nature. Farm buildings and cottages of local style and material sank into the soft landscape, and harmoniously diversified and adorned it. The fields, enclosed by hedges of bramble and hawthorn set with tall elms, and the new 'plantations' of oak and beech, were a fair exchange for the bare open fields, the heaths and thickets, of an earlier day.[46]

Trevelyan was not a vain man, but he was justifiably proud of his prose. Indeed, he once claimed that the 'writing of my books' was the only thing he had 'taken a good deal of pains with', and even at the peak of his powers, he still rewrote each paragraph four times before it was put on the typewriter. But his delight in creating patterns with words and sentences and paragraphs meant it was more a pleasure than a penance. For as A. L. Rowse has remarked, Trevelyan was a consummate literary craftsman, who was 'possessed' by the idea of writing.[47] Like Stanley Baldwin's oratory, his art was that which concealed his art. His mature prose never smelt of the lamp; but 'what was easy to read had been difficult to write.' And he was a singularly unostentatious writer, in that he never showed off just how much he knew. The learning, though invariably prodigious, was always lightly and felicitously borne. As David Knowles perceptively noted in his eightieth-birthday tribute:

> Behind the trilogy of Garibaldi and the volumes of Queen Anne lie years of travel in Italy, years of work in libraries, and a formidable bibliography; behind the *Social History* is a lifetime of reading, reflection and experience. Of this, the reader sees nothing.[48]

By virtue of the depth of his researches and the breadth of his erudition, the care with which he handled his evidence and the imaginative insight he brought to bear on it, and the style and authority of his prose, Trevelyan created a uniquely resonant kind of history – by turns wise and vivid, truthful and poetic, scholarly and passionate, powerful and accessible. Appropriately enough, it was in his inaugural lecture as Regius Professor that he conveyed, most cogently and most movingly, what he believed the study, the writing and the reading of history to be about:

> The appeal of history to us all is in the last analysis poetic. But the poetry of history does not consist of imagination roaming at large, but of imagination pursuing the fact and fastening upon it. That which compels the historian to 'scorn delights and live laborious days' is the ardour of his own curiosity to know what really happened long ago in that land of mystery which we call the past. To peer into that magic mirror and see fresh figures there every day is a burning desire that consumes and satisfies him all his life, that carries him each morning, eager as a lover, to the library and the muniment room. It haunts him like a passion of terrible potency, because it is poetic. The dead were and are not. Their place knows them no more, and is ours today. Yet they were once as real as we, and we shall tomorrow be shadows like them.[49]

Or, as he put it more succinctly on another occasion: 'Truth is the criterion of historical study; but its impelling motive is poetic. Its poetry consists in its being true.'[50]

II

But how 'true' was Trevelyan's history? Throughout his life, he was widely regarded as a Whig historian, and widely criticized for it, too. Even some of the less obsequious obituary notices suggested that his work was, in some way, fatally flawed because of its 'bias' and 'prejudice'.[51] It should be clear from the preceding chapters that it is too simplistic to describe him as a 'Whig', not only in terms of the sort of man he was, but also in terms of the kind of history he wrote. For his background and his circumstances were too diverse for him to espouse any narrow form of partisanship. On his extended family tree were to be found, among others, seventeenth-century Cavaliers, eighteenth-century Tories, nineteenth-century Evangelicals, and twentieth-century socialists. In his own life, Trevelyan was at different times an Old Whig, a New Liberal, a John Bright radical, a Baldwinite Tory, a Chamberlainite appeaser, a sceptical Churchillian, a guarded admirer of the postwar Labour governments, and a fierce critic of Sir Anthony Eden. And as an historian, he was far too scrupulous in his treatment of evidence, far too valiant for truth, to falsify the past to suit contemporary partisan ends.

The essence of Whig history as practised and preached in nineteenth- and twentieth-century Britain may be easily summarized.[52] It was fiercely partisan and righteously judgemental, dividing the personnel of the past into the good and the bad. And it did so on the basis of a marked preference for liberal and progressive causes, rather than conservative and reactionary ones. It assumed that Protestantism was more admirable than Catholicism, and also that the development of a secular society was a trend to be welcomed. It presumed that the past should be seen as leading inexorably to a triumphant present, and that the past was only of significance in that it led to such a triumphalist present. Whig history was, in short, an extremely biassed view of the past: eager to hand out moral judgements, and distorted by teleology, anachronism, and present mindedness. And Whig historians were men wise after the event but foolish in every other way: arrogant, vengeful, one-sided, intolerant of lost causes and disappointed hopes, and wilfully indifferent to the subtleties, dialectics and complexities of the historical process. How far was Trevelyan's history flawed in this way?

In one of his very earliest articles, on Thomas Carlyle, he spelt out his demanding notion of historical truth:

Inaccuracy is inevitable; dishonesty alone cannot be pardoned. If an author withholds the evidence against his side; if he chooses out one part of a document, which by itself bears a meaning it did not bear in the context; if, like Froude, he relates only what is creditable to one party, and only what is discreditable to another, it is just that he should stand in the pillory, and to the pillory, sooner or later, he is sure to come.[53]

And he made the same point in *Clio: A Muse*, published just before the First World War:

> History cannot rightly be used as propaganda even in the best of causes. It is not rightly taught by selecting such facts as will, it is hoped, point towards some patriotic or international moral. It is rightly taught by the disclosure, so far as is humanly possible, of the truth about the past in all its variety and many-sidedness.[54]

All his working life, Trevelyan was the inveterate enemy of 'the spirit of prejudice' and 'the abuses of partisanship' in the writing of history. 'The harm that one-sided history has done in the modern world is immense,' he sadly observed in his *Autobiography*. 'When history is used as a branch of propaganda, it is a very deadly weapon.' Since one of the prime purposes of history was to enable an educated citizenry to form broad views of political controversies, it was essential for the historian to 'study the past from as many angles as possible', so that all might gain 'in wisdom and understanding'.[55]

Like his friends the Hammonds, Trevelyan regarded his own history as part of a scientific enterprise. He never knowingly or wilfully suppressed material, or quoted documents out of context, to strengthen a case he wanted to make. The rules of evidence and method to which he adhered were part of an effort at objectivity which gave his work its scholarly value. To regard it and to dismiss it as mere Whig propaganda is an unwarranted slight upon his intellectual integrity. As Owen Chadwick has rightly noted:

> Trevelyan was not at all a man to avoid critical scholarship, and it is a misreading of character and aim to suppose that at any stage of his life, his ideal of historical writing was less than the highest, in the sense that he only wished to tell the truth, and knew that scientific methods were necessary to discover the truth.[56]

During the First World War, Trevelyan suggested that the ideal requirements for the general historian, the writer of textbooks, was 'acuteness of generalization, accuracy, sanity, fairness, [and] a sense of proportion'; and he always sought to ensure that they characterized his own work.[57]

But while Trevelyan believed that historians should see all aspects of a question and should present them all in their writings, this did not mean that they should be '"impartial" in the sense of thinking that all sides in the past were equally in the right.' On the contrary, he believed that the historian also had an obligation, having first laid out all the relevant facts, to reach his own conclusions and make his own judgements: 'we may, and we often should, feel that one side was on balance much more in the right than the other.' Like his father, Trevelyan 'had the Victorian belief in the emphatic difference between right and wrong conduct, whereupon he did not take much account of nuances.'[58] And like his Cambridge mentor, Lord Acton, he felt that 'it is a duty of the historian to display a bias for the moral law, impartially applied.' He had no time for 'the tone of artificial indifference to right and wrong, wisdom and folly, which some modern historians assume', partly because it 'saps mental and moral energy', and partly because it gave rise to 'a dangerous spirit of neutrality and fatalism'. For history, to Trevelyan, was all about morality: in particular, late-nineteenth-century, disinterested, altruistic morality. 'I have', he once remarked, 'no philosophy of my own to bring [to history], beyond a love of things good, and a hatred of things evil.' To him, morality was as simple as that.[59]

Nevertheless, while 'moral disapproval' was something of which the historian should not be afraid – and Trevelyan was never afraid to speak his mind – he recognized that 'its expression requires art and judgement to do it well.' When dealing with a religious war, it was unacceptable for an historian to condemn the 'crimes and persecutions' of one side, without doing the same vis-à-vis the other. It was essential to allow for the different standards of morality in different ages and different countries. But 'if the moral standards of an age were wrong, in theory as well as in practice, it is the business of the historian to point it out.' If the historian was confronted by someone totally wicked, like Adolf Hitler, then he had no alternative but to condemn him.[60] Indeed, Trevelyan once asserted that 'if all historians . . . had condemned aggressive wars, including those begun by their own kings and countrymen, we should not be where we are today.' For it was not just that Trevelyan believed historians must bring moral judgements to bear on the past: by so doing, he hoped historians might in turn help to create the morality of mankind.[61]

At the same time, Trevelyan recognized that no historian was ever fully free from his own personal predilections, however hard he might

try to correct for them. In later life, he admitted that his Garibaldi
books were 'reeking with bias': too well disposed to their hero and the
cause of romantic nationalism; and too hostile to the papacy, the
French and the Italian conservatives. This remark may partly have
been provoked by his sense of disillusionment with Italian affairs after
Mussolini took over. And it should also be remembered that in this
context Trevelyan had defined bias, rather idiosyncratically, as 'any
personal interpretation of events which is not acceptable to the whole
human race', by which criterion no history book could ever possibly
be free of it. But he also insisted that 'without bias I should never have
written [the Garibaldi books] at all.'[62] For he had been describing the
doings and achievements of an ardent, passionate, inspirational figure.
And to bring them vividly to life what had been needed was not the
cold, aloof impartiality of the detached historian, but imaginative sympathy, emotional involvement and a close sense of identity with the
subject.

In treating the past, therefore, Trevelyan tried to strike a difficult
but essential balance between dispassion and judgement, impartiality
and emotion, truth and opinion, objectivity and bias. And he took an
equally wise view about the extent to which the past could – and
should – be used to illuminate the present, and vice versa. Like most
late-nineteenth-century Liberals, Trevelyan took it as self-evident that
history's essential public function was to illuminate the present in the
light of the past, to enable people to understand themselves in time,
to help explain to the intelligent contemporary citizen something of
how the world he inhabited had come into being. Only history, he
noted in his *Autobiography*, could provide the necessary explanation 'of
the origins of the institutions, beliefs, habits and prejudices of the
various peoples of the world at the present day.' Without this essential
historical perspective, he went on, 'you cannot understand your own
country, still less any other.'[63]

But this does not mean that Trevelyan was crudely present-minded
and that he saw the whole of history as leading inexorably to the high
point of his own day. In part, this was because he recognized the
distorting effects of hindsight. 'The historian', he once observed, 'has
from time to time to stop himself, as it were, of his knowledge of what
came after.' In part, it was because his strong, poetic sense of the
transience of human life made it impossible for him to regard his own
generation as the triumphant final point of the historical process. On
the contrary, he felt nothing but 'humility for our petty and perishable

present, set in the vast succession of things past, and things to come.'[64] And in part, it was because he was, for much of his life, so genuinely 'out of love' with his own times, that he was incapable of writing history with such a simplistic and presentist teleology. Of course, Trevelyan had a preference for stories with 'happy endings'. But those had occurred in the past: 1688, 1714, 1745 and 1832. There was nothing in *British History in the Nineteenth Century*, or in the *History of England*, or in the *English Social History*, which celebrated the years since 1914: quite the reverse.[65]

Put the other way, Trevelyan also believed that the purpose of history was to bring home the *unlikeness* of past worlds to the present. One of the historian's prime functions, he insisted, was to teach the reader 'to understand that other ages had not only a different social and economic structure, but also correspondingly different ideals and interests from those of his own age.' This was partly why he so admired the work of Frederic Maitland, because he 'showed us that the past, when we suddenly see a piece of it close at hand, was so different from the present that we no longer feel confidence in reconstructing the thirteenth century from the analogy of our own experience and observation in a different age.'[66] Every historian should follow Maitland, and try to 'get inside the minds of the people of the Middle Ages, and of the Tudor times, and of the eighteenth century, and see their problems as they saw them, not as we see them now.' And Trevelyan practised what he preached. In 1926, he gave a paper to the Historical Association entitled 'Some Points of Contrast Between Medieval and Modern Civilization'. And in the *History of England*, and again in the *English Social History*, he was constantly pointing out how important – and how difficult – it was for the reader to appreciate the difference between the present, and the past, vanished worlds he was describing. That was what he meant when he observed that 'the social historian of today cannot really describe the people of the past; the most he can do is to point out some of the conditions under which they lived.'[67]

One of the ways in which the past differed from the present was that religion had then mattered a great deal more, and Trevelyan, for all his early and militant agnosticism, never doubted its force in history. For as he later explained, he 'retained a love of the Bible, and an understanding of the beauty and tenderness of religious feelings', even when he was 'most emphatic in my unbelief.' 'Otherwise,' he rightly noted, 'I could not in my early years have written *England in the Age of Wycliffe* or *England Under the Stuarts*.'[68] For in both of those books, it is religious thought, religious feeling, that provides the mainspring of the historical drama: in the fourteenth century because of popular hostility to the papacy and the medieval Church; and in the seventeenth because the Civil War was a war of ideas, which were themselves mostly religious in origin. One of the reasons he welcomed the new books on sixteenth-century England by A. F. Pollard and H. A. L. Fisher was that they explained so cogently the real significance of the Reformation, and showed the importance of 'Protestantism in history . . . coupled with the name of *Truth*.' And in his biography of Bright, Trevelyan set out to depict him as being first and foremost a religious crusader. It was, he insisted, 'the Quaker side of his life' which was 'the real secret of it all.'[69]

In his later writings, Trevelyan continued to stress the importance of religion. In his Romanes Lecture at Oxford, he argued that religious differences were the key to understanding the history of the two parties in Britain: the Tories were fervently loyal to the Church of England, the Whigs and Liberals were more concerned to protect and promote Dissenters' rights. And in the *History of England* and the *English Social History*, religion was placed at the very centre of the story. It was, Trevelyan noted, 'impossible . . . for the English historian to ignore religion.' This was self-evidently true for the whole period down to the Restoration. But Trevelyan was at pains to suggest that religious feeling continued to be significant thereafter. 'It is a common error', he noted, 'to regard the eighteenth century in England as irreligious.' It was not an error which Trevelyan made. For as he explained in a letter to Mary, 'one of the new ideas brought out by recent historical work is the religious character of the English eighteenth century.'[70] Nor, as the scion of one of the great Evangelical families, was he likely to underrate its importance in the nineteenth, where it remained 'an imposing fabric' until the Darwinian revolution. And in his *Autobiography*, Trevelyan pointed out that for all his brilliance, Gibbon was a 'one-sided' historian, because he 'was by nature insensitive to religious feeling.' Trevelyan never was. For him, religion was one of the 'supreme efforts of the human spirit.'[71]

Even at his most radical, in the years before the First World War, Trevelyan was, on the whole, more subtly and sensitively Whiggish than his detractors have sometimes depicted him as being. He was too imaginative, too compassionate, too much in love with the past, too much duty-bound to seek the truth, to adhere to a dogma which divided men into progressive sheep and reactionary goats, which presumed that the present was self-evidently better than the past, and which regarded religion with secular indifference; between the wars, his vision and his human understanding only broadened still further. Of course, like any historian, he did not always live up to his own exacting precepts as fully as he might have wished. As a young Liberal zealot, he was too much the friend of progress and the enemy of anachronism. His biography of Grey of the Reform Bill was certainly distorted by the knowledge of the nineteenth-century parliamentary democracy that flourished after 1832. And even in his more emollient interwar period, he never really understood Roman Catholicism, still less Anglo-Catholicism. But no historian has ever possessed total tolerance, total empathy, total understanding. Trevelyan's exceptional imaginative gifts meant he possessed these qualities more than most.

Appropriately enough, it was Trevelyan himself who provided the most judicious comment on his own bias and balance, in words which were written about his friend G. P. Gooch, but which seem equally applicable in his own case:

> During his long life, he has devoted himself to historical study and to the cause of goodwill among nations. I think his two qualities are width of knowledge and exact scholarship on the one hand, and a marvellous fairness of mind, seeing all sides of a controversy, while feeling and expressing his own ultimate judgement.[72]

And the most perceptive comment on the Whig historians, and the best riposte to their critics, has been provided by Eric Evans, whose words apply with peculiar force to Trevelyan:

> History is not, or should not be, the story of progress from a lesser to a greater state which can be plotted almost as a line moving steadily upward on a graph. The cruder varieties of such writing have been termed 'Whig history'. The phrase is intended to be dismissive. In fact, it traduces a generation of meticulous and imaginative scholars from the late nineteenth century, whose work is no longer much read (hence the crude facility with which it can be misleadingly parodied), but who laid the foundations for the emergence of history as a scholarly profession in the twentieth century.[73]

III

As Trevelyan said of Macaulay, so it might be said of him: 'In his view of history, he was not such a Whig as he has been painted.' Nevertheless, it was a label which stuck to Trevelyan all his life. When reviewing the *English Social History*, Raymond Mortimer described him as 'the latest, though I hope he will not be the last, of the great Whig historians.'[74] Yet within ten years of his birth, the Whigs had ceased to be a force in British politics, and by the First World War the Liberal Party had entered irretrievable decline. In politics Conservatism was in the ascendant, and in historical scholarship the Whig interpretation came under increasing attack – so much so that, when writing *England Under Queen Anne*, Trevelyan felt moved to wonder 'whether full-dress histories of a period will please the present generation.'[75] Two men, in particular, did not find such books to their taste: Herbert Butterfield and Lewis Namier. The first attacked the underlying presuppositions of the Whig historians. The second mounted a detailed empirical assault on Whig history at one of its most pivotal (and vulnerable) points. To the limited extent that they are known, Trevelyan's relations with both of these anti-Whig historians are instructive.

Trevelyan and Namier were very different men in their backgrounds, in their temperaments, in their careers – and thus in their attitudes to history. Indeed, it is no exaggeration to say that they came from totally different worlds.[76] For whereas Trevelyan's was a life of privilege, accomplishment, success and honour, Namier's was one of unhappiness, rejection, disillusion and disappointment. He was born in 1888, a Polish Jew, the son of a minor Galician landowner. But his father disinherited him, and the family estates were eventually lost to the Russians in 1945. While studying history at Balliol, Namier fell obsessively in love with the English way of life, became a British subject in 1913, and thereafter craved the acceptance of the nation's ruling Establishment which he so rarely got. For most of the 1920s he was without a job, and although he finally obtained academic preferment at a provincial university, the chair at Oxford or Cambridge, on which he had set his heart, always eluded him. In part this may have been because of lingering anti-Semitisim. But it was also that, even by the standards of Oxbridge, Namier was not an easy man. He was boring, rude, cynical, arrogant and unforgiving. He was an incorrigible snob and social climber, obsessed with landed estates and country houses. Yet he remained all his life the alienated outsider, the exiled misfit.

It is not clear when Trevelyan first came across him. It may have been during the First World War, when they were both at different times in close contact with the Foreign Office. Or it may have been during the 1920s, since one of Namier's patrons, Blanche Dugdale, was also a relative of Trevelyan's. But whenever they met, it must soon have become clear that they had little in common.[77] Trevelyan believed passionately in liberty and freedom: Namier thought them, like all ideas, 'cant terms'. Trevelyan was by then 'an ex- or semi-Liberal': Namier despised such men. Trevelyan much regretted the failure of the 1848 revolutions: Namier rejoiced that they had not succeeded. Trevelyan was at best ambivalent about the British Empire: Namier adored it. Trevelyan thought the Treaty of Versailles too harsh on Germany: Namier thought that no terms, however vindictive, could be harsh enough. Trevelyan believed that, during the 1930s, some form of 'appeasement' was the only realistic policy towards Hitler: Namier did not understand the complexities of the problems, or the limitations on British power, and believed that Hitler must be opposed at every point. Trevelyan admired and supported Chamberlain: Namier was on Churchill's side, and had nothing but 'bitter contempt' for the National Government.[78]

During the late 1920s, Trevelyan and Namier were both working on the eighteenth century: Trevelyan on the earlier part for his books on Queen Anne, Namier on the late 1750s and early 1760s. But while Trevelyan had no novel views to propound for the 1700s, Namier came up with a fundamental reinterpretation of his period, which duly appeared in two books published in 1929 and 1930: *The Structure of Politics at the Accession of George III* and *England in the Age of the American Revolution*. They made no impact on the general public; but in academic circles they caused a minor sensation which was to last for the next thirty years. For they blew sky-high most of the Whig presumptions about eighteenth-century politics concerning constitutional monarchy, responsible government and the two-party system – presumptions which Trevelyan (and even more so his father) had largely shared. According to Namier, the sovereign still wielded real power, parliamentary supremacy was not yet fully established, party labels were virtually meaningless, and party organization was almost non-existent. But Namier's greatest bombshell concerned George III: far from being a tyrant, who had sought to subvert the constitution, Namier insisted that his political practice differed scarcely at all from that of George II and George I. The real villains of the time, Namier argued, neatly turning the tables, had been the contemporary Whig polemicists, whose self-serving and disingenuous propaganda had misled generations of historians.[79]

Trevelyan's response to Namier's work was both generous and perceptive. Although not an expert on the period, he agreed to review *England in the Age of the American Revolution* in the *Nation*, 'in order to have the opportunity of expressing my admiration for the work and its author', and also because he feared that Namier might be 'deserting history for practical affairs'.[80] He felt that the book was too 'involved and long drawn out', and thought that some of Namier's conclusions were 'not quite as novel as he thinks, and others, perhaps, will be modified as he proceeds (if he ever does proceed) with the later story of George III's "personal government".' The argument that George III was a nontyrannical king had, Trevelyan observed, been made many times before, while the claim that his constitutional behaviour was exactly the same as that of George I and George II did not 'really emerge from the facts and doings [Namier] so faithfully and so fully marshalls for our benefit.' And while Namier had dealt with 'the moment when the rival traditions of the two parties appeared to be dead', Trevelyan thought that this quietus was more apparent than real, since party consciousness and party warfare revived very soon after.

Nevertheless, Trevelyan insisted that the main purpose of his review was 'to praise Mr Namier, not to question him'. He greatly admired the first chapter, on the 'social foundations' of English parliamentary life, picturing the 'strong, free, many-coloured life of the England of that day', which he thought 'full, profound and felicitous in generalization, based upon a great store of learning.' And he had no doubt that Namier's account of the political events of 1760 to 1762 would become definitive. Even more importantly, Trevelyan felt sure that Namier's approach – combining detailed analysis of the structure of politics with a day-by-day narrative of events – amounted to a whole new way of viewing the past:

> There is a touch of something unique in Mr Namier, a new method of tasting the intellectual pleasures of history. There are so many different ways in which things happen, or can truly be described as happening. Gibbon's is one, Carlyle's another, Macaulay's a third. Each is true, yet taken by itself each is false, for no one of them is the whole truth. In Mr Namier's narrative, things 'happen' in yet another new way – the Namier way. And it is one of the truths.

Of course, Trevelyan seemed to be implying, it was not 'the whole truth': there was no single, infallible method of unravelling the complex mysteries of the past. But he was willing to conclude that 'Mr Namier is a new factor in the historical world.'

This review, at once generous and guarded, was the only statement about Namier's work that Trevelyan ever made in print. In private, he seems to have been less well disposed. He can hardly have approved of Namier's politics, and he certainly disliked his adversarial method of history writing and his incorrigible vindictiveness as a reviewer. In 1937, Namier produced a devastating critique of Sir John Fortescue's edition of the correspondence of George III, and Trevelyan was appalled. 'No one', he observed, 'should write about a man like Sir John Fortescue as Mr Namier has done.'[81] But Trevelyan's desire to keep Namier in the profession seems to have been genuine, and his review helped to get him the Chair of Modern History at Manchester University in 1930. Namier, in turn, was deeply grateful: when talking on that subject, he spoke of Trevelyan with genuine warmth. But this appreciation was personal rather than professional. In later life, Namier claimed that he showed the full measure of his gratitude by refraining from reviewing any of Trevelyan's books, which he regarded as too liberal, too Whiggish, too superficial and too sentimental. Indeed, on one occasion, Namier described Trevelyan as being 'representative of all that is worthless in history.'[82]

Half a century on, Trevelyan's doubts about Namier seem to have been well borne out. No one today would seriously maintain that the constitutional practice of George III differed not at all from that of George I and George II. Party labels, party identity and party ideology have been put back at the very centre of eighteenth-century politics, which was where Trevelyan believed they had always belonged.[83] And while his own account of party development, in his Romanes Lecture at Oxford, was certainly too synoptic, his broad conception of how the history of party should be studied and written ('a new method of approach to English history as a whole') showed a range of vision far superior to Namier's myopically idiosyncratic approach.[84] As Trevelyan once remarked, Namier had 'no sense of the past', and no sense of human reality. And his gifts were more forensic and polemical than creative or expositional. He never did write a sequel to *England in the Age of the American Revolution* (it had been a very shrewd guess on Trevelyan's part that he wouldn't), let alone a comprehensive history of eighteenth-century politics. For all his unrivalled erudition, Namier

lacked creative gifts. He could not write narrative. In some fundamental sense, he could not really write history. Trevelyan's considered
judgement was neither unfair nor unjust. Namier: 'great researcher,
no historian.'[85]

Trevelyan and Butterfield were in their ways as different as
Trevelyan and Namier. Butterfield was a Nonconformist Yorkshire-
man, born in 1900, the son of the chief clerk in a Keighley wool firm,
who was educated at the local Trade and Grammar School. Even
allowing for Trevelyan's Manchester connections via his mother, these
two men were as far apart sociologically as Trevelyan and Namier were
geographically. But while Namier's career as an academic faltered,
Butterfield advanced inexorably from one triumph to another. He went
up to Peterhouse, Cambridge, in 1919, took a double First in history,
and was elected a Fellow in 1923. He was soon appointed to a university
lectureship, and in 1944 to the Chair of Modern History. Eventually,
he became Regius Professor of Modern History and Master of Peterhouse. Yet despite these impeccable establishment offices, Butterfield
wielded little influence outside Cambridge, least of all in Oxford or
London. He never lost his youthful scorn for orthodoxy, and retained
to the end of his life an almost Stracheyesque aura of irreverence and
irresponsibility. He was anti-Liberal, anti-Establishment, and took an
almost perverse delight in the paradoxes and contradictions of history.
And during the Second World War he regarded Hitler with a neutrality bordering on indifference.[86]

In short, Butterfield's was not a personality likely to endear itself to
Trevelyan on his return to Cambridge as Regius Professor. In 1931,
just after the publication of *Blenheim* and *England in the Age of the
American Revolution*, Butterfield produced a slight, confused, repetitive
and superficial work entitled *The Whig Interpretation of History*. It was
written with all the verve and outrage of a young man's polemic, and
sweepingly dismissed the Whig view of the past as 'a gigantical optical
illusion'. Much greater expositional skill and imaginative sympathy,
Butterfield argued, had been lavished by historians on Whigs, progressives and Protestants than on Tories, reactionaries and Catholics. Revolutions had been too much praised and progress too much celebrated,
with the result that history was all too often 'a ratification, if not a
glorification, of the present'. Such Whig history was too abridged, too
dramatic and too judgemental, as the historian arrogated to himself
the task of 'avenging god', 'dividing the world into the friends and
enemies of progress'. Only by detailed historical research, by studying

the past for its own sake and by unfolding the story in full detail, could such errors and distortions be eradicated.[87]

The authors of such misleading works, and the targets of Butterfield's attack, were 'textbook historians who have inherited the top hat and the pontifical manner', and 'the great patriarchs of history writing', who were 'the very model of the nineteenth-century gentleman', who embodied 'the humanistic Whiggism and elevated Liberalism endemic in the generation before his own', which were to Butterfield 'contemporary obstacles to historical understanding.'[88] He always denied that he had Trevelyan in mind when he wrote *The Whig Interpretation*, and that it was Acton who was the real target. But Trevelyan, who by this time regarded himself, in some ways rightly, in other ways wrongly, as 'the last Whig historian in the world', was sure that Butterfield's strictures were also meant for him. Indeed, it has even been suggested that Butterfield had been put up to writing his book by his friend and mentor Harold Temperley, who was also a Fellow of Peterhouse, and at that time Reader in History, and who resented the fact that he had been passed over for the Regius Professorship in favour of Trevelyan.[89] Whether Butterfield did have Trevelyan in mind we shall never know. But if not, he must have been astonishingly naïve to suppose that Trevelyan would not think himself implicated.

Some of the criticism in it certainly applied to Trevelyan, but more to his earlier than to his later work. In the years before 1914, he had been an admirer of the French and the English revolutions, the self-proclaimed champion of progress and scourge of obscurantism. Nor was Trevelyan ever afraid of dispensing moral judgements – though with the passing of time they became less intransigent. But even as an angry young man, Trevelyan was possessed of 'insight and sympathy and imagination', and this, combined with his fierce belief in the pursuit of truth, already transcended the grosser distortions of partisan history.[90] And by the interwar years, there was little in Butterfield's critique which could be applied to the eirenic, conservative, national historian which Trevelyan had become. By then, he was no longer intent on praising the Whigs at the expense of the Tories, and he never wrote of the past so as to glorify or ratify the present. Instead, he was concerned with those very things which Butterfield regarded as the prime tasks of the historian: with 'the elucidation of the unlikenesses between past and present', and with the compassionate study of men and women 'entangled in the net of time and circumstance.'[91]

In any case, within a decade, Butterfield had recanted of his youthful polemic. In 1944 he published a series of wartime lectures, entitled *The Englishman and His History*, 'an avowedly "Whig" book', in which he celebrated England's 'good fortune' and historical uniqueness: 'the continuity of our history', the growth of liberty, 'our national genius for compromise', 'our love of precedent', 'our affection for tradition', and the English passion for preserving 'the silt of bygone ages in the fabric of the present.' All this, he concluded, was 'the gift of the Whigs – partisan at first, perhaps, but later qualified, and finally absorbed into a tradition that is nationwide.'[92] This almost reads like a tongue-in-cheek pastiche of Trevelyan, as does his claim that this broader, Whig interpretation of Britain's history, was the only credible view of Britain's past: it 'tugged at the heartstrings of every Englishman', it was 'part of the landscape of English life, like our country lanes, our November mists, or our historic inns', and it had never been more vivid than 'in the great speeches of 1940'. As a display of wartime Whiggery, *The Englishman and His History* makes Trevelyan's *Social History*, which was published in the same year, seem remarkably subtle and nuanced by comparison. 'We are all of us', Butterfield proclaimed, 'exultant and unrepentant Whigs.'[93]

In fact, Butterfield changed his mind so often that it is not clear how much weight should be attached to his views about Trevelyan at any particular stage in his career. Having denounced teleology and abridgement, and having declared that 'history is not the study of origins', he later went on to write a book on *The Origins of Modern Science* which was far more Whiggish and present-minded than anything Trevelyan ever wrote.[94] Having urged that Pitt the Younger needed more historical attention than his famous adversary, Butterfield devoted himself after 1945 to studying Fox's papers, in the hope that he might produce the definitive biography. And having argued so vehemently that historians should not make value judgements, he later revised this opinion, arguing instead that it was only the limitations of their evidence which prevented historians from reaching morally authoritative verdicts on the events and personalities of the past.[95] In such a morass of confusion and contradiction, revisions and reversals, Butterfield's opinions of Trevelyan loom neither large nor significant; and well before the end of his career, he had effectively withdrawn every criticism of Trevelyan he had ever made during his earlier years.

However upset he may have been by *The Whig Interpretation of History*, Trevelyan never doubted Butterfield's cleverness, and as

Regius Professor and Master of Trinity did his utmost to promote his career and encourage his work. His great fear was that Butterfield was wasting his talents on insubstantial pamphlets of ephemeral polemic, instead of producing important books of enduring quality. In 1939, he produced a biography of Napoleon, and Trevelyan was delighted. 'Now, for the first time', he wrote, 'I am *sure* you will be a remarkable historian, and do big things, if you will get along and write some larger books.' In 1944, he helped to elect Butterfield to the Chair of Modern History, in the hope that this would encourage him to 'get on with your larger tasks.'[96] And so, for a time, it did. When *The Origins of Modern Science* appeared in 1949, Trevelyan wrote to 'say how delighted I am at your great productivity in the line of books of permanent value.' And later in the same year, Butterfield published his most substantial work, *George III, Lord North and the People*, which he dedicated to Trevelyan. 'It gives me the warmest pleasure', Trevelyan wrote, 'to see how productive of important works you have made your professorship. Your range is extraordinary, and so now is your performance.'[97]

Trevelyan's encouragement also took more practical forms, especially as Butterfield began to develop what seemed to be a major research interest in the eighteenth century. When he took up the task of writing the definitive biography of Charles James Fox, Trevelyan did not hesitate to make available to him the papers which he had inherited from his father, and urged him to 'do for Fox the historical duty that has never yet been performed in his case.'[98] And Trevelyan would certainly have sympathized with the criticisms that Butterfield began to mount, during the 1950s, on Namier's interpretation of eighteenth-century politics. Indeed, much of *George III and the Historians*, one of Butterfield's later and most successful books, reads like an elaboration of the doubts about Namier first ventilated in Trevelyan's review of 1929. Inevitably, there was a swipe at Sir George Otto, whose picture of George III as a power-crazed sovereign whose misguided policies brought his country to the verge of ruin, was dismissed as 'the more extreme form of the Whig interpretation'.[99] But Butterfield's main concern was to demonstrate in detail what Trevelyan had already hinted at: that much of Namier's argument had been made before; that the divisions between the Whigs and Tories really did matter; and that George III did have ideas which, while not unconstitutional, certainly differed from those of his two predecessors.

Yet it is difficult to believe that Trevelyan can have had much

sympathy with Butterfield's general approach to the past. For the
giggling, chain-smoking iconoclast, who seemed to be permanently
about thirty-five years old, never really matured into a seriously productive scholar or a major historian in the way that Trevelyan had
hoped and expected. Despite his dislike of Namier, Butterfield had
much in common with him: both were incapable of writing large-scale
works, and both lacked 'the power to create at the heart of the story'.[100]
After his two books of 1949, Butterfield produced very little solid
history, and the biography of Charles James Fox failed to materialize.
Instead, he devoted himself obsessively to studies of historiography,
and attempts to reconcile Christianity, history and the increasingly
secular contemporary world, endeavours for which Trevelyan can have
had little sympathy, not least because they were written in prose 'which
at times reached a point of such Delphic ambiguity that attentive
readers were baffled.'[101]

For his part, Butterfield's views about Trevelyan remain elusive. It
is never really clear what he thought, and perhaps he himself did not
know. But for what it is worth, here is his final summing up, written
shortly before Trevelyan's death:

> George Macaulay Trevelyan remains the Grand Old Man of English
> historiography . . . He has not been the greatest technician amongst
> our historians, and some of his books seem to me to be rather weak.
> But when I put together what I have seen and what I have read of
> him, I wonder whether he is not the one [historian] who most defi-
> nitely bears the marks of greatness.
>
> My feeling about this becomes assured if, to the qualities of sheer
> intellect, I add the ones that come from what I should call grandeur
> of the soul . . . From his combination of qualities – from the whole
> man – there comes a deep human wisdom which is his commentary
> on the story he narrates. His capacity for 'historical resurrection' –
> his ability to make the past live again – and his gift for narrative
> are not to be despised by the academic historian. And few of his
> contemporaries achieved such moments of poetry.
>
> Trevelyan has become the Grand Old Man, and everything seems
> to be forgiven – all criticism seems to be suspended – once one
> reaches the age of seventy-five or eighty. But he suffered a good
> deal in his youth because he was regarded as a literary man and a
> popularizer, rather than a technician in the field of research . . . He
> belongs to an urbane world that is really Edwardian, and as a survival
> of that world he is beyond price.[102]

IV

Butterfield's phrase 'despised by the academic historians' also serves as a reminder that Trevelyan's critics not only took exception to what they mistakenly believed was his incorrigible Whiggery: they also dismissed him as an amateur, a gentleman-scholar, who was hostile to, and largely ignorant of, the increasing professionalization of history.[103] To some extent, this was an impression which Trevelyan himself self-deprecatingly helped to foster. For he was, like Lord Acton, one of his predecessors in the Regius Chair, 'determinedly unprofessional', and made plain his dislike of narrow-minded intellectuals and their scholarly organizations. In his *Autobiography* he depicted himself as a 'traditional historian', who was lazy 'about everything except writing'. He once told Arthur Bryant that he was 'by nature much less academic than literary.' He claimed that the duties of the Regius Professorship at Cambridge were so undemanding that they had left him 'plenty of time for his own work'.[104] In his Clark Lectures on English Literature, he took delight in presenting himself as 'a layman – a "lewed man" as Chaucer would call me – not a professional scholar and critic at all.' And in his installation speech as Chancellor of Durham University, he described himself as 'a man of letters disguised as a don'. Yet while there was some truth in this amateur self-image, it was by no means the whole of it.[105]

As the self-appointed bearer of the family standard of literary history, Trevelyan certainly regarded himself as a lonely and embattled figure at the beginning of his career. 'When I started life,' he later told Arthur Bryant, 'I was very much alone, or looking backwards towards my father.'[106] For during the late nineteenth and early twentieth centuries, the cult of 'scientific' history seemed to be gaining an inexorable momentum. In part, this was because the expansion of undergraduate history courses, not just in Oxford, Cambridge and London, but in the new generation of provincial redbricks, encouraged university teachers to see themselves primarily as professional scholars rather than as men of letters. In part, it was because of the growing influence of the rigorous methods of German scholarship which meant 'the English tradition of history written for the general reader was thrown aside for the crabbed German ideal of the learned man who has nothing to do with literature.' And in part, it was because the increased prestige and popularity of the natural sciences encouraged some historians, eager to defend the status and standing of their subject, to stress in turn the 'scientific' nature of their own discipline. For all these reasons, Trevelyan believed that the 'reaction against "literary history", as it was scornfully called', was 'rampant' at the turn of the century, when he 'commenced [sic] historian.'[107]

This was the background to his impassioned response to J. B. Bury's inaugural lecture as Regius Professor of Modern History, delivered at Cambridge in January 1903. In the course of his remarks, Bury made it plain that he welcomed these new developments, whereby history was ceasing to be the province of literary artists and men of letters, and was becoming instead an increasingly rigorous, professionalized, scholarly endeavour. 'So long as history was regarded as an art', he opined, implicitly endorsing Seeley's denunciation of Macaulay as a 'charlatan', 'the sanction of truth and accuracy could not be severe.' But history, he insisted, as it was now being written and taught, was 'not a branch of literature'. On the contrary, it was giving up its 'old irresponsible ways', and was in the process of becoming 'a science, no less and no more'. The 'furtherance of research' was henceforth to be 'the highest duty of universities', and that research was to be based on the 'discovery, collection, classification, and interpretation of the facts.' This was the new idea of history 'which is gradually being accomplished', and while it was not yet 'universally or unreservedly acknowledged', Bury believed it was only a matter of time before history was 'enthroned and ensphered among the sciences.'[108]

Trevelyan, who was actually present in the audience, responded to these remarks with scarcely concealed rage. It was not at all coincidence that he left Cambridge for London later in the same year, and soon after he published an angry reply to Bury in an early number of the *Independent Review*. If the Regius Professor was correct, Trevelyan opined, then history was nothing but 'a chronicle of bare facts arranged on scientific principles', and 'literature, emotion and speculative thought' would be 'banished' from mankind's examination of his own past. But how could history possibly be regarded as a science, when it was of no practical utility, when no laws of general application could be deduced from it, and when it was impossible to establish cause and effect in a rigorous way? Yet this 'crusade' against the 'artistic and emotional treatment of the whole past of mankind' seemed to Trevelyan to be carrying all before it, so much so that there was a real danger of 'the complete annihilation of the few remaining individuals' who still believed that history was an art.[109] Nearly a decade later, Trevelyan rewrote the essay as the eponymous article for *Clio:*

A Muse. He removed all of the personal references to Bury, and 'immensely improved it', because 'a great deal of it was not good enough.' But the essential message remained the same, and it made 'some people at Cambridge – and doubtless at Oxford – very angry', which was precisely what Trevelyan wanted.[110]

In writing as he did, Trevelyan certainly seems to have overreacted against Bury's words, not least because Bury had expressed himself rather badly. Bury was certainly not 'opposed in principle to the literary art', nor to the use of 'sympathetic imagination'. In vindicating 'the claims of history to be regarded as a science', he 'never meant to suggest a proposition so indefensible as that the presentation of the results of historical research is not an art, requiring the tact and skill in selection and arrangement which belong to the literary faculty.'[111] And for his part, Trevelyan never denied that history was 'both a science and an art.'[112] How could he possibly have done so, given the trouble he took with his own research? His real objection was to the exaltation of the scientific aspect of history at the expense of the creative, and to the uncritical veneration of German historical methods which went with it. For Trevelyan had no wish to see British historians 'drilled' into 'so many Potsdam guards of learning'. And one of the reasons why he rejoiced at the defeat of Germany in 1918 was because he thought it discredited 'German ' "scientific" history', which had 'led the nation that looked to it for political prophesy and guidance' such a merry dance.[113]

But provided it did not seek to establish exclusive claims on the historian's task, Trevelyan was far less hostile to the ethos of 'scientific history' than his words may be taken as implying. Indeed, he devoted an impressive amount of time and effort to some of the more arid tasks of historical scholarship. He published extensive collections of original documents as by-products of his research for *England in the Age of Wycliffe* and *England Under Queen Anne*. Although he described the *English Historical Review* as 'the enemy's organ – the organ of "scientific" history', that did not prevent him from publishing and reviewing in its pages.[114] He may have wished historians to produce their best work for the public rather than the profession, but he never denied the value of the detailed, scholarly monograph. On the contrary, he regarded it as 'the deep foundation of the temple of history.' When H. W. C. Davis, Trevelyan's opposite number at Oxford, died before his Ford Lectures had been published, Trevelyan saw them through the press as *The Age of Grey and Peel*. And he rescued from oblivion the Fellowship dissertation of one of his lamented contemporaries, Roderick Geike, and in 1930 persuaded Cambridge University Press to publish it as *The Dutch Barrier, 1705–1719*.[115]

Indeed, throughout his time as Regius Professor, Trevelyan was far from being the Merovingian King of Cambridge mythology, whose influence was 'largely indirect, for he attended faculty meetings as seldom as possible.'[116] In his *Autobiography*, he gave the impression that he had little to do; but in fact, he took his professorial responsibilities very seriously. He was Chairman of the Faculty Board from 1930 to 1934, was an assiduous examiner, marking two hundred and fifty scripts a summer, and was closely involved in such dreary faculty chores as Tripos reform.[117] To be sure, it is difficult to believe that he did any of these things with relish, but he was far too public-spirited to have shirked his obligations. He played a major part in the creation of new professorships in Political Science, Economic History, Modern History and Medieval History, and certainly had a hand in the election of Admiral Sir Herbert Richmond to the Chair of Imperial and Naval History in 1934. (Richmond's wife, incidentally, was a sister of Mary Bell, who was married to Trevelyan's eldest brother, Charles.) And among senior figures in the Faculty, Trevelyan was in close harmony with John Clapham, the economic historian, and Ernest Barker, who shared his own sense of a non-partisan and all-embracing national past.[118]

It is also still widely believed in Cambridge that Trevelyan was an appalling lecturer. But again this is too simplistic a view. During his early years as a junior Fellow of Trinity, he was generally regarded as a brilliant performer on the rostrum. His lectures were vigorous, eloquent and iconoclastic, 'a joy to all the young men who flocked to hear him.'[119] When he returned as Regius Professor, he was certainly less inclined to put so much effort into his delivery. But he was characteristically zealous in the fulfilment of his obligations. He ran a Special Subject on the reign of Queen Anne and gave broad outline courses on British and imperial history from 1688 to the twentieth century. One of the reasons he was unable to begin the biography of Edward Grey immediately after he had completed *England Under Queen Anne* was that he had to write a new course of fifty-four lectures.[120] And it is worth quoting an account of Trevelyan on the rostrum, written in the 1930s, by the young Eric Hobsbawm. He admitted that the lectures lacked 'that air of revivalism that pervaded Postan's nine o'clocks in Mill Lane, or the massiveness of Kitson Clark.' But the renown of the lecturer, and his unfashionable interest in the constitution and liberty, compelled attention. 'One couldn't think of playing noughts and crosses', Hobsbawm noted. 'One hardly likes to doodle ... one writes.'[121]

Equally important for Trevelyan as Regius Professor was the encouragement of research: given the weight he placed on it in his own work, how could it have been otherwise? Back in 1904, he had supported C. H. Firth in his call that graduate students needed proper training in 'scientific historical methods'. He was involved from the very beginning in the establishment of the Institute for Historical Research, and in 1937 wrote an extended article in *The Times*, explaining the scholarly importance of its work, and appealing for funds on its behalf.[122] In the same year, he urged Stanley Baldwin to leave his papers to Cambridge, 'because the great difficulty of our history school here is the want of original material for our researchers to work at.'[123] And Trevelyan had good cause to know. It remains one of Cambridge's most enduring myths, put about by friend and foe alike, that Trevelyan had only one research student: the young J. H. Plumb, who was working on Parliament in the reign of William III. In fact, he supervised nine research students between 1928 and 1940, a greater number than any other professor except Harold Temperley. And three of them went on to enjoy academic careers of great distinction: J. H. Plumb himself, H. J. Habakkuk, and W. R. Brock.[124]

As Trevelyan's career thus vividly demonstrates, there was no clear-cut division between those 'professionals' who stressed research and craftsmanship, and those 'amateurs' who preferred to stress imagination and artifice.[125] Despite his attack on Bury, it was Trevelyan himself who once urged that there was no point in the scientists and the artists 'forever abusing each other as Dry-as-Dusts on the one hand, and shallow featherheads on the other.'[126] All his life, Trevelyan insisted that history was a science and an art, and judged by the standards of his time, his history was as 'scientific' as anyone else's. But his particular, self-appointed task was to reconcile the evidential rigour of the professional historian with the broad appeal and educative function of the literary historian, to write 'scholarly but readable history.'[127] Nevertheless, attacks on the 'amateurishness' of the literary historians remain to this day part of the stock in trade of the more belligerent and hard-nosed professionals. And especially in the years since his death, Trevelyan has been made the whipping boy by scholars who seem to feel that the best way to exalt their own brand of history is to denigrate what they mistakenly believe to have been his.

The most persistent and pejorative of these scholarly snipers has been Sir Geoffrey Elton, who eventually succeeded Trevelyan in the Regius Chair at Cambridge, but who has rarely been able to write about his most illustrious predecessor with anything other than scarcely concealed contempt. He asserts that Trevelyan was appointed Regius Professor 'without ever having taught anyone before': but this is simply incorrect.[128] He describes Trevelyan as a 'not very scholarly' writer: but Trevelyan's concern for evidence and for truth makes nonsense of this charge. He 'despises' the 'soothing pap' Trevelyan 'lavishly doled out' to 'a large public': but this is merely boorish abuse. He writes of his 'resentment' at Trevelyan's 'offences against moral and intellectual standards': but this is more a comment on Elton's bad temper than Trevelyan's good history.[129] He condemns Trevelyan's 'easy saunter around problems of intellectual gravity': but this is to take an easy saunter around the intellectual gravity of Trevelyan's work.[130] He thinks Trevelyan 'should have been a poet' instead of an historian: but who is Elton to offer gratuitous advice about that? And he claims Trevelyan failed 'to advance the cause of historical understanding': but that says more about the limitations of Elton's vision of the past than about the breadth and range of Trevelyan's.

Professor J. P. Kenyon is no less dismissive, and in the pages of *The History Men* presses home his attack with equally misguided relish. He maintains that Trevelyan did no archival work before he was fifty, that he never wrote a learned article, and that he had only one 'officially accredited research student'. Each of these statements is demonstrably untrue.[131] He contends that the *Social History* 'could have been written in 1900': but even a cursory glance at the references would have shown how up to date Trevelyan's reading had been. He asserts that Trevelyan possessed only 'moderate literary gifts': but there is no evidence to suggest that Kenyon is a reputable guide to stylistic accomplishment.[132] He claims that Trevelyan was an 'insufferable snob', overwhelmed by 'mandarin complacency': but this is unsubstantiated – and unsubstantiatable – character assassination. He thinks that Trevelyan's postwar attitudes were 'socially retrograde': but this ignores his guardedly appreciative view of the Labour government of 1945–51. And he dismisses Trevelyan's love of the countryside as 'bucolic excess': but those concerned with preserving the environment may be forgiven for taking a more appreciative view.[133]

Most recently, there has been Dr J. C. D. Clark, whose views about Trevelyan are no less disobliging. He claims Trevelyan 'unthinkingly absorbed Marxism': but offers no evidence in support of this bizarre assertion. Nor would it be easy to do so, since Trevelyan was rightly sceptical of any claims to have found a single key to historical expla-nation. He dismisses as 'disastrous' Trevelyan's view that the Whig and Tory Parties continued between 1660 and 1714: but this catas-trophe exists more in Dr Clark's mind than in Trevelyan's work, since recent research has done much to confirm Trevelyan's earlier belief.[134] He berates Trevelyan for not paying sufficient attention to the tra-ditional élites of eighteenth-century England: but Trevelyan is wholly innocent of this charge, and his essay which Dr Clark cites lends no support to this accusation.[135] And he indicts Trevelyan for 'shal-lowness', 'superficiality' and 'glibness', for his 'willingness to skate over ignorance with a commonly received form of words', and for 'evad[ing] important problems with a well-turned generalization': but this seems a more accurate description of Clark's views of Trevelyan.[136]

Even as a relatively young man, Trevelyan believed that 'professors' quarrels' were 'always ridiculous and unedifying', and after his early exchange with Bury, he did not venture into the treacherous waters of academic controversy again.[137] But as a result, the attacks made on him during his life went essentially unanswered, and they have only gathered further momentum in the period since his death. Indeed in recent years they seem to have taken on a life of their own, as the same accusations have been tediously repeated, by the older and the younger generations of militant conservative empiricists, even though in most cases they lack any evidential foundation whatsoever. How ironic it is that these self-appointed upholders of scholarly standards are so eager to berate Trevelyan that they seem unable to get right even the most elementary facts about his life and work. Once again, Trevelyan's words on Macaulay seem apposite: 'an undistinguishing condemnation of him' was for a time 'the shibboleth of English historians who destroyed the habit of reading history among their fellow country-men.'[138]

V

Judged by the standards of his own time, Trevelyan was neither the crude Whig nor the superficial amateur that his more extravagant critics have caricatured him as having been.[139] But there is more substance in the claim that he was, as he himself admitted, a 'traditional' historian. Having formed his mind on the great staples of a late-nineteenth-century liberal education, he did not feel any urge to keep up with new, or newly fashionable writing. There is no evidence that he read Marx or Freud or Max Weber or Durkheim or Pareto. He was not interested in debates about the philosophy of history or historical methodology: he believed that narrative was the 'bedrock' of history, and did not set out to look at the past in a self-consciously new and different way, in the manner of, say, Marc Bloch, R. H. Tawney – or Lewis Namier.[140] In the preface to the first volume of *England Under Queen Anne*, he made it plain that he had reached no novel conclusions:

> If I have not produced a new and startling theory about the politics and personalities of the Whigs, the High Tories, and the Moderate Tories, about the characters of Anne and Marlborough, I can only plead, to those to whom the plea may seem relevant, that any new and startling theory would have been wrong.

So it is not surprising that a recent book, devoted to 'historians who had made outstanding contributions to the development of the subject' ignores Trevelyan completely.[141]

Because Trevelyan's major concern was writing for the general public, he never regarded research as an end in itself. He was anxious to keep up with new work in his own field, and did so assiduously after he returned to Cambridge as Regius Professor, but he had a healthy scepticism for the enduring value of 'the latest article'. For he did not see history as a succession of technical exercises in games playing or problem solving. Of course, he wanted to get the facts right and to weigh the evidence. But interpretational questions arising out of his research were most appropriately consigned to the appendices of his books. Since the Second World War, by contrast, historians have been seduced by the allure of inventing problems. Was there a Tudor revolution in government? Were the gentry rising or falling in the seventeenth century? Did the standard of living in England improve or decline between 1800 and 1850? But the scholars who have asked these questions have not been particularly successful at solving them, while the debates thus initiated have often degenerated into arid and acrimonious controversy, and have made no impact on the general public. For Trevelyan, this was neither the right way to pursue historical inquiry nor a very helpful way of getting important history written. The narrative was the thing.

The result was that in Trevelyan's work, the questions are always implicitly embedded in the narrative or biographical treatment he provides, rather than explicitly posed or addressed head on. The Garibaldi books set out to explain the Italian revolution. The biography of Earl Grey was concerned to account for the final triumph of parliamentary reform. The *History of England* was about the growth of a national community. The Queen Anne trilogy described Britain's rise to greatness as a world power. The life of Grey of Fallodon gives the reasons why Britain went to war in 1914. And so on. In each case, the dynamic to Trevelyan's books was narrative vigour rather than explanatory rigour. This was (and is) what friends and foes alike meant when they describe Trevelyan's history as being in some sense 'simple-minded', and lacking in intellectual bite. But it would be more accurate to say that Trevelyan did not subscribe to the view that history was primarily about analysis and explanation. In evoking the past, in unfolding a narrative, and in capturing the imagination of a broad general public, the asking of questions was an important but essentially subordinate activity.

Yet although Trevelyan set great store by intuition and imagination, he was not powerfully gifted with insight into human character or motivation. He admitted that this had been a weakness of Macaulay's, and it was one he shared. His compassion for humanity in the mass was boundless; but as befitted someone not good at personal relationships, he was less successful in dealing with individual historical personalities. Moreover, as a man who 'lived by admiration', and who 'could not easily see faults in a friend', he was ill-equipped to cope with individuals who were – as most people are – a mixture of good and bad.[142] And he had no intention of probing the inner recesses of people's lives and minds in the way that Lytton Strachey made fashionable. So, for all the ardent, imaginative sympathy he displayed, he admitted to Bob that he never got 'quite inside Garibaldi'.[143] His biographies of Bright and Grey of the Reform Bill do not bring their characters fully to life. Both Manin and Marlborough were too complex, too devious, too flawed in their character to lend themselves to Trevelyan's heroic and admiring view. And Grey of Fallodon was too much a labour of love for him to do full justice to the harder, more ambitious side of Grey's temperament.

Trevelyan's traditionalism also came out in the fact that apart from

biographies he only wrote national histories. He took it for granted
that that was the framework within which he should write, and on six
occasions, he produced books with 'Britain' or 'England' in the title.[144]
Indeed, to his critics overseas, this was the most glaring fault in his
work. One American reviewer found the *History of England* to be
'ardently national', characterized by a 'militant assertiveness of the
superiority of English institutions over those of other nations', which
savoured of the late nineteenth century. And in his review of the *Social
History* for the *Annales*, François Crouzet dismissed it as '*un pamphlet
de propagande nationaliste et xénophobe*', written in a tone of '*complaisance
et d'autosatisfaction.*'[145] No doubt to the French, smarting after the
defeat of 1940, it was. But naturally Trevelyan saw things rather differ-
ently. For he was certain that compared with the histories of most
other European countries, Britain had indeed been fortunate. Even
during the first half of the twentieth century, much of which Trevelyan
had not found personally congenial, he still recognized that this was
the case. And he certainly took patriotic pride in saying so.

But he was no crude xenophobe. Thanks to the influence of his
father, he was more a child of the mid-Victorian era of liberal internationalism than of the late-nineteenth-century world of great power
rivalry. Despite his dislike of German 'military despotism', he had a
strong, almost Gladstonian 'European sense'. He travelled widely on
the Continent, and was at ease in every major European language.
Notwithstanding the family connection with the Raj, he was never
enamoured of Britain's imperial mission, and took no delight in 'the
white man's burden'. And for the time in which he wrote, he was
exceptionally sensitive to the relations between the constituent parts
of the United Kingdom. As a son of the Border country, an admirer
of Sir Walter Scott and a friend of John Buchan, he regarded Scottish
history as 'a subject always interesting to me.'[146] In both the *History
of England* and the *Social History*, there were separate chapters on Scotland, and the Union of 1707 was the central theme of the second
volume of his Queen Anne trilogy. Nor could he have been indifferent
to Ireland, considering that his grandfather, his father and his brother
all did public service there, and that Phoenix Park was one of his own
earliest memories. In *England Under the Stuarts*, he was unsparing in
his condemnation of Cromwell's Irish policy. In *British History in the
Nineteenth Century*, he was strongly on the side of Home Rule. And he
also gave Ireland extended treatment in his two general surveys. Only
when describing the controversial part played by his grandfather in

administering public works in the aftermath of the famine was he somewhat unsure of his ground.[147]

It was in his delight in military history, rather than in his ardent nationalism, that Trevelyan most showed himself a child of the late nineteenth century. (Here, again, incidentally, was a link with Winston Churchill.) As a small boy, one of Trevelyan's greatest pleasures was in playing elaborate war games with his brothers, according to carefully worked-out rules.[148] 'I keep dreaming', he wrote to Bob in 1934, 'these nights that we three brothers are playing soldiers again on the top floor [at Wallington]. I always get tremendously excited about it.' Many of the soldiers remain at Wallington today, and Trevelyan never doubted that it was this youthful pastime which was 'one reason why I afterwards enjoyed studying and describing the campaigns and battles, in my histories of Garibaldi and Marlborough.'[149] In 1907, when he was deep in the Garibaldi story, he told Charles of 'the pleasure of constructing, pulling to pieces, and reconstructing the story of a battle or march', from 'a score of more or less contradictory accounts.' And when writing *Queen Anne*, he confided to Bob that he was 'terrified by the fear of its becoming a "drum and trumpets" history, especially in these antiwar times, and especially as I like drums and trumpets so much, provided they were blown a good hundred years ago.'[150]

In retrospect, it is also clear how much Trevelyan was influenced by his upbringing as a member of the late-nineteenth-century landowning classes. From his earliest days, he naturally preferred the country to the town, and towards the end of his life, told A. L. Rowse that he 'disliked practically everything since the Industrial Revolution.'[151] All his books are pervaded by a tone of paternalistic decency which today seems slightly condescending. The too-frequent allusions to 'sturdy yeomen' in the early chapters of the *Social History* certainly pall after a time, and it is tempting to recall Peter Warlock's comment about Vaughan Williams's music, that it was 'all just a little too much like a cow looking over a gate.'[152] But Trevelyan's picture of the countryside never degenerated into the rural nostalgia so ignorantly beloved of the surburban middle class. For all his delight in nature, he never denied that it was red in tooth and claw. Despite his spiritual veneration for agriculture, he recognized that a long day's labour in the fields was backbreaking work. And although he preferred the country to the city, he knew that rural life – in the present no less than in the past – was often lonely, miserable and squalid.

Trevelyan has also been taken to task for his efforts at social history, and especially for his description of the subject as 'the history of the people with the politics left out', which has been much quoted, more often derided, and almost invariably misunderstood.[153] What Trevelyan actually said was that social history *might* be described that way, and he himself only adopted that essentially working definition with some reluctance at the behest of Robert Longman, who wanted a book that would complement, but not overlap with, the earlier *History of England*, in which the politics had understandably predominated. In the preface to his *Social History*, Trevelyan was careful to insist on the close links between economic, social and political change, and he took pains to delineate his subject in catholic and comprehensive terms:

> Its scope may be defined as the daily life of the inhabitants of the land in past ages: this includes the human as well as the economic relation of different classes to one another, the character of family and household life, the conditions of labour and of leisure, the atti- tude of man to nature, the culture of each age as it arose out of these general conditions of life, and took ever-changing forms in religion, literature and music, architecture, learning and thought.[154]

Even when it first appeared, and especially since the expansion of social history during the 1960s and 1970s, Trevelyan's survey has been widely condemned by professional historians, for its blandness, for its lack of concern with class conflict, for not really being social history at all. Arthur Marwick called it Trevelyan's 'greatest disservice to historical studies' (whatever that means).[155] Eric Hobsbawm thought its 'residual view' of the past 'no longer acceptable, if it ever was.' And Sir Geoffrey Elton averred that 'the book sired nothing: when English historians came really to concern themselves with the history of their society, they had to begin by forgetting the smooth sentimentalities of Trevelyan's "history of the people with the politics left out"'.[156] Beyond question, the book has its weaknesses. As in most of Trevelyan's general surveys, the economic side is inadequately treated, and the narrative is moved forward by literary artifice rather than by the momentum of the histori- cal process itself. And half a century's detailed research makes Trevel- yan's treatment of many subjects seem as 'inadequate and faulty' as he himself admitted it was.[157]

But like most criticisms of Trevelyan, these comments fail to take note of the time in which he was working. When he set out to write the *Social History*, the subject scarcely existed. There were the famous passages by Walter Scott and Macaulay, there were numerous inferior 'histories of everyday things', and there were the articles and monographs which, between the wars, had slowly been appearing. In attempting a broad survey of six centuries, Trevelyan's work was, no doubt, 'premature'. But far from closing down the subject, it opened it up. *Pace* Professor Elton, much of the social history done during the last generation has been concerned to look at the subjects Trevelyan enumerated in his introductory remarks. His concern for the victims of the industrialization process, which owed so much to the Hammonds, has continued to illuminate the work of such historians as E. P. Thompson and Eric Hobsbawm. And Trevelyan's final warning, in his speech on the presentation of his festschrift, against the excesses of crude class analysis, has increasingly been taken to heart in recent years.[158] Although postwar social historians seem unaware of it, or unwilling to acknowledge it, most of their work has been carried on in Trevelyan's shadow. The greatest practitioner of the 'old' social history was the first to foresee the scope, the strengths – and the pitfalls – of the 'new'.

In a letter to William Roscoe Thayer at the time of the Parliament Bill crisis, Sir George Otto Trevelyan noted with pride that his son 'relies on the old arts' in his work as an historian.[159] In the years since the Second World War, those 'old arts' were forgotten, ignored or derided by many professional historians. They no longer sought to argue that history was a science, but that it was a *social* science, and to that particular Brave New World, Trevelyan's work had nothing to contribute except silently eloquent reproach. Learned articles, doctoral dissertations, and scholarly monographs, which had been to Trevelyan the means to a greater end, became ends in themselves. Analysis took the place of narrative, jargon superseded fine prose, and seminars and conferences proliferated, with the result that historians became increasingly self-absorbed, and preferred to write for each other rather than for the educated laity. And so it became all too easy for a new generation of grammar-school academics to caricature Trevelyan as a patrician amateur, who strolled in from the Northumberland hills, dashed off a few superficial, mellifluous paragraphs, and then returned to his country walk.

But even during this period of unprecedented expansion and remorseless proliferation, there were still some historians who shared Trevelyan's views: Sir Steven Runciman, Sir Arthur Bryant and Dame Veronica Wedgwood outside the academy; Sir John Plumb, Professor

Owen Chadwick and Lord Briggs within; Dr A. L. Rowse somewhere in between. And in his inaugural lecture as Regius Professor of Modern History at Oxford, Hugh Trevor-Roper reminded his audience that the ultimate purpose of history was to educate and edify a non-professional audience.[160] The last decade has seen a growing recognition that professional history is in danger of collapsing under the weight of its unwieldy erudition; that more and more historians know more and more about less and less; that most scholarly articles and monographs have a readership of twenty and a shelf life of five years; and that academic history, as taught and practised in universities, increasingly appears to outsiders to be at best incomprehensible, at worst ridiculous. Put more positively, there has in recent years been a growing interest in the revival of narrative history, in the imaginative aspects of historical research and writing, and thus in the lives and works of the great past masters of history writing.[161] If these welcome trends continue and intensify, then Trevelyan seems sure to come into his own again.

VI

It should by now be clear why Trevelyan deserves to be rescued from that literary mausoleum inhabited by 'the great unread', and from that dismissive oblivion to which his detractors have so zealously, so ignorantly and so unappreciatively consigned him. But still the question remains: why should we bother to read him today? Unlike poetry or music or literature, the art of history is cumulative: its most recent practitioners tend to know more about the problems of the past than their predecessors, however accomplished. No one today, if they were seeking up-to-date information, would first turn to Thucydides on the Peloponnesian War, Gibbon on the fall of the Roman Empire, Tocqueville on *ancien régime* France, Macaulay on 1688 – or Trevelyan on Garibaldi or Queen Anne. But there remain good reasons why these patriarchs should still be read.

To begin with, like Thucydides, like Gibbon, like Tocqueville, like Macaulay, Trevelyan possessed a mind of remarkable range, power, erudition and creativity. He sought to mediate between the past and the present, and to render the one intelligible in the light of the other. His output was prodigious and his range astonishing, and no British historian since has written so widely or so confidently or so influentially. He wrote passages of greater lyrical beauty and greater poetic feeling than any other historian in the English language, and he never ceased to try to keep the spiritual and imaginative life in touch with reason and scholarship. In his power to recreate the past, and to inspire in others the passion to explore it further, he had no equal in his own day, and he has had no equal since. Throughout his writing, 'one encounters that mixture of learning, personal voice, view of the world and human nature, and knowledge of the past, filtered through mind and art', which is the unmistakable hallmark of a great artist and a great historian.[162] He occupies an assured place in Clio's Hall of Fame.

Trevelyan remains well worth reading not only because of his unrivalled vision of the past, but also because of the perspective his life and work affords on his own times. For half a century, he brooded, with wisdom and compassion, hope and confidence, insight and bewilderment, anxiety and melancholy, on the human dramas and political events of his own day and generation. At one level, his history may be read, like his letters, as a sustained commentary on these contemporary events. At another, it may be seen as a monumental effort to reorient himself intellectually, as all the certainties and landmarks and presuppositions of his youth inexorably disappeared, and as he was constantly obliged to come to terms with developments that he did not like and often did not understand. The fact that Trevelyan was an historian gave him greater insight in understanding that the world of his youth was dying: but it gave him precious little help in accommodating to the new world that was coming into being. To the extent that he did so, the way in which Trevelyan made his terms with his times is one of the most remarkable aspects of his life.

But Trevelyan was that even rarer person: a great historian who was also a great man. He was not without his faults and limitations, and he cannot have been an easy man to know or to be with. But he loved his country: its people and its places, its literature and its landscape. He wrote big books, on large subjects, that were widely read. He was a man of 'absolute integrity, a devastating candour, no nonsense, genuine high-mindedness amounting to nobility, rare justice of mind.' 'It is the duty of man', he once remarked, 'to be intellectually severe to himself.' But that should not prevent us from returning a less austere and more appreciative verdict. In his memoir of his father, Sir George Otto, Trevelyan quoted these words of Macaulay: 'He is a man of genius, a man of honour, a man of rigid integrity, and of a very kind heart.' They were written about Charles Trevelyan.[163] They apply with equal appropriateness to his grandson, George Trevelyan.

Trevelyan was not just a great historian and a great man: he was also an authentic phenomenon. There never has been anyone in British public life quite like him since, and as he recedes into the distance that fact becomes all the more clear and all the more remarkable. No historian since his time has been so well connected, or wielded such unchallenged cultural authority. Even among his contemporaries, the only figure who can be compared with him is the Harvard historian, Samuel Eliot Morison.[164] Both were patricians, at ease with the great men of their day. Both were nature-loving hero-worshippers: in Trevelyan's case it was the hills and Garibaldi, in Morison's, the ocean and Columbus. Both believed that history was about research, imagination, and fine writing, that the Ph.D., the learned article, and the scholarly monograph were the means to those ends, not the ends in themselves. Both were convinced that the writing of history was a public duty, and that they had an obligation to reach the broadest possible audience. And when they died, both were mourned as being the last of their line.

Yet like Morison, Trevelyan lives on, in his books, and his essays, his journalism and his letters, which cast a spell that captivates the mind, haunts the emotions, and lingers in the memory.[165] Appropriately enough, the particular nature of that spell has best been described by Trevelyan himself, in words which were written about Lord Acton, but which are much more applicable to him. For like Acton, but in much richer and more creative measure, Trevelyan possessed

> a width of outlook on the drama of history, a deep insight into the effect of principles upon action, and of ideas upon events, a sense of great issues and their significance, [and] a passionate feeling about right and wrong.[166]

Among his own generation of historians, there was no one who could rival him in possessing 'the largest grasp of intellect, the warmest human sympathy, the highest imaginative powers.'[167] And it remains a constant source of pleasure and enrichment to read books written by an historian so abundantly endowed with such remarkable gifts of mind and spirit.

Like Morison again, Trevelyan also lives on because in helping his contemporaries understand themselves in time, he left his mark indelibly on his times, as his histories written for the first half of the twentieth century have themselves become part of the history of that era. Early in the 1900s, when still at the beginning of his career, Trevelyan declared that what his generation needed was

> a man with a historical style as effective for our age as Macaulay's was for his, who could make the best results of the modern history school familiar to hundreds of thousands, and influential on all the higher thoughts and feelings of the day.[168]

For the next half century, Trevelyan was himself that man, those were the things that he set out to do, and those were the things that he accomplished. That is why he mattered in his time. That is why he matters if we would truly understand his time. And that is why his time matters if we would truly understand him.

APPENDIX A

The Trevelyans of Wallington

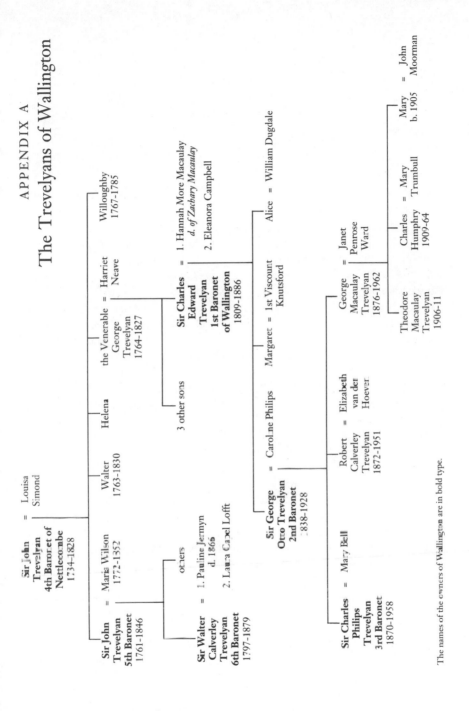

Sir John = Louisa
Trevelyan   Simond
4th Baronet of
Nettlecombe
1734-1828

Sir John Trevelyan 5th Baronet 1761-1846

Maria Wilson 1772-1852

Walter 1763-1830

Helena

the Venerable = Harriet
George   Neave
Trevelyan
1764-1827

Willoughby 1767-1785

Sir Walter Calverley Trevelyan 6th Baronet 1797-1879
= 1. Pauline Jermyn d. 1866
  2. Laura Capel Lofft

others

3 other sons

Sir Charles Edward Trevelyan 1st Baronet of Wallington 1809-1886
= 1. Hannah More Macaulay d. of Zachary Macaulay
  2. Eleanora Campbell

Margaret = 1st Viscount Knutsford

Alice = William Dugdale

Sir George Otto Trevelyan 2nd Baronet 1838-1928
= Caroline Philips

Sir Charles Philips Trevelyan 3rd Baronet 1870-1958
= Mary Bell

Robert Calverley Trevelyan 1872-1951
= Elizabeth van der Hoever

George Macaulay Trevelyan 1876-1962
= Janet Penrose Ward

Theodore Macaulay Trevelyan 1906-11

Charles Humphry 1909-64
= Mary Trumbull

Mary b. 1905
= John Moorman

The names of the owners of Wallington are in bold type.

Dr Trevelyan's Love of Letters

BY E. M. FORSTER

Dr Trevelyan's Clark Lectures for 1953, now issued in book form,* were a great event. The lecture room was filled, not only by his contemporaries, but by the young, and it remained full to the end of the course, which does not always happen with Clark Lectures. A distinguished historian, indeed our most distinguished, was speaking to us as a lover of letters, and that in itself was a draw. But the big draw was the lecturer's personality: his sincerity, his enthusiasm, his unforced courtesy towards his audience, the abrupt changes in his voice, the unobtrusiveness of his arrivals and departures, his occasional silences, and his occasional colloquies with the clock. No nonsense here whatsoever. The lectures abounded in quotations. Some of the quotations touched my heart, some of them missed it. But whether they hit or missed, they possessed inward life, because of the ardour with which they were delivered.

In a book, the lectures have naturally lost some of their magic. They remain personal; so much so that it is difficult not to review them personally. To take one point, Dr Trevelyan's literary loves have more loyalty about them than I can detect in mine. They are more deeply rooted in the experiences of his youth, in the hills he then climbed, in the Border-country or the Surrey he then tramped, in the poems or novels he then discussed with his friends. He has read constantly. But those early experiences have been the core round which subsequent loyalties have accreted, whereas I have practised what I venture to call respectful infidelity. The Bible calls it whoring after strange gods. Anyhow, neither Shelley nor Browning nor Meredith nor Clough nor Housman mean what they did to me, though I respect them. They mean as much as they ever did to Dr Trevelyan.

Though his response to books is personal, it never becomes capricious or arbitrary. He never falls into the error of smaller men who say 'I like that, I dislike that, I may be wrong, but that's how I feel,' and think they are being frank. So they are, but they are discrediting frankness and making it flimsy and unacceptable. Their confessions of faith contract one's heart. Dr Trevelyan's expand it, for he can amplify and illustrate. He is a scholar who respects

---

* *A Layman's Love of Letters.* By G. M. Trevelyan, O. M. (Longmans.) 11s 6d. Source: The *Cambridge Review*, 13 February 1954, p. 292. The original manuscript is in the Forster Papers, 09794F, Rare Book and Manuscript Library, Columbia University.

scholarship, he comes of intellectual and creative stock, he is the son of G. O. Trevelyan, and the great-nephew of Macaulay, and in his recommendations there is a touch of ancestral authority. That is no reason for agreeing with them, but it gives them desirable weight, they proceed from his entire being.

It is significant that he favours the English Tripos. When first it was mooted, he and his friends were against it as 'low'; an exam paper on *Arethusa* or on *Saul?* Never!! But he has come to believe that, with changing conditions, the tradition and study of literature might disappear if it had no fastness in the Universities. And characteristically he adds 'For these reasons, though a layman, I am all for an endowed priesthood, provided there are no articles for the clergy to sign, and no dogmas for them to impose on us.' Who is to endow the priests? 'The modern British State has a generous kindness of a truly liberal sort,' he says, and he may be right, though I wish the British State would not curtail access to the British Museum.

Dogmas lead him to debunking, of which activity he vehemently disapproves. He equates it with excommunication, and with organized attacks on the writers of the past at the behest of some contemporary fashion. I am with him thus far. Organized attacks are bad, and anyone who teaches the young how to snipe teaches amiss. Unorganized debunking, on the other hand, is good, and I defend it. It is a natural activity for each new generation. As a rule, young people resent the immediate past and the gods of the immediate past. It has a nasty smell for them which their elders cannot detect. They want to clear the carrion away, and they ought not to be chidden or hushed into reverence for established names. In the long run their purges do not signify, provided the carrion is merely literary. (When it is architectural other considerations intervene.) So I only share in part Dr Trevelyan's dislike of debunking. On the whole I'm for it, and I'm glad that in one of his lectures he debunks Mr Raymond Mortimer for debunking Kipling, and that in another he debunks me for debunking Scott. He carries out his fell work of destruction with immense spirit, courtesy, and charm, and he leaves me feeling that we have all of us been very well employed.

The heart of this robust course lies (it seems to me) not in its literary recommendations, and not in its incidental judgements, but in its insistence that prose and poetry are both here to be enjoyed, and that our enjoyment of them may be strengthened and stabilized by extraneous knowledge. History may help. Geography may help. Our own early experiences may help, even dictate. 'Literature has been to me a great part of the value of life, and may it be the same to you,' the lecturer concluded, and we believed him and believed in his good wishes. No platform-smarm. We partly believed him because of the timbre of his voice, and on one occasion, when it broke into a jolly crack and 'Bang – whang – whang goes the drum, tootle – te – tootle the pipe' exploded over the astonished audience, I felt that we were near the heart of the course, very near, and I wished that his fellow O. M.s could have been present to join in the fun.

APPENDIX C

The Speech of George Macaulay Trevelyan made on the 12th November 1955 at the dinner in Christ's College, Cambridge, given by Mr Mark and Lady Elizabeth Longman, to celebrate the publication of *Studies in Social History: A Tribute to G. M. Trevelyan**

Mr Chairman, Lady Elizabeth Longman, My Lord, Ladies and Gentlemen:

What a lovely occasion! Here we are, a set of friends, feasting, by favour of the Master and Fellows, in the sanctum of Plumb's College – the College of Milton, of Darwin and, let me add, of Gunning, a name dear to all historically minded Cantabs, and we have been feasting on the Walpole venison by favour of Lady Cholmondeley.

The word Walpole reminds me that I have among my friends tonight Kitson Clark and Plumb, the two men who are at last writing adequate histories of England's two great Sir Roberts, the Whig who placated the Tories and attached them to the modern State, and the Conservative who did so much of the work of the Liberals.

I have received very high honours, both from the Crown and from the University, but this honour, coming from my own friends and fellow-reapers in the field of history, goes nearer to my heart.

Veronica Wedgwood is the daughter of my oldest undergraduate friend, to whom I was devoted at Trinity long years before Adrian came up; she is now one of our most distinguished historians, doing impartial justice to the Cavaliers and Roundheads of the heroic period of our history. Plumb and Habakkuk I well remember as promising young students. They have both now gone very far. As to Kitson Clark, I reported on his Fellowship dissertation. As to Notestein, I can only say that I am deeply honoured that so great an American historian of England should have thought fit to associate himself with this affair. Oxford is well represented by Rowse and Hoskins.

It was only on Thursday afternoon that Plumb gave me my first sight of this volume which you now officially present to me. So far I have only had time to read Plumb's introduction, which says in beautiful English all that I

---

* Source: Longman MS, Part III, 67/20. Note: In addition to Trevelyan, and Mr Mark and Lady Elizabeth Longman, those attending were the Master of Trinity and Lady Adrian, Professor J. R. M. Butler, Professor Donald Robertson, Mr Noël Annan, Mr Cyprian Blagden, Mr G. S. R. Kitson Clark, Professor, H. J. Habakkuk, Dr W. G. Hoskins, Professor Wallace Notestein, Dr J. H. Plumb and Miss C. V. Wedgwood.

have long wished to think of myself, but hardly expected anybody else to say. Therefore, as you can imagine, I like it. The other essays I shall begin to read tomorrow, and I am glad to see that my eyesight, now beginning to fail, will have no difficulty with Longmans' excellent print.

The reason why I have not yet read these essays, as I so greatly look forward to doing, is that Plumb told me there were to be speeches, and I thought I ought to leave time to distil something suitable to the occasion out of my slow old brains. You remember that when Brougham was called on to defend a radical editor for his attack on the Durham clergy, the famous advocate was found on the night before the trial beside the dark waters of Wear. His friend asked him what he was thinking about, and Brougham replied, 'I am distilling venom for the clergy of Durham.' He did it so effectually and so frightened the poor clergy of Durham, that a few years later they gave a large part of their superfluous wealth to found the University of which I have now the honour to be Chancellor.

Well, I thought that I ought to spend the last two days in distilling something for this occasion, but it will be neither so venomous nor so effectual as Brougham's brew. There are, however, one or two little things that I should like to say in reply to the very kind words that have been spoken tonight.

In the first place, Mr Chairman, about Longmans. There is nothing in my life as an historian that has been a greater source of pride and advantage to me than my co-operation with Longmans, a tradition in my family of more than a century and a quarter. Longmans have not only brought out my books, but printed them again when they were destroyed by the blitz, even those volumes which were the least popular but not perhaps the worst.

My *Social History* was indeed profitable, both to author and publisher, but the genesis of that volume was due to Robert Longman, who suggested to me to write such a book. At first I thought it impossible to tear the close-woven fabric of history so as to isolate its social side. However, I took Robert Longman's advice, and it seemed to be just what the public wanted. There is no doubt people are seriously interested now in social history, and I hope this excellent volume with which you present me will have the success which is its due with the public.

And if social history in particular is popular now, more generally speaking history is what people want. My own opinion is that modern conditions of great city life and mechanized occupation have destroyed poetry and imaginative literature. On the other hand, history seems to have come into its own with the public, and I think we may all be proud and glad that we belong to the historical profession which is now so flourishing and important.

But to go back to the question of social history, there is no doubt that it has now a much more solid basis in economic history, which I consider was only begun as a serious academic subject by Dr Cunningham of Trinity at the time when I was an undergraduate. But social history is older than that. It owes a great deal to Macaulay, who in 1826 wrote in the *Edinburgh Review* that historians were leaving to the novelists (meaning Scott) realms that ought to be a part of the fabric of history, and he himself in his *History of England* not only wrote his third chapter, which with all its faults was a great contribution to popular knowledge, but interspersed his political narrative with sections of social history, like that of the Bank, the Recoinage, and the East India Company affairs. A generation later, J. R. Green's very popular *Short History of the English People* was almost as much a social as a political history.

There is only one warning about social history which I feel inclined to give, though this warning is not addressed to any of you here this evening. I mean that some people are inclined to suppose that a larger part of history is social than is really the case. Constitutional, legal, political, ecclesiastical and religious history, though affected by the growth of classes, each has a life of its own, and moves actually in its own orbit to a degree that some recent historians have not been willing to recognize. But, as I say, this is not addressed to any of you.

Although I have not had time to read any of the essays in this book, I see that my friend Noël Annan has written on the families of the intellectual aristocracy of the later nineteenth century. I have no doubt that he has treated it learnedly and well, and it is a very good subject. For whereas the best historical approach to the England of the eighteenth and early nineteenth centuries is the territorial and political aristocracy, the best approach to the last half of Queen Victoria's reign is the intellectual aristocracy, if we may use so very inexact a term.

This development is typified, and was to some degree caused, by the selection of civil servants by competitive examination, a change in which I am glad to think my grandfather, Sir Charles Trevelyan, took a leading part. In the pages of *Punch*, when you get to the 1870s, you find in du Maurier's pictures of social life a type of handsome bearded man, the new intellectual aristocracy, that dominates the scene in the last thirty years of the century.

The difficulty is under modern conditions to get a traditional aristocracy of any kind, and that is why I particularly value the universities and rejoice at their constant increase. For in the universities there is at least the recognition of the value of quality, otherwise disappearing with the disappearance of all forms of aristocratic tradition.

In the third chapter of *The Decline and Fall*, Gibbon wrote that history 'is little more than the register of the crimes, follies and misfortunes of mankind.' When I first read these words as a Harrow boy in 1889, I thought they were untrue. I think so less now, I fear, but we must add that history is also the register of the splendour of man, and of his occasional good fortune, of which our island has had more than its share.

Well, I can't thank you all enough. Your kindness in the matter of this book has given me not only great pleasure, but encouragement when I am beginning to need courage.

King George V's Silver Jubilee Speech

WESTMINSTER HALL, 9 MAY 1935

My Lords and Members of the House of Commons:*

I thank you from My heart for your loyal Addresses and for the words of devoted affection which you have used in speaking of Myself, of the Queen, and of our Family.

Your presence here today, accompanied by the Prime Ministers of the Dominion of Canada, the Commonwealth of Australia, the Dominion of New Zealand, and the Union of South Africa, gives rise to many memories and many thoughts. The Mother of Parliaments, and her children grown to full estate, stand now upon equal terms in common allegiance to the Crown. The unity of the British Empire is now no longer expressed by the supremacy of the time-honoured Parliament that sits here at Westminster. The Crown is the historic symbol that unites this great family of nations and races, scattered over every quarter of the earth.

The United Kingdom and the Dominions, India, the numerous Colonies and Dependencies, embrace such wide varieties of speech, culture, and form of government, as have never before in the world's history been brought into a Commonwealth of Peace. In these days, when fear and preparation for war are again astir in the world, let us be thankful that quiet government and peace prevail over so large a part of the earth's surface, and that under our flag of freedom, so many millions eat their daily bread, in far distant lands and climates, with none to make them afraid. I especially welcome here today representatives of My Indian Empire.

This, My Palace of Westminster, in the mighty heart of our Empire, is the very cradle of our envied parliamentary institutions. Here is the anvil whereon our Common Law was forged, to become the joint inheritance of the United States of America and our own community of peoples. Beneath these rafters of medieval oak, the silent witnesses of historic tragedies and pageants, we celebrate the present under the spell of the past.

It is to me a source of pride and thankfulness that the perfect harmony of our parliamentary system with our Constitutional Monarchy, has survived the shocks that have in recent years destroyed other Empires and other liberties.

---

* Source: *Hansard*, 9 May 1935, columns 1109–1111.

Our ancient Constitution, ever adaptable to change, has, during My Reign, faced and conquered perils of warfare never conceived in earlier days, and has met and satisfied new democratic demands both at home and overseas. The system bequeathed to us by our ancestors, again modified for the needs of our age, has been found once more, as of old, the best way to secure government by the people, freedom for the individual, the ordered strength of the State, and the rule of Law over governors and governed alike.

The complex forms and balanced spirit of our Constitution were not the discovery of a single era, still less of a single party or of a single person. They are the slow accretion of centuries, the outcome of patience, tradition and experience, constantly finding channels, old and new, for the impulse towards justice and social improvement inherent in our people down the ages.

When My Grandmother, Queen Victoria, of illustrious memory, rejoiced with Her people on the occasion of Her two Jubilees, She gave thanks for a long period of unbroken prosperity. Such periods cannot always recur. In looking back over twenty-five years of My Reign, the thankfulness that I feel today is chiefly for escape from danger greater than ever before threatened our land. I can never forget how the peril from without at once united all the parties, classes, governments and races of the Empire; men and women played their parts; the ranks were closed; and, in the issue, strength upheld the free. Let us not, in this hour of thanksgiving, fail to remember those who gave their lives, or who live now maimed or blinded that we might continue to enjoy the blessings of life.

Through later years, our path has led uphill. In the aftermath of war, in a world exhausted by its ordeals and impoverished by its destruction, we set ourselves to resume our normal ways, to re-create the structure of our industry and commerce, and to respond to the urgent desire to improve the conditions of life. We were treading unfamiliar and broken ground, for there had been far-reaching changes, especially in economic conditions. Everywhere a feeling of uncertainty and lack of confidence hung like a shadow over human endeavour. But we have made headway by the earnest goodwill, prudence and stability of My people, and today the Country has attained to a measure of industrial success which gives it confidence in the future.

I am very conscious that these years have brought hardship and often disappointment, and I have been moved with profound admiration for the great-heartedness of My people, and for the steadfast fortitude and unbending will to overcome, which they have ever shown in their anxieties. I sympathize deeply with those who have endured the sadness and burden of unemployment. It is a source of comfort to Me to feel that from these times of trial, there has grown up throughout our community a stronger feeling of fellowship one with another.

I have been pleased in all My work in having beside Me My dear Wife, of whom you have spoken so kindly. I give thanks to Almighty God, Who has thus far sustained Me and My people, and I pray that we may continue to pursue the cause of freedom and progress in a spirit of peace, tolerance, and understanding.

Trevelyan's Major Publications

I BOOKS: AS AUTHOR:

England in the Age of Wycliffe (1899)
England Under the Stuarts (1904)
The Poetry and Philosophy of George Meredith (1906)
Garibaldi's Defence of the Roman Republic (1907)
Garibaldi and the Thousand (1909)
Garibaldi and the Making of Italy (1911)
The Life of John Bright (1913)
Clio: A Muse and Other Essays (1913)
Scenes From Italy's War (1919)
The Recreations of an Historian (1919)
Lord Grey of the Reform Bill (1920)
British History in the Nineteenth Century (1922)
Manin and the Venetian Revolution of 1848 (1923)
History of England (1926)
England Under Queen Anne;
   Blenheim (1930)
   Ramillies and the Union with Scotland (1932)
   The Peace and the Protestant Succession (1934)
Sir George Otto Trevelyan: A Memoir (1932)
Grey of Fallodon (1937)
The English Revolution, 1688–89 (1938)
Trinity College: An Historical Sketch (1943)
English Social History (1944)
An Autobiography and Other Essays (1949)
A Layman's Love of Letters (1954)

2 BOOKS: AS EDITOR:

The Peasants' Rising and the Lollards (with E. Powell, 1899)
English Songs of Italian Freedom (1911)
The Poetical Works of George Meredith (1912)
Macaulay's Lays of Ancient Rome and Other Historical Poems (1928)

Select Documents for Queen Anne's Reign Down to the Union with Scotland,
   1702–7 (1929)
Bolingbroke's Defence of the Treaty of Utrecht (1932)
The Seven Years of William IV: A Reign Cartooned by J. Doyle (1952)
Carlyle: An Anthology (1953)
Meredith: Selected Poetical Works (1955)

3 BOOKS: AS CONTRIBUTOR:

'Past and Future', in C. F. G. Masterman (ed.), *The Heart of The Empire* (1901),
   pp. 398–415.
'The Work of the Unit', in Anon, *The Record of the First British Red Cross Unit
   for Italy* (n.d., ?1919), pp. 9–53.
'The Age of Johnson', in A. S. Turberville (ed.), *Johnson's England: An Account
   of the Life and the Manners of His Age* (1933), pp. 1–13.
'Amenities and the State', in C. Williams-Ellis (ed.), *Britain and the Beast*
   (1937), pp. 183–6.

4 ESSAYS, LECTURES AND PAMPHLETS:

De Haeretico Comburendo, or the Ethics of Religious Conformity (1911)
The Servians and Austria (1914)
***Englishmen and Italians: Some Aspects of Their Relations, Past and Present* (1919)
The War and the European Revolution in Relation to History (1920)
The Historical Causes of the Present State of Affairs in Italy (1923)
*****The Two-Party System in English Political History* (1926)
****The Present Position of History* (1927)
Must England's Beauty Perish? (1929)
*****The Calls and Claims of Natural Beauty* (1931)
*****History and the Reader* (1945)
Biography: A Reader's Guide (1947)
English Literature and Its Readers (1951)
*The Speech of George Macaulay Trevelyan, made on the 12th November 1955 at
   the dinner in Christ's College Cambridge, given by Mr Mark and Lady Elizabeth
   Longman, to celebrate the publication of* Studies in Social History: A Tribute
   to G. M. Trevelyan (1955)

5 ARTICLES:

'An Account of the Rising of 1381', *English Historical Review*, xiii (1898),
   pp. 509–22.
'Carlyle as an Historian', *Nineteenth Century*, xlvi (1899), pp. 493–503.
'Alexander Leslie and Prince Rupert', *Edinburgh Review*, cxci (1900),
   pp. 429–54.

'Restoration Regime in Scotland', *Edinburgh Review*, cxcii (1900),
   pp. 478–504.
**'The News of Ramillies', *Cambridge Review*, (1901), pp. v–vii.
'The White Peril', *Nineteenth Century*, l (1901), pp. 1043–55.
*'The Latest View of History', *Independent Review*, i (1903–4), pp. 395–414.
'The Phantom Crossways', *Independent Review*, ii (1904), pp. 493–6.
'The Poetry of George Meredith', *Independent Review*, iii (1904), pp. 234–55.
'Carlyle, Cromwell, and Professor Firth', *Independent Review*, iv (1904–5),
   pp. 302–8.
'Professor Firth's Inaugural Lecture', *Independent Review*, iv (1904–5),
   pp. 629–34.
'On Religious Conformity', *Independent Review*, iv (1904–5), pp. 374–92.
*'The Middle Marches', *Independent Review*, v (1905), pp. 336–51.
'Optimism and Mr Meredith: A Reply', *Independent Review*, vi (1905),
   pp. 42–56.
'The Great Conservative', *Independent Review*, vi (1905), pp. 224–9.
'Henry Sidgwick', *Independent Review*, vi (1905), pp. 231–40.
*'Poetry and Rebellion', *Independent Review*, vii (1905), pp. 101–20.
'Political History', *Independent Review*, vii (1905), pp. 356–60.
'Party Loyalty in Evil Days', *Independent Review*, viii (1906), pp. 348–52.
'Sentimentalist or Tiger', *Independent Review*, ix (1906), pp. 234–40.
*'If Napoleon Had Won the Battle of Waterloo', *Westminster Gazette*, xxx
   (1907), pp. 6–7.
'The War Journals of Garibaldi's Englishman: J. W. Peard', *Cornhill Magazine*,
   xcvii (1908), pp. 96–110, 812–30.
'Garibaldi in South America: A New Document', *Cornhill Magazine*, ciii
   (1911), pp. 391–6.
'A Holiday Among the Servians', *Contemporary Review*, civ (1913),
   pp. 153–63.
'Serbia Revisited', *Contemporary Review*, cvii (1915), pp. 273–83.
'Austria-Hungary and Serbia', *Fortnightly Review*, ciii (1915), pp. 978–86.
'From Waterloo to the Marne', *Quarterly Review*, ccxxix (1918), pp. 73–90.
'The Four Great Wars', *Edinburgh Review*, ccviii (1918), pp. 265–75.
**'The Two Carlyles', *Cornhill Magazine*, cxvii (1918), pp. 562–73.
'The Number of Casualties at Peterloo', *History*, vii (1922), pp. 200–5.
***'History and Fiction', *Cornhill Magazine*, cxxv (1922), pp. 527–39.
'History and Literature', *History*, ix (1924), pp. 81–91.
'Some Points of Contrast Between Medieval and Modern Civilization',
   History, xi (1926), pp. 1–14.
'Peterborough and Barcelona, 1705', *Cambridge Historical Journal*, iii (1931),
   pp. 253–9.
'The "Jersey" Period of the Negotiations Leading to the Peace of Utrecht',
   English Historical Review, xlix (1934), pp. 100–5.

'Sir George Otto Trevelyan', *DNB, 1922–30* (1937), pp. 853–6.

'Address to the Navy Records Society', *The Naval Review*, xxvi (1938), pp. 581–7.

'Sir Edward Grey', *DNB, 1931–40* (1949), pp. 366–75.

****'Admiral Sir Herbert Richmond', *Proceedings of the British Academy*, xxxii (1946), pp. 325–37.

****'Sir John Clapham', *Economic Journal*, lvi (1946), pp. 499–507.

****'Bias in History', *History*, xxxii (1947), pp. 1–15.

Note: This list makes no claim to comprehensiveness, and leaves out prefaces and introductions to books by other authors, all of Trevelyan's journalism, and his many reviews in scholarly periodicals and in newspapers. In recycling his early essays, Trevelyan was somewhat cavalier. They were first collected in *Clio: A Muse*, which was republished, with some pieces removed, and new items added, as *The Recreations of an Historian*. In 1930 a second edition of *Clio* was published, which contained further alterations and additions. A second selection was made, from among his later writings, for his *Autobiography and Other Essays*. To make matters more complex, Trevelyan often revised his essays before republishing, and also included pieces which had not been in print before. The location of the pieces that *were* reissued is as follows:

* in *Clio: A Muse*
** in *The Recreations of an Historian*
*** in *Clio: A Muse* (second edition)
**** in *An Autobiography and Other Essays*

APPENDIX F

Trevelyan's Papers

In the first paragraph of his brief and reticent *Autobiography*, Trevelyan included this stern injunction: 'May my malison alight on anyone who attempts to publish any of the scrawls that were once my letters.' And in his will, Trevelyan directed that 'my letters are never to be published, and that no life or memoir of me is to be written.' But extensive extracts from his letters have already been published by Owen Chadwick, Mary Moorman, Joseph M. Hernon, and Humphrey Trevelyan, and much of his correspondence survives in archives in Britain and North America. The following collections have been consulted during the preparation of this book:

Additional Manuscripts (Cambridge University Library)
Additional Manuscripts (Trinity College, Cambridge)
Lord Adrian Papers (in the possession of the present Lord Adrian)
Stanley Baldwin Papers (Cambridge University Library)
Berg Collection (New York Public Library)
Oscar Browning Papers (King's College, Cambridge)
Arthur Bryant Papers (Liddell Hart Centre for Military Archives,
    Kings College, London)
Herbert Butterfield Papers (Cambridge University Library)
James Bryce Papers (Bodleian Library, Oxford University)
John Buchan Papers (Queen's University, Kingston, Ontario)
Cambridgeshire Collection (Cambridge City Library)
Joseph Chamberlain Papers (University of Birmingham)
Willard Connely Papers (Harry Ransome Humanities Research Center,
    University of Texas at Austin)
Lord Crewe Papers (Cambridge University Library)
Geoffrey Dawson Papers (Bodleian Library, Oxford)
C. R. Fay Papers (King's College, Cambridge)
H. A. L. Fisher Papers (Bodleian Library, Oxford University)
Foreign Office Papers (Public Record Office)
E. M. Forster Papers (Rare Book and Manuscript Library, Columbia
    University, New York)
E. M. Forster Papers (King's College, Cambridge)
C. J. Fox Papers (British Library)

Roger Fry Papers (King's College, Cambridge)
J. L. and Barbara Hammond Papers (Bodleian Library, Oxford)
Maurice Hankey Papers (Churchill College, Cambridge)
Lord Kennet Papers (Cambridge University Library)
J. M. Keynes Papers (King's College, Cambridge)
Longman Papers (Reading University)
Houghton Mifflin Papers (Houghton Library, Harvard University)
Naomi Mitchison Papers (Rare Book and Manuscript Library, Columbia
    University, New York)
Lady Ottoline Morrell Papers (Harry Ransome Humanities Research
    Center, University of Texas at Austin)
Thomas Sturge Moore Papers (University of London)
Gilbert Murray Papers (Bodleian Library, Oxford University)
Allen Nevins Papers (Rare Book and Manuscript Library, Columbia
    University, New York)
A. F. Pollard Papers (University of London)
Grant Richards Papers (Library of Congress, Washington DC)
William Rothenstein Papers (Houghton Library, Harvard University)
Walter Runciman Papers (University of Newcastle upon Tyne)
Bertrand Russell Papers (McMaster University, Hamilton, Ontario)
Herbert Samuel Papers (House of Lords Record Office, London)
Siegfried Sassoon Papers (Harry Ransome Humanities Research
    Center, University of Texas at Austin)
R. W. Seton-Watson Papers (School of Slavonic and East European
    Studies, University of London)
J. T. Sheppard Papers (King's College, Cambridge)
Lord Simon Papers (Bodleian Library, Oxford University)
Thomas Marshall Spaulding Papers (Bentley Historical Library, University of
    Michigan)
J. A. Spender Papers (British Library)
Lytton Strachey Papers (British Library)
Joseph Sturge Papers (British Library)
William Roscoe Thayer Papers (Houghton Library, Harvard University)
C. P. Trevelyan Papers (University of Newcastle upon Tyne)
G. M. Trevelyan Papers (Harry Ransome Humanities Research Center,
    University of Texas at Austin)
G. M. Trevelyan Papers (in the possession of Mrs Mary Moorman)
G. O. Trevelyan Papers (University of Newcastle upon Tyne)
R. C. Trevelyan Papers (Trinity College, Cambridge)
Trevelyan Wills (Somerset House, London)
University Archives (University of Durham)
Leonard Woolf Papers (University of Sussex)
Francis Brett Young Papers (University of Birmingham)

A Note on Sources

All references to archival collections listed in Appendix F, and to works by Trevelyan included in Appendix E, are given in the notes in abbreviated form. Unless otherwise stated, all references to Trevelyan's books are to the first editions. Where Trevelyan's essays were republished, references are to the appropriate book and edition of collected articles, unless otherwise stated. Only those writings not listed in Appendix E are cited in full. Since the references to other secondary sources in each chapter constitute what is in effect a running bibliography, I have dispensed with a separate list of further reading. In each chapter, references to such works are given in full with every first citation, and are abbreviated thereafter. The place of publication is the United Kingdom, unless otherwise stated.

List of Abbreviations

THE TREVELYAN FAMILY:

MM	Mary Moorman (née Trevelyan)
CT	Lady Caroline Trevelyan (née Philips)
CPT	Sir Charles Philips Trevelyan
GMT	George Macaulay Trevelyan
GOT	Sir George Otto Trevelyan
HT	Humphrey, Baron Trevelyan
JPT	Janet Penrose Trevelyan (née Ward)
RT	Raleigh Trevelyan
RCT	Robert Calverley Trevelyan ('Bob')

OTHER ABBREVIATIONS:

AHR	*American Historical Review*
Chadwick	W. O. Chadwick, *Freedom and the Historian* (1969)
DNB	*Dictionary of National Biography*
EHR	*English Historical Review*
FO	Foreign Office
HRHRC	Harry Ransome Humanities Research Center
Moorman	Mary Moorman, *George Macaulay Trevelyan: A Memoir* (1980)
PBA	*Proceedings of the British Academy*
Plumb	*The Collected Essays of J. H. Plumb*, vol. i, *The Making of an Historian* (1988)
PRO	Public Record Office
Rowse	A. L. Rowse, *Memories of Men and Women* (1980)
TLS	*Times Literary Supplement*

Notes

NOTES TO THE PREFACE

1 GMT, 'Thomas Carlyle as a Historian', the *Listener*, 2 October 1947, p. 567.

2 For 'public moralists', see S. Collini, *Public Moralists: Political Thought and Intellectual Life in Britain, 1850–1930* (1991), esp. pp. 2–3, 57–58. For 'cultural authority', see R. Jann, 'From Amateur to Professional: The Case of the Oxbridge Historians', *Journal of British Studies*, xxii (1983), pp. 122–147.

3 Lord Adrian, 'George Macaulay Trevelyan, 1876–1962', *Biographical Memoirs of Fellows of the Royal Society*, ix (1963), pp. 315–321; Sir George Clark, 'George Macaulay Trevelyan, 1876–1962', *PBA*, xlix (1963), pp. 375–386; J. R. M. Butler, 'George Macaulay Trevelyan', *DNB*, 1961–70 (1981), pp. 1015–17. See also *The Times*, 23 July 1962.

4 Moorman; HT, *Public and Private* (1980), pp. 148–168.

5 A. Briggs, 'G. M. Trevelyan: The Uses of Social History', in *The Collected Papers of Asa Briggs*, vol. ii, *Images, Problems, Standpoints, Forecasts* (1985), pp. 236–252; idem, 'Introduction' to *History of England* (1973 edn.), pp. xxii–xxxiv; idem, 'General Introduction', to *English Social History* (1978 edn.), pp. ix–xvii; Chadwick; G. Kitson Clark, 'George Macaulay Trevelyan as an Historian: Charm'd Magic Casements', *Durham University Journal*, lv (1962), pp. 1–4; Plumb, pp. 180–204; B.

Wormald, 'Everybody's History', the *Listener*, 4 October 1962, pp. 505–507; J. Clive, 'Trevelyan: The Muse or the Museum?', the *Nation*, 16 February 1963, pp. 143–5, reprinted in idem, *Not By Fact Alone: Essays on the Writing and Reading of History* (New York, 1989), pp. 279–285; Rowse, pp. 94–132.

6 J. M. Hernon, 'The Last Whig Historian and Consensus History: George Macaulay Trevelyan, 1876–1962', *AHR*, lxxxi (1976), pp. 66–97.

7 W. L. Arnstein, 'George Macaulay Trevelyan and the Art of History: A Centenary Appraisal', *Midwest Quarterly*, xviii (1976), pp. 78–97; J. W. Osborne, 'The Endurance of "Literary" History in Great Britain: Charles Oman, G. M. Trevelyan and the Genteel Tradition', *Clio*, ii (1972), pp. 7–18; H. R. Winkler, 'George Macaulay Trevelyan', in W. S. Halperin (ed.), *Some Twentieth-Century Historians* (Chicago, 1961), pp. 32–55.

8 H. Butterfield, *The Whig Interpretation of History* (1931); idem, *The Englishman and His History* (1944); M. Cowling, *Religion and Public Doctrine in Modern England* (1980), pp. 222–228.

9 G. R. Elton, *The Practice of History* (1967), pp. 18–19, 106–107; G. R. Elton and R. W. Fogel, *Which Road to the Past? Two Kinds of History* (1984), pp. 75, 107; G. R. Elton, 'G. M. Trevelyan', in G. Smith (ed.), *1000 Makers of the Twentieth Century*

(1971), unpaginated entry; J. P. Kenyon, *The History Men* (1983), pp. 76, 172–177, 226–235; J. C. D. Clark, *English Society, 1688–1832* (1985), p. 43; idem, *Revolution and Rebellion: State and Society in England in the Seventeenth and Eighteenth Centuries* (1986), pp. 18–19, 144–145; A. Marwick, *The Nature of History* (1970 edn.), pp. 56–60.

10 Will of GMT, 1 March 1960, clause 3 (b).

11 *Autobiography*, p. 1; Will of GMT, 1 March 1960, clause 3 (b).

12 Bryce MS, 18 f 68, GOT to Bryce, 1 May 1915.

13 L. Colley, *Namier* (1989).

14 N. Nicolson (ed.), '*The Sickle Side of the Moon': The Letters of Virginia Woolf*, vol. v, *1932–1935* (1979), p. 368.

NOTES TO CHAPTER 1: The Life and the Man

1 For the general background, see D. Wooster (ed.), *Selections from the Literary and Artistic Remains of Paulina Jermyn Trevelyan* (1879); V. Surtees (ed.), *Reflections of a Friendship: John Ruskin's Letters to Pauline Trevelyan, 1848–1866* (1979); RT, *A Pre-Raphaelite Circle* (1978); N. Pevsner, *The Buildings of England: Northumberland* (1979 edn.), pp. 307–308.

2 CPT MS, 242, GMT to GOT and CT, 2 June 1918. See also GOT MS 94, GMT to GOT, 20 November 1901, and *Autobiography*, pp. 24–25.

3 HT, *Public and Private* (1980), p. 111.

4 A. Ryan, *Bertrand Russell: A Political Life* (1988), pp. 2–3.

5 GMT to RT, 4 March 1946, letter in the possession of RT.

6 HT, *Public and Private*, p. 107; *George Otto Trevelyan*, pp. 1–5.

7 J. Payne Collier (ed.), *Trevelyan Papers prior to 1558*, Camden Society, Old Series, vol. lxvii (1857); idem, *Trevelyan Papers*, Part ii, AD 1446–1643, Camden Society, Old Series, vol. lxxxiv (1863); Sir W. C. Trevelyan and Sir C. E. Trevelyan (eds.), *Trevelyan Papers*, Part iii, Camden Society, Old Series, vol. cv (1872); J. Burke and J. B. Burke, *A Genealogical and Heraldic History of the Extinct and Dormant Baronetcies of England, Ireland and Scotland* (2nd edn., 1841), pp. 63–64.

8 J. Bateman, *The Great Landowners of Great Britain and Ireland* (4th. edn., 1883, ed. D. Spring, 1971), p. 448.

9 K. Middlemas (ed.), *Thomas Jones: Whitehall Diary*, vol. 1, *1916–1925* (1969), pp. 268–269; D. Cannadine, *The Decline and Fall of the British Aristocracy* (1990), pp. 424–425; RT, *The Golden Oriole* (New York, 1988), p. 15.

10 E. J. Trevelyan, *The Law Relating to Minors in the Presidency of Bengal* (1878); idem, *The Hindu Laws of Inheritance* (1910); idem, *India and the War* (1914); idem, *The Constitution and Jurisdiction of Courts of Civil Justice in British India* (1923).

11 HT, *The Middle East in Revolution* (1970); idem, *The India We Left* (1972); idem, *Diplomatic Channels* (1973); idem, *Public and Private*, pp. 3–103; A. Nutting, 'Humphrey, Baron Trevelyan', *DNB, 1981–1985* (1990), p. 395; J. Pope-Hennessy, *Learning to Look* (1991), pp. 201–202, 206, 217–218.

12 G. Kitson Clark, 'Statesman in Disguise: Reflexions on the History of the Neutrality of the Civil Service', *Historical Journal*, ii (1959), pp. 19–39; I. Klein, 'Wilson vs Trevelyan: Finance and Modernization in India after 1857', *Indian Economic and Social History Review*, vii (1970), pp. 91–107.

13 J. Hart, 'Sir Charles Trevelyan at the Treasury', *EHR*, lxxv (1960), pp. 92–110; E. T. Hughes, 'Sir Charles Trevelyan and Civil Service Reform, 1853–5', *EHR*, xliv (1949), pp. 53–88, 206–234; C. E. Trevelyan, *The Purchase System in the British Army* (1867); RT, *Golden Oriole*, p. 13; Rowse, pp. 101, 119.

14 *George Otto Trevelyan*, pp. 138–139, 143–144; D. G. Gordon, 'Sir George Otto Trevelyan', in H. Ausubel, J. Bartlet Brebner and E. M. Hunt (eds.), *Some Modern Historians of Britain: Essays in Honour of R. L. Schuyler* (New York, 1951), pp. 172–173. Many of TR's letters to GOT are printed in E. E. Morrison and J. M. Blum (eds.), *The Letters of Theodore Roosevelt* (8 vols., Cambridge, Mass., 1951–4).

15 For a full account of his life, see A. J. A. Morris, *C. P. Trevelyan, 1870–1958: Portrait of a Radical* (1977).

16 *Autobiography*, pp. 42–43. Between them, GOT and CT left £703,000.

17 G. M. Young, *Last Essays* (1950), p. 73; CPT MS 237 (3), GMT to CPT, 23 December 1905.

18 RT, *Golden Oriole*, pp. 144–50, 332–337, 375–381, 389–397; HT, *Public and Private*, pp. 123–125; *George Otto Trevelyan*, pp. 91–92, 120–121.

19 HT, *Public and Private*, pp. 129–130, 132–134; C. V. Wedgwood in the *Observer*, 22 July 1962.

20 Rowse, pp. 100, 114; Sir John Habakkuk to the author, 21 September 1990.

21 The correspondence is in PRO, FO 369/20, file 35,235, nos. 35,235; 39,794; 40,211; covering the period 18 October 1906 to 4 December 1906.

22 Thayer MS, GMT to Thayer, 30 September 1910; MM, GMT MS, GMT to MM, 6 March 1934; *Autobiography*, p. 47.

23 GOT, Will, 10 February 1928, clauses 10–11; *The Times*, 6 December 1928; Fox MS, vol. xliii, ff 148–50, G. Parsloe to GMT, 28 January 1932; Butterfield MS, Box T, GMT to Butterfield, 16 March 1951, 23 April 1951; *The Times*, 28 July 1951.

24 See King's College, E. M. Forster MS, GMT to Forster, 15 May 1956, on the publication of E. M. Forster, *Marianne Thornton: 1797–1887: A Domestic Biography* (1956).

25 N. Annan, 'The Intellectual Aristocracy', in J. H. Plumb (ed.), *Studies in Social History: A Tribute to G. M. Trevelyan* (1955), pp. 242–287; idem, *Leslie Stephen: The Godless Victorian* (New York, 1984), pp. 1–15.

26 S. Collini, *Public Moralists: Political Thought and Intellectual Life in Britain, 1850–1930* (1991), pp. 14–19.

27 Ursula Vaughan Williams, *RVW: A Biography of Ralph Vaughan Williams* (1988 edn.), pp. 1–7, 34–41, 46–51, 164–170, 236, 252, 327, 343, 375. See also the references to GMT in R. Vaughan Williams, *National Music and Other Essays* (1963 edn.), pp. 54, 154, 168, 241–242.

28 Fisher MS, 213/134, GMT to Mrs H. A. L. Fisher, 18 April 1940.

29 R. Clark, *The Life of Bertrand Russell* (1975), p. 490.

30 J. Huxley, *Memories* (1970), pp. 38–39; J. Sutherland, *Mrs Humphry Ward: Eminent Victorian, Pre-Eminent Edwardian* (1990), pp. 59, 177–178.

31 Janet Trevelyan, *Evening Play Centres For Children: the Story of their Origin and Growth* (1920); idem, *Life of Mrs Humphry Ward* (1923); idem, *Two Stories* (1954),

pp. 145–222; *The Times*, 20
January 1922, 4 July 1924, 13 and
19 November 1931, 10 and 15
September 1956.

32 J. Lees-Milne, *Ancestral Voices*
(1975), p. 106.

33 See Beatrice Webb's comments on
GOT, in N. and J. Mackenzie
(eds.), *The Diary of Beatrice Webb*,
vol. i, *1873–1892*, '*Glitter Around
and Darkness Within*' (1982),
pp. 194–199.

34 Rowse, p. 96; Sir Steven Runciman
to the author, 9 January 1991; HT,
Public and Private, p. 128.

35 Morris, *C. P. Trevelyan*, pp. 9–10;
N. and J. Mackenzie (eds.), *The
Diary of Beatrice Webb*, vol. iv, *1924–
1943*, '*The Wheel of Life*' (1985),
p. 350.

36 HT, *Public and Private*, pp. 128–
140; Sir Steven Runciman to the
author, 9 January 1991; B. Pimlott
(ed.), *The Political Diaries of Hugh
Dalton, 1918–40, 1945–60* (1986),
pp. 45, 170; N. and J. Mackenzie
(eds.), *The Diary of Beatrice Webb*,
vol. ii, *1895–1905*, '*All the Good
Things of Life*' (1983), pp. 181–182.

37 *The Collected Works of R. C.
Trevelyan*, vol. i, *Poems* (1939), vol. ii,
Plays (1939); M. Lago and P. N.
Furbank (eds.), *Selected Letters of
E. M. Forster*, vol. i, *1879–1920*
(1983), pp. 59–63, 159; RT, *Golden
Oriole*, pp. 444–455.

38 HT, *Public and Private*, pp. 141–
147; N. Mariano, *Forty Years with
Berenson* (1966), pp. 24–26, 37, 67–
70, 83–84, 94–96, 199, 202, 217,
228; H. and M. Cecil, *Clever Hearts:
Desmond and Molly MacCarthy: A
Biography* (1990), pp. 41–42, 197,
228, 239.

39 *Diary of Beatrice Webb*, vol. ii, p. 183.

40 Moorman, pp. 109–110;
Autobiography, p. 29; Thayer MS,
GMT to Thayer, undated
[postmarked 23 April 1911]. See also

GOT MS, 103, GMT to GOT, 24
June 1911: 'There was to have been
another generation – or so at least
my fancy had it.'

41 Since the basic outlines of GMT's
life are well established, I have only
provided references for specific
details and quotations in this section.

42 *Autobiography*, pp. 7, 19–20.

43 For GMT's letters to Lord Acton,
see Cambridge University Library,
Add. MS, 8119/I/T101, May 2
[?1897]; 8119/I/T102, May 11
[?1897]; 8119/I/T105–6 [?1898];
G. P. Gooch, *Under Six Reigns*
(1958), pp. 30–31; GOT MS, 11,
GMT to GOT, 11 October 1898.

44 *The Times*, 27 and 30 December
1915. For the award of the Medal for
Military Valour in 1915, see PRO,
FO 327/688, file 190,615. For the
award of the Order of St Maurice
and St Lazarus in 1918, see PRO, FO
372/1139, file 98,485, and FO 372/
1141, file 171,416.

45 Moorman, pp. 177–8;
Autobiography, p. 40.

46 For a brief history of Hallington see
J. Crawford Hodgson, *A History of
Northumberland*, vol. iv,
Hexhamshire, Part ii (1897),
pp. 238–44; *Autobiography*, pp. 42–
44.

47 *The Times*, 19 July 1927, 29
September 1927; G. N. Clark,
'George Macaulay Trevelyan,
1876–1962', *PBA*, xlix (1963),
p. 382.

48 For GMT's letters about accepting
the Mastership see: MM, GMT
MS, GMT to MM, 27 September
1940, 2 October 1940; Trinity
College, Add. MS, GMT to G.
Kitson Clark, 7 October 1940;
Kennet MS, 58/34, GMT to
Kennet, 27 September 1940;
Sheppard MS, GMT to Sheppard,
7 October 1940.

49 *Autobiography*, pp. 49–50; *Library of*

Sir Isaac Newton: presentation by the Pilgrim Trust to Trinity College, Cambridge, 30 October 1943 (1944), pp. 5–12; Nevins MS, GMT to Nevins, 18 December 1941; HRHRC, Connely MS, GMT to Connely, 4 December 1942, 12 November 1944, 20 August 1946; PRO, FO 371/26,246, file 2068, paper 5395, ff 12–26, GMT to T. N. Whitehead, 28 June 1941, T. N. Whitehead to GMT, 4 July 1941, and ensuing correspondence. For GMT's concern about the prompt release of university premises after the war, see PRO, FO 371/34,190, file 1156, paper 10,440, ff 122–131, GMT to N. Butler, 9 November 1943; GMT to R. A. Butler, 9 November 1943; R. A. Butler to GMT, 29 November 1943.

50 Forster's review, which gives an unforgettable picture of GMT in old age, is printed in full as Appendix B, pp. 234–235.

51 *The Times*, 28 December 1959.

52 The *Scotsman*, 23 July 1962; Cambridgeshire Collection, C35.7, 'Order of Proceedings, Presentation of the Grant of the Office of High Steward of the Borough to Dr G. M. Trevelyan, O. M., Litt. D., 22 October 1946'.

53 The *Times*, 7 December 1949, 20 May 1950. For a vivid account of GMT's installation, see H. Nicolson, 'Marginal Comment', the *Spectator*, 2 June 1950, p. 755.

54 The *Listener*, 26 May 1949; the *Spectator*, 28 May 1949; C. V. Wedgwood, 'History as Literature', *TLS*, 6 January 1956, p. xi; D. Knowles, 'George Macaulay Trevelyan', the *Spectator*, 17 February 1956, pp. 209–210.

55 *The Times*, 16 February 1956, 1 March 1957, 19 October 1957; Plumb, p. 280.

56 *The Times*, 11 May 1961; *Cambridge Daily News*, 23, 24, 26, July 1962, 19 and 23 November 1962.

57 Anon [W. E. Gladstone], review of GOT, *Life and Letters of Lord Macaulay*, *Quarterly Review*, cxlii (1876), p. 2; GOT MS, 94, GMT to CT, 8 October 1901.

58 Fisher MS, 59/254–7, GMT to Fisher, 5 July 1911; CPT MS, 238, GMT to Walter Morley Fletcher [?draft], 6 June 1911; J. R. M. Butler, 'George Macaulay Trevelyan', *DNB*, 1961–70 (1981), p. 1017; Clark, 'George Macaulay Trevelyan', p. 375.

59 MM, GMT MS, GMT to MM, 2 October 1940.

60 Vaughan Williams, *RVW*, pp. 206–207, 322–323.

61 Adrian MS, GMT to E. D. Adrian, 14 December 1954.

62 'Restoration Regime in Scotland', p. 479; GOT MS, 103, GMT to GOT, 18 November 1911; GMT to Francis Acland, 15 January 1915, published in D. Lloyd George, *War Memoirs*, vol. i (1933), pp. 398–401.

63 J. R. Colville, *The Fringes of Power: 10 Downing Street Diaries, 1939–55* (1985), pp. 185–186, 239–240, 250–251, 253, 296.

64 F. Eyck, *Gooch: A Study in History and Politics* (1982), p. 11.

65 *The Times*, 29 February 1940; MM, GMT MS, GMT to MM, 7 March 1940.

66 *George Otto Trevelyan*, pp. 58–61; *Autobiography*, pp. 15–16.

67 For Bowen, see HRHRC, GMT MS, GMT to CT, 14 April 1901, and J. Bryce to GMT, 15 April 1901. For Browning, see Browning MS, GMT to Browning, undated [1895–7]. For Sidgwick, see 'Henry Sidgwick'. For Butler see *George Otto Trevelyan*, pp. 27–28; *Trinity College*, pp. 107–113.

68 For a piece of paternal advice given

by GMT, see King's College, Forster MS, GMT to Forster, 9 May 1902.

69 Woolf MS, GMT to Woolf, 12 June 1924, 9 May 1925; N. Nicolson (ed.), *'The Sickle Side of the Moon': The Letters of Virginia Woolf*, vol. v, *1932–1935* (1979), p. 402.

70 R. Deacon, *The Cambridge Apostles: A History of Cambridge's Elite Intellectual Secret Society* (1985), pp. 118, 125; A. Boyle, *The Climate of Treason* (1979), pp. 116, 152.

71 Sir I. de la Bère, *The Queen's Orders of Chivalry* (1964), pp. 168–170; GOT MS, 103, GMT to GOT 24 June 1911.

72 RCT MS, 13/233, GMT to RCT, 5 June 1930.

73 Murray MS, 89/201, GMT to Murray, 1 January 1941.

74 Baldwin MS, 171 f 324, GMT to Baldwin, 3 November 1936.

75 J. Gross, *The Rise and Fall of the Man of Letters* (1969), p. 130.

76 Longman MS: Sales Ledgers, 1925–36 and 1926–30; Part II, 67/10, Memorandum by Robert Longman, 23 May 1946.

77 E.g. *Yorkshire Post*, 20 May 1950.

78 For the background see A. Briggs, 'Introduction: At the Sign of the Ship', in A. Briggs (ed.), *Essays in the History of Publishing in Celebration of the two Hundred and Fiftieth Anniversary of the House of Longman, 1724–1974* (1974), pp. 3–28; Longman MS, Part II, 67/16, GMT to T. N. Longman, 21 August 1928.

79 Longman MS, Part II, 67/18, GMT to R. G. Longman, 26 July 1944.

80 Longman MS, Part II, 67/12, R. G. Longman to GMT, 24 May 1946; Appendix C, pp. 236–238.

81 *The Times*, 15 December 1928, 19 September 1929, 29 February 1940, 16 March 1944, 11 January 1947, 7 December 1951, 13 March 1958.

82 *The Times*, 3 and 9 June 1933, 17 October 1933.

83 GMT, 'The Novelist as Historian', *The Times*, 21 September 1932; idem, 'Marlborough: The Making of Great Britain', *The Times*, 6 October 1932; idem, 'The Great Days of Reform – I – Whig and Tory', *The Times*, 7 June 1932; idem, 'The Great Days of Reform – II – England's Way', *The Times*, 8 June 1932; idem, 'The Crown and the People: Twenty-Five Momentous Years', *The Times*, 3 May 1935; idem, 'Monarchy and the Constitution: A Historical Survey', and 'Coronation Oath: Reasons for Revision', *The Times*, 11 May 1937.

84 *The Times*, 21 June 1926, 3 June 1930, 10 March 1932, 5 October 1940, 24–26 May 1950, 23 July 1962.

85 See Dawson MS, GMT to Dawson, 18 July 1941.

86 J. R. Vincent (ed.), *The Crawford Papers: The Journals of David Lindsay, Twenty-Seventh Earl of Crawford and Tenth Earl of Balcarres, 1871–1940, during the years 1892 to 1940* (1984), pp. 504–506; A. Briggs, *The BBC: The First Fifty Years* (1985), pp. 49–53, 116.

87 GMT, 'The Parliamentary Union of England and Scotland, 1707', the *Listener*, 20 November 1929, pp. 669–671, 697–698, and *The Times*, 13 November 1929; idem, 'Thomas Carlyle as a Historian', the *Listener*, 2 October 1947, pp. 567–568; idem, 'Macaulay and the Sense of Optimism', the *Listener*, 12 February 1948, pp. 258–259; C. Scott, *A Historian and His World: A Life of Christopher Dawson, 1889–1970* (1984), pp. 159–161, 228.

88 GOT MS, 93, GMT to GOT, undated [1900]; CPT MS, 244, GMT to CPT, 8 June 1951.

89 Chadwick, p. 23; *George Otto Trevelyan*, p. 30.

90 MM, GMT MS, GMT to MM, 15 August 1937; Gordon, 'Sir George Otto Trevelyan', pp. 164–166, 168–169.

91 Moorman, p. 11; CPT MS, 241, GMT to GOT and CT, 13 January 1917.

92 *Autobiography*, p. 17; GOT MS, 103, GMT to GOT, 24 June 1911.

93 This matter is discussed more fully below in Chapter v, pp. 213–215.

94 GOT MS, 113, GMT to GOT, 17 March 1921; *George Otto Trevelyan*, p. 152.

95 Bryant MS, E3, GMT to Bryant, 16 August 1932; MM, GMT MS, GMT to MM, 28 August 1940; 'Macaulay and the Sense of Optimism', pp. 258–259.

96 Ibid., p. 258.

97 C. Petrie, 'England in Transition' [a review of *Blenheim*], *The Saturday Review*, 4 October 1930, p. 410; RCT MS, 14/43, GMT to RCT [undated].

98 *English Social History*, p. ix.

99 See below, pp. 113, 161.

100 J. Clive, *Thomas Babington Macaulay: The Shaping of the Historian* (1973), pp. 239, 492.

101 *George Otto Trevelyan*, pp. 96–98, 100–101.

102 'Introduction' to *Carlyle: An Anthology*, p. 1.

103 Moorman, p. 42; GMT MS, 93, GMT to CT, 19 June 1900; 'Carlyle as an Historian'.

104 CPT MS, 237 (2), GMT to CPT, 27 October 1900; 'Carlyle, Cromwell and Professor Firth'; 'The Two Carlyles', in *The Recreations of an Historian*, pp. 192–212; 'Thomas Carlyle as a Historian', pp. 567–568; *The Times*, 9 June 1934; Buchan MS, GMT to Buchan, 27 February and 3 March 1921.

105 'Introduction' to *Carlyle: An Anthology*, p. 2.

106 'The Two Carlyles', pp. 193, 199–201.

107 'The Two Carlyles', p. 192; A. Shelston (ed.), *Thomas Carlyle: Selected Writings* (1986), p. 25.

108 'The Two Carlyles', p. 194; 'Carlyle as an Historian', p. 499; 'Introduction' to *Carlyle: An Anthology*, p. 6.

109 'On Religious Conformity', p. 375; 'The Two Carlyles', p. 200. GMT's father was also given to hero-worship: *George Otto Trevelyan*, p. 68.

110 CPT MS, 238, GMT to CPT, 4 October 1907; Clark, 'George Macaulay Trevelyan', p. 382.

111 Shelston, *Carlyle: Selected Writings*, p. 8.

112 *Autobiography*, pp. 30–31; Cecils, *Clever Hearts*, pp. 41–43, 82–83; D. MacCarthy, *Portraits*, vol. i (1931), pp. 170–174. For the limited correspondence between GMT and Meredith which has survived, see C. L. Cline (ed.), *The Letters of George Meredith*, vol. iii (1970), pp. 1345–6, 1450–5, 1556–8, 1561, 1565. See also HRHRC, GMT MS, GMT to C. L. Cline, 1 March 1954.

113 For preliminary versions of the Meredith book, see 'The Poetry of George Meredith', and 'Optimism and Mr Meredith: A Reply'; GMT, 'England and Mr Meredith', the *Nation*, 8 February 1908, pp. 668–669; idem, 'George Meredith, 1828–1928', the *Nation and Athenaeum*, 11 February 1928, pp. 713–714.

114 *Poetry and Philosophy of George Meredith*, pp. 104–105, 114–115

115 'Optimism and Mr Meredith', p. 56; S. R. Gardiner, *History of the Civil War*, vol. iv (1893 edn.), p. 287.

116 *Poetry and Philosophy of George Meredith*, pp. 184, 191, 200–206.

117 *Poetry and Philosophy of George*

Meredith, pp. 208–209;
'Introduction' to *Selected Poetical
Works of George Meredith*, p. xii.

118 For 'history's blood royal', see *The
War and the European Revolution*, p. 8.
For 'a harsher air', see *The English
Revolution*, p. 240.

119 A. F. Watson, 'Meredith and Italy',
Fortnightly Review, cv (1919),
pp. 293–302.

120 P. Bartlett, *George Meredith* (1963),
pp. 24–25; 'Introduction' to
English Songs of Italian Freedom,
pp. xx-xxi.

121 *Autobiography*, pp. 3, 12–13.

122 *English Literature and Its Readers*,
esp. pp. 4–7.

123 HT, *Public and Private*, pp. 165–
166; H. A. Williams, *Some Day I'll
Find You* (1982), p. 91; CPT MS,
237+, GMT to CPT, undated
[?1902].

124 *Layman's Love of Letters*, pp. 2–4; J.
Dover Wilson, *Milestones on the
Dover Road* (1969), pp. 29–31.

125 'History and Literature'; *History and
the Reader; English Literature and Its
Readers*.

126 *Autobiography*, p. 13.

127 *Layman's Love of Letters*, pp. 2, 7.

128 *Layman's Love of Letters*, pp. 124–
125.

129 *George Otto Trevelyan*, pp. 14–17;
Chadwick, p. 29; GOT MS, 92,
GMT to GOT, 15 December 1899;
Kennet MS, 58/40, GMT to
Kennet, 27 August 1947.

130 CPT MS, 237+, GMT to CPT, 13
October 1912; 'On Religious
Conformity', pp. 374–392; *De
Haeretico Comburendo*, p. 20.

131 P. Jalland, *Women, Marriage and
Politics, 1860–1914* (1986), pp. 40,
78–80, 88; S. Hynes, *The Edwardian
Turn of Mind* (1968), p. 389.

132 Sutherland, *Mrs Humphry Ward*,
pp. 195, 250; GOT MS, 92, GMT
to GOT and CT, 27 December

1899; CPT MS, 237+, GMT to
CPT, 13 October 1902.

133 GOT MS, 96, GMT to CT, 13
August 1903; RCT MS, 13/76, CT
to RCT and Bessie Trevelyan, 20
March 1904; Sir Steven Runciman
to the author, 9 January 1991.

134 R. Speaight, *The Life of Hilaire Belloc*
(1957), pp. 409–430; A. N. Wilson,
Hilaire Belloc (1984), pp. 318–321,
335, 350.

135 Buchan MS, GMT to Buchan, 13
October 1937; Bryant MS, E3,
GMT to Bryant, 11 November
1932.

136 *De Haeretico Comburendo*, p. 16;
Autobiography, pp. 22–23.

137 MM, GMT MS, GMT to MM, 10
September 1926; Kennet MS, 58/
40, GMT to Kennet, 27 August
1947.

138 RCT MS. 14/112, GMT to RCT,
30 September 1929.

139 MM, GMT MS, GMT to MM, 10
October 1935, 2 February 1936;
Bryant MS, E3, GMT to Bryant, 10
April 1936.

140 Rowse, p. 103, HT, *Public and
Private*, p. 158.

141 Williams, *Some Day I'll Find You*,
pp. 89–90.

142 See D. Knowles, 'George Macaulay
Trevelyan', and in *The Times*, 7
August 1962.

143 P. Levy, *Moore: G. E. Moore and the
Cambridge Apostles* (1981 edn.),
pp. 139, 222–225, 228–232; D.
Wilson, *Leonard Woolf: A Political
Biography* (1978), pp. 16–28; L.
Woolf, *Sowing: An Autobiography of
the Years 1880–1904* (1961),
pp. 142–150.

144 Murray MS, 17/36–7, GMT to
Murray, 9 May 1910; 17/38–9,
GMT to Murray, 11 May 1910; 17/
116–7, GMT to Murray 15 October
1910; D. Newsome, *On the Edge of
Paradise: A. C. Benson the Diarist*

(1980), pp. 275–276; *The Times*, 26 July 1910.

145 RCT MS, 14/79, GMT to RCT, 24 May 1910; Fisher MS, 60/3–6, GMT to Fisher, 14 February 1902.

146 Rowse, pp. 129–130; R. F. Harrod, *The Life of John Maynard Keynes* (1951), pp. 254–275, 389–398; Keynes MS, GMT to Keynes, 24 April 1933.

147 J. M. Keynes, *Essays in Biography* (1933), p. 120; HRHRC, GMT MS, Harrod to GMT, 18 November 1951.

148 Woolf MS, GMT to Woolf, 14 July 1926, 27 May 1914, 4 May 1941; L. Woolf to L. Strachey, 8 April 1902, in F. Spotts (ed.), *Letters of Leonard Woolf* (1987), pp. 22–23; L. Woolf, 'Introduction' to CPT, *Letters from North America and the Pacific 1898* (1969), p. x; idem, 'English History', the *Nation and Athenaeum*, 10 July 1926, p. 418.

149 Rowse, pp. 103, 129; Levy, *Moore*, pp. 20–21; Annan, *Leslie Stephen*, pp. 159–162. It is difficult to imagine GMT having any sympathy for a woman who in 1919 could write this disparagingly and scornfully of the intellectual aristocracy (in *Night and Day* [1969 edn.], p. 33):
On the whole, in the first years of the twentieth century, the Alardyces and their relations were keeping their heads well above water. One finds them at the top of professions, with letters after their names; they sit in luxurious public offices, with private secretaries attached to them; they write solid books, in dark covers, issued by the presses of the two great universities; and when one of them dies, the chances are that another of them writes his biography.

150 Ryan, *Russell*, pp. 1–20, 26–28.

151 Anon. [B. Russell], 'Garibaldi's Defence of the Roman Republic',

Edinburgh Review, ccv (1907), pp. 489–507; Russell MS 710.056923, GMT to Russell, 23 May 1907; 710.056929, GMT to Russell, 22 December 1915.

152 R. Clark, *The Life of Bertrand Russell*, 23 May 1907; (1975), pp. 98, 102–103; HT, *Public and Private*, p. 159. Janet, incidentally, had sense, but no money, and left only £1, 472–3s-2d.

153 Russell MS, 710.056929, GMT to Russell, 22 December 1915.

154 Ryan, *Russell*, pp. 85–87, 97, 103–109, 112–114, 117–123, 124–126; HT, *Public and Private*, p. 159.

155 MM, GMT MS, GMT to MM, 7 December 1934; Russell MS, 710.056942, GMT to Russell, 9 June 1949

156 Ryan, *Russell*, pp. 156–157; Clark, *Russell*, pp. 483, 490; Russell MS, 710.056945, GMT to Countess Russell, 12 March 1943.

157 *Trinity College Annual Record* (1956), pp. 8–9; Russell MS 710.056944, GMT to Russell, 17 February 1956. Unfortunately, the *Listener* was not published that week, because of a strike, but for a brief summary of Russell's remarks, see *London Calling*, no. 861, 3 May 1956, p. 8.

158 Levy, *Moore*, pp. 20–21; Cannadine, *Decline and Fall*, pp. 424–425.

159 RT, *Golden Oriole*, pp. 411–412.

160 Strachey MS, f 180, GMT to Strachey, 2 March 1900; M. Holroyd, *Lytton Strachey: A Critical Biography*, vol. i, *The Unknown Years (1880–1910)* (New York, 1968), pp. 111–112.

161 Deacon, *Cambridge Apostles*, pp 53–54, 59–63, 69–71, 81–82; B. Russell, *The Autobiography of Bertrand Russell*, vol. i (1974), p. 74; R. Skidelsky, *John Maynard Keynes*, vol. i, *Hopes Betrayed, 1883–1920* (New York, 1986), pp. 124–126.

162 Strachey MS, ff 182–3, GMT to Strachey, 22 March 1902.

163 Holroyd, *Strachey: The Unknown Years*, pp. 221, 236–237.

164 Holroyd, *Lytton Strachey: A Critical Biography*, vol. ii, *The Years of Achievement (1910–1932)* (New York, 1968), pp. 78, 189.

165 Strachey MS, ff 195–6, GMT to Strachey, 12 August 1918; f 198, GMT to Strachey, 6 May 1921.

166 Strachey MS, ff 200–01, GMT to Strachey, 25 November 1928.

167 L. Strachey, *Portraits in Miniature* (1931), p. 203.

168 Holroyd, *Strachey: The Years of Achievement*, p. 666; Strachey MS, f 202, GMT to Miss Strachey 22 January 1932.

169 See GMT's muted – but coded – remarks in 'History and Literature' (1924), pp. 86–87:
Mr Strachey is not a man of deep historical learning, but he is a man of letters of the first order, and so there is a large public in England that 'wants' whatever he has to say about history. He is doing history a great service by connecting her again with literature, and by interesting the public in her themes. But I should be sorry if those who know most about history, those who give their whole lives to the study of history, relinquished the interpretation and exposition of history entirely to novelists and literary men who were not primarily historians.

170 *Biography: A Reader's Guide*, p. 4; Bryant MS, E3, GMT to Bryant, 19 December 1933.

171 *John Buchan, by His Wife and Friends*, p. 17; the *Scotsman*, 18 December 1944.

172 *Layman's Love of Letters*, pp. 7, 27–35, 96–105. For Forster's response, see Appendix B, pp. 234–235.

173 Strachey, *Portraits in Miniature*, p. 169.

174 S. C. Roberts, *Adventures with Authors* (1966), p. 121.

175 Bryant MS, E3, GMT to Bryant, 20 July 1932, 16 August 1932, 8 September 1932, 22 October 1932, 25 December 1932.

176 MM, GMT MS, GMT to MM, 30 June 1942.

177 Rothenstein MS, GMT on Élie Halévy [1937], for a volume of contemporary drawings.

178 MM, GMT MS, GMT to MM, 18 January 1943.

179 GOT MS, 92, GMT to GOT and CT, 6 July 1899.

180 Sir John Habakkuk to the author, 21 September 1991; HT, *Public and Private*, p. 168.

181 Rowse, p. 95; Plumb, p. 202; Longman MS, Part II, 316/17, ? to V. Matthews, 31 January 1956.

182 *Diary of Beatrice Webb*, vol. ii, pp. 85–86.

183 *Diary of Beatrice Webb*, vol. ii, pp. 183, 353; *Autobiography*, p. 8.

184 Sheppard MS, 4.4.1.

185 CPT MS, 237 (2), GMT to CPT, 15 September 1898; CPT MS, 237, GMT to CPT, 11 November 1904.

186 CPT MS, 238, GMT to Walter Morley Fletcher [?draft], 6 July 1911; CPT MS, 241, GMT to GOT and CT, 17 June 1917.

187 Cecils, *Clever Hearts*, p. 56; Rothenstein MS, H. A. L. Fisher on GMT for volume [1937] of contemporary drawings; Moorman, p. 225.

188 GOT 114, GMT to GOT and CT, 16 February 1922; J. Burrow, reviewing Moorman, *The Times*, 1 July 1980.

189 *The Times*, 26 July 1962.

190 *Autobiography*, p. 9; Levy, *Moore*, pp. 180, 186–189.

191 Rothenstein MS, GMT to Rothenstein, 8, 10 and 11 October 1912; Sir Steven Runciman to the author, 9 January 1991; CPT MS, 244, GMT to CPT, 8 June 1951.

192 Janet Trevelyan, *Two Stories*, pp. 1–

130, was an account of Theodore's life, written as late as 1954.

193 Rowse, p. 107; HT, *Public and Private*, pp. 160–161.

194 Sheppard MS, GMT to Sheppard, 3 August 1947. Humphry was the author of *The Popular Background to Goethe's Hellenism* (1934) and *Goethe and the Greeks* (1941). Much influenced by her father, Mary's first book was *William III and the Defence of Holland, 1672–4* (1930).

195 Among his articles, 'If Napoleon Had Won the Battle of Waterloo' and 'The News of Ramillies', are the only two which are deliberately light-hearted.

196 Sutherland, *Mrs Humphry Ward*, p. 280; *Diary of Beatrice Webb*, vol. ii, p. 181; Plumb, p. 181.

197 Cecils, *Clever Hearts*, p. 101; GOT MS, 86, GMT to GOT and CT, 26 June 1902.

198 Lees-Milne, *Ancestral Voices*, p. 198.

199 Chadwick, p. 2; L. Edel (ed.), *Henry James Letters*, vol. iv, *1895–1916* (1984), p. 747.

200 G. Kitson Clark, 'The Macaulay Tradition', *Trinity Review* (1976), p. 13.

201 Rowse, pp. 103, 107; HT, *Public and Private*, p. 166; Woolf, 'Introduction' to *Letters from North America*, p. x.

202 Williams, *Some Day I'll Find You*, p. 91; HT, *Public and Private*, p. 164.

203 Keynes MS, GMT to Keynes, February 1905, concerning the election of Arthur Hobhouse to the Apostles. See also Skidelsky, *Hopes Betrayed*, p. 127.

204 CPT MS, 242, GMT to CPT, 17 March 1934.

205 Rowse, p. 112; Collini, *Public Moralists*, pp. 60–90; Moorman, p. 54; Chadwick, pp. 29–30.

206 Williams, *Some Day I'll Find You*, p. 92.

207 *Diary of Beatrice Webb*, vol. iv, p. 350.

208 E.g. HRHRC, GMT MS, R. H. Hodgkin to GMT, 29 December 1935: 'A letter of praise from you is the most coveted honour of all historians.' See also HRHRC, GMT MS, J. E. Neale to GMT, 18 May 1953: 'As always, you are encouraging, kindly, magnanimous.'

209 For the help GMT gave Sassoon with Meredith, see HRHRC, Sassoon MS, GMT to Sassoon, 20 July 1947, 5, 10, 14, 19 November 1947, 2 December 1947.

210 See below, pp. 204–212.

211 Russell, *Autobiography*, vol. i, p. 175.

212 R. C. Trevelyan to B. Russell, in B. Russell, *Autobiography*, vol. ii (1967), pp. 242–243; N. Nicolson (ed.), *Harold Nicolson: Diaries and Letters, 1939–1945* (1967), p. 140.

213 D. Knowles in *The Times*, 7 August 1962; HT, *Public and Private*, p. 166.

214 *Grey of Fallodon*, p. vi.

215 Williams, *Some Day I'll Find You*, pp. 91–92.

216 R. Hart-Davis (ed.), *The Lyttelton-Hart-Davis Letters: Correspondence of George Lyttelton and Rupert Hart-Davis, 1955–56* (1978), p. 101.

217 Bryant MS, E3, GMT to Bryant, 16 May 1957. See also Fay MS, Misc 17/10, GMT to Fay, 27 July 1957.

218 J. Clive, 'Historians as Teachers' (unpublished paper), p. 3; HT, *Public and Private*, p. 167.

219 *Autobiography*, p. 1.

220 Thayer MS, GMT to Thayer, 26 September 1909.

NOTES TO CHAPTER II: The Liberal Internationalist

1 N. Pevsner, *The Buildings of England: Cambridgeshire* (1970 edn.), pp. 172–175; P. Gaskell and R. Robson, *The Library of Trinity College: A Short History* (1971), pp. 13–22. For GMT's own

account, see *Trinity College*, pp. 43–45.

2 *George Otto Trevelyan*, pp. 6–7, 13–14.

3 *George Otto Trevelyan*, pp. 71–78, 135–136.

4 R. Jenkins, *Asquith* (1967 edn.), p. 606.

5 A. J. A. Morris, *C. P. Trevelyan, 1870–1958: Portrait of a Radical* (1977), pp. 21–26.

6 B. Pimlott (ed.), *The Political Diaries of Hugh Dalton, 1918–40, 1945–60* (1986), p. 45.

7 G. P. Gooch, *Historical Surveys and Portraits* (1966), p. 255; CPT MS, 238, GMT to CPT, 1 February 1910; Moorman, pp. 19–22, 34–35; *Autobiography*, p. 9.

8 Moorman, p. 38; Morris, *C. P. Trevelyan*, p. 39; GOT MS, 92, GMT to GOT and CT, 1 March 1899; GOT MS, 98, GMT to CT, 21 November 1906; RCT MS 14/35, GMT to RCT, 2 March 1899; Thayer MS, GMT to Thayer, 20 January 1909, 21 November 1909.

9 CPT MS, 238, GMT to CPT, 28 January 1910, 28 October 1910; GOT MS, 100, GMT to CT, 30 November 1908; Thayer MS, GMT to Thayer, 28 November 1910, 13 December 1910, 8 January 1911.

10 Moorman, pp. 70–74; *Autobiography*, pp. 23–24.

11 GOT MS, 93, GMT to GOT, 17 October 1900; CPT MS 237 (2), GMT to CPT, 27 October 1900.

12 L. Masterman, *C. F. G. Masterman: A Biography* (1939), pp. 40–43.

13 G. P. Gooch, *Under Six Reigns* (1958), pp. 85–86; F. Eyck, *Gooch: A Study in History and Politics* (1982), pp. 72–76.

14 'Past and Future', pp. 408–415.

15 Murray MS, 9/27–28, GMT to Murray, 2 April 1903; CPT MS, 237, GMT to CPT, 11 November 1904; Moorman, pp. 79–80, 82–85.

16 Berg MS, GMT to Leonard Woolf, undated [c1903–1904]; Russell MS, 710.056911–5, GMT to Russell, undated [1903]; Sturge Moore MS, 32/50–55, GMT to Sturge Moore, 12 June 1902–30 January 1904.

17 'A Puritan Henry George', p. 341.

18 'Party Loyalty in Evil Days', and 'Poetry and Rebellion', passim.

19 Keynes MS, GMT to Keynes, February 1905.

20 *The Times*, 23 and 31 October 1901; RCT MS, 13/96, GMT to Elizabeth Trevelyan, 23 October 1901; Russell MS, 710.056910, GMT to Russell, 1 August 1900; M. Howard, *War and the Liberal Conscience* (1978), pp. 9–10; Moorman, pp. 74–75.

21 CPT MS, 237 (2), GMT to CPT, 20 October 1901; GMT MS 93, GMT to GOT and CT, 4 February 1900.

22 GOT 98, GMT to CT, 23 July 1906; Keynes MS, GMT to Keynes, February 1905.

23 *The Times*, 25 October 1919; Runciman MS, GMT to Runciman, 19 October 1910; GOT MS, GMT to CT, 4 November 1910; HRHRC, Lady Ottoline Morrell MS, GMT to P. Morrell, 15 October 1909.

24 Eyck, *Gooch*, pp. 146–148; GOT MS, 104, GMT to CT, 26 October 1912; GOT MS, 105, GMT to CT, 15 May 1913.

25 Moorman, pp. 120–123; 'A Holiday Among the Servians', pp. 157–158; GMT, 'The Servian Army and its Turkish Victories', the *Nation*, 19 July 1913, pp. 601–603; GMT in *The Times*, 18 September 1914; GMT, 'The Magyar Tragedy', the *Nation*, 10 October 1914, pp. 33–34.

26 *Autobiography*, p. 30.

27 H. G. Wells, *The New Machiavelli* (New York, 1919 edn.), pp. 237–238, 273–280, 289; Sturge Moore

Ms, 32/58, GMT to Sturge Moore, undated [1911].

28 Plumb, p. 187; Chadwick, pp. 20–21; *Autobiography*, p. 21.

29 GOT MS, 103, GMT to GOT, 24 June 1911.

30 See H. Rudman, *Italian Nationalism and English Letters: Figures of the Risorgimento and Victorian Men of Letters* (New York, 1940), passim.

31 *Garibaldi and the Thousand*, p. 22; J. Pemble, *The Mediterranean Passion: Victorians and Edwardians in the South* (1987), pp. 66, 98, 214–215.

32 Bryce MS, 18 f 49, GOT to Bryce, 27 May 1911; *George Otto Trevelyan*, pp. 79–85.

33 *Garibaldi and the Thousand*, pp. 24–25; D. Beales, 'Garibaldi in England: The Politics of Italian Enthusiasm', in J. A. Davis and P. Ginsborg (eds.), *Society and Politics in the Age of the Risorgimento: Essays in Honour of Denis Mack Smith* (1991), pp. 191–195, 210–211. I am most grateful to Professor Beales for sending me a copy of an exhibition catalogue from the Italian Institute on 'Garibaldi's visit to Newcastle in 1854', originally shown in the Berwick Gallery of the Central Library, Newcastle upon Tyne, from 15 March to 14 April 1954, which contains annotations in GMT's own hand.

34 For a recent analysis of this painting, see P. Usherwood, 'William Bell Scott's Iron and Coal: Northern Readings', in Laing Art Gallery, Newcastle upon Tyne, *Pre-Raphaelites: Painters and Paintings in the North-East* (1989), pp. 39–56.

35 E. Samuels, *Bernard Berenson: The Making of a Connoisseur* (1979) and *Bernard Berenson: The Making of a Legend* (1987), passim; *George Otto Trevelyan*, p. 135; *Autobiography*, pp. 27–28.

36 Sturge Moore MS, 32/48, GMT to Sturge Moore, undated [?1901–2]; Mrs G. M. Trevelyan, 'Wandering Englishmen in Italy', *PBA*, xvi (1930), pp. 61–84; *Autobiography*, pp. 31–33; R. Pares, *The Historian's Business and Other Essays* (1961), p. 43.

37 Fisher MS, 59/6–7, GMT to Fisher, undated [early 1905].

38 *Garibaldi's Defence of the Roman Republic*, p. 70; *Garibaldi and the Thousand*, p. 3.

39 *Garibaldi and the Making of Italy*, pp. 31, 33–34.

40 C. F. Delzell (ed.), *The Unification of Italy, 1859–1861: Cavour, Mazzini or Garibaldi?* (1965), p. 1.

41 *Garibaldi's Defence of the Roman Republic*, pp. 4, 14–15, 23–24.

42 *Garibaldi's Defence of the Roman Republic*, pp. ix, 22.

43 H. A. L. Fisher, 'The Whig Historians', *PBA*, xiv (1928), pp. 303–4. See also Fisher MS, 66/165, GMT to Fisher, 1 November 1928.

44 Anon., 'Garibaldi and the Thousand', the *Nation*, 2 October 1909, p. 22.

45 *Garibaldi's Defence of the Roman Republic*, p. 74; *Garibaldi and the Thousand*, p. 2.

46 *Garibaldi's Defence of the Roman Republic*, pp. 8, 227; *Garibaldi and the Making of Italy*, p. 59.

47 *The Times*, 5 July 1907.

48 GMT, 'The Festival of Italian Unity', *The Times*, 27 March 1911; *Garibaldi and the Making of Italy*, p. 294.

49 PRO, FO 371/2377, file 72,694, no. 72,816, ff 198, 202, Sir Rennell Rodd to Sir Arthur Nicolson, 5 and 6 June 1915.

50 S. J. Woolf, *The Italian Risorgimento* (1969), pp. 10–13.

51 W. Miller, review of *Garibaldi's Defence of the Roman Republic*, *EHR*, xxii (1907), p. 816.

52 *Garibaldi and the Thousand*, pp. 3–4; *Garibaldi and the Making of Italy*, pp. 263–264, 295–296.

53 GMT, 'Epilogue' to W. J. Stillman, *The Unification of Italy, 1815–1895* (1909 edn.), pp. 394–398.

54 RCT MS, 14/82, GMT to RCT, undated; RCT MS, 14/83, GMT to RCT, undated [postmarked 4 October 1911]. See also Murray MS, 403/63, GMT to Murray, 27 January 1912.

55 Fisher MS, 59/259–60, GMT to Fisher, 1 November 1911.

56 *The Times*, 1 and 3 November 1911; 'Introduction' to *English Songs of Italian Freedom*, pp. xv, xxx–xxxi.

57 P. F. Clarke, *Liberals and Social Democrats* (1978), p. 155.

58 Plumb, p. 190.

59 *Garibaldi's Defence of the Roman Republic*, p. 191.

60 D. Mack Smith, *Cavour and Garibaldi 1860: A Study in Political Conflict* (1985 edn.), p. 228.

61 *Garibaldi and the Thousand*, p. 27; GMT, 'Mr Thayer's *Life of Cavour*', *Atlantic Monthly*, cix (1912), pp. 226–227.

62 GOT MS, 103, GMT to CT, 4 October 1911.

63 *John Bright*, preface, and pp. 75, 131–132, 259 note 1; CPT MS 238, GMT to CPT, 17 January 1913; Plumb, p. 193; *George Otto Trevelyan*, pp. 78–79, 85–87.

64 CPT MS, 238, GMT to CPT, 7 April 1910; HRHRC, GMT MS, GOT to GMT, 3 October 1912; GOT MS, 104, GMT to GOT, 1 November 1912.

65 GOT MS, 105, GMT to GOT and CT, 26 May 1913.

66 Moorman, p. 15.

67 *John Bright*, pp. 1, 104, 116.

68 *John Bright*, pp. 217–218; *Autobiography*, p. 34.

69 *John Bright*, pp. 3, 90, 258.

70 *John Bright*, pp. 60, 342, 415.

71 *John Bright*, pp. 15, 47.

72 *John Bright*, pp. 49–55, 254, 268.

73 Bryce MS, 4 f 71, Bryce to Dicey, 20 August 1914.

74 A. G. Porritt, review of *Life of John Bright*, *AHR*, xix (1913), p. 352.

75 *John Bright*, pp. 223, 262–267.

76 *John Bright*, p. 278.

77 *John Bright*, pp. 189, 333–334.

78 See Bodleian Library, MS Eng. Hist, c. 659 ff 170–1, GMT to Arthur Ponsonby (a radical Liberal), 17 November 1913: 'I often thought of you in writing about Bright. Your causes are so very much his.'

79 HRHRC, GMT MS, Morley to GMT, 29 June 1913.

80 Morris, *C. P. Trevelyan*, pp. 90–91. For the broader background, see D. Cannadine, *The Decline and Fall of the British Aristocracy* (1990), pp. 313–314, 333–334; G. Searle, *Corruption in British Politics, 1895–1930* (1987), esp. pp. 145–200.

81 *John Bright*, p. 1.

82 Russell MS, 710.056924, GMT to Russell, 22 July 1910, where he writes of the 'late lamented' *Independent Review*.

83 Jenkins, *Asquith*, p. 203; Morris, *C. P. Trevelyan*, pp. 73–75; Runciman MS, 21, GMT to Runciman, 13 April 1908.

84 GOT MS, 104, GMT to CT, undated [1912]; Bodleian Library, MS Eng. Hist, c. 659, ff 170–1, GMT to A. Ponsonby, 17 November 1913.

85 J. Huxley, *Memories* (1970), p. 101; Clarke, *Liberals and Social Democrats*, p. 165; Morris, *C. P. Trevelyan*, pp. 99–117; Moorman, p. 126–127; *The Times*, 2 August 1914; CPT MS, 239+, GMT to CPT, 31 July 1914.

86 CPT MS, 60, GMT to CPT, 8 August 1914; GOT MS 106, GMT to GOT, 8 August 1914; RCT MS 14/204, GMT to RCT, 28 August

1914; Bodleian Library, MS Autographs, c. 25, f 233, GMT to Carr Bosanquet, 2 September 1914.

87 Russell MS, 710.056928, GMT to Russell, 14 October 1914; Fisher MS, 62/249–50, GMT to Fisher, 16 December 1916.

88 Morris, *C. P. Trevelyan*, p. 127; CPT MS, 60, GMT to CPT, 13 August 1914; CPT MS, 239, GMT to CPT, 15 March 1915; CPT MS, 239+, GMT to CPT, 17 October 1923; CPT MS 242, GMT to GPT, 17 March 1934.

89 Clarke, *Liberals and Social Democrats*, pp. 166–168; CPT MS, 60, GMT to CPT, 16 August 1914.

90 Russell MS, 710.056928, GMT to Russell, 14 October 1914.

91 Moorman, pp. 129–33; H. and C. Seton-Watson, *The Making of a New Europe: R. W. Seton-Watson and the Last Years of Austria-Hungary* (1981), pp. 112–117; PRO, FO 371/1906, file 81,051, ff 84–88, minutes and correspondence concerning Serbian visit, 7–10 December 1914; Seton-Watson MS, GMT to Seton-Watson, 7 November 1914; GOT MS, 106, GMT to GOT and CT, 10 December 1914.

92 *The Times*, 26 February 1915; *R. W. Seton-Watson and the Yugoslavs: Correspondence, 1906–1941*, vol. i, *1906–1918* (1976), pp. 197–198; GMT to F. Acland, 15 January 1915, published in D. Lloyd George, *War Memoirs*, vol. i (1933), pp. 398–401; M. and E. Brock (eds.), *H. H. Asquith: Letters to Venetia Stanley* (1982), pp. 386, 429–30. See also 'Serbia Re-Visited' and 'Austria-Hungary and Serbia', passim; PRO, FO 371/2241, file 214, paper 6, 110, ff 364–8, minutes and correspondence re Serbia, 15–16 January 1915.

93 S. Gwynn, *The Letters and Friendships of Sir Cecil Spring-Rice: A Record* (Boston, 2 vols., 1929), vol. ii, p. 263; Runciman MS, 136, GMT to Runciman, 9 March 1915; Houghton Mifflin MS, GMT to Houghton Mifflin, 23–25 March 1915; GOT MS, 107, GMT to GOT, 13 April 1915; Bryce MS, 18 ff 68–71, GOT to Bryce, 1 and 13 May 1915.

94 Houghton Mifflin MS, GMT to F. Greenslet, 21 May 1915; GOT MS, 107, GMT to GOT, 6 June 1915; PRO, FO 371/2377, file 72,694, ff 196–206, correspondence, 5–11 June 1915; GMT, 'Italy at War', the *Nation*, 10 July 1915, p. 482.

95 Moorman, p. 159; *Scenes From Italy's War*, p. 40; Bryce MS, 18: f 88, GOT to Bryce, 20 October 1915; f 110, GOT to Bryce, 29 September 1916; f 117, GOT to Bryce, 24 November 1916.

96 PRO, War Office, 106/808, 'Mr G. M. Trevelyan on the Condition of the Italian Army, 1915–1917'; GOT MS, 110, GMT to GOT and CT, 26 December 1918.

97 *Scenes from Italy's War*, pp. 1–22, 28–41; Woolf, *Italian Risorgimento*, pp. 13–14; CPT MS, 241, GMT to GOT and CT, 23 August 1917.

98 GMT, 'Englishmen and Italians: Some Aspects of their Relations Past and Present', *PBA*, ix (1919–20), pp. 93, 97.

99 See also PRO, FO 395/311, file 734, 'Remarks on anti-British feeling in Italy', minute from Cecil Harmsworth, reporting visit from Mr and Mrs G. M. Trevelyan to him in the House of Commons.

100 GMT, 'Englishmen and Italians', *PBA*, p. 108.

101 Moorman, pp. 187–188; *The Times*, 8 September 1923.

102 Morris, *C. P. Trevelyan*, p. 143; Bryce MS 145, f 143, GMT to Bryce, 19 June 1919.

103 Delzell, *Unification of Italy*, p. 93.

104 Woolf, *Italian Risorgimento*, pp. 91–93; *Garibaldi's Defence of the Roman Republic*, p. 163.

105 *Historical Causes of the Present State of Affairs*, p. 8.

106 *Historical Causes of the Present State of Affairs*, pp. 9, 17.

107 *Historical Causes of the Present State of Affairs*, pp. 16, 19–20.

108 Plumb, p. 192; *Manin and the Venetian Revolution*, pp. 22, 29.

109 *Autobiography*, p. 38; CPT MS, 239, GMT to CPT, 10 October 1923; *Manin and the Venetian Revolution*, pp. 207–208.

110 *Manin and the Venetian Revolution*, pp. vii-viii, 199, 244. For an earlier articulation of this view, see 'From Waterloo to the Marne', pp. 78–79. A. J. P. Taylor recalled that in describing 1848 as 'the year when German history reached its turning point and failed to turn', he was 'unconsciously stealing the phrase from Trevelyan'. See A. J. P. Taylor, *A Personal History* (1983), p. 190.

111 RCT MS, 14/102, GMT to RCT, 26 October 1923; CPT MS, 239, GMT to CPT, 8 October 1925.

112 *Autobiography*, pp. 29, 38; MM, GMT MS, GMT to MM, 27 February 1926 and 18 November 1926; CPT MS 242, GMT to CPT, 28 March 1939.

113 GMT, 'Italy June 10th', the *Spectator*, 14 June 1940, pp. 803–805; MM, GMT MS, GMT to MM, 14 June 1940; HT, *Public and Private* (1980), p. 154.

114 *Autobiography*, p. 27; *Poetry and Philosophy of George Meredith*, p. 21.

115 *Autobiography*, pp. 34, 38; RCT MS, 14/205, GMT to RCT, 31 August 1914.

116 *The War and the European Revolution*, pp. 12–13, 41.

117 'From Waterloo to the Marne', pp. 74, 79; CPT MS, 241, GMT to GOT and CT, 8 and 16 July 1917.

118 GOT MS, 14, GMT to CT, 8 April 1917.

119 Fisher MS, 206/95, GMT to Fisher, 10 March 1919; Thayer MS, GMT to Thayer, 8 December 1919; *The War and the European Revolution*, p. 14.

120 CPT MS, 241, GMT to CPT, 22 February 1918; GOT MS, 111, GMT to GOT, 25 February 1919.

121 Bodleian Library, MS Eng. Hist., c.668, f 11–12, GMT to A. Ponsonby, 7 May 1920; Buchan MS, GMT to Buchan, 27 February 1921.

122 GOT MS, 111, GMT to GOT, 25 February 1919; GOT MS, 112, GMT to CT, 16 February 1920.

123 *British History in the Nineteenth Century and After* (1941 edn.), p. 485; *Autobiography*, p. 38.

124 GOT MS, 113, GMT to CT, 24 October 1921.

125 *Garibaldi's Defence of the Roman Republic*, p. 1; *George Otto Trevelyan*, pp. 145–146.

126 CPT MS, 241, GMT to CPT, 18 May 1918; CPT MS, 239, GMT to CPT, 10 March 1921; MM, GMT MS, GMT to MM, 29 May 1926.

127 Runciman MS, 249, GMT to Runciman, 6 November 1931; *British History in the Nineteenth Century and After*, p. 483.

128 *George Otto Trevelyan*, p. vi.

129 *The Times*, 28 January 1938. See also two of GMT's reviews: of J. L. Hammond, *Gladstone and the Irish Nation* (1938), in *EHR*, liv (1939), pp. 345–348; and of D. Ogg, *Herbert Fisher, 1865–1940: A Short Biography* (1947), in *EHR*, lxiii (1948), pp. 119–120.

130 Keynes MS, GMT to Keynes, June [?1904], also quoted in R. F. Harrod, *The Life of John Maynard Keynes* (1951), pp. 99–100; and in R. Skidelsky, *John Maynard Keynes*, vol. i, *Hopes Betrayed, 1883–1920* (New York, 1986), p. 124.

131 Hammond MS, J. L. to Barbara Hammond, 19 June 1922, quoted in Clarke, *Liberals and Social Democrats*, p. 207.

132 MM, GMT MS, GMT to MM, 5 May 1926, 26 September 1926, 6 and 20 October 1926; CPT MS, 242, GMT to CPT, 17 March 1934.

133 MM, GMT MS, GMT to MM, 23 May 1945, 5 June 1945; CPT MS, 243, GMT to CPT, 8 July 1945; RCT MS, 14/193, GMT to RCT, 31 July 1945; CPT MS, 244, GMT to CPT, 1 March 1950.

134 MM, GMT MS, GMT to MM, 10 October 1935, 10 November 1935, 17 December 1935, 14 April 1936, 23 November 1936.

135 *The Times*, 19, 21 and 25 April 1938; Murray MS, 232/156, GMT to Murray, 6 May 1930; W. O. Chadwick, *Hensley Henson: A Study in the Friction Between Church and State* (1983), pp. 249, 253.

136 MM, GMT MS, GMT to MM, 20 May 1940. PRO, FO 371/24, 951, file 60, paper 6,173, ff 40–54, includes correspondence between Halifax and the BBC, and the text of GMT's broadcast.

137 *The Times*, 24 August 1940, 16 January 1942, 7 January 1943, 28 June 1943, 11 May 1945; Murray MS, 88/165, GMT to Murray, 22 August 1940.

138 MM, GMT MS, GMT to MM, 2 April 1947; CPT MS, 243, GMT to CPT, 21 April 1947.

139 Murray MS, 98/208, GMT to Murray, 26 November 1947; Moorman, p. 237.

140 J. Nehru, *An Autobiography* (1980 edn.), p. 19; M. Edwardes, *Nehru: A Political Biography* (1973), pp. 20–21; S. Gopal, *Jawaharlal Nehru: A Biography*, vol. i, *1899–1947* (1975), p. 21.

NOTES TO CHAPTER III: The Whig Constitutionalist

1 N. Pevsner, *The Buildings of England: Northumberland* (1970 edn.), p. 249.

2 *Grey of the Reform Bill*, p. 250.

3 *Autobiography*, pp. 11, 34.

4 *George Otto Trevelyan*, p. 128.

5 P. Scott, *Knowledge and Nation* (1990), pp. 187–188.

6 H. A. L. Fisher, 'The Whig Historians', *PBA*, xiv (1928), p. 310.

7 Fisher, 'The Whig Historians', p. 318.

8 *George Otto Trevelyan*, pp. 66–68, 94–95, 102–105; Fisher, 'Whig Historians', p. 328.

9 Chadwick, pp. 23–24; Fisher, 'Whig Historians', pp. 334–336; *George Otto Trevelyan*, pp. 137–138.

10 *Autobiography*, p. 20; *England in the Age of Wycliffe*, pp. 1–2.

11 *England in the Age of Wycliffe*, pp. 22, 67, 352.

12 *England in the Age of Wycliffe*, pp. 1, 80.

13 CPT MS, 237 (2), GMT to CPT, 10 March 1898; *England in the Age of Wycliffe*, p. 291.

14 *England in the Age of Wycliffe*, pp. 2, 68, 255.

15 J. Tait, review of *England in the Age of Wycliffe*, *EHR*, xv (1900), p. 161.

16 *England in the Age of Wycliffe*, pp. 10, 13, 15, 184, 338.

17 Anon., 'The Peasants' Rising of 1381', *Edinburgh Review*, cxci (1900), pp. 87, 105.

18 *England Under the Stuarts*, pp. 1–2.

19 *England Under the Stuarts*, pp. 62, 65, 74, 195.

20 *England Under the Stuarts*, pp. 191, 225–226, 228–230, 270, 291.

21 *England Under the Stuarts*, pp. 196, 272, 327.

22 *England Under the Stuarts*, pp. 365, 469.

23 D. Underdown, *Somerset in the Civil*

War and Interregnum (1973), pp. 70–72, 81, 93, 127, 185–186, 192.

24 P. B. M. Blaas, *Continuity and Anachronism: Parliamentary and Constitutional Development in Whig Historiography and in the Anti-Whig Reaction Between 1890 and 1930* (1978), pp. 121–122.

25 *England Under the Stuarts*, pp. 2, 153, 196, 438, 516.

26 GOT MS, 105, GMT to GOT and CT, 30 May 1913; GMT to GOT, 6 July 1913.

27 *Autobiography*, p. 34; Bryce MS, 19 f 24, GOT to Bryce, 2 January 1920; GOT MS, 111, GMT to CT, 17 February 1919.

28 'The Great Conservative', 'Party Loyalty in Evil Days', 'Poetry and Rebellion', passim; N. and J. Mackenzie, *The Diary of Beatrice Webb*, vol. ii, *1895–1905*, *'All the Good Things of Life'* (1983), p. 353.

29 Sturge Moore MS, 62/16/23, GMT to Sturge Moore, undated [1920].

30 *Grey of the Reform Bill*, pp. 72, 148.

31 *Grey of the Reform Bill*, pp. 143, 192; Moorman, pp. 123–124.

32 *Grey of the Reform Bill*, pp. 141, 230.

33 *Grey of the Reform Bill*, pp. viii, 33.

34 *Grey of the Reform Bill*, pp. 220, 368.

35 *Grey of the Reform Bill*, pp. 16, 106–107, 207, 246, 253.

36 *Grey of the Reform Bill*, p. 29.

37 W. Hunt, review of *Grey of the Reform Bill*, *EHR*, xxxv (1920), pp. 457–458.

38 C. E. Fryer, review of *Grey of the Reform Bill*, *AHR*, xxvi (1920), p. 91.

39 *England Under the Stuarts*, p. 391; *Grey of the Reform Bill*, p. 345.

40 *England in the Age of Wycliffe*, p. 181.

41 *Autobiography*, pp. 34, 38. See also CPT MS, 241, GMT to GOT, 11 November 1917; Bryce MS, 18, f 142, GOT to Bryce, 2 December 1917, where GOT noted that 'all his life [his son] had been looking at world-shaking events through one end of the telescope. He now had seen them at the other.'

42 The last recorded mention of a possible book on the French Revolution in GMT's surviving correspondence is CPT MS, 239, GMT to CPT, 16 July 1921.

43 Moorman, p. 206.

44 Buchan MS, GMT to Buchan, 30 June 1926.

45 Chadwick, pp. 34–35; R. C. Richardson, *The Debate on the English Revolution Revisited* (1988), pp. 72–73.

46 *The War and the European Revolution*, pp. 8–9, 13.

47 Moorman, p. 201; MM, GMT MS, GMT to MM, 14 January 1925, admitting that the original book tailed off after 1660.

48 Cf. the first edition of *England Under the Stuarts*, pp. 290–291, with the 1925 edn., p. 240.

49 Cf. the first edition of *England Under the Stuarts*, pp. 466–468, with the 1925 edn., pp. 384–388. See also GMT, review of K. Feiling, *A History of the Tory Party, 1640–1714* (1924), *EHR*, xl (1925), pp. 132–134.

50 *British History in the Nineteenth Century*, pp. 17, 35–36, 141.

51 *British History in the Nineteenth Century*, pp. viii, 69, 108, 231.

52 *British History in the Nineteenth Century*, pp. 269, 339, 410.

53 *British History in the Nineteenth Century*, pp. xiv, 192, 242.

54 *British History in the Nineteenth Century*, pp. 224, 423–424.

55 *British History in the Nineteenth Century*, pp. vii, 140, 243.

56 *British History in the Nineteenth Century*, pp. 72, 225, 292–295.

57 *British History in the Nineteenth Century*, p. xvi; G.Hedger, review of *British History in the Nineteenth*

58 *British History in the Nineteenth Century*, *AHR*, xxviii (1923), pp. 114–115.

58 *British History in the Nineteenth Century*, pp. 214, 381; GOT MS, 113, GMT to GOT and CT, 28 October 1921.

59 *The Times*, 25 May 1922; The *Spectator*, 1 July 1922, p. 57.

60 É. Halévy, review of *British History in the Nineteenth Century*, *History*, vii (1923), p. 310; G. B. Hurst, review of *British History in the Nineteenth Century*, *EHR*, xxxviii (1923), pp. 116–118.

61 CPT MS, 241, GMT to GOT and CT, 1, 17 and 19 June 1917.

62 L. Woolf, 'English History', The *Nation and Athenaeum*, 10 July 1926, p. 418.

63 *History of England*, p. 136.

64 *History of England*, pp. xvii, 178.

65 *History of England*, pp. 380, 636, 640.

66 *History of England*, pp. 250–252.

67 *History of England*, pp. 301–302.

68 *History of England*, pp. 101, 340, 375.

69 *History of England*, pp. 272, 324.

70 *History of England*, pp. 272, 378.

71 *History of England*, pp. 473, 578.

72 *History of England*, pp. xix, 376.

73 *History of England*, pp. 514, 646.

74 *History of England*, pp. 69, 102, 198, 288; MM, GMT MS, GMT to MM, 30 November 1926.

75 E. R. Cheyney, review of *History of England*, *AHR*, xxxii (1926), p. 570, T. F. Tout, review of *History of England*, *History*, xi (1926), pp. 236–237.

76 MM, GMT MS, GMT to MM, 14 February 1926; Buchan MS, GMT to Buchan, 30 June 1926.

77 Anon., 'The Politics of the Nineteenth Century', the *Nation and Athenaeum*, 8 July 1922, p. 508; E. R. Cheyney, review of *History of England*, pp. 571–572.

78 *History of England*, p. 693.

79 *The Times*, 17 June 1926; *History of England*, p. 703.

80 *Autobiography*, p. 19; Murray MS, 403/51–2, GMT to Murray, 28 October 1910.

81 *Autobiography*, p. 46; MM, GMT MS, GMT to MM, 1 September 1926; RCT MS, 14/129, GMT to RCT, 27 October 1932.

82 *Blenheim*, pp. 1, 70–71.

83 *Ramillies*, pp. ix, 2; *The Peace*, pp. 207, 318, 320.

84 *Ramillies*, p. viii; GMT, 'The Parliamentary Union of Scotland and England', the *Listener*, 20 November 1929, pp. 669–671, 697–698.

85 *Ramillies*, p. 285.

86 *Blenheim*, p. 248; *Ramillies*, p. 161; *The Peace*, p. 4.

87 *Ramillies*, p. 162; *The Peace*, p. viii; *Autobiography*, p. 46.

88 *Blenheim*, p. 178; *Ramillies*, pp. vii, 7, 130, 135.

89 MM, GMT MS, GMT to MM, 28 October 1926

90 *Blenheim*, pp. vii, 169, 184, 188.

91 *Blenheim*, pp. 185, 336; *Ramillies*, p. 406; MM, GMT MS, GMT to MM, 29 September 1926.

92 *Blenheim*, pp. 115–116; *Ramillies*, p. 404.

93 *Blenheim*, p. 189; *The Peace*, pp. 230, 317.

94 *The Peace*, p. 321.

95 *Blenheim*, p. vii.

96 *The Peace*, pp. 96, 128, 206, 315–316.

97 *Autobiography*, p. 34.

98 Bryant MS, E3, GMT to Bryant, 25 July 1935, 1 August 1935.

99 A. Bryant, 'Our Notebook', *Illustrated London News*, 30 April 1938, p. 738; Bryant MS, E3, GMT to Bryant, undated [postmarked 1 May 1938].

100 Moorman, p. 206; É. Halévy, review of *The Two Party System in English Political History*, *History*, xii (1927), p. 278.

101 *Autobiography*, pp. 184–185.

102 These phrases were in the original, published edition of 1926, at pp. 12–13; but they were cut out of the reprinted version: *Autobiography*, p. 188.

103 *Autobiography*, pp. 191, 194–195.

104 *Autobiography*, p. 197.

105 *Autobiography*, p. 35.

106 GMT, 'The Great Days of Reform – I – Whigs and Tories', *The Times*, 7 June 1932; GMT, 'The Great Days of Reform – II – England's Way', *The Times*, 8 June 1932.

107 GMT, 'The Crown and the People: Twenty-Five Momentous Years', *The Times*, 3 May 1935.

108 MM, GMT MS, GMT to MM, 25 May 1935.

109 For the full text, see Appendix D, pp. 239–240.

110 A. J. P. Taylor, *English History, 1914–1945* (1967 edn.), p. 378, note 1; J. M. Hernon, 'The Last Whig Historian and Consensus History: George Macaulay Trevelyan, 1876–1962', *AHR*, lxxxi (1976), pp. 86–87.

111 MM, GMT MS, GMT to MM, 17 May 1935, 10 June 1935; Bryant MS, E3, GMT to Bryant, 25 February 1936.

112 E. Longford, *Victoria RI* (1964), p. 387; *Grey of the Reform Bill*, p. 40.

113 Moorman, p. 224; MM, GMT MS, GMT to MM, 15 November 1936.

114 Bryant MS, E3, GMT to Bryant, 27 December 1936.

115 Moorman, pp. 224–225; GMT, 'Monarchy and the Constitution: A Historical Survey' and 'Coronation Oath: Reasons for Revision', both in *The Times*, 11 May 1937.

116 For a full and very illuminating discussion of GMT's book, in the context of recent later Stuart historiography, see J. S. Morrill, 'The Sensible Revolution', in J. Israel (ed.), *The Anglo-Dutch Moment: Essays on the Glorious Revolution and Its World Impact* (1991), pp. 73–104.

117 *The English Revolution*, pp. 7, 9, 175, 240–243.

118 Chadwick, p. 33; Blaas, *Continuity and Anachronism*, p. 117.

119 RCT MS, 14/141, GMT to RCT, 18 October 1938.

120 Chadwick, p. 6; *England Under the Stuarts*, p. 533; Murray MS, 403/51–2, GMT to Murray, 28 October 1910; MM, GMT MS, GMT to MM, 5 August 1937.

121 'The Four Great Wars', p. 265; *The War and European Revolution*, esp. pp. 18–24.

122 *British History in the Nineteenth Century*, pp. 140–41.

123 *History of England*, pp. 585–586.

124 *The Peace*, p. 230.

125 *British History in the Nineteenth Century and After* (1941 edn.), pp. 480–485.

126 MM, GMT MS, GMT to MM, 23 November 1936, 15 August 1937; RCT MS, 14/143, GMT to RCT, 22 October 1938.

127 MM, GMT MS, GMT to MM, 7 April 1934, 8 July 1934, 22 October 1934, 10 March 1940.

128 Keynes MS, GMT to Keynes, 24 April 1933; MM, GMT MS, GMT to MM, 25 May 1935; Lord Beveridge, *A Defence of Free Learning* (1959), pp. 2–5; D. Wilson, *Rutherford: Simple Genius* (1983), pp. 483–489.

129 MM, GMT MS, GMT to MM, 5 May 1935.

130 CPT MS, 242, GMT to CPT, 31 October 1935; MM, GMT MS, GMT to MM, 14 October 1935, 14 April 1936.

131 MM, GMT MS, GMT to MM, 25 October 1938.

132 MM, GMT MS, GMT to MM, 23 November 1936; CPT MS, 243, GMT to CPT, 19 June 1940.

133 *Autobiography*, p. 11; R. S. Churchill,

Winston S. Churchill, vol. i, *Youth, 1874–1900* (1966), p. 383.

134 CPT MS, 238, GMT to CPT, 8 August 1909.

135 Buchan MS, GMT to Buchan, 23 October 1937; Moorman, p. 212; W. S. Churchill, *Marlborough: His Life and Times* (4 vols., 1933–8).

136 W. S. Churchill, *My Early Life* (New York, 1939 edn.), p. 112; *Autobiography*, p. 46.

137 Berg MS, GMT to Eddie Marsh, 14 October 1930; Moorman, p. 212.

138 The correspondence between GMT and Churchill for the years 1936 to 1938 is printed in M. Gilbert, *W. S. Churchill*, companion vol. v, part iii (1982), pp. 318–319, 733–734, 910, 917.

139 GMT in TLS, 19 October 1933; MM, GMT MS, GMT to MM, 16 February 1938.

140 GMT to Churchill, 10 October 1937 and 8 September 1938, both printed in Gilbert, *Churchill*, companion vol. v, part iii, pp. 784, 1153.

141 Plumb, p. 225.

142 GOT MS, 106, GMT to GOT, 5 December 1914; M. Gilbert, *Winston S. Churchill*, vol. iii, *1914–1916* (1971), pp. 1141–44.

143 Baldwin MS, 170 f 262, GMT to Baldwin, 6 July 1935; MM, GMT MS, GMT to MM, 5 and 6 July 1935, 20 September 1938.

144 S. W. Roskill, *Hankey: Man of Secrets*, vol. iii, *1931–1963*, (1974), pp. 43–44, 277, 557, 597; Hankey MS, General Correspondence, 4/27 f 5, GMT to Hankey, 7 May 1935: 'you are if I may say so, one of my national heroes of the twentieth century, as I read it'; P. Addison, 'The Political Beliefs of Winston Churchill', *Transactions of the Royal Historical Society*, 5th. series, xxx (1980), p. 25; Dawson MS, 81/101, GMT to Dawson, 18 July 1941.

145 MM, GMT MS, GMT to MM, 12 November 1935; Bodleian Library, MS Eng. Hist., d. 400, f 24, GMT to W.M. Crook, 11 February 1936.

146 Simon MS, 67/78, GMT to Simon, 6 December 1930.

147 MM, GMT MS, GMT to MM, 1 February 1935.

148 Baldwin MS, 168 f 271, GMT to Baldwin, 13 October 1933.

149 MM, GMT MS, GMT to MM, 23 February 1938.

150 MM, GMT MS, GMT to MM, 24 March 1938.

151 MM, GMT MS, GGMT to MM, 12 May 1938.

152 MM, GMT MS, GMT to MM, 20 September 1938, 1 and 4 October 1938.

153 Hernon, 'The Last Whig Historian', p. 89; MM, GMT MS, GMT to MM, 20 September 1938.

154 MM, GMT MS, GMT to MM, 7 March 1940; Bryant MS, E3, GMT to Bryant, 12 April 1940; RCT MS, 14/159, GMT to RCT, 12 July 1940.

155 *British History in the Nineteenth Century and After*, postscript, p. 486; MM, GMT MS, GMT to MM, 26 May 1940.

156 CPT MS, 243, GMT to CPT, 19 June 1940.

157 GMT, 'All in the Front Line Now: Are We Ready Heart and Soul?', *Sunday Times*, 7 July 1940. For one appreciative response to a 'fine article' see H. Henson, *Retrospect of an Unimportant Life*, vol. iii, *1939–46, The Years of Retirement* (1950), p. 122.

158 J. R. Colville, *The Fringes of Power: 10 Downing Street Diaries, 1939–55* (1985), p. 253.

159 Berg MS, GMT to Eddie Marsh, 8 October 1940.

160 *British History in the Nineteenth Century and After*, p. 487.

161 MM, GMT MS, GMT to MM, 18 January 1943.

162 MM, GMT MS, GMT to MM, 11 May 1940, 27 November 1940.

163 CPT MS, 243, GMT to CPT, 30 January 1942; MM, GMT MS, GMT to MM, 17 February 1941, 30 June 1942. One of the reasons GMT supported Lord Tedder for the Chancellorship of Cambridge University in 1950 was that he thought him 'a wise and humane man, and against the Bomber Harris policy': MM, GMT MS, GMT to MM, 31 October 1950.

164 MM, GMT MS, GMT to MM, 25 December 1944, 23 May 1945, 5 June 1945.

165 MM, GMT MS, GMT to MM, 5 October 1942; *Trinity College*, preface.

166 *Trinity College*, pp. 8–9, 15, 41, 115.

167 *Trinity College*, pp. 73, 86, 89.

168 *Trinity College*, pp. 36, 108.

169 *Autobiography*, p. 51; *The Times*, 5 June 1947; MM, GMT MS, GMT to MM, 8 June 1947.

170 Kennet MS, 58/38, GMT to Kennet, dated VE Day.

171 Hammond MS, 28/205, GMT to J. L. Hammond, 5 November 1947; MM, GMT MS, GMT to MM, 26 June 1948.

172 Viscount Simon, *Retrospect* (1952), esp. pp. 156–166, 175–204, 238–254; Simon MS, 100/118, GMT to Simon, 10 June 1952; 100/126, GMT to Simon, 13 June 1952.

173 Lord Moran, *Churchill: Taken from the Diaries of Lord Moran: The Struggle for Survival, 1940–1965* (New York, 1966), pp. x-xi.

174 Moorman, p. 212; Bryant MS, E3, GMT to Bryant, 17 February 1956.

175 M. Gilbert, *Winston S. Churchill*, vol. viii, *'Never Despair', 1945–1965* (1988), pp. 1194–1195, 1225.

176 Bryant MS, E3, GMT to Bryant, 22 March 1957. The letter is partly printed in P. Street, *Arthur Bryant: Portrait of a Historian* (1979), p. 153, note 1.

177 *The Times*, 10 February 1948; MM, GMT MS, GMT to MM, 10 February 1948.

178 Moorman, p. 240; *The Seven Years of William IV*, pp. 3–4. For the correspondence concerning the publication of this book, see HRHRC, GMT MS, GMT to A. Bott, and A. Bott to GMT, February 1951 to September 1952.

179 J. Ehrman, *The Younger Pitt: The Years of Acclaim* (1969), p. xiv.

180 Chadwick, p. 37.

181 See Appendix C, pp. 236–238.

182 Fisher, 'The Whig Historians', p. 304.

NOTES TO CHAPTER IV: The Rural Elegist

1 The guides to Northumberland are legion. I have used those from Trevelyan's time: *Tomlinson's Comprehensive Guide to the County of Northumberland* (1910 edn.), pp. v-xi; J. E. Morris, *Northumberland* (1916), pp. 1–9; A. G. Bradley, *The Romance of Northumberland* (1933 edn.), pp. 1–13.

2 For Northumberland's remoteness before the nineteenth century, see L. and J. C. F. Stone, *An Open Elite? England, 1540–1880* (1984), pp. 40, 47–50.

3 Quoted in A. Mee, *The King's England: Northumberland* (1952), p. 11.

4 K. V. Thomas, *Man and the Natural World: Changing Attitudes in England, 1500–1800* (1983), p. 13.

5 MM, GMT MS, GMT to MM, 23 July 1926; CPT MS, 243, GMT to CPT, 17 February 1949.

6 GOT MS, 95, GMT to GOT, undated [1902]; MM, GMT MS, GMT to MM, 3 October 1945.

7 H. A. L. Fisher, *James Bryce* (2 vols., 1927), vol. i, pp. 280–282.

8 *Autobiography*, pp. 11, 14–15.

9 Moorman, p. 90.

10 *Autobiography*, p. 15; Moorman, pp. 67–70.

11 Samuel MS, B/7/3e, [?M and C. Trevelyan], *The Hunt, 1898–1937* (privately printed, 1937), pp. 3–8, 9–23, 39.

12 MM, *William Wordsworth: A Biography* (2 vols., 1957–65); Moorman, pp. 95–96, 245–246; Will of GMT, 1 March 1960, clause 1.

13 Moorman, pp. 124–125; *The Times*, 15 June 1912, 22 October 1913.

14 See GMT's essay, 'Walking', in *Clio* (2nd edn.), pp. 1–18, and his obituary in the *Alpine Journal*, lvii (1962), pp. 399–401.

15 *Autobiography*, pp. 25–27; Moorman, p. 93; HT, *Public and Private* (1980), p. 160; B. Russell, *The Autobiography of Bertrand Russell*, vol. i (1967), p. 65.

16 Thomas, *Man and the Natural World*, p. 13.

17 MM, GMT MS, GMT to MM, 10 September 1926.

18 The essay was re-published in *Clio* (2nd edn.), p. 19.

19 *England Under the Stuarts*, pp. 5–7, 35.

20 *John Bright*, pp. 12–14, 255, 412–413.

21 *Grey of the Reform Bill*, pp. 1–2; Chadwick, p. 7.

22 *Clio* (2nd. edn.), pp. 3–6; *Autobiography*, p. 28; *The Times*, 3 June 1932.

23 Chadwick, p. 8; *Garibaldi and the Thousand*, pp. 31–34, 329–330; Kennet MS, 58/5, GMT to H. Young, 16 January 1907; 58/9, GMT to H. Young, 23 June 1909; HRHRC, GMT MS, G. Young to GMT, 13 October 1908.

24 For the broader historical background see A. Offer, *Property and Politics, 1870–1914: Landownership, Law, Ideology and Urban Development in England* (1981), pp. 328–349.

25 R. C. K. Ensor, 'The English Countryside', in L. Oldershaw (ed.), *England: A Nation* (1904), pp. 107–108; C. F. G. Masterman, *The Condition of England* (1909), p. 203.

26 L. Wilkes, *John Dobson: Architect and Landscape Gardener* (1980), passim; N. Pevsner, *The Buildings of England: Northumberland* (1970 edn.), pp. 55–58, 222–223, 241–251.

27 GOT MS, 94, GMT to CT, 8 October 1901.

28 'Past and Future', pp. 399–401, 404–405.

29 'The White Peril', pp. 1045, 1046, 1054.

30 RCT MS, 14/45, GMT to RCT, 23 December 1901; Fry MS, vii, GMT to Fry, 23 December 1901; GOT MS, 94, GMT to GOT, 4 December 1901.

31 D. Cannadine, *The Decline and Fall of the British Aristocracy* (1990), pp. 103–112, 153–167, 355–369.

32 *British History in the Nineteenth Century*, pp. viii, xvi, 159, 230.

33 *British History in the Nineteenth Century*, pp. xiii, 398, 405.

34 *History of England*, p. 87.

35 *History of England*, p 691.

36 *History of England*, pp. 601, 693, 703.

37 *The Times*, 21 June 1926; RCT MS, 14/107, GMT to RCT, 27 October 1926.

38 *Autobiography*, pp. 40–41; Moorman, pp. 207–208; J. Gaze, *Figures in a Landscape: A History of the National Trust* (1988), pp. 68–71.

39 *The Times*, 24 February 1926, 15 July 1927.

40 *The Times*, 21 June 1926.

41 Gaze, *Figures in a Landscape*, pp. 44–47.

42 Gaze, *Figures in a Landscape*, pp. 47–48.

43 See the obituary notice by D. M. Matheson, Secretary of the Trust from 1934–45, in the National Trust, *Annual Report* (1961–2), pp. 6–7.

44 Just before GMT retired, James Lees-Milne described him as 'the worst chairman I have ever witnessed' (J. Lees-Milne, *Caves of Ice* [1983], p. 110). But perhaps he had not yet recovered from his earlier, unhappy experience at Wallington. See above, pp. 10–11.

45 Gaze, *Figures in a Landscape*, pp. 114–116; *The Times*, 18 May 1929, 29 June 1931, 23 April 1937, 28 June 1937.

46 Fisher MS, 69/57–9, GMT to Fisher, 1 September 1931; Marquess of Zetland, *'Essayez'* (1956), pp. 164–165.

47 *The Times*, 18 January 1929.

48 *Must England's Beauty Perish?*, pp. 9, 14, 18–20.

49 Moorman, pp. 217–220; *The Times*, 28 April 1926, 26 June 1926, 7 December 1928, 23 July 1929.

50 *The Times*, 18 February 1929, 31 March 1933, 22 May 1933, 14 November 1934, 6 February 1936, 1 October 1936, 11 December 1936, 23 December 1937; Gaze, *Figures in a Landscape*, pp. 118–120.

51 *The Times*, 15 January 1927, 16 April 1930, 14 January 1936.

52 *The Times*, 27 January 1930, 11 October 1930, 16 February 1933, 23 April 1934, 24 October 1934, 18 October 1937; J. R. Vincent (ed.), *The Crawford Papers: The Journals of David Lindsay, Twenty-Seventh Earl of Crawford and Tenth Earl of Balcarres, 1871–1940, during the Years 1892 to 1940* (1984), pp. 521, 582.

53 *The Times*, 10 June 1931; Hammond MS, 23/186, GMT to Hammond, 5 May 1931.

54 See the obituary notice by J. Catchpool in *The Youth Hosteller*, xxx (1962), pp. 10–12.

55 *The Times*, 21 January 1933, 30 March 1936; GMT, 'Breakfasted, Booted and on the March', *The Rucksack*, i (1932), p. 3.

56 'Address by Professor G. M. Trevelyan, O. M., The President of the Association, on the wireless, January 21st 1931', pp. 2–4, 6.

57 *The Times*, 27 October 1931.

58 *Autobiography*, pp. 101. 106.

59 Moorman, pp. 195–196; CPT MS, 239, GMT to CPT, 29 May 1920; R. W. Pfaff, *Montague Rhodes James* (1980), pp. 366–7.

60 Vincent, *Crawford Papers*, pp. 2–3, 472–473.

61 P. Scott, *Knowledge and Nation* (1990), p. 188; Cannadine, *Decline and Fall of the British Aristocracy*, pp. 326–338, 369.

62 Buchan MS, GMT to Buchan, 21 September 1913, 25 July 1922, 9 September 1922, 23 August 1925, 1 August 1926, 16 October 1928, 20 July 1931, 6 March 1932, 17 December 1937.

63 Buchan MS, GMT to Buchan, 27 February 1921, 3 March 1921, 6 October 1926; Janet Trevelyan to Buchan, 26 May 1921.

64 J. Adam Smith, *John Buchan: A Biography* (1985 edn), p. 471; *John Buchan, by his Wife and Friends* (1947), pp. 11–17. See also GMT's additional obituary notice in *The Times*, 15 February 1940, saluting 'the peculiar nature of Lord Tweedsmuir's public services, and the quality of John Buchan's mind and heart as author and friend.'

65 Adam Smith, *Buchan*, p. 306. In return, GMT dedicated *Ramillies* to Buchan.

66 D. Cannadine, 'Politics, Art and

Propaganda: The Case of Two "Worcestershire Lads"', *Midland History*, iv (1978), pp. 97–107.

67 MM, GMT MS, GMT to MM, 18 October 1925; Baldwin MS, 161 f 227, GMT to Baldwin, 17 June 1926.

68 T. Jones, *A Diary with Letters, 1931–1950* (1969), pp. 29, 141, 285; Baldwin MS: 165 f 334, GMT to Baldwin, 22 February 1930; 165 f 336, GMT to Baldwin, 14 October 1930; 45 f 133, GMT to Baldwin, 28 January 1931; 170 f 260, GMT to Baldwin, 18 February 1935; 171 f 322, GMT to Baldwin, 22 January 1936.

69 MM, GMT MS, GMT to MM, 5 and 6 July 1935; Baldwin MS: 170 f 62, GMT to Baldwin, 6 July 1935; 171 f 324, GMT to Baldwin, 3 November 1936.

70 Baldwin MS, 170 f 261, GMT to Baldwin, 31 March 1935.

71 Baldwin MS, 173 f 163, GMT to Baldwin, 27 October 1937; MM, GMT MS, GMT to MM, 27 September 1940, 10 November 1941; Jones, *Diary with Letters*, pp. 516, 523.

72 H. M. Hyde, *Baldwin: The Unexpected Prime Minister* (1973), pp. 564–565.

73 *Autobiography*, pp. 47–48; MM, GMT MS, GMT to MM, 22 March 1934, 28 August 1934.

74 MM, GMT MS, GMT to MM, 8 March 1935, 25 May 1935.

75 *Grey of Fallodon*, pp. vi, 337–338.

76 Baldwin MS, 168 f 271, GMT to Baldwin, 13 October 1933; Jones, *Diary with Letters*, p. 326.

77 *Grey of Fallodon*, pp. 53, 245–246.

78 *Grey of Fallodon*, p. 339; MM, GMT MS, GMT to MM, 25 May 1935.

79 MM, GMT MS, GMT to MM, 25 May 1935, 23 September 1935.

80 Chadwick, p. 36; *Grey of Fallodon*, pp. 51–52.

81 *Grey of Fallodon*, pp. 17, 53, 341.

82 Chadwick, p. 8.

83 *Grey of Fallodon*, pp. vii, 364–365; Hammond MS, 25/117, GMT to Hammond, 22 March 1937.

84 *Grey of Fallodon*, pp. 96–97, 267, 281.

85 *Grey of Fallodon*, pp. 107–120.

86 MM, GMT MS, GMT to MM, 7 December 1934; Crewe MS, Crewe to GMT, 3 June 1935.

87 *Grey of Fallodon*, p. 254, note 1.

88 R. Mortimer, *New Statesman and Nation*, 13 March 1937, pp. 445–446; *Grey of Fallodon*, p. 365; K. Robbins, *Sir Edward Grey: A Biography of Lord Grey of Fallodon* (1971), p. 125.

89 Crewe MS, GMT to Crewe, 17 May 1936; Seton-Watson MS, GMT to Seton-Watson, 12 May 1936.

90 *Grey of Fallodon*, pp. 68–69, 82, 254–257, 268–269, 280–282.

91 *Grey of Fallodon*, pp. 355–357.

92 Baldwin MS, 171 f 323, GMT to Baldwin, 6 April 1936.

93 *Grey of Fallodon*, pp. 107–120, 266–267.

94 J. Harvey (ed.), *The Diplomatic Diaries of Oliver Harvey, 1937–40* (1970), pp. 23–24. This makes it plain that both Harvey and Eden had read *Grey of Fallodon*. For Henderson, the evidence is circumstantial, but persuasive: see A. Roberts, *'The 'Holy Fox': A Biography of Lord Halifax* (1991), p. 68.

95 S. Roskill, *Hankey: Man of Secrets*, vol. iii, *1931–63* (1974), p. 277; Hankey MS, General Correspondence, 4/29, Hankey to GMT, 23 May 1937, reporting that 'everyone' seemed to have read the book.

96 Murray MS, 232/156, GMT to Murray, 6 May 1938; MM, GMT MS, GMT to MM, 27 September 1938.

97 RCT MS, 14/149, GMT to RCT, 4 October 1939.

98 MM, GMT MS, GMT to MM, 1 May 1940, 14 June 1940.

99 RCT MS, 14/159, GMT to RCT, 12 July 1940.

100 RCT MS: 14/158, GMT to RCT, 27 September 1940; 14/173, GMT to RCT, 6 August 1940; MM, GMT MS, GMT to MM, 5 February 1941.

101 Dawson MS, 81/101, GMT to Dawson, 18 July 1941; Woolf MS, GMT to Woolf, 4 May 1941; MM, GMT MS, GMT to MM, 5 February 1941, 4 April 1942.

102 Kennet MS, 58/33, GMT to Kennet, 4 September 1940; MM, GMT MS, GMT to MM, 13 August 1940.

103 Gaze, *Figures in a Landscape*, pp. 122, 126–127, 129–131, 174–175; MM, GMT MS, GMT to MM, 8 April 1941.

104 GMT, 'Presidential Address', *The Rucksack*, ix (1941), pp. 1–3.

105 *The Times*, 3 February 1944, 12 April 1944.

106 GMT, 'Fifty Years of the National Trust', *Country Life*, 12 January 1945, pp. 62–64. See also Crewe MS, Crewe to GMT, 7 February 1945; GMT to Crewe, 13 February 1945.

107 *Autobiography*, pp. 48–49.

108 Two earlier sections, on the Romans and the Anglo-Saxons, were later published as separate chapters in his *Autobiography*.

109 MM, GMT MS, GMT to MM, 13 July 1941, 27 May 1942, 7 July 1944.

110 *English Social History*, pp. 96, 252, 265, 367, 398, 508.

111 *English Social History*, pp. ix, 15, 230, 503.

112 *English Social History*, pp. 19, 147, 317.

113 *English Social History*, pp. 50–51, 157.

114 *English Social History*, p. 139.

115 *English Social History*, pp. 401, 523.

116 *English Social History*, pp. 4, 10, 18, 28, 123.

117 *English Social History*, pp. 125, 236.

118 *English Social History*, pp. 304, 330, 339–340, 367.

119 *English Social History*, pp. 304–308, 392, 398, 405.

120 *English Social History*, pp. x, 255, 371, 463–464, 476.

121 *English Social History*, pp. 373–374, 474, 483.

122 *English Social History*, pp. 521–522, 535, 553, 578.

123 *English Social History*, pp. 117, 522–524, 527–528.

124 *English Social History*, pp. 269, 585–586.

125 MM, GMT MS, GMT to MM, 10 March 1940; *English Social History*, pp. 450, 585–586.

126 *English Social History*, p. 24; Plumb, p. 251; M. Wiener, *English Culture and the Decline of the Industrial Spirit, 1850–1980* (1981), p. 87.

127 *English Social History*, p. 586, note 6.

128 *English Social History*, pp. 88, 131, 139, 273–274.

129 MM, GMT MS, GMT to MM, 17 March 1947.

130 *English Social History*, p. 26; Hammond MS, 28/205, GMT to Hammond, 5 November 1947.

131 RCT MS: 20/56, GMT to MacCarthy, 1 April 1951; 13/138, GMT to Elizabeth Trevelyan, 18 June 1952.

132 'Amenities and the State', pp. 183–186; *The Times*, 7 July 1945.

133 CPT MS, 243, GMT to CPT, 22 May 1946; B. Pimlott, *Hugh Dalton* (1985), pp. 455–456.

134 Pimlott, *Dalton*, pp. 84, 455–6, 544.

135 *The Times*, 17 November 1947.

136 CPT MS, 244, GMT to CPT, 1 March 1950; Pimlott, *Dalton*, pp. 578–580.

137 B. Pimlott (ed.), *The Political Diary*

of *Hugh Dalton, 1918–40, 1945–60* (1984), p. 474.

138 *The Times*, 2 June 1945, 2 July 1945; Gaze, *Figures in a Landscape*, p. 145; Longman MS, Part II, 67/13, GMT to R. Longman, 18 May 1946.

139 *The Times*, 22 October 1947, 26 October 1948, 13 November 1948, 18 and 24 July 1951.

140 *The Times*, 27 December 1945, 2 August 1949, 11 May 1951.

141 Gage, *Figures in a Landscape*, p. 177; National Trust, *Annual Report* (1948–9), pp. 21–22.

142 *The Rucksack*, xix (1951), p. 1. See also GMT's valedictory 'Introduction' to O. Coturn, *The Youth Hostel Story* (1950), pp. 1–2.

143 Durham University MS, 'Proceedings on the 24th and 25th May, 1950, in connection with the Installation of Dr G. M. Trevelyan as Chancellor', pp. 4–5, 12.

144 Kennet MS, 58/31, GMT to Kennet, 3 July 1934; MM, GMT MS, GMT to MM, 8 July 1934.

145 CPT MS, 242, GMT to CPT, 17 March 1934.

146 Murray MS, 103/122, GMT to Murray, 4 October 1952.

147 CPT MS, 244, GMT to CPT, 29 October 1951.

148 *Layman's Love of Letters*, pp. 48–49; Appendix C, pp. 236–238.

NOTES TO CHAPTER V: The Historian and the Reputation

1 N. Pevsner, *The Buildings of England: Cambridgeshire* (1970 edn.), pp. 42, 44, 46, 48, 217–218.

2 See, for example, J. Morley, *Diderot and the Encyclopedists*, vol. ii (1923 edn.), pp. 201–202; idem, *Critical Miscellanies*, vol. iii (1886), p. 9.

3 'The Latest View of History', p. 403; *Clio*, p. 178. (All references to *Clio* in this chapter are to the second [1930] edition.)

4 *Autobiography*, p. 80; 'The Latest View of History', pp. 407–408.

5 *Clio*, pp. 155–156, 178; 'The Latest View of History', p. 410.

6 Chadwick, p. 5; *Autobiography*, p. 80.

7 *Clio*, pp. 151–152; *Autobiography*, p. 65.

8 *Clio*, p. 160.

9 *Autobiography*, p. 68; 'History and Literature', p. 90; *Clio*, pp. 160, 192.

10 HRHRC, GMT MS, GMT to CT, undated [1900s]; *Autobiography*, p. 447.

11 *Garibaldi and the Thousand*, pp. 329–330.

12 G. W. E. Russell, 'Garibaldi', in his *Sketches and Snapshots* (1910), p. 115; Anon., 'Garibaldi and the Making of Italy', *Contemporary Review*, c (1911), p. 887.

13 MM, GMT MS, GMT to MM, 6 March 1934.

14 *The Times*, 19 January 1952; GMT, 'Foreword' to *National Film Archive Catalogue*, Part 1, *Silent News Films* (1951).

15 Chamberlain MS, 5/7/60–1, GMT to Austen Chamberlain, undated and 29 November 1911; Sturge MS, ff 210–13, GMT to Sturge, 2 January 1912, 8 October 1913, 5 August 1913.

16 Crewe MS, GMT to Crewe, 28 April 1936; Baldwin MS, 171 f 323, GMT to Baldwin, 6 April 1936.

17 Rowse, p. 117.

18 *Autobiography*, p. 117.

19 *England in the Age of Wycliffe*, pp. 364–365.

20 *Garibaldi and the Thousand*, pp. 346–347.

21 *Grey of the Reform Bill*, pp. 376–378.

22 'The Number of Casualties at Peterloo', passim.

23 *Ramillies*, pp. 412–416.

24 C. D. Hazen (ed.), *The Letters of William Roscoe Thayer* (Boston, 1926), prints only one to GMT, 27

September 1909, pp. 180–181. But see also pp. 158–161, 182–185.

25 Thayer MS, GMT to Thayer, 21 January 1909, 1 April 1909, 30 September 1909, 22 October 1910.

26 Thayer MS, GMT to Thayer, 10 June 1910, 4 July 1910, 30 January 1911, 11 August 1911.

27 Thayer MS, GMT to Thayer, 4 July 1910, 4 November 1910.

28 'The Latest View of History', p. 400.

29 MM, GMT MS, GMT to MM, 30 November 1926.

30 MM, GMT MS, GMT to MM, 5 September 1926.

31 *Autobiography*, p. 13; Plumb, p. 184.

32 GMT, 'The English Reformation', The *Nation*, 15 October 1910, p. 130.

33 D. Knowles, 'George Macaulay Trevelyan', the *Spectator*, 17 February 1956, p. 210.

34 Chadwick, p. 9.

35 *Clio*, p. 156.

36 *Autobiography*, p. 32; MM, GMT MS, GMT to MM, 1 September 1926.

37 'The Latest View of History', p. 397.

38 *Clio*, p. 162; 'The Latest View of History', pp. 401–402.

39 RCT MS, 14/43, GMT to RCT, undated; GOT MS 11, GMT to GOT, 19 November 1898.

40 *England in the Age of Wycliffe*, p. 13.

41 'The Reformation Regime in Scotland', p. 478.

42 *Autobiography*, p. 29; RCT MS, 14/37, GMT to RCT, 26 April 1900.

43 *England Under the Stuarts*, p. 430.

44 *History of England*, p. 533.

45 *Grey of Fallodon*, pp. 1–2.

46 *English Social History*, pp. 400–401.

47 *Autobiography*, p. 1; A. L. Rowse to the author, 18 July 1990.

48 *Clio*, p. 162; Knowles, 'George Macaulay Trevelyan', p. 210.

49 *Clio*, p. 196.

50 'History and Literature', p. 91.

51 The *Guardian*, 23 July 1962; *Glasgow Herald*, 23 July 1962.

52 P. B. M. Blaas, *Continuity and Anachronism: Parliamentary and Constitutional Development in Whig Historiography and in the Anti-Whig Reaction, Between 1890 and 1930* (1978), pp. 1–34.

53 'Carlyle as an Historian', p. 494.

54 *Clio*, pp. 178–179.

55 'The Latest View of History', p. 405; *Autobiography*, pp. 63–65.

56 P. F. Clarke, *Liberals and Social Democrats* (1978), p. 252; Chadwick, p. 20.

57 'From Waterloo to the Marne', p. 75.

58 *Autobiography*, p. 65; George Otto Trevelyan, p. 16.

59 'The Latest View of History', p. 406; *Autobiography*, pp. 78–79, 82.

60 Hon. W. G. Runciman [now Lord Runciman] to the author, 12 January 1990.

61 *Autobiography*, pp. 78–80.

62 *Autobiography*, pp. 69, 77.

63 *Autobiography*, pp. 59, 62.

64 'The Latest View of History', p. 410; *Autobiography*, p. 77.

65 GOT MS, 15, GMT to GOT, undated [1900s]; *Autobiography*, p. 34.

66 *Clio*, pp. 153, 181–182.

67 *Autobiography*, p. 77; *English Social History*, pp. 4, 131, 204.

68 *Autobiography*, pp. 22–23.

69 Fisher MS, 59/51–5, GMT to Fisher, 14 January 1907; Birmingham University Library, GMT to Dr Hodgkin, 23 March 1912, letter inside Hodgkin's copy of GMT's *Life of John Bright*.

70 *English Social History*, p. 353; MM, GMT MS, GMT to MM, 8 December 1940.

71 *Autobiography*, p. 73; *British History in the Nineteenth Century*, p. vii.

72 GMT to F. E. Hirsch, 27 November 1953, quoted in F. E. Hirsch, 'George Peabody Gooch', *Journal of Modern History*, xxvi (1954), p. 271.

73 E. Evans, *Britain Before the Reform Act: Politics and Society, 1815–1832* (1989), p. 96.

74 *Clio*, p. 167; R. Mortimer, 'Books in General', *The New Statesman and Nation*, 19 August 1944, p. 123.

75 Brett Young MS, 3384, GMT to Brett Young, 20 November 1934.

76 J. Namier, *Lewis Namier: A Biography* (1971), passim; L. Colley, *Namier* (1989), esp. pp. 6–20.

77 Colley, *Namier*, pp. 21–45.

78 D. C. Watt, 'Sir Lewis Namier and Contemporary European History', *Cambridge Journal*, vii (1954), esp. pp. 580–582, 584–585, 588–591, 598–599.

79 For the historiographical background, see Colley, *Namier*, pp. 46–71; E. A. Reitan (ed.), *George III: Tyrant or Constitutional Monarch?* (1964).

80 GMT, 'Mr Namier and the Mid-Eighteenth-Century', the *Nation and Athenaeum*, 15 November 1930, p. 238. All the quotations in this and the following paragraph are from this article.

81 J. P. Kenyon, *The History Men* (1983), pp. 257–258.

82 N. Annan, *Our Age: Portrait of a Generation* (1990), p. 270.

83 B. W. Hill, *The Growth of Parliamentary Parties, 1689–1742* (1976); idem, *British Parliamentary Parties, 1742–1832* (1985); J. Brewer, *Party Ideology and Popular Politics at the Accession of George III* (1976).

84 *Autobiography*, p. 184.

85 Plumb, p. 9; Rowse, p. 131.

86 Annan, *Our Age*, p. 270; Plumb, p. 7.

87 H. Butterfield, *The Whig Interpretation of History* (1973 edn.), pp. 9, 11, 13, 24, 71, 79, 83–85.

88 Butterfield, *Whig Interpretation*, p. 13; *DNB, 1971–80* (1986), p. 116; M. Cowling, *Religion and Public Doctrine in Modern England* (1980), pp. 223–224.

89 Plumb, p. 254; Chadwick, pp. 37–38; G. R. Elton, 'Herbert Butterfield and the Study of History', *Historical Journal*, xxvii (1984), pp. 732–733.

90 Chadwick, pp. 37–38; Butterfield, *Whig Interpretation*, p. 70. For all GMT's early sympathy with the Roundheads, his essay 'Alexander Leslie and Prince Rupert' contains (pp. 441–2) an extravagant, proto-Garibaldian passage on Rupert himself:

It was he who organized the cavalry, who filled them with his own spirit of endurance, confidence, and dashing valour, who led them with extraordinary strategic as well as tactical genius . . . All this he did at the age of twenty-two to twenty-three, a record almost unequalled in the annals of youthful achievement. All the immense weight of business and responsibility he had not only carried off successfully, but had impregnated with his own ideas and his own character, at an age when Bonaparte, a forward youth enough in his own way, had only carried out a small though important operation against the fort at Toulon.

And further on in the same article, GMT's treatment of Rupert's later, sadder years, is no less sympathetic.

91 Butterfield, *Whig Interpretation*, pp. 12, 17, 21.

92 H. Butterfield, *The Englishman and His History* (1944), pp. v–vii, 72, 82–84, 98–101, 110, 114–117, 137–138; V. Mehta, *Fly and Fly-Bottle* (1963), pp. 201–204; Cowling, *Religion and Public Doctrine*, pp. 227–228.

93 Butterfield, *Englishman and His History*, pp. 2–3.

94 Butterfield, *Whig Interpretation*,
p. 40; Elton, 'Herbert Butterfield',
p. 736.
95 Butterfield, *Whig Interpretation*,
pp. 13, 29; H. Tulloch, *Acton* (1988),
pp. 108–109.
96 Butterfield MS, Box T, GMT to
Butterfield, 5 December 1939, 26
June 1946.
97 Butterfield MS, Box T, GMT to
Butterfield, 7 and 8 July 1948, 10
and 29 October 1949.
98 Butterfield MS, Box T, GMT to
Butterfield, 28 September 1949, 11
October 1949. For the (limited) use
that Butterfield made of GMT's
Fox papers, see H. Butterfield, 'C. J.
Fox and the Whig Opposition in
1792', *Historical Journal*, ix (1947),
p. 314, note 68.
99 H. Butterfield, *George III and the
Historians* (1959 edn.), pp. 166–167.
100 Elton, 'Herbert Butterfield',
pp. 729, 739.
101 Mehta, *Fly and Fly-Bottle*, pp. 205–
206; Annan, *Our Age*, p. 270.
102 Butterfield MS, Box 73,
'Historiography in England'
[1962], pp. 1–2.
103 G. Kitson Clark, 'George Macaulay
Trevelyan as an Historian:
Charm'd Magic Casements',
Durham University Journal, lv
(1962), pp. 3–4.
104 Tulloch, *Acton*, p. 89; *Autobiography*,
pp. 1, 14, 42, 45; Bryant MS, E3,
GMT to Bryant, 25 July 1935.
105 *Layman's Love of Letters*, p. 1;
Durham University MS,
'Proceedings on the 24th and 25th
May, 1950, in connection with the
Installation of Dr G. M. Trevelyan
as Chancellor', p. 4.
106 Bryant MS, E3, GMT to Bryant, 30
November 1944.
107 *Autobiography*, pp. 54–56.
108 J. B. Bury, 'The Science of History',
in H. Temperley (ed.), *Selected

Essays of J. B. Bury (1930), pp. 4–6,
9, 13, 16, 22.
109 'The Latest View of History',
pp. 395–400.
110 CPT MS, 238, GMT to CPT, 11
August 1913, 31 December 1913.
See the very similar argument made
by Theodore Roosevelt in 'History
as Literature', *AHR*, xvii (1912–13),
pp. 473–487. The fact that TR was
a close friend of GOT's was not just
coincidence.
111 J. B. Bury, *Life of St Patrick* (1905),
p. viii, note 1; H. Temperley, 'The
Historical Ideas of J. B. Bury', in
Selected Essays of J. B. Bury, pp. xv-
xvi, xxviii-xxxi.
112 'Professor Firth's Inaugural
Lecture', p. 630; 'History and
Literature', p, 91; *Clio*, p. 159.
113 *Recreations of an Historian*, p. 8; *Clio*,
p. 142. For a judicious discussion of
the Bury-GMT controversy, see
W. H. Walsh, *An Introduction to
Philosophy of History* (1967), pp. 170–
187.
114 *The Peasants' Rising and the Lollards*;
*Select Documents for Queen Anne's
Reign Down to the Union with
Scotland*; *Bolingbroke's Defence of the
Treaty of Utrecht*; GOT MS, 104,
GMT to GOT, 28 October 1912.
115 'Professor Firth's Inaugural
Lecture', p. 630; GMT,
'Introduction' to H. W. C. Davis,
The Age of Grey and Peel (1929),
pp. vii-ix; *Autobiography*, p. 20.
116 T. E. B. Howarth, *Cambridge
Between Two Wars* (1978), p. 114.
117 MM, GMT MS, GMT to MM, 14
April 1934, 12 June 1934, 10 June
1935.
118 J. Stapleton, 'The National
Character of Ernest Barker's
Political Science', *Political Studies*,
xxxvii (1989), pp. 171–189; see also
GMT's appreciative obituary
notices of Clapham and Richmond,

NOTES TO PAGES 216-221

reprinted in *Autobiography*, pp. 213–234.

119 J. Dover Wilson, *Milestones on the Dover Road* (1969), p. 29.

120 MM, GMT MS, GMT to MM, 22 March 1934, 7 April 1934, 28 August 1934.

121 E. J. Hobsbawm, 'Professor Trevelyan Lectures', *The Granta*, 27 October 1937, p. 61.

122 'Professor Firth's Inaugural Lecture', p. 634; 'History and Literature', p. 89; GMT, 'The Archives of London: A World Centre for Research: History Truly Taught', *The Times*, 16 December 1937.

123 Baldwin MS, 173 f 163, GMT to Baldwin, 27 October 1937.

124 Dr P. Higgins in the *TLS*, 27 July 1989, and to the author, 6 August 1989.

125 S. Collini, *Public Moralists: Political Thought and Intellectual Life in Britain, 1850–1930* (1991), pp. 216–219, and the references cited therein.

126 'Professor Firth's Inaugural Lecture', p. 630.

127 Baldwin MS, 171 f 324, GMT to SB, 3 November 1936.

128 G. R. Elton, 'George Macaulay Trevelyan', in G. Smith (ed.), *1000 Makers of the Twentieth Century* (1971), unpaginated.

129 G. R. Elton and R. W. Fogel, *Which Road to the Past? Two Views of History* (1984), pp. 75, note 2, 107.

130 G. R. Elton, *The Practice of History* (1967), pp. 18, 107.

131 Kenyon, *The History Men*, pp. 227, 231.

132 Kenyon, *The History Men*, pp. 177, 234.

133 Kenyon, *The History Men*, pp. 228, 233, 235.

134 J. C. D. Clark, *Revolution and Rebellion: State and Society in England*

in the Seventeenth and Eighteenth Centuries (1986), pp. 144–145.

135 J. C. D. Clark, *English Society, 1688–1832* (1985), p. 43, citing GMT, 'The Age of Johnson'. In fact, this essay was concerned to demonstrate three self-evident truths about eighteenth-century England: the vigour of its mercantile life, and of its economic and imperial expansion; the greater degree of freedom which existed in England, compared with most Continental nations; and the sustained dominance of the traditional landowning classes. Not surprisingly, Dr Clark's attempt to 'despatch' and 'delete' what he regards as such 'hapless arguments' has met with rather limited success.

136 Clark, *Revolution and Rebellion*, pp. 18–19.

137 Pollard MS, 3 15 GMT to Pollard, 24 November 1914.

138 *Clio*, p. 167.

139 For more than a century, it has been the standard ploy of militant empiricists to exaggerate the scholarly shortcomings of their predecessors: see Collini, *Public Moralists*, p. 217.

140 *Clio*, p. 149; Sir John Habakkuk to the author, 21 September 1990.

141 *Blenheim*, p. vii; J. A. Cannon, 'Preface', in J. A. Cannon (ed.), *The Historian at Work* (1980), p. ix.

142 Sir George Clark, 'George Macaulay Trevelyan, 1876–1962', *PBA*, xlix (1963), p. 382.

143 RCT MS, 14/86, GMT to RCT, 13 July 1913. In fairness, it should be added that GMT also thought Garibaldi was never 'quite inside himself'.

144 W. L. Arnstein, 'George Macaulay Trevelyan and the Art of History: A Centenary Reappraisal', *Midwest Quarterly*, xviii (1976), pp. 79–80.

145 E. P. Cheyney, review of *History of*

England, AHR, xxxii (1926), p. 571;
F. Crouzet, 'Tout va Très Bien
Madame l'Angleterre', *Annales,
ESC*, iii (1948), p. 39.

146 Buchan MS, GMT to JB, 24
November 1913, 18 November
1925. See also the perceptive
obituary of GMT in the *Scotsman*,
23 July 1962.

147 J. M. Hernon, 'The Last Whig and
Consensus History: George
Macaulay Trevelyan, 1876–1962',
AHR, lxxxi (1976), p. 82.

148 Chadwick, p. 6; *Autobiography*,
pp. 3–4.

149 RCT MS, 14/133, GMT to RCT, 7
December 1934.

150 CPT MS, 238, GMT to CPT, 6
September 1907; RCT MS, 14/129,
GMT to RCT, 27 October 1932.
For Trevelyan's views on naval, as
distinct from military history, see
'Address to the Navy Records
Society'.

151 Rowse, pp. 101, 110.

152 R. Taylor, 'Vaughan Williams and
English National Music', *Cambridge
Journal*, vi (1952–3), p. 620. Like
GMT's history, Vaughan
Williams's music was both more
varied and more robust than
his detractors were inclined to
claim.

153 C. Hill, *Reformation to Industrial
Revolution* (1969), p. 14; S. T.
Bindoff, 'Political History', and
H. J. Perkin, 'Social History', both
in H. P. R. Finberg (ed.), *Approaches
to History* (1969), pp. 1, 51. But
GMT's most recent successor as
Regius Professor at Cambridge got it
right: P. Collinson, *De Republica
Anglorum: Or, History with the Politics
Put Back* (1990), pp. 13–14.

154 *English Social History*, pp. vii–viii.

155 A. Marwick, *The Nature of History*
(1970), p. 59. For a full discussion of
Marwick's idiosyncratic views of
GMT, see Hernon, 'The Last Whig
Historian'. pp. 93–94, esp. note
104.

156 Elton, 'George Macaulay
Trevelyan', unpaginated; E. J.
Hobsbawm, *Industry and Empire*
(1969), pp. 366–367; idem, 'From
Social History to the History of
Society', in M. W. Flinn and T. C.
Smout (eds.), *Essays in Social History*
(1974), p. 2.

157 *Autobiography*, p. 49.

158 See Appendix C, p. 236.

159 Thayer MS, GOT to Thayer, 14
December 1909.

160 H. R. Trevor-Roper, *History:
Professional and Lay* (1957).

161 L. Stone, 'The Revival of Narrative:
Some Reflections on a New Old
History', *Past and Present*, no. 85
(1979), pp. 3–24; H. R. Trevor-
Roper, *History and Imagination*
(1980); J. Clive, *Not By Fact Alone:
Essays on the Writing and Reading of
History* (New York, 1989).

162 Clive, *Not By Fact Alone*, p. ix.

163 Rowse, p. 115; HRHRC, GMT MS,
GMT to CT, 14 March 1901;
George Otto Trevelyan, p. 9.

164 G. M. Pfitzer, *Samuel Eliot Morison's
Historical World: In Search of a New
Parkman* (Boston, 1991), passim.
Like GMT, Morison did not want
his biography written.

165 Clive, *Not By Fact Alone*, p. xiv.

166 *Clio*, pp. 184–185.

167 'The Latest View of History',
p. 400.

168 Quoted in Arnstein, 'George
Macaulay Trevelyan', p. 83.

Index